# The Politics of the Chinese
# Cultural Revolution

This volume is sponsored by the
Center for Chinese Studies
University of California, Berkeley

The Center for Chinese Studies at the University of California, Berkeley, supported by the Ford Foundation, the Institute of International Studies (University of California, Berkeley), and the State of California, is the unifying organization for social science and interdisciplinary research on contemporary China.


RECENT PUBLICATIONS

Lowell Dittmer
Liu Shao-ch'i and the Chinese Cultural Revolution
The Politics of Mass Criticism

Angus W. McDonald, Jr.
The Urban Origins of Rural Revolution
Elites and the Masses in Hunan Province, China, 1911-1927

Dorothy J. Solinger
Regional Government and Political Integration
  in Southwest China, 1949-1954

Frederic Wakeman, Jr.
History and Will
Philosophical Perspectives of Mao Tse-tung's Thought

James L. Watson
Emigration and the Chinese Lineage
The *Mans* in Hong Kong and London

HONG YUNG LEE

# The Politics of the Chinese Cultural Revolution

A CASE STUDY

UNIVERSITY OF CALIFORNIA PRESS

Berkeley · Los Angeles · London

University of California Press
Berkeley and Los Angeles, California
University of California Press, Ltd.
London, England
Copyright © 1978 by
The Regents of the University of California
First Paperback Printing 1980
ISBN 0-520-04065-1
Library of Congress Catalog Card Number: 76-19993
Printed in the United States of America

3 4 5 6 7 8 9

*To My Parents and Whakyung's Parents*

# Contents

# Tables

# Acknowledgments

This study would not have been possible without the generous assistance that I have received from many people in the last several years. Though any shortcomings contained herein are solely my responsibility, I would like to share any credit with those who have assisted me in various ways.

I owe a particular personal and intellectual debt to Tang Tsou of the University of Chicago, who has for many years guided my intellectual growth and rendered his unstinting help at every stage in the preparation of this study, including a painstaking reading with extensive comments on every chapter in a long series of preliminary drafts. My special thanks go to Chalmers Johnson, who has read my dissertation and encouraged me to revise it for publication. For their careful readings and valuable comments and criticisms, I am grateful to Michel Oksenberg, Frederic Wakeman, John Starr, and John Service. Robert Scalapino and Joyce Kallgren were unsparing in giving me encouragements and suggestions. As the members of my dissertation committee, Lloyd Rudolph and William Parish helped in laying down the basic framework of this study. David Milton and Nancy Milton generously shared their rich experiences in Peking with me in a series of stimulating discussions. I profited greatly from the exchange of opinions with my friends, Lowell Dittmer, Mitchell Meisner, Brantly Womack, and Marc Blecher.

The Center for Chinese Studies at the University of California generously provided the financial support that made it possible for me to spend the academic years 1973-1975 revising the final draft. Mr. Paul Weisser has done a marvelous job of editing and typing the final draft.

Finally, I must acknowledge the help that I received from Whakyung Lee, my wife, who not only courageously shared hardship and difficulty with me, but also showed unwavering confidence in me. Sonya and Sunyoung Lee have also contributed to this study by sacrificing their due share of my time.

Though all of the aforementioned helped me well beyond my ability to express my debt to them in an acknowledgment, none should be held responsible for any errors of fact or interpretation that remain.

# Abbreviations Used in the Notes

CB     *Current Background*
CFCP     *Chieh-fang chün-pao*
CNS     *China News Summary*
CQ     *China Quarterly*
DR     *Daily Report*
DSJP     *Daily Summary of Japanese Press*
JMJP     *Jen-min jih-pao*
JPRS     *Joint Publication Research Service*
KMJP     *Kuang-ming jih-pao*
NCNA     New China News Agency
PR     *Peking Review*
SCMM     *Selections from China Mainland Magazines*
SCMMS     *Supplement to Selections from China Mainland Magazines*
SCMP     *Survey of China Mainland Press*
SCMPS     *Supplement to Survey of China Mainland Press*
URS     *Union Research Service*

"Record"     "Wu-ch'uan chieh-chi wen-hua ta ko-ming ta-shih chi" [The Great Proletarian Cultural Revolution—Record of Major Events]. This monograph was originally published by Chingkangshan in February 1967 and translated in the *Joint Publication Research Service*, no. 42,349 (August 25, 1967).

# Introduction

In a meeting on July 27, 1968, with five representatives from the Peking Red Guards who were protesting the workers' intervention in the students' sphere of the Cultural Revolution, Mao Tse-tung declared that "the 'black hand' is nobody else but me." This statement virtually marked the end of the Great Proletarian Cultural Revolution that had thrown all of China into turmoil and disarray for more than two years. Why did Mao start the Cultural Revolution by mobilizing the Chinese students into Red Guards, and then end it by using the workers to control the students? What were the objectives and how did he actually lead the mass movement? Did the mass movement take the course that its initiator had planned? If not, how must we conceptualize the actual proceedings of the Cultural Revolution? These questions are not only intellectually challenging, they are also crucial for understanding the Chinese political system which followed the Cultural Revolution.

The Great Proletarian Cultural Revolution was certainly one of the most complex political events in the entire history of the Chinese Communist Party. It involved virtually all of the Chinese people, raised debates on a wide range of issues, and revealed a multitude of conflicts at various levels. Although the elite groups initiated the mass mobilization, once the masses were mobilized the movement gained its own momentum. The elite groups endeavored to manipulate the masses, but the masses found numerous ways to express themselves spontaneously. The Cultural Revolution manifested every conceivable type of human problem and every kind of political behavior. It was a study in contrasts, as emotional outbursts challenged rational calculations, individual demands opposed group interests, and personal loyalties undermined organizational allegiances. As the struggle developed,

1

the discrepancy widened between ideological pronouncements, on the one hand, and actual motivations and actions, on the other.

Because of this complexity, interpretations of the Cultural Revolution among Western scholars have differed widely. Alternative theories have dubbed it a great purge arising from a power struggle; an ideological struggle coupled with policy differences; a crisis caused by the regime's declining legitimacy; a confrontation between a charismatic leader and a bureaucratic organization; a simple two-line struggle between proletarian revolutionaries and capitalist revisionists; and an expression of Mao's personal idiosyncrasies (which urged him to idealize permanent revolution and a revival of the "Yenan spirit").

For all its complexity, however, one can readily observe certain attributes unique to the Cultural Revolution. First of all, Mao Tse-tung mobilized the masses to attack the Communist Party, the party of which he was Chairman, and which was the instrument for ruling as well as revolutionizing Chinese society. Mao's unique and decisive role distinguishes the Cultural Revolution from the typical revolution in which a rising counter-elite mobilizes the masses to seize power from a ruling elite.

Second, the Cultural Revolution involved a large segment of the general population and all the ruling groups, both in the government and in the Party, from the Central Committee down to Party branches in the schools and factories. Moreover, a wide variety of issues was raised, discussed, and debated. These included broad ideological and political questions, as well as specific questions on economic, cultural, and educational policy.

Third, the Cultural Revolution lasted more than two years, during which it passed through several stages. Each stage exhibited its own unique features in terms of the dominant actors, issues, and coalitions. In turn, each actor tried to adjust himself to the changing situation by improvising new tactics and forming a new coalition.

Fourth, the Chinese masses, once freely mobilized, usually split into two or more warring factions, and their factional struggle affected the course of the Cultural Revolution more than any other factor. The warring factions emerged in almost all of the existing occupational and social units, and a fragment of one social unit often formed an alliance with a faction from the other. Moreover, the mass organizations, the basic units in the factional struggle, came into existence, merged with one another, and disappeared, as their membership and the issues they debated underwent constant change.

Consistent with these characteristics, we hypothesize that the Cultural Revolution started with an elite conflict and split over the dispute on how to cope with the widening gap between the elite and the masses in a socialist China. One group of Chinese leaders—headed by Mao—considered the narrowing of the gap not only essential for the continuing Communist revolution, but also necessary for the effective operation of the Chinese political system. But the Party organization was less willing than Mao to take drastic measures to reduce the gap, because it was thought that the radical egalitarianism might interfere with the "principle of efficiency" and the rapid economic development of Chinese society.

These different perspectives reflected two diverse interpretations of Marxism: a strict economic interpretation of Marxism justified the Party's position; whereas the Maoists justified their view by stressing the Marxist concepts of voluntarism and political consciousness. This dispute was not a mere ideological debate, but was intimately related to the power position of each group in the Chinese political system. Obviously, the Party organization's interpretation of Marxism, combined with the Leninist notion of a vanguard party, tended to overlook the rising elitism of the Party, which was the major locus of political power in the society.

The Cultural Revolution can thus be best described as Mao's attempt to resolve the basic contradictions between the egalitarian view of Marxism and the elitist tendencies of Leninist organizational principles. By drawing the Chinese masses into the political process, Mao wanted to reverse the trend toward restratification caused by the bureaucratization of the Party, and he also wanted to build a mass consensus on the future direction of the society.

Yet, to Mao's apparent disappointment, when he removed or weakened the control exercised by the Party organization (until that time, the major instrument for regulating Chinese public opinion), all the latent tensions and contradictions in the society surfaced. The Chinese masses quickly polarized into two factions: one interested in the radical restructuring of the Chinese political system, and the other in maintaining the political status quo. As the Cultural Revolution unfolded along its unexpected course, the Chinese elite was further divided over the constantly arising political and socio-economic issues. Soon the Maoist coalition at the top also split along conservative-radical lines, thus forming a "vertical cleavage" which cut across the "horizontal cleavage" between the elite and the masses.

This book is an attempt to analyze the Cultural Revolution in its proper historical and social contexts as a stage in the continuing Chinese revolution. In particular, it attempts to recapture the dynamics of the mass movement by focusing on the vertical as well as the horizontal cleavages. Thus, conflict rather than consensus, and struggle rather than unity, occupy the larger portion of the analysis. A special effort has been made to explain the four characteristics of the Cultural Revolution mentioned above. The more specific questions examined in the book include these: What were the issues which created the deep cleavage among the Chinese elite? Were there any discernible patterns in the factional struggle among the mass organizations? If so, how do we explain the basic cleavages in the mass movement? What

Figure 1
*A Schematic Outline of the Cleavages and Coalitions
in the Great Proletarian Cultural Revolution*

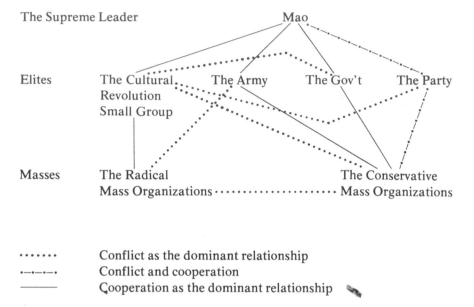

The Supreme Leader                Mao

Elites          The Cultural     The Army     The Gov't     The Party
                 Revolution
                 Small Group

Masses       The Radical                    The Conservative
               Mass Organizations · · · · · · · · · · · · · · · · · · · · Mass Organizations

· · · · · · ·          Conflict as the dominant relationship
·—·—·—·         Conflict and cooperation
————          Cooperation as the dominant relationship

were the relationships between the conflicts at the elite level and those at the mass level? And how was the elite conflict revealed to the Chinese masses?

Our approach examines the interactions of seven political "actors" (Mao, the Cultural Revolution Small Group, the People's Liberation Army, the Party organization, the government, the radical mass organizations, and the conservative mass organizations) operating on three different levels (the supreme leader, the elite, and the masses).

The political behavior of each group in the Cultural Revolution was largely determined by its ideology, its policies, and its power considerations. In turn, the internal structure of each group and its position in the hierarchy of the Chinese political system defined its interests and priorities. Of the seven political "actors," the Party, the government, and the Army began as organized institutional groups. The Cultural Revolution Small Group started as a semi-official group, but later developed into a well-established formal body. The radical and conservative mass organizations emerged and organized themselves more or less spontaneously, in the process manifesting previously latent conflicts in the society.

As the supreme leader with unchallengeable authority, Mao could concern himself primarily with broad ideological questions. In fact, he radicalized or deradicalized the prevailing official ideology depending on the nationwide situation of the movement, and he did this without being overly concerned with the effects his actions might have on his own or other groups' power interests. In contrast, the elite groups had to harmonize their power interests with the official ideology and policy at any given moment. In order to do so, each elite group utilized its own political assets: the Party organization utilized its decision-making powers; the Small Group, its proximity to Mao; the government, its essential supervision over day-to-day operations, especially in economic affairs; and the People's Liberation Army, its coercive power and its organizational capability as the only surviving organizational structure capable of carrying out the Peking leaders' will after the Party organization was completely destroyed.

The Party, the government, and the People's Liberation Army shared Mao's desire to maintain a certain degree of the regime's continuity and status quo. Hence, they could support Mao insofar as he was willing to respect their basic institutional interests. For instance, the People's Liberation Army could tolerate the radicalization of the Cultural Revolution only to the extent that this did not threaten its basic institutional interests. When the radicals later challenged the organizational integrity of the Army and its privileged position in China, the Army suppressed the radicals, despite Mao's and the Small Group's orders.

On the other hand, the ideology, policies, and power interests of the Small Group were extremely radical. Created outside the formal power structure of the Chinese political system, the Small Group as a whole had no special interests to protect and little stake in the political status quo. Yet, despite the differences of ideology, policy, and power considerations among themselves, the elite groups were obliged to take into account the basic interests of the regime as a whole against their various sectarian interests.

In contrast, the mass organizations were almost exclusively concerned with narrow group interests, particularly power interests. To them, ideological and policy considerations were mere means to advance their political interests. The mass organizations upheld the official ideology and policy of a given moment only if these coincided with their power interests, and they rejected them if not. Since they tended to push their own ideological viewpoints to extremes without considering their broader ramifications, the radical-conservative cleavage was much more clearly manifested at the mass than at the elite level.

It is one of our main theses that the radical mass organizations were largely composed of underprivileged social groups, whereas the conservatives were heavily drawn from the better-off social groups. The radicals attempted to change the political status quo as much as possible, whereas the conservatives strenuously defended the status quo. Mao declared that the conflict in the Center reflected the conflict in society, and not vice versa, when the radical Red Guards asserted that their factional struggle reflected the conflict among the elite. The coupling of the elite conflict with the latent conflict at the mass level gave rise to the vertical factional structure along radical-conservative lines.

In order to substantiate these hypotheses, I will try to identify the major issues over which the elite groups divided, and I will relate their positions to the interests of the various mass organizations. Since my aim was to write a comprehensive and balanced history of the Cultural Revolution in all its complexity and subtlety, rather than to provide a provocative new interpretation, I have organized the book chronologically. Concepts and insights from the social sciences have been freely drawn upon to illuminate various aspects of the movement, but caution has been taken not to overemphasize any particular thesis. This organizational format has the advantage, among others, of providing the reader with a clear view of each stage of the Cultural Revolution in which the dominant actors, issues, and patterns of coalition changed. Analytically speaking, the Cultural Revolution went through four different stages.

## The Politics of Bureaucracy: October 1965 to August 1966

It was during this period that the intra-elite conflict was deepening and the initial line of forces within the elite was taking on definitive shape. The main actor was the Party organization, which still exercised its traditional leadership over the incipient mass movement. Meanwhile, Mao was playing the game on two different levels: on the one hand, he tried in formal meetings to persuade the Party organization of the need to launch the Cultural Revolution; and on the other, he organized the Cultural Revolution Small Group and enlisted the support of the People's Liberation Army. Yet, the elite conflict by and large still took place within the boundaries of the existing rules and away from the public eye.

Unable to carry out Mao's demand to purge the "revisionist elements" within itself, the Party first adopted the evasive tactic of stressing procedural rules in decision-making. As the Maoists stepped up their pressure after June 1, 1966, the Party organization increasingly relied on the old bureaucratic strategy of "waving the red flag to oppose the red flag," and "obeying outwardly and disobeying inwardly." This meant that the Party organization was distorting Mao's wishes in the process of implementing them. As a result, the gap widened between the official ideology and the actual policy that the Party carried out, the ideology proclaiming the need for freely mobilizing the masses, while in fact the Party and the work teams restricted the mass movement by emphasizing Party leadership. Some rebellious students challenged the Party in the name of Mao's Thought, but they were ruthlessly suppressed.

Two chapters cover this period. Chapter One analyzes Mao's initial move against the Peking Municipal Party Committee (the most vulnerable spot in the entire Party organization) and the countermove of the Party leaders. Chapter Two examines how the Party organization carried out its own version of the Cultural Revolution through the work teams.

## The Politics of Manipulation: August 1966 to December 1966

In retrospect, this was the period when, as Mao asserted, the previously amorphous Cultural Revolution took on a definitive shape and its orientation was corrected. At first, however, an increase in the number of actors created uncertainty and suspense, as the masses, which soon split into conservatives and radicals, entered the already complicated political arena. The suspense was further heightened by new rules which stressed ideology over organization and mass initiative over Party leadership, coupled with the near absence of any clear-cut guidelines on the major tasks, participants, and targets of the movement. The power relationships between the Party and the Cultural Revolution Small Group at the elite level and between the conservative and radical mass organizations at the mass level were particularly undefined, but the trend for the elite groups to manipulate the mass organizations was clearly discernible.

The major issues at this time concerned the selection of targets, the evaluation of the work teams, the rehabilitation of those stigmatized by the work teams, and the membership qualifications for joining the Red Guards. Adjusting itself to the new rules of mass mobilization, the Party organization began to mobilize the pro-Party social groups and attempted to direct the movement toward relatively harmless targets and issues. By denouncing the practice of limiting Red Guard membership to students from "good" family backgrounds and by opening membership to students from "bad" family backgrounds, the Small Group rallied the discontented social groups to its side. The Small Group and the radicals also exaggerated the importance of the work team issue by making the criticism of the teams the major task of the Cultural Revolution. By the end of this phase, the radical Red Guards had captured the leadership of the movement from the original group of conservative Red Guards, and the main targets of the movement were the "power holders taking the capitalist road within the Party."

The People's Liberation Army, which hitherto had been collaborating with the Small Group against the civilian Party organization, vacillated in this period, refraining from taking a clear stand in the mounting disputes between the radical and the conservative Red Guards. Chou En-lai was also trying to keep in step with the changing situation, but the extension of the movement into the economic field inevitably drew his government functionaries into the mainstream of the struggle. Resenting the manipulation of the aggrieved workers by the Small Group, the government functionaries and local Party committees retaliated with "economism." Meanwhile, Mao, who at first appeared undecided on the future course of the movement, was finally convinced to take a radical course of action, swayed by the dynamics of the events.

Two chapters deal with this period. Chapter Three analyzes the changing political situation after the withdrawal of the work teams and also considers the major issues of the movement, which was still dominated by the conservatives. Chapter Four describes the rise of the radicals over the conservative Red Guards, as the movement shifted its principal focus to the campaign against the "power holders." The political and socio-economic characteristics of the radical workers are also analyzed in Chapter Four.

## The Politics of the Masses: January 1967 to August 1967

With the Cultural Revolution entering the stage of the "January Power Seizure," the unstable balance between the elite's control and the masses' spontaneity was shifted decisively in favor of the latter. Not only were the Chinese masses freed from the control of the elite, but they were actually encouraged to seize power from the ruling structures. In the process, the influence of the elite groups fell to an all-time low, and they found themselves suddenly the objects of attack by the masses.

The net result of this type of mass politics was chaos and anarchy. After taking control from the hands of the elite, the Chinese masses were drawn directly and suddenly into the political process without the benefit of previous experience. The leadership then created a power vacuum by failing to define the meaning of the power seizure or making clear what was to be done with the newly won power. On the other hand, the power holders shrewdly exploited the chaotic situation to protect their own interests, further intensifying the factional struggle among the masses.

In the face of a complete breakdown in order and production, Mao moderated the official policy of ordering the cadres and the People's Liberation Army to provide leadership for the power seizure. However, this new policy only exacerbated the factional struggle. The Army, the cadres, and the conservative mass organizations formed an alliance against the radicals and the Cultural Revolution Small Group and pushed the movement in the opposite direction from the radicalism of January, thus creating what the radicals later called the "February Adverse Current."

In March, the radical forces hit back, and by the end of the month the radical-conservative confrontation had reached a stalemate on both the elite and the mass levels. Meanwhile, the Peking leadership pursued two contradictory goals; (1) they tried to stabilize the situation by restricting the activities of the Red Guards; and (2) they tried to continue the power seizure. However, the attempt to pursue these two contradictory goals simultaneously was as ineffective as the attempt to pursue them sequentially had been. The radical and conservative mass organizations, both unable to justify their actions in terms of the official policy line, intensified their armed struggle until it culminated in the open revolt, in July 1967, of the Wuhan regional military force, which sided with the conservatives.

This period is covered by three chapters. Chapter Five analyzes the evolution of the January Power Seizure and the reasons for its failure. Chapter Six examines how the moderate official line in February prompted the government functionaries and the Army to suppress the radical mass organizations. And Chapter Seven describes the organizational structure of the Red Guards and analyzes their factional struggle in the context of the changing official line.

## The Politics of Factionalism: After September 1967

In order to avert a direct confrontation between the Small Group and the radical mass organizations, on the one hand, and the Army, the government functionaries, and the conservative mass organizations, on the other, Mao criticized both sides and then imposed a compromise solution on the elite groups. With Mao firmly backing a policy of retrenchment, there was no longer any room for the elite factions to manipulate the policy issues.

By October 1967, when it had become obvious that the mass mobilization would soon end, the issue at stake in the elite conflict was no less than who would dominate the Party organizations that were to be reconstructed—that is to say, who would rule China after the Cultural Revolution. Once power became the major bone of contention, Chou En-lai came out in support of the Small Group, despite its earlier attacks on him and despite his proximity to the Army on various substantive policy issues. Thereafter, the political process increasingly came to resemble a purely factional power struggle with ideological issues retiring into the background.

At this last stage of the mass movement, the most clearly discernible vertical cleavage was that between the Small Group, which had collaborated with the radicals, and the Army, which had collaborated with the conservatives. The Small Group and the Army made desperate moves to enhance or preserve the strength of their own mass organizations, since the strength of their client mass organizations had substantial bearing on their own power positions among the elite groups. In turn, the rise and fall of the mass organizations were ultimately determined by the relative power positions of their patrons among the central leaders and by their patrons' successes or failures in pursuing issues favorable to their clients. Thus, when the Red Guard organizations stepped up pressure on their respective patrons, the conflicts among the Red Guards were readily transposed to the elite groups, reinforcing the tension between the Small Group and the Army.

Since the radical and conservative mass organizations were closely affiliated with either the Small Group or the Army, it was impossible to resolve the conflict at the mass level without first solving it at the elite level. However, Mao could not afford to eliminate or decisively weaken either the Small Group or the Army. He needed the Army to maintain a semblance of order and discipline, since it not only possessed a monopoly on coercive power, but was also the only nationwide body with its organizational capability intact. But neither did he want to discredit the Small Group, which would have been tantamount to discrediting the Cultural Revolution as a whole. Furthermore, he could not impose his will organizationally from the top to the bottom, because that would have meant resorting to the very method he had criticized in the past.

Confronted with this dilemma, Mao temporized, but finally improvised a new method to resolve the conflict: the "Workers' Mao's Thought Propaganda Teams." Even though he succeeded in demobilizing the mass organizations through this ingenious method, the legacy of this period has continued to influence Chinese politics. The political structure of the country immediately following the Cultural Revolution displayed three distinctive but interrelated trends: the rise of the Army's political influence; a tendency toward decentralization of political power to the local leaders (mainly the regional Army leaders); and the rise of the mass groups which had fought in the Cultural Revolution on the conservative side. A coalition of these three forces, probably with Lin Piao as its leader, constituted the most powerful political force in China from 1968 to 1970.

Chapter Eight analyzes the intensifying power struggle between the Small Group and the Army, a struggle that centered on the control of the revolutionary committees. Chapter Nine describes the demobilization process, focusing on the Workers' Mao's Thought Propaganda Teams, the campaign to purify class ranks, and the rebuilding of the Party organization. Chapter Ten tests the hypothesis of the radical-conservative cleavage with data drawn from Kwangtung.

The author's major source of information has been the Red Guard newspapers, for which he has compiled an extensive index under the sponsorship of the Center for Chinese Studies at the University of Michigan. Since the present volume does not include a bibliography, interested readers may wish to consult *A Research Guide to the Red Guard Materials in the United States* (forthcoming in the Occasional Papers Series of the University of Michigan, Center for Chinese Studies).

# CHAPTER 1

# The Campaign Against Wu Han: The First Phase of the Cultural Revolution

The Great Proletarian Cultural Revolution started with the apparently insignificant criticism of Peking vice-mayor Wu Han, a well-known historian specializing in the Ming period. In 1961, Wu Han had written an historical play, *Hai Jui Dismissed from Office,* at a time when the Chinese Communist Party (CCP) had somewhat relaxed its control over society after the failure of the Great Leap Forward.[1]

In the play, Wu Han praised Hai Jui, a quasi-historical official of the Ming period who had been dismissed from office by the Emperor after returning lands to the peasants that corrupt officials had seized from them. At the beginning of the Cultural Revolution, the Maoists wanted to condemn the play as a veiled political attack on Mao's 1959 dismissal of P'eng Teh-huai, but the Party organization tried to divert the campaign against Wu Han into an academic debate. Gradually this apparently minor difference developed into an ideological and political controversy among the entire Chinese elite, which resulted in the reorganization of the Peking Party Committee and the purge of the Committee's first secretary, P'eng Chen.

## The Campaign Unfolds

At the CCP Work Conference held in September–October 1965, Mao proposed that criticism of Wu Han be made on two levels. First, he asked P'eng Chen, the head of the Group of Five in charge of revolutionizing literature and art, to criticize Wu Han at the official level. Second, he instructed the informal Chiang Ch'ing group to prepare a critique of Wu Han's play in complete secrecy. When P'eng Chen failed to act against his

1. *Pei-ching hsin wen-i,* 8 June 1967.

own vice-mayor, Mao arranged for an article entitled "Comments on the Newly Written Historical Opera, *Dismissal of Hai Jui"* to be published under the name of Yao Wen-yüan in the Shanghai *Wen hui pao* of November 11, 1965.

Although its tone was quite mild, this article nonetheless proved so alarming to P'eng Chen that he initially forbade the Peking newspapers to reprint it.[2] However, as it became clear that Mao was responsible for the article's original publication, P'eng Chen reluctantly lifted his ban, but only after he provided several safeguards to mitigate its impact on the public.[3]

First, he forbade the Peking newspapers to carry the article simultaneously.[4] Second, he gave the job of opening the debate to Teng T'o, who had joined Wu Han in criticizing Mao in 1961; P'eng Chen personally instructed Wu Han to "examine your thinking where you are wrong and persist where you are right to uphold truth and correct mistakes."[5] Third, he had *Pei-ching jih-pao* carry moderate editorial notes that defined the issue of Wu Han as a purely academic question.[6] Finally, he prepared to attack the radical intellectuals under Chiang Ch'ing on the grounds that they had formed a "faction" in the fields of literature and art.[7] In short, P'eng Chen was conceding, by the end of November, that Wu Han's play had raised some academic questions, but he still refused to take a political position on them.

Articles supporting and opposing Wu Han's academic views thereafter competed in the public news media. Probably dissatisfied with such an inconclusive debate, even when limited to academic questions, Mao revealed his own position in an interview with high party officials on December 21, 1965. After making a sweeping attack on the "policy of concession," "formal logic," and abstract philosophical thinking that had been evident in the debate thus far, Mao indicated that the matter of "dismissal" was the key question in *Hai Jui Dismissed from Office.*[8]

On December 24, however, P'eng Chen had an exclusive interview with Mao. Although no records of the meeting are available, P'eng Chen's subsequent behavior indicates that he succeeded in persuading Mao to delay the political conclusion of the controversy, while agreeing to criticize Wu Han's

2. Ting Wang, *Chung-kung wen-hua ta ko-ming tzu-liao hui-pien,* vol. 4 (Hong Kong: Ming-pao yüeh-kan-she, 1969), pp. 453-470.

3. One Red Guard newspaper reported that Chou En-lai pressured the Peking Party Committee to publish the article in the Peking newspapers. *Shou-tu hung-wei-ping,* 9 June 1967; *Pei-ching hsin wen-i,* 8 June 1968.

4. "Wu-ch'an chieh-chi wen-hua ta ko-ming ta-shih chi" [Great Proletarian Cultural Revolution—Record of Major Events] (hereafter "Record"), *Chingkangshan* (February 1967), in *Joint Publication Research Service,* no. 42,349, August 25, 1967.

5. Ibid.

6. Ting Wang, *Chung-kung wen-hua ta ko-ming tzu-liao hui-pien,* vol. 4, p. 425.

7. "Record," p. 3.

8. Ibid., p. 5.

academic position.[9] After this interview, P'eng Chen and Lu Ting-yi, the Director of the Propaganda Department, publicly declared that Wu Han was wrong in describing Hai Jui as an honest official, and that the play should be criticized on that account.[10] On orders from P'eng Chen and with help from Teng T'o, Wu Han prepared his self-criticism of his academic views.[11] Soon the bureaucratic intellectuals were busy writing articles denouncing Wu Han's academic views, and articles defending him disappeared.[12]

With the Party's position on academic questions clearly decided, the Propaganda Department moved to reassert its organizational leadership over the campaign. It ordered the news media to submit all the relevant articles to the Department for approval before publication; it sent out three volumes of reference materials to guide the academic debate; and it organized numerous conferences to transmit the official guidelines to the lower levels.[13]

At the same time, the Party organization moved to have its views adopted in a formal Party decision. Hsü Li-chün, the deputy director of the Propaganda Department of the Central Committee, prepared a draft outline of the opinions that had emerged in the various meetings organized by the Party.[14] On February 3, 1966, the document was submitted to the Group of Five, which approved it over K'ang Sheng's opposition.[15] On February 5, P'eng Chen obtained Liu's approval, and wrote on the cover that "[because of the pressures of time], this report has not been examined by every member of the Group of Five."[16]

On February 8, P'eng Chen, Wu Leng-hsi, and Hsü Li-chün (some sources also include Lu Ting-yi) took the Outline to Hangchow, where, according to the Red Guards, P'eng Chen verbally explained its general terms to Mao. When Mao raised the question of Wu Han's motivation, P'eng Chen attempted to mollify Mao by promising that the Party would first deal with the academic issues and then censure the intellectuals who criticized the Great Leap Forward.[17] On his return to Peking, P'eng Chen allegedly lied to Liu Shao-ch'i and Teng Hsiao-p'ing by stating that Mao had approved the document. On February 12, 1966, the "February Outline" was sent as an

9. At the end of the interview, P'eng Chen reportedly had said that "Chairman Mao said that the Wu Han problem can be concluded politically only after several months," *Pei-ching hsin wen-i*, 8 June 1967.

10. "Record," p. 5.

11. *Pei-ching hsin wen-i*, 8 June 1968.

12. For instance, Chou Yang and Liao Mo-sha collectively wrote an article entitled "What Kind of Ideology Did 'Hail Jui Dismissal' Represent" in the *Pei-ching jih-pao, Pei-ching hsin wen-i*, 8 June 1968.

13. *Tung-fang-hung pao*, 28 May 1967, "Press Campaign Against Chou Yang," *Current Background*, no. 802 (14 September 1966), p. 30.

14. *Shou-tung hung-wei-ping*, 21 May 1967; *Pei-ching hsin wen-i*, 8 June 1968.

15. *Hsin-wen chan-pao*, 10 June 1967.

16. *Tung-fang-hung pao*, 28 May 1967.

17. *Shou-tu hung-wei-ping*, 9 June 1967.

official document to all levels of the Party organization, and the Party convened numerous meetings to explain the "spirit" of the Outline.

While the Party organization vigorously propagated its duly adopted "February Outline," the Maoists worked through the People's Liberation Army (PLA) to develop an outlet for their own views. Delegated by Lin Piao to prepare the guideline for the PLA's literature and art work, Chiang Ch'ing, together with the Maoist intellectuals, produced the "Forum on Work in Literature and Art in the Armed Forces" (also known as the Shanghai Forum).[18] In contrast to the "February Outline," which was strictly a Party document prepared by Party bureaucrats, the Maoist intellectuals wrote the Forum under the name of the PLA and with extensive consultation with the members of the Military Affairs Commission (MAC).[19] Mao himself took an interest in the document's preparation and personally revised it three times with the help of Ch'en Po-ta. Chiang Ch'ing forwarded the document on March 16, 1966, to Lin Piao, who in turn submitted it to the Central Committee as an official document of the MAC on March 30. On April 10, the Central Committee sent it down to the *hsien*-level Party committees.

The content of the Forum opposed that of the Outline in almost every respect.[20] First, the Forum reaffirmed Mao's basic thesis that the political victory of the proletarian class would not automatically determine the outcome of the struggle in the superstructure. Hence the class struggle in the field of ideology was crucial in deciding which class would rule China. Then, the Forum judged the various academic questions in political terms and condemned the opponents' views as a "black line" that not only opposed Mao's ideas on literature and art but also imposed its own dictatorship over the field. By specifically denouncing the slogan of "literature for national defense," the document made it clear that the leader of the "black line" was none other than Chou Yang, the deputy director of the Propaganda Department.

With the Shanghai Forum in his hand, Mao ended the two-month moratorium on the political question of Wu Han and swiftly moved into final battle with P'eng Chen and the bureaucratic intellectuals. At a March 28 Politburo meeting, Mao unleashed his criticisms of P'eng Chen, the February Outline, and the Department of Propaganda and sought support from the MAC and Chou En-lai for P'eng's purge.[21] Informed by K'ang Sheng of

18. "Minutes of Forum on Literature and Art in the Armed Force Convened by Comrade Chiang Ch'ing on Comrade Lin Piao's Request," *Survey of China Mainland Press*, no. 3956 (9 June 1967), pp. 1-3.

19. Ibid., p. 4.

20. For the February Outline, see "This Is the Notorious February Outline," *SCMP*, no. 3952 (5 June 1967), pp. 1-3.

21. *T'i-yü chan-pao*, 21 April 1967; "Record," *JPRS*, no. 42,349, pp. 9-10.

Mao's resentment, P'eng Chen transmitted Mao's warning in general terms, but still defended his own innocence in a hurriedly convened meeting of the Peking Party Committee. The meeting authorized a small group to prepare a self-examination of the Peking Party Committee's past works, and it was decided to sacrifice Teng T'o.[22]

The Peking Party Committee's belated efforts to purge itself of its guilt for resisting Mao did not forestall outside measures to deal with its problems. First, a meeting of the Secretariat, presided over by Teng Hsiao-p'ing and attended by Chou En-lai, K'ang Sheng, and Ch'en Po-ta, finally decided to disband the Group of Five and annul the February Outline. Then, the Standing Committee of the Politburo, meeting in Shanghai on April 16, approved the Secretariat's decision and forwarded it to the Peking Party Committee.[23] Receipt of the document prompted the Committee to convene an emergency session.[24]

According to the charges of the Red Guards, the session did not follow the customary procedure of explaining instructions from the higher level so as to allow the participants to express their views without being influenced by the opinion of the Center.[25] Still defying the Center, the meeting attributed Mao's wrath to a conspiracy of K'ang Sheng and Chang Ch'un-ch'iao and concluded that there was nothing wrong with either the Peking Municipal Committee or the February Outline. The Center in Hangchow had to transmit five more documents on P'eng Chen's mistakes before the still defiant Peking Party Committee finally sent a delegate to see Li Fu-ch'un, the Central Committee member in charge of work in Peking, to learn the real attitude of the Center. The talk with Li finally persuaded the Peking Party Committee to reorganize itself.[26]

Meanwhile, the Peking Party Committee made a public gesture at self-criticism in a three-page editorial in the April 16 *Pei-ching jih-pao*. The editorial, written with Teng T'o's prior understanding, attacked the columns "Notes on a Three-Family Village" and "Night Talks at Yenshan," in which co-authors Teng T'o, Wu Han, and Liao Mo-sha had criticized Mao.[27] Although the Peking Party Committee admitted its own responsibility for permitting publication of the columns, it condemned them for their anti-Party, antisocialist content. Not surprisingly, the Center rejected this belated self-criticism.[28] On April 19, the Secretariat of the Central Committee notified all the units under the Peking Party Committee that the self-criticism

22. Ibid., 21 April 1967.
23. Ibid., 21 April 1967; *Hsin-wen chan-pao*, 6 June 1967.
24. *Pei-ching hsin wen-i*, 8 June 1967.
25. Ibid.
26. *T'i-yü chan-pao*, 21 April 1967.
27. *Pei-ching hsin wen-i*, 8 June 1967.
28. *T'i-yü chan-pao*, 21 April 1967.

was feigned and should be disregarded, and that all the newspapers should publish all their articles as planned, without being influenced by the self-criticism. It also instructed all the institutes of higher learning and all the other organs and units under the jurisdiction of the Peking Party Committee to stop implementing the Committee's decisions.[29]

On May 16, 1966, the Politburo held an enlarged meeting, probably to inform local Party leaders of P'eng Chen's fate. Lin Piao set the tone of the meeting with a kickoff speech in which he accused P'eng Chen, Lo Jui-ch'ing, and Lu Ting-yi of attempting a coup d'état to seize political power, and implied that the PLA would not tolerate any resistance from them.[30] No doubt, the Party organization was not convinced by Lin Piao's thesis of coup d'état. Even Mao was annoyed, at least according to the admittedly unreliable letter he is supposed to have sent to Chiang Ch'ing: "His [Lin Piao's] address was devoted entirely to a political coup. I was quite uneasy at some of his thinking. . . . I was driven by them to join the Liangshan rebel. . . . I expressed my opinion, which was different from that of my friend [Lin Piao]. I could do nothing else."[31]

After twelve days of debate, the meeting adopted the "May 16 Notice," which criticized the February Outline along the lines presented in the Shanghai Forum. After charging that the Outline distorted Mao's theory of class struggle in order to turn the movement against staunch leftists, the Notice redefined the goal of the Cultural Revolution:

> The whole Party must . . . thoroughly expose the reactionary bourgeois stand of those so-called "academic authorities" who oppose the Party and socialism. . . . To achieve this, it is necessary at the same time to criticize and repudiate those representatives of the bourgeoisie who have sneaked into the Party, the government, the Army, and all spheres of culture, to clear them out or to transfer some of them to other positions. Above all, we must not entrust them with the work of leading the Cultural Revolution. In fact, many of them have done and are still doing such work, and this is extremely dangerous. . . . Some of them [the representatives of the bourgeoisie] we have already seen through, others we have not. Some are still trusted by us and are trained as our successors; persons like Khrushchev, for example, are still nestling beside us. Party committees at all levels must pay full attention to this matter.[32]

The Notice, which was sent down to the *hsien* level and to the PLA regiment-level Party Committee, set up the Cultural Revolution Small Group, staffed mostly with radical intellectuals under the leadership of Chiang Ch'ing, who took control of the Party propaganda machine.

29. "Record," p. 11.
30. For Lin Piao's speech at the May 16 Politburo Meeting, see Martin Ebon, *Lin Piao: The Life and Writings of China's New Ruler* (New York: Stein and Day, 1970), pp. 252-269.
31. "Mao Tse-tung's Private Letter to Chiang Ch'ing," *Issues and Studies* 9, no. 4 (June 1973): 94-96.
32. For the May 16 Notice, see *Peking Review*, no. 21 (19 May 1967), pp. 6-9.

Taking a cue from the May 16 Notice, Nieh Yüan-tzu, a lecturer and a member of the Party Committee of the Department of Philosophy—the only department Party committee controlled by radicals—put up a big-character poster on May 25, 1966. Under the heading of "What the Peking University Party Committee Is Doing in the Cultural Revolution," Nieh accused the school Party Committee of suppressing the student movement on the pretext of "strengthening leadership."[33] Lu P'ing, the president of the University, immediately reported the matter to his superior, Li Hsüeh-feng, the newly appointed secretary of the Peking Party Committee. Li went to the University at midnight and ordered the school Party Committee to suppress the poster.[34] On the following day, the school Party Committee mobilized students through the Chinese Youth League (CYL) to counterattack Nieh and to pledge their support for the school Party Committee.[35] By May 27, when the campus was again calm, the Party Committee instructed every academic class to study the question "What lesson can be learned from the old lady [Nieh]?" On orders from the newly reorganized Peking Party Committee, the other Peking schools had banned dissemination of the big-character poster.

But the situation soon changed drastically. On June 1, Mao instructed K'ang Sheng to broadcast the content of the poster over Peking Radio, and the June 2 issue of *Jen-min jih-pao* (the People's Daily) carried the poster with commentators' notes explaining its implications. These events brought about the collapse of the Peking University Party Committee, paving the way for the eventual Red Guard movement.

## Analysis

So far, we have presented in a straightforward fashion the evolution of the Wu Han campaign. In the remaining part of this chapter we will discuss three questions which are crucial for interpreting the Cultural Revolution as a whole. They are (1) why Mao initiated the criticism of Wu Han; (2) what linkage one can establish between the criticism of Wu Han and the subsequent downfall of P'eng Chen and Lu Ting-yi; and (3) to what extent the moves and countermoves of the Maoist leaders and the Party bureaucrats were known to the public at the time.

### Mao's Motives

In retrospect, Mao seems to have had good reason to attack Wu Han. Undoubtedly, Wu Han's play was intended to criticize Mao's dismissal of

33. *Jen-min jih-pao,* 2 June 1966.
34. "Record," p. 12.
35. *JMJP,* 5 June 1966; *Kung-jen jih-pao,* 5 June 1966.

P'eng Teh-huai by using the classical technique of "borrowing from antiquity to criticize the present," the method that traditional Chinese scholars had used to censor their emperors.[36] Thus Mao might well have regarded Wu Han as typical of those Chinese intellectuals who had reached politically powerful positions but still derided Mao's Thought, his Great Leap Forward policy, and his personal power. Also Mao's motive might well have been to revolutionize Chinese literature and art. In the past he had personally initiated several well-known campaigns, including the ones against the legend of Wu Hsün and the writings of Yu P'ing-po.[37] In addition, Mao might also have intended the secret attack on Wu Han to give an impetus to his ongoing effort to revolutionize ideology—particularly the current Socialist Education Movement in the rural areas and the campaign to reform literature and art in the urban areas.[38]

Wu Han was an ideal opening wedge for a larger campaign. His position at the middle level of the Chinese political hierarchy was neither so high that it might force Party leaders to form an open anti-Mao bloc nor so low that it might allow the Party organization to shift the campaign to an attack on lower-ranking cadres, as it had already done in the Socialist Education Movement.

*The Purge of P'eng Chen*

If Mao had good political as well as personal reasons for criticizing Wu Han, did he foresee the purge of P'eng Chen? In other words, was his attack on Wu Han the initial move against P'eng Chen? There are three different theories on this question. The "test" theory suggests that Mao used the Wu Han issue to test the loyalty of his associates. This interpretation credits Mao with some genuine concern for revolutionizing the superstructure, while recognizing his supreme power over his associates. The "plot" theory explains Mao's demand for an attack on Wu Han as the initial move in a larger plan to "trap" those Party opponents he wanted to purge, in order to consolidate his power. A third theory conceives of the whole process as a full-fledged power struggle between Mao and the Peking Party Committee supported by Liu.

Although conflicts between Mao and the Party preceded the Cultural Revolution, and maneuvers on both sides were readily apparent, there is still not enough evidence to support the contention that Mao intended from the

36. James R. Pusey, *Wu Han: Attacking the Present Through the Past* (Cambridge, Mass.: East Asian Research Center, Harvard University Press, 1969), p. x.
37. For Mao's instructions regarding these campaigns, see "Long Live Mao Tse-tung's Thought," *CB*, no. 891 (8 October 1969), pp. 14, 19-21.
38. For Mao's effort to revolutionize superstructure in 1962-1964, see Merle Goldman, "The Chinese Communist Party's Cultural Revolution of 1962-1964," in *Ideology and Politics*, ed. Chalmers Johnson (Seattle: Washington University Press, 1973), pp. 219-254.

beginning to purge the Party leaders.[39] It seems more likely that when Mao initiated the attack on Wu Han he had only an extremely vague idea of its implications, and that the subsequent unfolding of events, to which the Party, the PLA, and Chiang Ch'ing's informal group also contributed, led to the purge of P'eng Chen. At the beginning, Mao appears to have been undecided even on the issue of Wu Han.

Although the official publications and the Red Guard newspapers maintain that P'eng Chen had defied Mao's specific instruction to criticize Wu Han—"Chairman Mao's instruction regarding Wu Han"—it is more likely that Mao had merely expressed some general wish, instead of a specific instruction. According to a detailed account of the dialogue between Mao and P'eng Chen, Mao merely indicated his suspicion of Wu Han: "Can Wu Han be criticized?"[40] P'eng Chen himself argued that Mao was indecisive, even on the February Outline. "At that time my view was correct; otherwise I would not have sent [the February Outline] to seek Chairman Mao's criticism. At that time Chairman Mao neither affirmed nor rejected [the February Outline]."[41]

Mao's ambiguous attitude might be interpreted as an attempt to test P'eng Chen's loyalty, but if so, it seems unlikely that P'eng Chen would not have noticed Mao's intention. P'eng Chen's subsequent behavior suggests that he assumed that Mao was under conflicting pressures and that his own (P'eng's) position could eventually prevail. Or the Party bureaucrats might well have believed that if they made decisions according to the proper procedures Mao would not openly repudiate the decisions even if he disliked them. In fact, Mao did not move against the Party organization until the Chiang Ch'ing group produced the competing official document, the Shanghai Forum.

Even if Mao initiated the criticism of Wu Han with a limited purpose, the Party organization had good reason to worry about the campaign. As shown in the subsequent developments, the Maoists actually broadened the issue to encompass Wu Han's political motivation for writing the play—his opposition to Mao's Thought and Mao's Great Leap Forward policy. Once questions were raised about Wu Han's political motivations, they were bound to reflect on the Party organization's responsibility for accepting the play in the first place in 1961, and on its failure, despite pressure from the radicals, to criticize the play during its extensive efforts to revolutionize literature and art in the preceding two years. More important, if Wu Han could be attacked for his opposition to Mao's Thought and the Great Leap Forward, those Party leaders who privately had entertained similar critical views would also be

39. Lowell Dittmer, *Liu Shao-ch'i and the Chinese Cultural Revolution* (Berkeley and Los Angeles: University of California Press, 1974), pp. 63-66.
40. "Record," p. 2.
41. *Chung-kung wen-hua ta ko-ming chung-yao wen-chien hui-pien* (Taipei: Chung-kung Yen-chiu, 1973), p. 3.

unsafe. The Party organization therefore attempted to limit the Wu Han issue to the academic questions alone. This in turn prompted Mao to expand the Wu Han issue, since the Party's attempt constituted an apparent diversion in his eyes. After all, Mao had already made clear his position on such academic issues as how to evaluate "clean historical officials."[42]

Apart from these political implications, Mao's demand for criticism of Wu Han also spotlighted other ideological issues. For one, it brought to the fore the question of subsystem autonomy free of political interference—that is, in Chinese jargon, the proper relationship between politics and functional work. With regard to literature and art, criticism of Wu Han raised the question of whether artistic projects should be evaluated by artistic and aesthetic criteria, by political criteria, or by both, and in what proportions. Another ideological issue related to the problem of mass participation in the decision-making process: specifically, who should make decisions in the functional fields. Logically, the arguments favoring some sort of subsystem autonomy would give specialists and professionals a greater voice in evaluating end products. On the other hand, the notion of "politics in command" allowed the masses to render final judgment, even on art and literature.

It is paradoxical that the Party organization found itself supporting the intellectuals' position on these ideological issues, for when the Chinese elite had been tightly united under Mao the Party bureaucrats had suppressed the dissident intellectuals—such as Yu P'ing-po, Hu Feng, and Ting Ling—who demanded autonomy for cultural endeavors. In the Hundred Flowers campaign, Mao, not the Party organization, was willing to allow the intellectuals to speak out freely. But the coalition pattern had changed by 1966, when many of the Party leaders found themselves privately questioning Mao's wisdom and many intellectuals were co-opted into powerful positions within the Party organization. In other words, the new coalition between intellectuals (experts) and Party bureaucrats (reds) reflected a widening division between those with and those without power in Chinese society, as well as the alienation from Mao of both the intellectuals and the Party leaders since the Great Leap Forward. Thus, in the Wu Han issue, the bureaucrat-intellectuals and the Party leaders found their common interests in resisting Mao's wishes.

Only some young ambitious intellectuals, who had not published critical articles about the Great Leap Forward and Mao's Thought, saw Mao's call as an opportunity to advance their political ambitions. Recruited by Chiang Ch'ing, these young radicals set themselves up as the "true leftists" and helped challenge the Party establishment. This informal radical group had another ally in the PLA. Since Lin Piao's success in restoring the morale of

42. *Mao Tse-tung ssu-hsiang wan-sui* (n.p., preface dated August 1969), p. 397.

the PLA with political education, he had been the leading advocate of the "politics in command" slogan and the cult of Mao Tse-tung's Thought. By September 1965, Lin Piao had established himself as the interpreter of Mao's orthodoxy by advocating the now famous "four firsts," and had consolidated his power within the PLA by purging Lo Jui-ch'ing, the Chief of Staff, who had probably resisted Lin's attempt to politicize the PLA. During the Cultural Revolution, the PLA squarely challenged the Party over ideological issues such as "politics in command" and mass participation, and provided important support for the Maoist group led by Chiang Ch'ing.

In retrospect, it seems undeniable that Mao collaborated with Chiang Ch'ing's informal group and the PLA, but it is still difficult to prove that Mao manipulated the PLA in order to purge his political opponents. Rather, the PLA (and Lin Piao in particular) seems to have exploited the conflict between Mao and the Party organization for its own advantage. The PLA's controversy with the Party organization over "politics in command" ended with the expansion of the PLA's political influence. By claiming to be a faithful follower of Mao's Thought, Lin Piao emerged as the most powerful political leader after Mao. At that time, when Mao wanted only "to over-throw a part (it is not possible to overthrow all) of the rightists in the Party and throughout the country," he appeared to be uneasy with Lin Piao's attempt to use Mao Tse-tung's Thought for his own political advancement. Mao revealed his worry over Lin Piao in his letter to Chiang Ch'ing: "The higher a thing is blown up, the more seriously it is hurt when it falls. . . . I never believed that several booklets I wrote would have so much supernatural power."[43]

### Revelation of the Conflict to the Masses

The Chinese leadership's maneuvers and countermaneuvers took place behind the public scene; yet gradually the conflict became known to the Chinese masses. The first indication of the dissension among the elite was exposed in a mild rivalry between the *Jen-min jih-pao*, the Party organ, and the *Chieh-fang chün-pao* (the Liberation Army Daily). At that early stage of the Cultural Revolution, the *Jen-min jih-pao* lagged behind the *Chieh-fang chün-pao*, not only in the number of articles relevant to the Cultural Revolution, but also in the militancy of its content.[44] The *Chieh-fang chün-pao* advanced the radical thesis that "politics in command" was not merely a slogan to encourage high-level performance in functional work, but the goal itself, the realization of which would determine the progress of the socialist

43. "Mao Tse-tung's Private Letter to Chiang Ch'ing," *Issues and Studies* 9, no. 4 (June 1973): 94-96.

44. Ting Wang, *Collection of Essays on the GPCR* (Hong Kong: Contemporary Chinese Research Center, 1976), p. 7.

society.[45] In contrast, the *Jen-min jih-pao* echoed Liu Shao-ch'i's views on organization by arguing that, first, functional work was an inevitable consequence of division of labor in modern society; second, "politics in command" meant to do one's functional work well, since all functional work in a socialist country was still for the revolution; and third, the reason for "bringing politics to the fore" and mobilizing the masses was to increase production.[46] Moreover, the *Jen-min jih-pao* stressed Mao's teaching on practice, which it interpreted as observing and experimenting with nature rather than actually participating in social and political struggle. Consequently the *Jen-min jih-pao* made Mao's Thought into something closer to a philosophy of passive empiricism than a revolutionary ideology.[47]

As the campaign against Wu Han intensified in late April 1966, the *Jen-min jih-pao* moved to reduce its differences with the PLA by advancing the theory of the unity of politics and functional work. It explained that politics was the goal and functional work the means; hence politics should be closely integrated with functional work: "[If] politics are not realized in and integrated with functional work, then politics will fall through and the political aim will not be achieved. There is neither functional work without politics nor political work without functional work."[48] This revised position, however, was still unacceptable to the PLA: "To say, on the one hand, that politics should command functional work and, on the other hand, that politics should be realized in functional work is to deny the supremacy of politics and place politics in a subordinate position."[49] This veiled criticism of the *Jen-min jih-pao* by the *Chieh-fang chün-pao* prompted some politically sensitive Chinese to suspect the elite discord.

More direct revelation of the conflict came on April 18—the day when the *Pei-ching jih-pao* made a public self-criticism—when the *Chieh-fang chün-pao* published excerpts from the Shanghai Forum in its editorial with only minor changes and an omission of the most explosive sentence.[50] In effect, the editorial finally made public the most radical argument against the Party's insistence on dealing with the Wu Han problem as an academic discussion—the thesis that neglect of the class struggle in ideological fields

45. "Forever Bring Politics to the Fore," *Chieh-fang chün-pao,* 4 February 1966, in *SCMP,* no. 3644 (24 February 1966), pp. 1-5.

46. *JMJP,* 22 October 1965; 8 January 1966.

47. Chao Ts'ung, *Wen-ko yün-tung li-ch'eng shu-lüeh* (Hong Kong: Yu-lien yen-chiu-so, 1971), vol. 1, p. 113; *Shou-tu hung-wei-ping,* 9 June 1967.

48. *JMJP,* 22 April 1966.

49. "Bringing of Politics to the Fore Must Be Implemented in Ideological Revolution," *Chieh-fang chün-pao,* 17 May 1966, in *SCMP,* no. 3706 (26 May 1966), pp. 1-5.

50. "Hold High the Great Banner of Mao Tse-tung's Ideas and Take Active Part in the Great Socialist Cultural Revolution," *CFCP,* 18 April 1966. It was the first public use of the terms "Socialist Cultural Revolution" and "anti-Party, antisocialist black line."

could result in the loss of political power. The PLA also pledged itself to perform an important role in the Great Socialist Cultural Revolution and made a public hint at the targets of the movement by labelling "literature on national defense" a reactionary slogan.

On May 8, the *Chieh-fang chün-pao* and the *Kuang-ming jih-pao* launched a final frontal assault on the Peking Party Committee with a rejection of the *Pei-ching jih-pao*'s self-criticism. The *Chieh-fang chün-pao* further called upon old comrades in high places to engage in self-criticism to maintain the spirit of the old days, and invited the Party secretaries to boldly take responsibility for their committee members' mistakes.[51] Kuo Mo-jo, the most prominent figure in Chinese literary circles, responded with a drastic self-criticism, and Chou En-lai publicly supported the Maoist position.[52] The provincial and city Party committees, which had not yet been affected, began to mobilize the masses to display their indignation toward the Peking Party Committee. Although Teng T'o was the only person yet actually named, his major crime—opposition to the Great Leap Forward— clearly implied that the purge of other Party leaders would follow. Use of terms such as "black gang," "black line," and "bourgeois line" to refer to yet unidentified targets heightened the atmosphere of excitement and created a witch-hunting mentality among the masses.

In addition to the expansion of the targets and issues, the Maoist leaders began to expose inner-Party discussion to the public, in violation of the Party regulations.[53] This Maoist move in effect amounted to an open call upon the masses to criticize those who had led the mass movement up to that time to the academic debate. Thus, what had once been the legitimate official line became the object of criticism, and all the lower-level Party units that had faithfully carried out the official line of the February Outline became vulnerable to mass criticism. This changed situation no doubt threatened the whole organizational structure of the school Party committees, since most of them had carried out the now repudiated policy either because it was the official decision of the Party or because they supported it. Whatever their reasons, many school Party committees had suppressed spontaneous student participation in the Wu Han controversy; they had resisted any attempt to question the political motivation of Wu Han; they had instructed the students to write only small-character posters—good, well-argued articles; they had prohibited the students from writing big-character posters and holding

51. "Open Fire on the Anti-Party and Anti-Socialist," *CFCP*, 8 May 1966, in *Daily Report*, 9 May 1966, pp. CCC1-3.

52. *JMJP*, 14 April 1966.

53. "Smash Teng T'o's Conspiracy of Inciting Youth to Oppose the Party in the CR," *Chung-kuo ch'ing-nien pao*, 14 May 1966, in *SCMP* no. 3709 (1 June 1966), pp. 1-6.

political meetings; and they had stipulated that any article by students to the newspapers had to be censored by the school Party committees.[54]

While encouraging the masses to criticize the Party leadership, the Maoist leaders also pressed the Party to allow the masses to mobilize freely. For the lower Party units that had taken the February Outline as a legitimate official decision, this Maoist demand—which was actually tantamount to asking the Party to mobilize the masses to criticize itself—was most unfair. To overcome the resistance of the Party units at the lower levels, the Maoists argued that if those who had carried out the wrong decision rectified their mistakes by exposing the wrong-doing of the higher units and sincerely making self-criticism, they would be exonerated.

This formula, however, was not easy for the school Party committees to follow. First, there were genuine dissenters in every school who would exploit the self-criticism of the school Party committee to discredit it completely. Second, admitting its mistake would raise the complicated problem of how retroactive the Party committee's self-criticism should be—that is to say, whether a school Party committee should admit its mistakes in actions taken before the Cultural Revolution or not. Third, the policy line of the newly organized Peking Party Committee was not clear, and the school Party committee could not know what would be the outcome of the struggle between the Maoist leaders and the Party leaders at the top level. Fourth and most important, the school Party committees that had maintained particularly close relationships with the now purged leaders knew well that they would not survive a sincere self-criticism.

The political situation in the last part of May was confusing not only for the Chinese students but also for the school Party committees. The Peking Party Committee, now defunct, was no longer issuing guidelines on how to deal with the various problems, including the discussions of P'eng Chen. The surviving members of the Peking Party Committee were busy protecting themselves, and no one was willing to assume responsibility. While the news media made it legitimate to expose the inner-Party discussion, the Party organization was still defending its organizational legitimacy. Sung Shih, the Director of the University Work Department of the Peking Committee, issued a directive to Lu P'ing:

The Party organization of the school is urged to strengthen its leadership and to hold its position firmly. . . . If the masses are indignant and ask for a meeting, do not suppress them, but lead them to hold group discussions, to study documents, and to publish wall papers in small character.[55]

54. *JMJP,* 14 May 1966; 5 and 11 June 1966.
55. *Hsin kang-yüan,* 6 March 1967.

To summarize, then, by early May 1966, the Wu Han campaign had undergone parallel expansions on several levels: the academic criticism among professionals rapidly changed into a mass campaign against anti-Party and antisocialist elements within the Party; the Wu Han question spread to encompass the Peking Party Committee; and the issues involved in the historical play *Hai Jui Dismissed from Office* were applied to all other cultural fields.

Not only Mao, but also the Party bureaucrats, the Cultural Revolution Small Group, and the PLA contributed to this evolution of the Wu Han campaign, all of them maneuvering and countermaneuvering to lead the movement to their own political advantage. P'eng Chen tried to contain the Wu Han question, if not openly protect Wu Han himself, but this backfired by pushing Mao into close cooperation with the Chiang Ch'ing group and the PLA. Mao's repudiation of the February Outline, once regarded as the legitimate official document, made the leadership of lower-level Party units vulnerable to the challenge of the masses. To deal with the leadership problem and to lead the students in the Cultural Revolution, the Party organization sent out work teams, the subject of the following chapter.

# CHAPTER 2

# The Work Teams and the Student Revolt: Early Summer, 1966

In this chapter we will analyze the incipient student revolt in June and July of 1966, which constitutes the background of the eventual emergence of the Red Guards and, more important, of the conservative-radical split in the Red Guard movement. At that time Mao had not yet returned to Peking and taken command of the Cultural Revolution, and the newly organized Cultural Revolution Small Group had not gained its full strength. Yet, as a result of the earlier confrontation with the Party organization, the Maoists were in partial control of the Party propaganda machine, but the Party organization still retained power in other fields and implemented concrete policy decisions under the leadership of Liu Shao-ch'i and Teng Hsiao-p'ing through the work teams. Later the Maoists condemned the Party leaders for having carried out a "bourgeois reactionary line" during this "fifty days of white terror," and used the charges to purge the Party leaders.

We will begin this chapter by examining the general orientation of the work teams, as reflected in the "anti-interference campaign." This first section of the chapter will also consider some major events of the period. We will then discuss in the second section the differences between the Maoists and the Party leaders over the desirability of dispatching the work teams, and the actual operation of the work teams will be the concern of the third section. The fourth section will reconstruct the Maoists' view of the movement, as reflected in the official news media, which, we believe, precipitated the student revolt against the work teams. The most crucial issue of who should be purged and who should be allowed to participate in the movement will be dealt with in the fifth section. The chapter will conclude with a summary of the student revolt.

## The Anti-Interference Campaign

The Party organization's trouble in the Great Proletarian Cultural Revolution began in earnest with Nieh's big-character poster, which the Maoists aptly called "the first Marxist-Leninist big-character poster in the twentieth century."[1] It represented the first time that an individual Party member had challenged the organization in the name of correct ideology. Its official publication—which Mao claimed "stirred up the whole world"—suggested a number of points to the Chinese students.[2] First, it was clear that the regime intended to encourage the students to revolt against "revisionist" school Party committees. Second, the term "revisionist" applied to those who opposed Mao's Thought, as, for example, Wu Han did when he wrote his play. Third, it was legitimate for students to put up big-character posters attacking school Party committees. Fourth, it was wrong for the school Party committees to invoke organizational principles or to manipulate the students. Fifth, these points were certainly backed by Mao, if not by the Party organization.[3]

Given these implications, the Chinese students only had to decide whether their school Party committees fell within Nieh's specifications for "revisionist." If so, they had not only the right but the obligation to criticize their school Party committees. Some courageous students put up big-character posters intimating that their school Party committees had lacked zeal in the Wu Han campaign. Instead of admitting their mistakes and issuing self-criticisms, as the Maoist leaders expected, the attacked Party committees took defensive measures: they convened secret Party meetings and mobilized students close to them—the members of the Party and the Chinese Youth League and children of cadres—to sway student opinion over to their side.[4] Soon the students stopped attending classes in order to engage in the debates over whether their school Party committee members represented Mr. Ma (Marxism) or Mr. Hsu (revisionism).[5]

Confronted with the students' challenge to their legitimacy, the school Party committees urgently asked the higher Party units to send out the work teams. In accordance with past practice, Liu Shao-ch'i, who was in charge of the daily work of the Party organization, routinely dispatched the work teams. This time, however, he sent them out hastily without adequate

1. For Nieh's big-character poster and its implication, see *JMJP*, 2 June 1966.
2. "Speech at the Work Conference of CC," *CB*, no. 891 (8 October 1966), p. 75.
3. For instance, many Party leaders opposed the publication of Nieh's big-character poster. Ch'en I was reportedly opposed to it on the ground that it "let all the Party secret out." *Wai-shih hung-ch'i*, 8 May 1967.
4. *Tung-fang-hung pao*, 24 October 1967.
5. William Hinton, *Hundred Day War* (New York: Monthly Review Press, 1972), p. 20.

preparation and without carefully weighing their desirability.[6] The work teams, composed mainly of personnel from the Party and Chinese Youth League organs and the Socialist Education Work Teams, were large in size and low in quality.[7] Worse still, they were not even briefed on what "general and specific work" they were expected to perform on the campuses.[8]

The students, particularly those who had challenged the school Party committees, warmly welcomed the work teams initially with expectations that the work teams would resolve the problem of their school Party committees. Their hopes diminished, however, as they observed the work teams in operation, and soon some students began to criticize the work teams. The work teams reacted promptly and excessively to the initially mild anti-work-team big-character posters, which merely questioned the work team operations and stated the students' own views. Students critical of the work teams were put under close surveillance, while pro-work-team students were mobilized against the others.[9]

On June 18, some students at Peking University defied the work team's restrictions by staging violent meetings against the targets they freely selected in the fashion suggested by Mao's "Hunan Reports."[10] Considering this spontaneous student action to be a challenge to its leadership, the work team quickly denounced the incident as a "prepared, planned, and guided counterrevolutionary incident."[11] Nonetheless, by June 20 the anti-work-team movement had developed into a full-fledged student movement encompassing thirty-nine of the fifty institutes of higher learning in Peking.[12]

In response to the students' criticism that the work teams "basically do not carry out the instructions from the Party Center and Chairman Mao,"[13] the Party organization tried to improve the quality of the work teams by reducing their size and setting up elaborate training programs for their members. Wang Kuang-mei joined the Tsinghua work teams, and Liu Shao-ch'i personally took charge of the movement at Tsinghua University, the Radio Broadcast Institute, the Building Construction Institute, and the

6. "Liu Shao-ch'i's Self-Criticism Made at the Work Conference on the CCP Central Committee," *Issues and Studies* 6, no. 9 (June 1970): 90-98.

7. *Tung-fang-hung pao,* 15 February 1967.

8. "Teng Hsiao-p'ing's August 2 Speech at the People's University," *CB,* no. 819 (10 March 1967), pp. 4-7.

9. For the development of the anti-work-team activities in Tsinghua, see "Selected Big Character Posters of Tsinghua," *Supplement to Selections from China Mainland Magazines,* no. 20 (18 March 1968), pp. 1-59.

10. *Tung-fang-hung pao,* 24 October 1966.

11. "Li Hsüeh-feng Is the Executioner Suppressing the CR in Peking Municipality," *Supplement to Survey of China Mainland Press,* no. 162 (14 February 1967), pp. 16-22; *Chan-tou pao,* 15 February 1967.

12. *Tung-fang-hung pao,* 14 October 1967.

13. *KMJP,* 7 April 1967.

Girls' Middle School attached to the Peking Normal University.[14] At the same time, the Party organization stiffened its attitude toward the revolting students by labelling them "monsters and freaks." Declaring that, "in many units, not all freaks and monsters were wiped out, but freaks and monsters were wiping out everything," the reorganized work teams advanced the slogan "Sweep out all obstacles to the Cultural Revolution."[15] The movement was thus turned into an "anti-interference campaign" designed to eliminate the opposition to the work teams.

At first glance, the anti-interference campaign appeared to be a relatively unimportant, temporary measure, but in fact it represented a subtle shift of the Cultural Revolution targets from the elites to the masses—from the "bourgeois authorities" and "black gangs" to those who "pop up their heads" (students who visited other campuses in violation of a ban imposed by the work teams). Later the Maoists charged that the Party leaders intentionally changed the targets to protect the power holders and, in the process, created a situation in which the masses were fighting against themselves.

The Party organization justified the anti-interference campaign on two grounds. First, as Li Hsüeh-feng, the newly appointed first secretary of the Peking Party Committee, asserted, the Party leaders regarded the anti-work-team students as rightists:

The backgrounds of the anti-work-team [forces] are complicated; counterrevolutionaries, black gangs, conservatives, bourgeois authorities, their defenders, and rightist students came out to seize the leadership power of the work teams, taking advantage of the chaos.[16]

If this diagnosis was true, the Party's only choice was to spearhead a movement against the rightists. Comparing the Great Proletarian Cultural Revolution to the anti-rightist campaign of 1957, Li declared that, "[as] we did in [the] 1957 [anti-] rightist offensives, we should call on old Communist Party members to come out at the critical moment to prevent a coup."[17]

As a second justification for the anti-interference campaign, the Party claimed that the real intention of the anti-work-team forces was to protect the black gangs and bad elements in the school Party committees: "The black gangs are the rabbits and the masses are grass," and hence it is necessary to "peel them off level by level and unit by unit."[18]

14. "Record," pp. 18-22.
15. *Tung-fang-hung pao,* 14 October 1967.
16. Ibid.
17. "Record," p. 19. Liu Shao-ch'i shared Li's view: "Now that they [the rightists] have begun to take the offensive, this is a good thing. When the enemies come out, they are like snakes coming out of holes, and it will be easier for you to eliminate them." Ibid.
18. *JMJP,* 30 August 1967; "Liu Shao-ch'i's Daughter Writes to Expose Her Father," *CB,* no. 821 (16 March 1967), pp. 1-25.

Chang Ch'eng-hsien, the head of the Peking University work team, prepared a report on the June 18 incident, which Li Hsüeh-feng incorporated
into his report to the Work Conference of the Peking Municipal Party
Committee. The document, together with materials on the anti-interference
campaign and the rationale behind it, were transmitted through the organizational channels to the lower Party units. An accompanying instruction read
that, "upon discovering a similar phenomenon in other areas, it can be
handled according to the measures taken at Peking University."[19] As might
be expected, the organization's policy line pleased the lower Party committees and the work teams, who praised it as a "good example of living study
and living application to Mao's Thought," and urged all the Party members
to carry out the "spirit" of the policy.[20] The anti-interference campaign thus
became the official policy.[21]

By mid-July, the anti-interference campaign had succeeded in sapping the
anti-work-team forces; in some schools the radical forces were reduced to
only ten persons. Even a stubborn radical like K'uai Ta-fu, the leader of the
anti-work-team students at Tsinghua University, began to show signs of
diminishing vigor in offering to compromise with the work teams. As the
students' excitement abated, the campuses regained a semblance of order.
Yet, with the reestablishment of order, the students also lost their revolutionary élan. Obviously satisfied with the restored order, Liu Shao-ch'i
declared that the "danger had passed" and called for the prompt restoration
of the school Party committee leadership and preparations for the reopening
of classes.[22]

The Party's confidence soon proved unfounded. Mao, who was probably
watching the Cultural Revolution in Peking from Hangchow, made his
famous "sixty-five-minute, nine-mile swim" in the Yangtze on July 16, and
came to Peking on July 18. On that day, the work teams abruptly declared
the end of the anti-interference campaign, and returned to the original work
of the Great Proletarian Cultural Revolution.[23] On July 22, without any
explanation, the Tsinghua work team released the radicals it had placed
under confinement, including K'uai Ta-fu. Meanwhile, Mao, who hesitated
to discredit the Party organization during his first four days in Peking, called
a series of high-level Party meetings. At the meetings, he echoed the views of

19. "Record," pp. 18. The Cultural Revolution Small Group raised objection to the "June 20
Report." *JMJP*, 13 August, 1967. T'ao Chu nevertheless argued with the CRSG that it was
approved by the CC of the CCP, and the CRSG had no power to object to it. *Chan-tou pao*, 15
February 1967.

20. *Hung-se tsao-fan pao*, 20 January 1967; *JMJP*, 13 August 1967.

21. For instance, Wang Jen-chung, the first secretary of Hupeh Provincial Party Committee,
issued a directive instructing the middle school of Hupeh to launch the anti-rightist struggle.
*Tung-fang-hung pao*, 14 October 1967.

22. "Record," p. 24.

23. Ibid., p. 28.

the anti-work-team students in a point-by-point criticism of the policies the Party organization had been pursuing: he criticized the Party leaders for their failures to live up to the mass line; he stressed that the Cultural Revolution "must be led by the cultural revolution teams of schools, as organized by revolutionary teachers, students, and neutrals, who are the only people in the schools who know anything at all"; and he specifically denounced Liu Shao-ch'i's slogan "Make a distinction between inside and outside [the Party]."[24]

The Party organization, however, persisted in defending the anti-interference campaign. Liu Shao-ch'i and Po I-po ordered the work teams to sum up their "good experiences,"[25] while the Cultural Revolution Small Group interviewed the students at Peking University to collect materials critical of the work teams. At a July 24 meeting, Liu Shao-ch'i presided and Party leaders such as T'ao Chu and Po I-po dominated the floor. At the end of the five-hour session, Liu Shao-ch'i decided against withdrawing the work teams.[26] The next day, however, Mao personally convened another meeting with Liu Shao-ch'i and the Cultural Revolution Small Group, and the decision to withdraw the work teams was finally made.[27]

On July 27, the Cultural Revolution Small Group held a mass rally at Peking University to denounce the work teams.[28] The next day, the Peking Party Committee formally promulgated the "Circular on the Withdrawal of the Work Teams," thus ending the initial stage of the Cultural Revolution.[29] On that day, Liu Shao-ch'i was so upset that his daughter reported that she had never seen her father so "vexed."[30] The following day, Wang Kuang-mei volunteered to serve the Tsinghua students by serving potatoes at the school cafeteria, but her last desperate gesture to "serve the masses" saved neither her nor her husband from disgrace.[31]

## Mao and the Work Teams

A crucial question concerning this period of the Cultural Revolution and the work teams is why Mao would permit the Party organization to lead the

24. Jerome Ch'en, *Mao Papers* (New York: Oxford University Press, 1970), pp. 24-26; "Speeches and Statements Alleged to Have Been Made by Chinese Communist Leaders," *CB*, no. 891 (8 October 1969), pp. 1-84.

25. When the decision on the work teams was reversed, the Party leaders changed the wording in their reports and destroyed the materials showing their support of the work teams. *Tung-fang hung pao*, 15 February 1967; *Chan-tou pao*, 15 February 1967.

26. "Record," p. 28.

27. Ibid., p. 29.

28. Ibid., p. 29.

29. Ibid., p. 30.

30. "Liu Shao-ch'i's Daughter Writes to Expose Her Father," *CB* no. 821 (16 March 1967), pp. 1-25.

31. William Hinton, *Hundred Day War* (n. 5 above), p. 66.

mass movement in the wrong direction for "fifty days." Did he intend to trap the Party leaders by allowing them to make mistakes? Or did he gradually become critical of the work teams as he watched their actual operations? Although the available evidence is inconclusive, the second proposition seems to be more plausible.

The work team usually has a more difficult task than the ordinary Party units. Since the work team is employed when the operations of the basic-level leadership are in doubt, it must balance the various expectations of the higher Party units and the basic Party units, and carry out the official policy without antagonizing either the basic-level leadership or the masses. Analytically speaking, the work team's relationship with the basic Party units and the masses depends on the specific goal of a given movement. In a campaign intended to rectify a condition in which a locality has a vested interest, the masses and the local Party leadership are apt to unite against the work team. When the basic-level cadres are the object of rectification, the work teams and the masses share common interests. If the campaign is aimed at one segment of the masses (such as rightists or landlords), the basic-level cadres collaborate with the work teams against those outside the Party.

In reality, however, no campaign has only one analytically discernible task. All campaigns that have involved the work teams in China have gone through various stages in which the balance among work teams, basic-level cadres, and the masses has shifted. During the land reform period, the work teams collaborated first with the basic-level cadres to carry out the land reform policy, and then with the masses to rectify the basic-level cadres.[32] Finally, the masses and the basic-level cadres criticized the work teams.

During the Socialist Education Movement, the respective roles of the three groups changed according to shifts in the nature of the movement.[33] The First Ten Articles did not even mention work teams. The Revised Ten Articles acknowledged their role, but provided safeguards so that the work teams would not push aside the basic-level cadres. The Later Revised Ten Articles, however, written by Liu on the basis of Wang Kuang-mei's T'aoyüan experience, increased the importance of the work teams at the expense of the other groups. Mao then cautioned the Party organization against its heavy reliance on the work teams: "In short, we must rely on the masses, not the work teams. The work teams either do not understand the situation or are ignorant. Some of them become bureaucrats and obstruct the movement. Some people on the work teams are not dependable."[34]

32. William Hinton, *Fanshen* (New York: Monthly Review Press, 1966), passim.

33. For the different emphasis on the function of the work teams between Mao and Liu during the Socialist Education movement, see Richard Baum, *Prelude to Revolution* (New York: Columbia University Press, 1975).

34. *Mao Tse-tung ssu-hsiang wan-sui* (n.p., preface dated August 1969), p. 612.

In a campaign specifically designed to rectify the basic-level cadres, the work teams had to achieve a delicate balance in carrying out their various tasks. First, they had to prevent the public from developing their criticism of cadres into a larger struggle against the Party or a personal struggle against individuals. Second, they had to operate in such a way as not to undermine the morale and leadership of the basic-level cadres. And third, they had to alleviate the fears of political reprisal so the masses would say what was on their minds.[35]

To successfully discharge these conflicting duties, a work team had to be keenly aware of the diverse goals of the movement and strongly motivated toward them. Otherwise, the team would commit the mistake of "commandism," which sapped the initiative and enthusiasm of the masses, or "formalism and tailism," which resulted in failure to implement the official policy. Considering the difficulties confronting the work teams under ordinary circumstances, it is not surprising that the Cultural Revolution work teams, so hastily dispatched with such ill-defined tasks, failed to live up to the expectations of the Maoist leaders.

When the official publication of Nieh's big-character poster created chaos in the schools, the Party leaders had two options: to send out work teams to "seize the power from the black gangs, suspected black gangs, or capitalist authoritarian elements"; or to "let the people in the respective units promote their revolution and throw everything into confusion for a period."[36] Not surprisingly, the Party leaders chose the first option. It enabled them to perform an orderly and limited surgical operation in the lower units without undermining the organization's legitimacy in the eyes of the public. It also curtailed meaningful mass participation in the movement.

The second option would have given the masses a free hand in the movement but weakened the Party organization's control. In addition to the obvious objection that no organization likes chaos and unpredictability, the Party organization could not politically afford to allow the masses complete freedom in determining the fate of the Party committees. Too many Party leaders had written or uttered remarks critical of Mao's Thought and wholeheartedly supported the "February Outline." Permitting the masses to mobilize freely and expose the leaders' "mistakes" would certainly have caused problems for high-ranking Party leaders and undermined "a primary need of any organization—security for the organization as a whole in relation to the social forces and its environment."[37] As early as June 1966, some students began to criticize top leaders for what they had written and said. Instead of

35. Hinton, *Fanshen*, p. 130.
36. "Premier Chou En-lai's Speech at Tsinghua University," *JPRS*, no. 41,313 (8 June 1967), pp. 14-21.
37. A. Selznick, "Co-optation: A Mechanism for Organizational Stability," in *Reader in Bureaucracy*, ed. Robert Merton (New York: Columbia University Press), pp. 135-140.

admitting their mistakes, the criticized leaders "denounced and persecuted" the revolting students, regarding their criticisms as a challenge to the Party organization itself.[38]

If the Party organization had good reasons for sending out the work teams, Mao had equally good reasons for his hesitation. His ideology has always attached more importance to internal forces (self-reliance) and heightened consciousness than to external forces and superficial compliance with imposed changes. Politically, Mao enjoyed direct mass support, but he did not have firm control over the Party organization at that time. Moreover, if he intended to purge the revisionists hidden in the Party rather than only specific persons, his purpose would be better served by allowing the masses to mobilize freely; they knew best about the leadership in their own units.

Even when Mao agreed to use the organizational format of the work teams, his expectations differed from those of other Party leaders. Consistent with his tendency to view any phenomenon in its totality, Mao expected the work teams to provide proper guidance to the lower levels and to correct any of their leadership mistakes, thus strengthening, not weakening, the existing leadership. As early as the land reform period, Mao had ordered: "Work teams must be sent out, but it must be stated clearly that they are being sent to help local Party organs, not to replace them."[39]

The CCP departed from the Soviet practice of relying on outside cadres by leaning heavily upon basic-level cadres during collectivization.[40] Even when investigating the cadres' backgrounds in the 1943 rectification campaign, the CCP consistently stressed the role of the masses and the members of basic units, while downgrading the importance of the work teams sent down by the upper level.[41] For an organizational man like Liu Shao-ch'i, however, other work-team functions were secondary to their primary function of supervising the lower-level leadership. Therefore, the Party organization tended to acquiesce in the work teams' take-over of the lower-level leadership functions and their use of secret agents to gather information.[42] In brief, Mao evaluated the work teams according to the correctness of their leadership style; the Party leaders evaluated their ability to carry out official decisions.

38. A student from Wuhan had written a letter to Wang Jen-chung, the first secretary of Hupeh, in which the student had criticized an article Wang had published in the *Hupeh jih-pao.* Li Hsüeh-feng had also been criticized in a big-character poster for his May 25 speech in which he had attacked Nieh's big-character poster. Instead of admitting his mistake, Li denounced and "persecuted" the authors of the posters, asserting that "whoever opposed the new Peking Party Committee opposed the Party Central Committee." "Record," p. 14.

39. Stuart R. Schram, *The Political Thought of Mao Tse-tung* (New York: Praeger Publishers, 1969), p. 321.

40. Thomas Bernstein, "Leadership and Mass Mobilization in the Soviet and Chinese Collectivization Campaign of 1929-1930 and 1955-1956: A Comparison," *China Quarterly,* no. 31 (September 1967), pp. 1-47.

41. *Kuan-yü ch'ing-li chieh-chi tui-wu tzu-liao hui-pien* (n.d.) pp. 11-12.

42. Liu's view on the work teams was crystalized in T'ao-yüan experience. For the operation of the work teams led by Wang Kuang-mei, see *Tung-fang-hung,* 7 May 1967.

There are some ambiguities in Mao's initial attitude toward the Cultural Revolution work teams. The various Red Guard newspapers contended that Mao actually opposed sending out the work teams; he reportedly warned the Party leaders on June 9, 1966, not to send out the teams hastily.[43] K'ang Sheng and Ch'en Po-ta also allegedly objected to sending out the work teams, but without revealing that this reflected Mao's opinion.[44] Yet, there is no convincing evidence that Mao unequivocally ordered the Party not to send out the work teams. It seems that he initially took a wait-and-see attitude. Like Chiang Ch'ing, who frankly admitted the gradual change in her views of the work teams, Mao became increasingly critical of the teams as he observed their actual operation. In fact, it was only when the students clashed with the work teams that K'ang Sheng and Ch'en Po-ta unequivocally demanded their withdrawal, but Liu Shao-ch'i refused.[45]

It seems clear, therefore, that at least some of the Party leaders became aware of the Cultural Revolution Small Group's role in the anti-work-team movement. Why, then, did they still refuse to withdraw the work teams? Did they not believe that the Cultural Revolution Small Group was speaking for Mao? Or did they intend to oppose Mao? By the time the Cultural Revolution Small Group demanded the withdrawal of the work teams, the Party leaders might well have made too heavy a commitment to the teams to repudiate their own policy without undermining their own prestige and power. But a more likely reason was their confidence in due policy-making procedures.

It must be remembered that the Party leaders were acting in their official capacity, making decisions through the regular channels and implementing them through the legitimate Party machinery.[46] In contrast, the Cultural Revolution Small Group was carrying out secret, factional, anti-Party activities, bypassing the well-established government and Party channels. Liu Shao-ch'i denounced those who backed the radical students as promoters of

43. *P'i T'ao chan-pao*, 4 March 1967; *Tung-fang-hung*, 7 May 1967.

44. "Teng Hsiao-p'ing's Self-Criticism at the Work Conference of CCP Central Committee on 23 October 1966," *Issues and Studies* 6, no. 1 (September 1970): 84 90. T'an Chen-lin later argued that Liu had no reason to listen to Ch'en, because Ch'en did not say that the objection was Mao's idea. *Hsin nung-tu*, 11 and 17 March 1967.

45. Liu argued that "at the present nobody has any experience. No rules can be produced to govern this new type of work In dealing with the work teams, the question is one of help, and not of withdrawal. The work teams cannot be done away with, but it is all right to employ a small number of people," "Selected Edition of Liu Shao-ch'i's Counterrevolutionary Revisionist Crimes," *Selections from China Mainland Magazines*, no. 652 (28 April 1969), p. 54. But later Liu was compelled to change his view. "We should not have sent people from outside to do everything themselves and to establish organs to lead the masses in implementing the CR. If the masses insisted that we should send some people, then we should have sent a few liaison men to evaluate the situation, to view it from the various quarters and take over [the leadership], and to preserve the data, and to perform certain administrative work of the former Party Committee." "Liu Shao-ch'i's Self-Criticism," *Issues and Studies*, June 1970, pp. 90-98.

46. Mao acknowledged this point. Ch'en, *Mao Papers*, p. 45.

factionalism: "Who is behind all this? Why do they refuse to listen to the work teams and the Party? Anyone rejecting the Party is engaging in the illegal underground activity of instigating the masses."[47] The Party leaders might have surmised, as P'eng Chen did, that Mao would not dare to repudiate the policy decisions made by the legitimate authorities through the legitimate processes and implemented through the regular government and Party channels, since such a repudiation would cause far-reaching repercussions throughout the entire political process.

To summarize, the work teams that the CCP customarily dispatched when the leadership of the basic units was in doubt confronted a more difficult task than the ordinary Party units. Because of his ideology and political interest, Mao was more reluctant than the Party leaders to use the work teams, and when they were used he expected them to help rather than weaken the basic-level leadership. From the viewpoint of the Party organization, however, the work teams were the most effective and efficient instruments for carrying out the top leaders' decisions and resolving the lower-level leadership problems. Despite this difference, Mao failed to raise any specific objection to sending out the teams in the Cultural Revolution. It was only two months later that he ordered their withdrawal. We conclude, therefore, that the crucial difference between Mao and the Party leaders centered not so much on the organizational format of the work teams as on their actual operation.[48]

## The Work Style of the Work Teams

The Maoists charged that the work teams, by restricting mass mobilization, diverting the major campaign target downward to the masses, and following a strategy of "hitting at many in order to protect a few," had practiced a "bureaucratic style" of leadership to impose a "bourgeois reactionary line." This broad indictment contains three specific charges: (1) the work teams actually acted as "fire-brigades" to dampen the revolutionary zeal of the students; (2) the top Party leaders like Liu Shao-ch'i and Teng Hsiao-p'ing were responsible for the behavior of the work teams; and (3) they intentionally pursued the "bourgeois reactionary line." Admittedly, these points are difficult to verify, partly because quantitative data are lacking, and partly because what material is available all comes from the

47. "Record," p. 19.
48. Even Chiang Ch'ing, the most outspoken critic of the work teams, conceded: "The problem of the work teams lies not in their format, but in their line and policy. Some units did not have work teams and relied on their existing leadership for the movement, but they still made the same mistakes. A few work teams adopted the correct line and policy and did not make mistakes." *Chung-kung wen-hua ta ko-ming chung-yao wen-chien hui-pien* (Taipei: Chung-kung Yen-chiu, 1973), p. 292.

anti-work-team side. Yet, the circumstantial evidence seems to support the first two points, but not the third one.

As soon as the work teams arrived on campus, they pushed aside the existing cadres and either took over the leadership of the Party committees themselves or reorganized the Party committees with hand-picked members whose qualifications were questionable in the eyes of the students.[49] Then the work teams insisted that the mass movement be conducted "step by step" and "unit by unit" under the strong leadership of the Party. For that purpose, they laid down a set of prescriptive rules designed to keep the development of the movement within manageable boundaries and inhibit student mobilization.[50] On the pretext of improving the quality of the campaign, the work teams stressed small group meetings over large ones. According to an alleged quote from Wang Kuang-mei, even a meeting of "a few staunch loyal work team groups" was unlawful because the work teams had not been notified.[51] Big rallies were authorized only when they were well prepared in advance—that is, when the work teams had examined and approved the program and the speeches.

In a further effort to contain the movement, the work teams imposed a "news black-out" to isolate each group of students from the others.[52] Even after the official publication of Nieh's big-character posters, the work teams continued their attempt to compartmentalize each academic class, department, and school, and confined the big-character posters to the boundaries of each campus. "The school gate was strictly guarded, and inspection teams patrolled day and night."[53] Moreover, a work team member was assigned to each academic class. When the students complained about being cut off from the movement elsewhere, the work teams argued that news from one school was irrelevant to conditions at another.[54] Students who disregarded the compartmentalization were suppressed as "wandering fishes."

To give an appearance of spontaneity to the student movement, the work teams employed a "two-handed tactic"—the device of handing out an idea to "loyalist" students, and then receiving it back as though it had genuinely come from the masses.[55] To manipulate the content of big-character posters, they mobilized the "loyalists" to counter the posters critical of the work

49. *JMJP*, 31 March 1967; *T'i-yü chan-hsien*, 6 May 1967; *T'ieh-tao hung-ch'i*, 21 May 1967.

50. *JMJP*, 30 March 1967.

51. "Liu Shao-ch'i's Daughter Writes to Expose Her Father," *CB*, no. 821 (16 March 1967), pp. 1-25. Hinton, *Hundred Day War*, p. 45.

52. "Selected Big Character Posters of Tsinghua University," *SCMMS*, no. 20 (18 March 1968), pp. 1-59.

53. "Li Hsüeh-feng Is the Executioner Suppressing the CR in Peking Municipality," *SCMPS*, no. 162 (14 February 1967), pp. 16-22.

54. "Kuan Feng's Speech," *JPRS*, no. 41,313 (8 June 1967), pp. 2-3.

55. The radicals insisted that "to hand out" is to decorate one's house and to "receive" is to preserve oneself. This was an attempt to make the movement proceed under their control. "Selected Big Character Posters of Tsinghua," *SCMMS*, no. 20 (18 March 1968), pp. 13-14.

teams with their own complimentary posters. The work teams also employed some less subtle methods to deal with the anti-work-team forces. At the height of the anti-interference campaign, they put the leaders of the radical forces under house arrest and coerced them into admitting that they had committed "anti-Party crimes." They also subjected the radical leaders to carefully prearranged, school-wide struggle meetings. At Tsinghua, Wang Kuang-mei allegedly used her daughter, Liu T'ao, and Ho Lung's son, Ho P'eng-fei, to organize a school-wide meeting to "drag out K'uai Ta-fu."[56]

The majority of the students were highly offended, however, by the teams' practice of classifying all students as rightists, middle-roaders, or leftists, mainly on the basis of the students' attitude toward the work teams.[57] Their methods for collecting information on the students were especially objectionable. Although Mao had criticized secret information-gathering during the Socialist Education Movement, the top Party leaders again encouraged the practice during the Great Proletarian Cultural Revolution.[58] The Party organization and the work teams relied not only on their own organizational resources, but also on the public security forces to keep track of who was writing what kind of big-character posters. Sometimes they even took pictures of the students at a mass rally.[59]

Such compilation of "black materials" not only inhibited the students from raising issues sensitive to the Party organization at the time, but also presented a serious and continuing personal threat to the students whose names appeared on the "black lists." The slogan "Settling accounts after the autumn harvest" further heightened the students' resentment of the "black materials" and intensified their fear of their own future. The slogan meant that the crucial issue of who was right and who was wrong would be determined only after the campaign ended and normality was restored.

Thus, the Party cadres could intimidate their attackers with a threat of retaliation: "Now you rectify us, but we will return what you have given to us"; or, "In the later period of this movement, those who were officials will still be officials, those who were foot soldiers will still be foot soldiers, and those who should be rectified will not escape rectification."[60] Such remarks reminded the Chinese of the previous abrupt shift from the Hundred Flowers campaign to the Anti-Rightist campaign. The early phase of the Great

56. Neal Hunter, *Shanghai Journal* (New York: Praeger, 1969), pp. 61-62.
57. Ibid.
58. T'an Chen-lin reportedly instructed the work teams to collect materials on radicals secretly so that they could not notice. *Chung-hsüeh wen-ko pao,* 1 April 1967. Also the underlying assumption of Liu Shao-ch'i's slogan "luring out snakes from the hole to hit hard" was that the Party organization would allow the students to criticize the Party tactically and temporarily to find out who had grudges against the organization.
59. *Chieh-fang pao,* March 1968; *JMJP,* 15 January 1967.
60. *JMJP,* 27 February 1967; 16 January 1967.

Proletarian Cultural Revolution even resembled the Hundred Flowers campaign, which created deep skepticism among the students about the real intention behind the pronouncement "Allow free mobilization of the masses." With their vivid memories of the bitter experiences during the Anti-Rightist campaign, the older teachers warned students not to get actively involved in the Cultural Revolution.[61]

There is no doubt that the work teams failed to live up to the Maoists' expectations in so far as "freely mobilizing the masses" was concerned. Whether intentionally or not, the teams' highly manipulative operation and "bureaucratic leadership style" resulted in the restriction of spontaneous expression among the students, particularly alienating those with independent minds. As a matter of fact, Liu Shao-ch'i acknowledged in his self-criticism that the work teams had pursued the mobilization by forcing ideas to filter down from the top: "At the very outset, they [the work teams] asked the broad masses who had been aroused to act according to the plans and steps which we and the work teams [had] conceived on the basis of our subjective wishes."[62] It is also equally clear that, as Teng Hsiao-p'ing admitted, the work teams had "widely adopted measures that Chairman Mao had criticized and repudiated during the Four Clean Up movement in the rural areas and factories.[63]

The top Party leaders, including Liu Shao-ch'i and Teng Hsiao-p'ing, were responsible for the erroneous line that the work teams pursued. As noted, the two top Party leaders dispatched the work teams without proper preparation, were personally involved in the work team operations in several Peking educational institutes, and tacitly approved the anti-interference campaign. If they did not specifically instruct the work teams to suppress the student movement as such—they did sanction the suppression of anti-work-team students—at the very least, they failed to provide detailed guidelines to the work teams, and they took a confusing and equivocal attitude toward the Cultural Revolution.

No Party leader ever publicly raised the issue of power holders or unreservedly declared support for "free mobilization of the masses."[64] At most, they treated the Cultural Revolution with levity. Liu Shao-ch'i portrayed it mainly as an educational reform that would last only a few months,[65] Such an

---

61. Gordon Bennett and Ronald Montaperto, *Red Guard: The Political Biography of Dai Hsiao-ai* (New York: Doubleday, 1971), p. 41.

62. "Liu Shao-ch'i's Self-Criticism," *Issues and Studies*, June 1970, pp. 90-98.

63. "Teng Hsiao-p'ing's Self-Criticism at the Work Conference of the CCP Central Committee on 23 October 1966," *Issues and Studies*, September 1970, pp. 84-90.

64. The radicals later insisted that the Party leaders "closed their mouths and never mentioned that the major task was to rectify inside the Party."

65. *Chieh-fang pao*, March 1968; *Pao-feng pao*, March 1968. Liu Shao-ch'i stipulated that "many teachers of the middle school practice military training, have first and second year

ambiguous attitude among the top Party leaders suggests that they were intentionally derelict in their failure to instruct the work teams clearly on how to lead the mass movement.

The top Party leaders did, however, unequivocally accentuate the need for leadership, order, and discipline in those areas in which Maoist pressure was greatest, such as the educational, propaganda, and cultural fields[66] They even justified their narrow definition of movement targets with Mao's dictum: "Concentrate forces to annihilate the enemy." Liu Shao-ch'i allegedly instructed the work teams: "Schools and individuals should both be grouped. . . . Every move should lead to the output of products and by-products. . . . In this case, the by-products are the detection of some counter-revolutionaries."[67]

The Peking Party Committee elaborated on Liu's views in the instructions it issued: (1) Prohibit big-character posters in the streets; (2) Prohibit rallies; (3) Prohibit parades in the streets; (4) Prohibit encirclement of residences; (5) Make a distinction between the inside and the outside. (6) Prohibit manhandling and the insulting of others. (7) Guard against sabotage by bad elements. (8) Prevent the movement from developing in undesirable directions.[68]

The theoretical justification for restraining the spontaneous mass movement was the slogan, allegedly attributed to Liu Shao-ch'i, "Make a distinction between inside [the Party] and outside [the Party]," which means that the Party organization must resolve its own internal matters without outside interference. The basic idea of the phrase can be easily found in the Leninist notion of a vanguard party, but it is interesting to note that it also accurately reflected the typical behavioral disposition of any organization to minimize both uncertainty of mass movement and the changes a movement might produce within the system. The more significant point is that the slogan served the organizational interests of the Party, for in the setting of the Cultural Revolution the slogan meant that the work teams should first distinguish between the struggles inside and outside the Party, and then

---

students take a vacation or be sent to the rural area and factories, and some other students practice military training." "Liu Shao-ch'i's Self-Criticism," *Issues and Studies*, June 1970, pp. 90-98. Many party leaders regarded the cultural revolution as an anti-rightist movement, thereby justifying the shift of the target from the power holders to the teachers. "Selected Big Character Posters of Tsinghua," *SCMMS*, no. 20 (18 March 1968), p. 14.

66. For instance, T'ao Chu, who was promoted to be director of the Propaganda Department as of June 6, instructed the Central South Regional Bureau Party Committee to concentrate its purge on the "propaganda, educational, cultural, journalism, and academic fields and the units dealing with these fields in the Party and government organs at the provincial and municipal and district levels," while exempting the other fields except where there were serious problems. *Chieh-fang pao*, March 1968; *I-yüeh feng-pao*, 1 March 1968; *P'i T'ao chan-pao*, 26 April 1967.

67. "Record," pp. 9-17.

68. Ibid., p. 14.

apply different methods to each—a strategy that effectively eliminated the opportunity for the students to voice their opinion on cadre problems.

Yet, the controlled mobilization organized by the work teams did not depart from the CCP's past practices, as Teng Hsiao-p'ing aptly conceded in his apologistic phrase, "Old cadres confront new problems."[69] What had changed in the Cultural Revolution were Mao's expectations. When the CCP responded to the "new problems" (Mao's radical expectation that the Party organization could negate its own interests for the sake of revolution), the old methods were dysfunctional, at least in the eyes of the Maoist leaders. The following section will examine Mao's radicalized expectations and how they were made known to the Chinese students.

## The Official Ideology of the Cultural Revolution

The work team period witnessed a widening of the gap between the official ideology advocated in editorials and the policy that the Party and the work teams actually pursued. In contrast to the actual policy the official ideology reached the masses directly without the mediation of the Party organization and portrayed the Cultural Revolution as an open-door rectification campaign directed at none other than the Party organization itself.

The official ideology made the Thought of Mao Tse-tung the sole criteria for judging between right and wrong, friend and enemy, and revolutionary and sham revolutionary.[70] Even the *Jen-min jih-pao*, which had clashed with the *Chieh-fang chün-pao* in the preceding stage, now accepted the cult of Mao's Thought. With the June 1, 1966, issue, the *Jen-min jih-pao* changed its format: it put a quotation from Chairman Mao next to the title in the place formerly occupied by the table of contents and the weather report.

The Thought of Mao Tse-tung, according to the official ideology, enabled the masses to "penetrate deeply into all things . . . and to determine the essence behind the outward appearance."[71] Those who "have grasped Mao Tse-tung's Thought are most skilled in waging struggle and in thoroughly

69. Ibid., p. 36.

70. For instance, see "Long Live Mao Tse-tung's Thought," *JMJP*, 1 July 1966. According to a Red Guard report, the initial draft written by Ch'en Po-ta extravagantly extolled the MTTT. However, Liu and Teng deleted from the manuscript the sentence that "Chairman Mao enjoys the highest of prestige among the people of the whole country and throughout the world." Also they added the names of Marx, Engels, Lenin, and Stalin to the sentence "A revolutionary leader who has experienced such a long, complex, violent, and multifarious struggle as Comrade Mao Tse-tung is rare in history." They also revised the sentence "They [bourgeois representatives] extended their hands very far to grasp power in the Party, the military, and the government" to read "They extended their hands very far, intending to grasp power in the Party, the military, and the government." "Record," pp. 22-23.

71. For instance, see "The Mao Tse-tung Thought Is the Telescope and Microscope of Our Revolutionary Course," *CFCP*, 7 June 1966, in *Daily Report*, 8 June 1966, pp. CCC1-4.

repudiating the representatives of the bourgeoisie with facts and reasoning."[72] Thus, one's attitude toward the free mobilization of the masses became an important criterion for determining whether one was revolutionary or counterrevolutionary in the "gigantic struggle between the two classes."[73]

Initially, the terminology used to define the targets of the Cultural Revolution was somewhat ambiguous: they were referred to as the "representatives of the bourgeoisie who have sneaked into the Party." But by June, 1966, this was changed to the "power holders taking the capitalist road within the Party," who "dressed themselves up as 'authorities' on Marxism [and] took advantage of their position . . . in order to peddle anti-Party and antisocialist ideas."[74]

At the same time, the public media made it clear that the bourgeois intellectuals, though not exempted from criticism, were not the major target of the movement:

Bourgeois academic ideas in general must, of course, come under criticism, but that is different from the treatment befitting anti-Party and antisocialist elements. . . . In dealing with ordinary bourgeois scholars, we shall go on providing them with suitable work conditions and let them remold their world outlook in the course of their work, provided they do not oppose the Communist Party and the people.[75]

The "bourgeois representatives," according to the editorials, could be spotted by their opposition to Mao's Thought and the Cultural Revolution: "Anyone who opposes Mao's Thought, now or in the future, will be an arch enemy of the revolution and the people, to be condemned by the whole Party and denounced by the whole nation."[76] One's formal position in the Party organization did not establish his loyalty to the Thought of Mao Tse-tung: "If a person acts against the Thought of Mao Tse-tung, regardless of how high his position and what kind of authority he may have, we must expose him, bring him to light, and refute him till he sinks."[77]

Opposition to Mao's line of "free mobilization of the masses" in the Cultural Revolution was a concrete example of the bourgeois representatives' opposition to Mao's Thought.[78] The struggle against them was a "struggle

72. Ibid.
73. "Trust the Masses, Rely on the Masses," *PR*, no. 28 (8 July 1966), pp. 28-30; *JMJP*, 16 June 1966.
74. "Long Live the Great Proletarian Cultural Revolution," *Hung ch'i*, no. 8 (8 June 1966), in *PR*, no. 25 (17 June 1966), pp. 7-12.
75. Ibid.
76. "Long Live Mao Tse-tung's Thought," *JMJP*, 1 July 1966, in *PR*, no. 27 (1 July 1966), pp. 5-14.
77. "Hold High the Great Red Banner of Mao Tse-tung's Thought," *CFCP*, 6 June 1966 in *CB*, no. 791 (21 June 1966), pp. 1-15.
78. "They resisted the current great Cultural Revolution initiated by the Party Central Committee and Chairman Mao in a well-organized, well-planned, and well-guided way. Before

for taking back the power of leadership, a struggle for transforming the bourgeois dictatorship into the proletarian dictatorship."[79] The official ideology also pointed out that the bourgeois representatives were not opposing Mao's Thought openly, but from behind the scenes—"waving the Red Flag to oppose the Red Flag. . . . They use the phrases of Marxism-Leninism and the Thought of Mao Tse-tung as a cover for their negative articles with which they smuggle in bourgeois and revisionist stuff. The enemies holding false red banners are ten times more vicious than enemies holding a white flag."[80]

The official ideology distinguished between "bourgeois organizational discipline" and "proletarian organizational discipline" as defined by Mao Tse-tung's Thought. The enemies used "bourgeois discipline" to oppose the Thought of Mao Tse-tung.[81] Hence, those who challenged the organizational legitimacy of the representatives of the bourgeoisie were not an anti-Party "black gang," but good comrades supporting Mao Tse-tung's Thought.[82] At the same time, the official ideology specifically warned the Party organization not to use its organizational discipline to check free mass mobilization: "Our Party must not be trammeled by erroneous, stereotyped ideas about ranks, past work experience, and age, but must organize the resolute Left as the backbone of its movement."[83] If the Party organization failed to lead the masses boldly, its leaders were useless.[84]

The message in the mass media was clear to the Chinese students: the principles guiding the Cultural Revolution were Mao Tse-tung's radical ideas that stressed free mobilization over controlled mobilization, democracy over centralism, division over unity, enthusiasm over discipline, change over order, destruction over construction, and struggle against the Party over struggle against the masses—in brief, the ideological legitimacy of Mao Tse-tung's Thought over the "structural legitimacy" of the Party organization.

---

the masses took action, they began to stir up ill winds, spread rumors, create confusion to divert the people's attention, and set up heavy obstacles to bind the hands and feet of the masses. Hardly had the proletarian leftists begun to speak and put up a few big-character posters when they flew into a rage and mounted joint attacks on the leftists by severely reprimanding and threatening the masses, turning up criminal charges against them, and subjecting them to political persecution." *JMJP,* 15 June 1966.

79. *JMJP,* 16 June 1966.

80. "The Mao Tse-tung Thought Is the Telescope and Microscope of Our Revolutionary Course" (n. 71 above).

81. "They use the strange logic that whoever exposes them, whoever stands opposed to their sinister gangs are 'opposing the Party' and 'opposing the Central Committee.' The result of doing this is exactly contrary to what they seek; it completely unmasks the real forces of these loyalists and counterrevolutionaries and sounds the death knell announcing their utter failure."

82. "To Be Proletarian Revolutionaries or Bourgeois Royalists," *KMJP,* 5 June 1967. "It was precisely a conscious respect for proletarian revolutionary organizational discipline that destroyed your organizational discipline. It was precisely a conscious support and defense of the leadership of the CCP headed by Chairman Mao that opposed your leadership." Ibid.

83. "Trust the Masses, Rely on the Masses," *PR,* no. 28 (8 July 1966), pp. 28-32.

84. Ibid.

The message of the public news media was unacceptable to the Party organization. The reason becomes clear if we consider Chester Bernard's four criteria for testing the acceptability of a communication to any organization: (1) the recipient must understand the communication; (2) at the time of decision, the recipient must believe that it is not inconsistent with the purpose of the organization; (3) the recipient must believe it to be compatible with his personal interests as a whole; and (4) the recipient must be mentally and physically able to comply with it.[85]

Many Party cadres, particularly low-ranking cadres, probably did not understand Mao's instructions (real intentions), and if they did understand them, they would have found the reasons for attacking the Party organization either incomprehensible or threatening. Thus, they would have hesitated to carry out Mao's wishes, since undermining the Party organization's "structural legitimacy" suited neither their personal interests nor those of the organization, which were characterized by taking "clearance and safety over initiative and risk."[86] Even if some Party members agreed with Mao on the need for the Cultural Revolution, the threat of expulsion from the organization dissuaded them from doing anything to challenge its structural legitimacy.

Unable to discard its organizational principles and structural legitimacy, the Party took the position that "any member represented the Party as a whole, that lower-level units represented the Party Center, and that the Party represented the proletarian class."[87] By selectively propagating editorials that stressed the leadership and legitimacy of the Party, the Party leaders insisted that "anyone bent on chasing away the work teams was determined to seize the power from the work teams, that is, to seize the power of the Party."[88] By further stretching the same logic, the Party organization actually subordinated ideology to the organization: "Whoever opposes the Party, regardless of what he may say, is invariably a feigned leftist, and true rightist."[89]

In contrast, the Maoist leaders replaced "structural legitimacy" with ideological legitimacy: "The leadership of the Party means the leadership of Mao Tse-tung's Thought and the Central Committee of the Party. Not every

85. Chester I. Bernard, "Definition of Authority," in *Reader in Bureaucracy* (n. 37 above), p. 181.

86. Robert Presthus, *Organizational Society* (New York: Vintage Books, 1962), p. 36.

87. *Chingkangshan,* 23 March 1967.

88. At the same time the work teams widely and enthusiastically propagated the editorials of 24 and 30 June 1966 in *JMJP,* and 30 June in *Pei-ching jih-pao* that stressed the importance of Party leadership and legitimacy. For the *Pei-ching jih-pao* June 30 editorial, see "Communist Party Members Must Stand Out at the Forefront of the Revolutionary Struggle," *SCMPS,* no. 154 (2 September 1966), pp. 6-8.

89. "Record," p. 20.

Party organization or individual Party member represents leadership by the Party."[90] The Maoist criteria for evaluating the work teams included the following: (1) whether the work team removed the lid boldly; (2) whether it made as many suggestions and put up as many big-character posters as possible; and (3) whether it allowed spontaneous and free mass mobilization.[91] The students were encouraged to revolt against any work teams failing to meet these requirements.

The Party organization found the Maoist methods for transmitting the official ideology as objectionable as the actual content. The structural legitamacy of the Party organization depended on its due decision-making procedures and its patterned communication channels for transmitting decisions. The big-character posters used by the Maoists and radicals, however, threatened the Party organization's well-established patterns of communication: they provided a means for direct communication between the top leaders and the masses which bypassed the Party organization; they were accessible to everyone, in contrast to the relatively limited audiences reached by newspapers or Party documents; and the amount and diversity of information they contained rendered it impossible for the Party organization to control them.

Although the big-character posters undermined the structural legitimacy of the Party organization, they well served the political purposes of the Maoist leaders in Peking, who did not have reliable organizational channels for gathering information on local conditions. From the big-character posters the Maoist leaders could grasp what was going on at the lower levels, which cadres were loyal to them, and what the general mood was. Moreover, the big-character posters were better suited to the purposes of mass mobilization than the conventional communication channels, because their content tended to be less ideological and stereotyped, and they dealt with specific problems that were of more interest to the general public.

The big-character posters were also effective in exposing "hidden enemies," since they could be directed at individuals who would then be forced to respond.[92] The official news media praised the big-character posters as the best means to "expose and vanquish enemies and to educate the masses and raise their political consciousness."[93] They also urged the Party leaders to encourage the big-character posters: "Are you a revolutionary? Then you

90. *Hung-se tsao-fan*, 26 December 1966.
91. *Hung-wei-ping*, 8 December 1966.
92. *JMJP*, 20 June 1966.
93. "These posters set all kinds of opinion and bring out all kinds of contradictions through which it is possible to understand the situation. . . . They concentrated twenty years of education for the masses in a day, particularly raising the proletarian consciousness of the young generation." *JMJP*, 20 June 1966.

have to welcome big-character posters, take the initiative in writing big-character posters, and freely allow the masses to write big-character posters and expose problems. If you are a conservative, then you will be afraid of big-character posters and [you will] sweat."[94] "All anti-Party, antisocialist counterrevolutionaries fear big-character posters the most."[95]

Given the obvious discrepancy between the official ideology and the actual policy line pursued by the Party organization, it is not surprising that some students challenged the work teams. The rebellious students simply parroted the newspaper editorials and sought to carry out the official ideology:

The Thought of Mao Tse-tung, or concretely speaking, the Chairman's books and recent editorials of the *People's Daily* are the highest instructions for our great Cultural Revolution. Things should be done if they conform to the instructions; otherwise they should be opposed. We will struggle against anyone who violates these instructions. . . .[96]

The radical students' commitment to struggle on the basis of the instructions in the official ideology led to an even more radical anti-organizational statement: "We must not treat proposals from certain persons or certain Party organizations as instructions from the Central Committee and Chairman Mao."[97] Moreover, if the work teams violated the Thought of Mao Tse-tung, the power of the work teams should be seized.

Once the Chinese students accepted the radical ideology with its far-reaching implications, their next task was to judge the operation of the work teams "on the basis of facts."[98] The "facts" amassed in the big-character posters on the actual operations of the work teams repudiated the work teams' claim that they were following the official ideology. K'uai Ta-fu, for instance, argued that, even though the work teams talked about large-scale exposure and criticism, the number of big-character posters had dropped sharply.[99] Confronted with "irrefutable facts," the work teams sometimes resorted to coercive moves and sometimes openly challenged the official ideology by criticizing the students for blindly following the newspaper editorials: "To whom will you listen, the Party Committee or the newspapers?"[100]

94. *Tung-fang-hung pao,* 14 October 1967.
95. Ibid.
96. "Selected Big Character Posters of Tsinghua University," *SCMMS,* no. 20 (18 March 1968), p. 4.
97. Ibid., p. 12.
98. To the radicals, "fact" meant the discrepancy between the Mao Tse-tung Thought (MTTT) and what the work teams were actually doing, whereas to the Party organization it meant the real condition in a school. Inevitably, the first never raised any question of the validity of the MTTT, whereas the latter view tended to allow for possible conflict between the MTTT and the reality.
99. "Selected Big Character Posters of Tsinghua," p. 4.
100. *Hung-wei-ping,* 24 October 1966.

The work teams also argued that free mobilization of the masses was a tactical move of the Party organization that the students did not understand: "You may be considered high intellectuals, but from what you have done you do not deserve the name, and you know nothing about the Party's tactics. The masses are just like mobs, like a flock of sheep. Your sense of organization and discipline is too low."[101] Such arguments further convinced the radicals that the work teams were not following Mao Tse-tung's Thought. They responded with the statement: "If there are problems that you cannot solve or explain, you must doubt boldly."[102]

As the conflicts between the work teams and the radical students intensified, they each developed a more personal stake in the outcome, which in turn further intensified the confrontation. The divergence between the official ideology and the policy was not merely doctrinaire; it involved the crucial question of who would purge whom in the Great Proletarian Cultural Revolution.

## Targets and Participants

In a sense, all the conflicts and cleavages in the Cultural Revolution stemmed from the question of whether one took part as an attacker (participant) or as an object of attack (target). This fundamental question defined the basic orientation of the movement, and served to crystalize the different views of the Maoist leaders and the Party organization. The Maoist leaders tended to accentuate the horizontal cleavage between the masses and the elites as the demarcation line between participants and targets. The Party organization stressed the vertical cleavage between inside and outside the Party.

The frontal clash between the two trends came gradually as the movement expanded through its various stages and the central issue shifted from Wu Han's play *Hai Jui Dismissed from Office* to the political problem of Wu Han himself, to the question of "bourgeois intellectuals" in academic fields, to "bourgeois authority" in general, to "black gangs" who protected the bourgeois intellectuals, and finally to the "power holders taking the capitalist road within the Party." The Maoist leaders provided impetus for the expansion, while the Party leaders endeavored to keep the targets as narrow as possible. Whenever the Maoist leaders initiated an expansion, the Party organization reacted by attempting to restrict the target to the one specified by the Maoists. Consequently, the Party organization was continually one step behind the Maoist leaders.

The gradual expansion of the official position resulted in a certain amount

101. "Selected Big Character Posters of Tsinghua," p. 4.
102. Ibid., p. 12.

of ambiguity, which further intensified the conflict among the various groups. By the work team period, the "May 16 Notice" had clearly specified that the "power holders" were the main target and the masses were the participants. But distribution of the Notice had been restricted to the *hsien*-level Party committees, and the Chinese public did not yet know of its existence.

The message in the official news media at the time was contradictory: while the general tone and ideological implication in the editorials clearly pointed to the Party leaders as the major target, they actually used such ambiguous words as "monsters and freaks."[103] As the official line continued to evolve even after the work team period, many ordinary people, not to mention the cadres, became involved in the movement as both accused and accuser. Some who were attacked at one stage later challenged their attackers and charged them with intentionally distorting the official line in order to protect themselves. Thus, legitimate participants at one time could subsequently become targets.

Compelled by the "May 16 Notice," which unequivocally called for the purge of power holders, the Party organization moved with reluctance to comply with Mao's wishes. It approached the unpleasant task in a purely organizational way, relying exclusively on the existing leadership at the various levels and on the inner-Party regulations regarding "management and evaluation of the cadres."[104] Moreover, it did not specify precisely who should be purged. The lack of a clear guideline left the work teams some room for personal discretion within the general criteria determined by the organization's selection. According to fixed quotas received from above,[105] chiefs at each level carried out the rectification of Party cadres: "Party factions rectified bureau chiefs, bureau chiefs rectified section chiefs, and section chiefs rectified the masses."[106] They also classified all the cadres as rightists, middle-roaders, or leftists.

This top-to-bottom mobilization allowed the chief cadres at each level to evade rectification. Even after the Cultural Revolution Committees were organized to insure fairness in target selection, "those with the title of chiefs were usually made members of the committees."[107] Consequently, suspected revisionists among the first secretaries or Party committee members were

103. Later Mao defined "monsters and freaks" as "unrepented four elements." *P'ing-fan tzu-liao hui-pien,* January 1968.
104. *Chieh-fang pao,* March 1968.
105. For instance, the Central South Regional Bureau ordered each province under its jurisdiction to purge three or four persons, mostly "reactionary intellectuals and power holders who did not hold important posts in the government and Party." *I-yüeh feng-pao,* January 1968.
106. *Pei-ching kung-she,* 27 April 1967. When the work teams arrived at the schools, they selected the targets themselves and sent down the targets to each class to struggle with. Some students disagreed with the work teams' verdict on cadres and this created a split among the students. *Hsin jen-ta,* 2 April 1967.
107. *Pei-ching kung-she,* 12 and 27 April 1967.

entrusted with the task of purging revisionists. Radicals later termed this ironic phenomenon a "rightist opportunist line of relying upon black gangs to struggle against the black gangs."[108]

Worse still, the existing leadership selected targets secretly without seeking the opinions of the masses. Instead, they frequently relied on confidential and irrelevant information obtained through personal files such as personal dossiers, personal reports on one's ideology, records of activities in past campaigns, and secret files prepared by ordinary cadres on others.[109] Some of the materials had been voluntarily submitted. Much of the information dealt with past rather than present behavior, problems on which the organization had already taken action, or such trivial questions as personal habits and friendships. The targets thus selected fell into certain discernible groups: lower-ranking cadres, "dangerous elements," and those with bourgeois class backgrounds.

As the Maoist leaders insisted, the top Party leaders may well have concentrated on purging the lower-ranking cadres while intentionally protecting the high-ranking cadres.[110] Since the higher-ranking cadres symbolized the "structural legitimacy" of the organization, their purge would have had a more far reaching and disruptive impact on the organization as a whole.

At the same time, several factors acted to minimize the resentment of lower-ranking cadres. First, as members of the organization, the lower-level cadres shared a common interest with the higher-ranking cadres in protecting the "structural legitimacy" of the organization. Furthermore, they were probably well accustomed to this kind of organizational discipline. Or, as the Maoists argued, the lower-level cadres might have been "corrupted" by Liu's organizational principle that one should carry out even a wrong decision so long as it comes down from the higher levels through legitimate organizational channels. In any case, if the lower-ranking cadres knew that the Maoist radicals had forced the disciplinary action upon the Party organization, they also could hope that they would be reinstated after the movement.

The "dangerous element" targets were those with some grievances against

108  Ibid.; *Chih-pa ch'un-lai pao,* 26 February 1967.
109. *Pei-ching kung-she,* 12 April 1967.
110. For instance, "In the organs of the Honan Provincial Party Committee alone, many mechanics, cooks, health officers, communication agents, ushers, carpenters, and boiler room hands were criticized, judged, and struggled with." "The Evil Deeds of the Anti-Party and Antisocialist Element and Counterrevolutionary Double Dealer," *JPRS,* no. 43,357 (16 November 1967), pp. 7 52. In the Ministry of Commerce, only 3 out of 21,000 big-character posters were aimed at the Party Committee of the Ministry. *Pei-ching kung-she,* 2 April 1967. In the organs under the direct jurisdiction of the Kwangtung province, 30 percent of the masses [low ranking cadres] were struggled with, whereas only a bureau chief was rectified. *I-yüeh feng-pao,* January 1968. When the students raised the question regarding the school Party Committees, the work teams replied: "You understand little about the school Party Committee and don't understand [what goes on] inside the Committee. Your best interest lies in the problems of departments and classes. You should be much more concerned with the problems in your department and class." *Hsin jen-ta,* 2 April 1967.

the leadership of each unit, perhaps over some past Party disciplinary action or the handling of "historical problems." Such discontented elements constituted a threat to the Party's organizational interests; they were the ones who were willing to risk their personal safety to expose the secrets of the organization and challenge its organizational legitimacy. Therefore, the Party organization constantly cautioned its cadres to guard against the "dangerous elements who might take advantage of muddy water to catch fish [take revenge]."[111]

In fact, the Party organization had previously used the same argument to oppose Mao's demands for an open-door rectification campaign during the Hundred Flowers period and the Socialist Education Movement. Mao, however, had specifically refuted this Party view by pointing out that the Chinese revolution could not have succeeded without the participation of the discontented.[112] Nevertheless, the Party organization continued to worry about the potential harm which "bad persons" could do to the organization during an uncertain period. Therefore, during the Cultural Revolution it used such slogans as "Cadres should draw fire to lure the snake out of its hole," and placed stress on one's motivation rather than his actions. Even after the disintegration of the Party, the conservatives persisted in using this kind of slogan.

Most conspicuous among the Party-selected targets were those with a bourgeois class background. Their selection reflected both the Party's reliance on personnel dossiers in picking the targets and the Party leaders' understanding of "class" as a purely economic category. The Central South Regional Bureau allegedly issued three documents stressing the rectification of the "four [categories of] bad elements" during the Cultural Revolution.[113] Once the bourgeois class was designated as the major target, even the innocent bourgeoisie—those who "in the past had voluntarily handed over their problems" and whose "cap" had been removed in accordance with the legal requirements—were indiscriminately attacked.

Both the school Party committees and later the work teams pursued basically the same line at the schools. The school Party committees had defined the Cultural Revolution as a campaign to rectify the four bad elements and turned the movement against the "academic authorities," many of whom, particularly the older teachers, had such obvious bourgeois backgrounds that they were less powerful in the schools.[114] When the movement further expanded, student enthusiasm increased, and the Party committees came to feel threatened, they simply added more teachers and a few

111. *Ko-ming wen-i chan-pao,* 15 May 1967.
112. *Mao Tse-tung ssu-hsiang wan-sui* (n. 34 above), pp. 591, 595.
113. *Ts'ui-hui tzu-fan hsien,* February 1968; *Chieh-fang pao,* March 1968.
114. For this point, see *JMJP,* 26 April 1967; *KMJP,* 7 April 1967; *Ping-t'uan chan-pao,* 10 April 1967; *Pei-ching kung-she,* 12 April 1967; *Chung-ta hung-ch'i,* 30 April 1967.

Party cadres with obviously "bad" backgrounds to their list of targets.[115] After the work teams arrived, they publicly declared that the major targets were those who "were criticized nationwide—the reactionary teachers, and some cadres and masses who jumped out in the movement—[and that the] students' distrust of their teachers indicated that they were fully mobilized."[116]

A brief look at the position that the bourgeois intellectuals occupied prior to the Cultural Revolution will help explain the apparent paradox of why the Party organization, criticized by the Maoists for protecting the "bourgeois authorities," should, in fact, turn the Cultural Revolution against them. Basically, the intellectuals belonged to the traditional ruling elite in China. After several campaigns designed to eliminate their identity as a social stratum and their role as independent critics, they were co-opted into the system, where, in exchange for their skills and knowledge, they again enjoyed power and privilege.

Particularly after the Great Leap Forward, the Party organization stepped up its efforts to recruit intellectuals into the Party in order to utilize their talents. Under the slogan of "red and expert," the Party waived the regular background requirement, since "all intellectuals had a complicated history."[117] At Peking University, four of the thirty-two high-ranking professors who joined the Party quickly became vice-presidents; the others became members of the standing committee for the general school Party committee or Party branch secretaries.[118]

Paralleling the influx of intellectuals into powerful positions, the power of the school shifted from the Party committees to the School Council, which was composed primarily of professors. Soon the authority of the School Council had expanded at the expense of the school Party branch, and included jurisdiction over "matters regarding overall plans for school development, size, teaching plans, scientific development, and organization."[119] Since the Party leaders were preoccupied with rapid economic development and modernization, they were willing to allow the bourgeois intellectuals a certain amount of power, privilege, and functional autonomy.[120]

To Mao, who was worried that even the Party might form a new ruling elite, the rise of the bourgeois intellectuals in the Party organization meant

115. *Tung-fang-hung pao*, 12 April 1967; *Hung pei-ying*, 25 May 1967; *T'i-yü chan-pao*, 6 May 1967.
116. *Ping-t'uan chan-pao*, 10 April 1967.
117. In Peking University half of all those who joined the Party from 1959 to 1964 came from exploiting families. *Hsin pei-ta*, 7 January 1968.
118. *Hsin pei-ta*, 25 November 1967; *Hung-ch'i*, 9 December 1967.
119. *Hsin pei-ta*, 25 November 1967.
120. For the different attitudes of Mao and Liu toward the establishment, see Tang Tsou, "The Cultural Revolution and the Chinese Political System," *CQ*, no. 38 (April-June 1969), pp. 63-91.

not only their re-emergence as an elite group, but also the spread of bourgeois ideology. Thus, although Mao readily acknowledged the political impotence of the bourgeoisie and advocated lenient treatment of them,[121] he constantly warned against the dangers of bourgeois ideology.

Whenever Mao renewed his vigilance over the class struggle, the Party's attitude toward the bourgeoisie abruptly changed from acceptance to harsh treatment, particularly toward those who were outside the power structure and hence a part of the masses rather than the elite. During both the Hundred Flowers campaign and the Socialist Education Movement, the Party directed the major thrust of its campaign against the bourgeoisie, as though they had been the major target of the movement. During the Cultural Revolution, the Party organization did initially try to protect those bourgeois intellectuals closely associated with it, but as the targets expanded to include "black gangs" and "power holders," the Party endeavored to cut its losses by sacrificing the bourgeois intellectuals.

In fact, some cadres understood the inextricable relationship between the reds and the experts and carried out Mao's line even at the early stages of the Cultural Revolution. For instance, a cadre from the Peking Municipal Party Committee argued over the question of student participation in target selection: "Expose what you see. As in the case of shooting, if you cannot hit the distant target, hit the near target. All departments and classes in your institute have power holders, and you may expose first those in power whom you know best. When they are exposed, they will have no alternative but to expose the higher levels. Then the problems will be brought to light."[122]

Over the controversy concerning who were the "monsters and freaks," this cadre declared, "Some Party committees have accused professors of being freaks and monsters and bourgeois authorities. Some professors have accused the Party committees of being bourgeois authorities. For the present, we should direct the spearhead of the movement against the Party committees."[123] When the work teams defended themselves and the school Party committees on the grounds that they were "blind executors of a mistaken line" and "everybody has a share of mistakes," he declared: "Party committee [members] must accept the mass test. If they are not new revisionists, they at least at one time carried out the revisionist line, and this should be brought to light."[124]

Among the most serious charges that the Maoists made against the work teams was that they had "aimed their spearhead downward" at the masses.

121. *Mao Tse-tung ssu-hsiang wan sui* (see note 34 above).
122. "The Wrong Must Be Redressed," *SCMPS*, no. 161 (17 January 1967), pp. 3-12.
123. Ibid.
124. Ibid. For the work teams' view, see "Selected Big Character Posters of Tsinghua," *SCMMS*, no. 20 (18 March 1967), pp. 1-59.

According to Red Guard sources, 800 persons at Tsinghua University and 829 persons at the Peking Mining College were attacked as "rightists."[125] In Canton, the radicals claimed that the work teams "stigmatized 220,000 innocent persons."[126] The tactic of "aiming the spearhead downward" was a logical consequence of the emphasis on "class background" as well as on the structural legitimacy of the Party organization and the view that the anti-work-team students were "rightists" challenging the Party organization out of a hatred for communism.

As we noted earlier, there is a grain of truth in the Party's basic premise for the anti-interference campaign. Yet, for the Maoists, who saw the real danger of revisionism in the growing elitism among the Party leaders—regardless of whether they were "bourgeois specialists," "black gangs," or "power holders"—the concentrated attack on the "bourgeois academicians" and students from bourgeois families was, at best, a misunderstanding of "class struggle." At worst, "aiming the spearhead downward" was a "sinister scheme to save their own skin" on the part of the power holders, who were as guilty of revisionism as the "bourgeois academicians." Not surprisingly, some students challenged the work teams on the grounds that "political and crucial problems are being evaded, and the black gangs that cause great harm are going free."[127]

Were there any discernible groups of students who were likely to resent the authoritarian operations of the work teams and the division of the targets into the bourgeoisie and the masses? Did those who revolted against the work teams, and who subsequently became the targets of the work teams in the anti-interference campaign, show any common characteristics?

Perhaps the most obvious group was the students from "bad" family backgrounds. They were particularly angry when the work teams directed the spearhead of the movement against the teachers and professors, rather than against the power holders. Worse still, they themselves were attacked because of their bad class background. Later they charged that the work teams "did not do class analysis on the students and teachers from bad family backgrounds, made all of them 'bad eggs' and 'rightists,' . . . blurred class boundaries, created splits between the teachers and students, incited the students to struggle against the old teachers, and tried to evade the basic direction of the movement."[128]

For all the discussion on the class background issue, the work teams

125. *Studies on Chinese Communism* 11, no. 5 (May 1968): 78-93; *Ping-tuan chun-pao*, 10 April 1967; *Hung-wei-ping*, 25 November 1966.
126. *Ts'ui-hui tzu fan-hsien*, 2 August 1967; *Chieh-fang pao*, March 1968.
127. "Selected Big Character Posters of Tsinghua," *SCMMS*, no. 20 (18 March 1968), p. 20.
128. *Tung-fang-hung pao*, 12 April 1967; *Hung pei-ying*, 25 May 1967; *T'i-yü chan-pao*, 6 May 1967; *KMJP*, 7 April 1967.

actually considered it of secondary importance compared with the attitude a student displayed toward the work teams. One Red Guard newspaper made the following observations on how the work teams' criteria actually worked: (1) If students from bad class origins dared to revolt, the work teams considered their motivations impure (class revenge); (2) if students from a good family background revolted, the work teams insisted that they were ambitious and arrogant and wanted to seize power; and (3) if one's background was bad, but he supported the work teams, they said that he passed the tests.[129] Thus, one had to go beyond "class background" to identify the potentially rebellious students—those who held grievances against the school Party committees. Among the most discontented were those who had been sent to rural areas.[130]

Originally, the ideological goal in Mao's *hsia-fang*[131] instructions was to reduce the "three major differences" between "town and countryside," "mental and manual labor," and "workers and peasants." In the process of implementing the policy, however, practical considerations, such as the alleviation of unemployment and population congestion in the urban areas, outweighed the ideological goal and changed the criteria for determining who should be sent to the rural areas. According to the original goal, competent and able individuals in various fields should be sent to the countryside. Since nobody volunteered to go, the Party organization sent those who did not do well in school or other social areas—the "social dregs."[132]

Several groups were likely to be sent: urban residents of peasant background;[133] demobilized soldiers who could not secure permanent urban jobs; graduated youths who had come from the countryside to the city for their education; and urban youths who had failed to enter higher education or find urban jobs. Although it is difficult to establish the class backgrounds of these various groups, we do know that the urban residents of rural background tended to be former landlords and rich peasants who had moved to the city during collectivization.[134]

There was one discernible group, however, that was exempted from this policy—the children of cadres and army officers who obtained preferential

129. *Chingkangshan.* 23 March 1967. K'ang Sheng confirmed this point. "Kang Sheng's Speech to the Middle School Red Guards," *CB,* no. 891 (8 October 1968), pp. 1-3.

130. Lynn White, "Shanghai Polity in the Cultural Revolution," in *The City in Communist China,* ed. John Wilson Lewis (Stanford: Stanford University Press, 1971), pp. 325-370.

131. *Hsia-fang* refers to sending the urban students to the rural areas.

132. John Gardner, "Educated Youth and Urban-Rural Inequalities, 1958-1966," in *The City in Communist China,* pp. 235-286.

133. John Philip Emerson, "Manpower Training and Use of Cadres," in *The City in Communist China,* pp. 183-214.

134. Ibid. Though we do not have definitive evidence, it is highly likely that bourgeois students were more probably being sent to the rural areas. Gardner seems to imply this point too (in "Educated Youth and Urban-Rural Inequalities").

treatment in education as well as in job assignment.[135] As a matter of fact, at the initial stage of the Cultural Revolution the original Red Guards from the "five red categories" forced the bourgeoisie and other "undesirable elements" to leave the urban areas for the rural areas.[136]

When the *hsia-fang* policy shifted from its original lofty goals into a program for eliminating the "undesirable elements" from the urban areas, the peasants understandably resented the policy because it increased the financial burden on the already strained rural economy and demeaned their areas by making them the "dumping grounds for the social dregs" of urban society. In the early stages of the Cultural Revolution, these educated youths were politically discriminated against as a potentially explosive group.[137]

Once the school Party committees had been criticized, many of the students who had been sent to the countryside returned to their original units to join the Cultural Revolution. According to one report, six thousand students returned to their original units as soon as Nieh's big-character poster was broadcast. Eight hundred students and teachers from Peking University who had been sent to Szechwan came back in the excitement to participate in the mass movement. Although we do not have information regarding the activities of this group during the work team period, the fact that the Peking Municipal Party Committee organized a mass rally on August 13 to denounce *liu-mang* ("riffraff") suggests that they were still regarded as a major target.

If the students sent to the rural areas and those from the "bad" family backgrounds—the most underprivileged groups among the Chinese students—revolted against the work teams because of their discontent with the political status quo, a third group probably responded primarily to the ideological appeal of the Maoist leaders. The gap between the official ideology and the actual policy was so wide that it was readily apparent to any careful reader. Undoubtedly, some students from "good" families or in minor leadership positions in the schools genuinely felt that the work teams were guilty of "waving the Red Flag to oppose the Red Flag."

K'uai Ta-fu probably fits into this category of students from the privileged strata with "good" backgrounds, who nevertheless took their cue from the official ideology and revolted against the work teams. K'uai Ta-fu was from a poor peasant family and was a member of the Chinese Youth League. According to his own explanation, he had been inspired to challenge the

135. *Ch'un lei.* 16 May 1967. It is interesting to note that even after the CR the cadres could still use their position to give their children preferential treatment in this matter. See *JMJP,* 29 January 1974.

136. "Chin-chi t'ung-chih" ("Urgent Notice" of the Peking Second Middle School), 26 August 1966.

137. For the activities of this group in the CR, see *Chih-nung hung-ch'i,* 7 October 1967 and 6 January 1968; *Ko-ming ch'ing-nien,* 10 November 1967; *32.111 Chan-pao,* 31 October 1967.

work teams after his contact, on June 2 and 3, 1966, with the radical students at Peking University, and after he read *Chieh-fang chün-pao*'s June 5 editorial entitled "Hold the Great Banner of Mao Tse-tung's Thought."[138] It is equally possible, as the work teams charged, that he saw an opportunity to achieve his political ambitions in the mass movement.

In social science terminology, a receiver who holds a view different from that of the sender of a message prefers an ambiguous message, whereas a receiver, who shares the sender's view prefers a more explicit message.[139] When a message is implicit, opinion leaders play a decisive role in its interpretation. The implicit message in the official news media required some explicit interpretation in order to galvanize the students to action, and this was done by the Maoist leaders through secret communication channels.[140]

The clearest indication of the secret communication channels was the "Incident of the Letter from Peking."[141] Kao Hsiang, who became the leader of the Canton Third Headquarters, wrote a letter to his friends in Canton while he was visiting in Peking on June 24, 1966. In the letter, he specified that the "major target of the movement is a handful of power holders taking the capitalist road within the Party." He added that "we must examine everything, analyze everything with Mao Tse-tung's Thought," and that "our task is the seizure of power from the power holders taking the capitalist road within the Party."[142] This bold suggestion drew an immediate retaliation from the Kwangtung Party Committee.

In keeping with the Party organization's attempt to protect itself, it tended to restrict mobilization in the Cultural Revolution to selected, privileged groups which shared the Party's interest in maintaining the basic pattern of power distribution in China. These privileged groups were less susceptible to Maoist ideology, which, in effect, called for the end of their privileges. At the same time, they could be counted on, even when freely mobilized, not to challenge the structural legitimacy of the Party organization and not to ask for a restructuring of the Chinese political system.

138. "Selected Big Character Posters of Tsinghua," *SCMPS* no. 20 (18 November 1967), p. 34.
139. B. J. Fine, "Conclusion Drawing, Communication Credibility," *Journal of Abnormal and Social Psychology* 54, no. 3 (March 1959): 63-73.
140. There is an unconfirmed report that Nieh's big-character poster was actually written by K'ang Sheng's wife. Also it is very likely that Lin Chieh, a member of the CRSG and a graduate of the Peking Normal University, had established the contact with the anti-work-team force in the school. In addition, the mysterious telephone incident in Tsinghua of which the K'uai group stubbornly made an issue, his confident and almost arrogant tone in his big-character posters, and K'uai's false use of the Shanghai address in the letter to some students in the Girls' Middle School attached to the Peking University, all seemed to indicate that he had received some sort of assurance from the CRSG.
141. *Hung-ch'i pao*, 24 June 1967.
142. Ibid.

The selected mobilization pattern became apparent during the anti-interference campaign. On Liu Shao-ch'i's instruction to mobilize Party members for a counterattack on the critics of the Party, the work teams turned loose selected cadres after they had written a self-examination and openly denounced the radicals attacking the work teams.[143] Among the students, the work teams first mobilized ordinary Party and Chinese Youth League members, "exploiting their profound love for Chairman Mao."[144] With the slogan "Workers have risen to speak," which was used against the rightist students during the Hundred Flowers campaign, the work teams actively sought support among the workers, "exploiting the workers' profound class feelings."[145]

The students thus mobilized by the work teams were all from the "five red categories," which officially constituted the proletarian class and its allies in China.[146] In actual social position, however, the first two groups—workers and poor and lower-middle peasants—occupied low positions in terms of power and economic wealth, while the other three—cadres, army men, and martyrs—obviously belonged to the privileged groups. The work teams, stressing the theme of the "responsibility of sons of cadres to stave off the attack on the Party," actively mobilized children of cadres as the "most reliable groups."[147]

Most of the children of cadres had initially supported the school Party committees, but when the work teams arrived, they suddenly "changed and started uprising [against the school Party committees], claiming that they were deceived."[148] Contrary to the radical students' expectations, the work teams continued to support and rely on the "loyalists," instead of the students who had originally challenged the school Party committees and had consequently been subjected to reprisals.

In some schools, the work teams immediately convened secret meetings, at which they passed out students' files to the children of cadres so that they might check their classmates' class background.[149] In other places, the children of cadres simply took out the files on their own initiative.[150] When the work teams set up the Cultural Revolution Committees at the schools, the children of cadres were placed in all the high positions. In the Cultural Revolution Committee of the middle school attached to the Peking Normal

143. "Liu Shao-ch'i's Daughter Writes to Expose Her Father," *CB*, no. 821 (16 March 1967), pp. 1-25.
144. "Record," pp. 21-24.
145. "Selected Big Character Posters of Tsinghua," *SCMMS*, no. 20 (18 March 1968), p. 14.
146. "Five Red Categories" refers to the children of poor and lower-middle peasants, workers, the People's Liberation Army, revolutionary martyrs, and revolutionary cadres.
147. "Record," p. 21-24.
148. "Selected Big Character Posters of Tsinghua," p. 3.
149. *Hung-chün chan-pao*, 8 March 1968.
150. *JMJP*, 17 May 1967; *T'ieh-tao hung-ch'i*, 2 May 1967.

University, one of Liu Shao-ch'i's daughters was the chairman, and all twenty-one members were the children of cadres.[151] Most of the members of the three-person nuclear groups established in each class were also the children of cadres.[152] The Cultural Revolution Small Group objected to the practice. When Ch'en Po-ta visited the middle school, he tried to persuade the children of cadres to resign from their posts; instead, the children of cadres mobilized thirty thousand people to debate with him.[153]

While the Party organization emphasized class background, affiliation with the Party organization, and loyalty to its structural legitimacy in selecting participants, the Maoists advocated a diametrically opposed line. They declared that "whoever is revolutionary is to be relied upon. Nobody has made it a rule to rely on the Party or Chinese Youth League branches. You do not know whether they are revolutionary or not."[154] When the conservative students from the "five red categories" countered that the revolt of students from bad family backgrounds constituted "class revenge," the Maoists replied:

Whatever their aim and origin, bold exposure of problems means response to the call from the Party and Chairman Mao. If [a] questionable person rise[s] up and devotes himself to revolution, those whose origin is not good should be more than welcome to express problems and devote themselves to the revolution.[155]

Thus, the Maoists stressed action over motivation, the view constantly echoed by the radicals throughout the Cultural Revolution.

To sum up, when Mao applied pressure on the Party organization to rectify itself from bourgeois influence and to elminate the danger of revisionism, the Party organization moved to propitiate Mao, while protecting its own personnel and its own "structural legitimacy." For the selection of targets it employed a purely organizational method, which inevitably entailed shifting the targets to the lower-ranking cadres, the dangerous elements, and those with a bourgeois class background.

In the eyes of the Maoist leaders, the organizational method, in addition to selecting the wrong targets, was itself wrong, for it excluded the involvement of the masses, the most important mechanism for revolutionary action and hence for legitimizing the action of the Party organization in the eyes of the Chinese masses. When the Maoist leaders discredited the actions of the Party organization, those who had been attacked by the Party organization—whether or not the attack had been justified—rose to revolt and demanded that their verdicts be reversed, thus confounding the already complicated

151. "Liu Shao-ch'i's Daughter Writes to Expose Her Father," *CB*, no. 821 (16 March 1967), pp. 1-25; *Pei-ching fu-lun*, April 1967; *Ping-tuan chan-pao*, 27 April 1967; *KMJP*, 7 April 1967.
    152. Ibid.
    153. *Ping-t'uan chan-pao*, 27 April 1967.
    154. "The Wrong Must Be Redressed," *SCMPS*, no. 161 (17 June 1967), pp. 3-12.
    155. Ibid.

problem of who were the good cadres and who were the bad cadres deserving to be purged.

## Summing Up the Student Revolt

So far, we have examined the early differences that emerged among the Chinese elites over the various issues regarding the mass mobilization and the repercussions these differences had on the student revolt. The newspaper editorials, reflecting the views of the Maoist leaders, called for "free mobilization of the masses" and dropped ample hints that the Party leaders themselves were the major targets. The Party organization endeavored to maintain its leadership over the mobilization process, and this resulted in a series of policies that had the effect of restricting mass mobilization and deflecting the thrust of the movement onto the lower-ranking cadres and the masses outside the Party organization.

The Party organization was particularly eager to retain authority in selecting the participants for mobilization, and it displayed a tendency to limit these participants to "bourgeois authorities." The Maoists, on the other hand, opted for a broad interpretation of the Thought of Mao Tse-tung. The Party organization denied participation to social groups holding grievances against the Party organization. The Maoists, contrarily, viewed the masses' criticisms of the ruling elites as a vital function of the Cultural Revolution and exhibited a more tolerant attitude toward the revolt of the aggrieved social groups.

The Party organization justified its policies on the grounds that its "structural legitimacy" was inviolable. The Maoists subordinated the "structural legitimacy" of the organization to the Thought of Mao Tse-tung, which they extolled as the highest principle. These two different perspectives no doubt reflected the basic human dilemma between ends (ideology) and means (organization).

Indeed, the Maoists violated well-established Leninist organizational principles in the name of Marxist goals. In reaffirming that the ends (ideology) would determine the means (organization), not vice versa, the Maoists tended to restore to the individual the right to make judgments which the Communist Party had arrogated to itself in the name of Leninist principles. In this respect, the Cultural Revolution represented a noble attempt to resolve an ironical situation in which the Communist Party, initially established to carry out the Communist revolution, became itself the goal of the revolution. At the same time, it broke the long-standing myth that Marxist ideology and Leninist organization are necessarily tightly united.

The conflict between the Maoists and the Party organization did not entirely stem from the two different ideological perspectives, but was compounded by the divergent political interests of each group. The stress on ideology served the political interests of the supreme leader and his followers, who enjoyed the direct support of the masses but did not have effective control over the Party organization. On the other hand, the stress on the structural legitimacy of the Party organization served the political interests of the Party leaders, whose major power base was obviously the Party itself.

As obvious as the differences were between the two views, the conflict was still relatively contained at the time of the anti-interference campaign, and only developed into a full-fledged confrontation at a later stage in the movement. Therefore, it is difficult to conceptualize the actual conflict.

The Maoists claim that, from the beginning, the Cultural Revolution was a struggle between two lines—the bourgeois line led by Party leaders like Liu Shao-ch'i, and the proletarian line led by Mao. The implication of this claim is that the two groups confronted each other with different sets of ideological systems and a full awareness of their conflicts. This tends to be supported by previous experience. For example, when Mao Tse-tung's Thought proved to be dysfunctional vis-à-vis the Chinese reality during the Great Leap Forward, the Party organization moved subtly to elevate the more pragmatic and organization-oriented philosophy of Liu Shao-ch'i to the position of official ideology. Moreover, it is readily discernible that the orientiation of the Party organization during the work team period bore the marks of Liu's ideology rather than Mao's.

The thesis of full-fledged conflict, however, overlooks the fact that the conflict was still a latent and limited one. Each group maneuvered behind the scenes, avoiding a square confrontation until the end of the work team period. Mao tolerated the Party organization's domination of the movement through its organizational arms, the work teams. Divorced from Mao's Thought as the Party policy was, at least publicly the Party organization still acknowledged the supremacy of Mao Tse-tung's Thought, and defended its "structural legitimacy" on the grounds that it was congruent with that Thought.

Instead of openly challenging Mao's Thought, then, the Party organization resorted to the technique of passive resistance: the leaders first tried to interpret Mao's Thought in so moderate a way that it would be consistent with their own organizational interests, and then they tried to moderate Mao's Thought in the process of translating it into actual policy.

Rather than actively leading the mass movement in the direction opposed to Mao, the Party leaders simply neglected to instruct the work teams on "free mobilization of the masses," so that the work teams followed the typical organizational mode of operation and consequently led the movement in the direction that the Party leaders wanted. The Maoist leaders countered the passive resistance of the Party with further mobilization of the masses, a strategy that was most effective in exposing the Party's double-handed tactics of "waving the Red Flag to oppose the Red Flag."

It is obvious that the revolt of the Chinese students against the Party organization was a revolt against its norms and operational codes, and in confirmation of the values defined by the official Maoist ideology. Confronted with the discrepancy between ideology and policy, the students resolved the dissonance in favor of the official ideology. In addition to their preference for Mao's ideology over the Party's, some of the students were also directly manipulated by the Maoist leaders. But once the students accepted and used the radicalized version of Mao Tse-tung's Thought to evaluate the behavior of the Party organization and the work teams, it was obvious that the work teams were not carrying out what they claimed. The radical students used these "facts" to write big-character posters, to challenge the work teams, and to sway the opinion of other students to their side.

On a more general level, the student revolt can be viewed as a revolt of the individual against the impersonal structure of the organization. By specifically subordinating the organization to ideology, Mao's Thought profoundly changed the students' perception of the Party. It was seen no longer as the ultimate source of legitimacy, but only as a means of achieving political goals. This change in their perception enabled the students to attack the Party while still proclaiming their dedication to Communism.[156]

The unique role of the supreme leader and his ideology distinguishes the revolt of the Chinese students during the Cultural Revolution from other student revolts largely induced by the alienation of youth from the existing value system. The Chinese students revolted, not because they were alienated from the prevalent value system, but because they wanted to conform with it. In their behavior they displayed what the regime had tried to instill in their minds, such as the ideas of "class struggle," "one dividing into two," participatory democracy, concern with the fate of collectives, and above all, the demands of high-level self-consciousness. Although one can notice in their behavior a certain persistence of traditional Chinese social traits, such as loyalty to and love for leaders, group cohesion, and a small-group mentality, these features were overshadowed by modern, positive attitudes which stood out most prominently when compared with those of their counterparts in other developing countries.

The Chinese students rejected a "slave mentality" and followed their individual judgments rather than the lead of the organization. They aptly utilized "mass line" techniques to draw the support of the public, and they displayed a high level of awareness of their own interests and how these interests conflicted with the interests of the collective. They developed the ability to articulate and rationalize their own views in terms of Communist ideology, and they demonstrated a remarkable cooperativeness in setting up

156. Ronald Montaperto, "From Revolutionary Successor to Revolutionaries: Chinese Students in the Early Stage of the CR," in *Elites in the People's Republic of China,* ed. Robert Scalapino (Seattle: University of Washington Press, 1971), pp. 576-605.

their own organization. Moreover, they confronted the difficult choice between individual and collective interests, thus clearly making a break with traditional, passive, submissive, and particularistic attitudes.

Characterization of the value pattern discernible in the Chinese students' behavior, however, does not mean that the Chinese value system based on the Thought of Mao Tse-tung was well integrated in its inner structure and in its relations to norms and rules. On the contrary, as a system of thought, Mao Tse-tung's Thought contains contradictory and hence dynamic elements. Even if Mao had wanted to provide a well-integrated value system with a specific set of norms and rules within the framework of Marxism-Leninism, it is most unlikely that he could have succeeded.

This inability is underscored by the contradictory tendencies in the official treatment of Mao Tse-tung's Thought, which absolutized it, while insisting on its creative application. Mao's own insistence that the revolutionary successors should be knowledgeable in Marxism-Leninism, as well as experienced in politics and applying the mass line, eloquently indicates his keen awareness of the problem and his desire to maintain the basic value system of communism while adapting it, through continuous practice, to the changing environment. Thus, Mao seems to have hoped that, through a continuous study of "dialectics," the Chinese youth would internalize the two opposing values, combining Marxist ideology with pragmatic strategy and conformity with creative thinking.

If the intrinsic contradictions in the Thought of Mao Tse-tung gave it flexibility, they also drastically diluted its capacity for exercising control, especially when the Party organization lost its customary role as the authoritative interpreter of Mao Tse-tung's Thought and the masses were given direct access to it. During the Cultural Revolution, all the political actors interpreted the Thought of Mao Tse-tung differently, according to their own political interests. Underprivileged social groups saw that the radicalization of Mao's Thought served their interests, whereas the privileged social groups saw their interests served by a moderate interpretation. Each fought the other in the name of Mao Tse-tung's Thought. Even when presumably all the Chinese students were exposed to the dual communications and subject to cognitive dissonance, it was only a small number of students who resolved their ambivalence by revolting against the Party organization rather than accepting its authority.

Contrary to the generally held assumption that the Red Guard movement was essentially a revolt, only a minority of the radicals could be considered genuine rebels. In their relentless challenge to the "structural legitimacy" of the Party organization, this minority of the students gradually heightened "the political consciousness" of their apathetic fellow students, enabling them to see the subterfuge of the power holders. This indicates that psychological and communication theories alone are incapable of answering the next logical question of who were the minority students who were so suscep-tible to the radicalized version of Mao's Thought.

Our examination of the targets and participants has revealed that those who held grievances against the political status quo in general and the Party committees in particular readily subscribed to Mao's Thought. Varied as their grievances were, the discontented groups found the cause of their problems in a common source—the power holders—thus approximating what William Gamson has called "the situational interest group."[157] Mao's Thought provided these groups with the opportunity to express their griev-ances in the name of revolution.

Confronted with a potential challenge to its legitimacy, the Party organi-zation resorted to classical methods: on the one hand, it pre-empted poten-tial threats within the organization; and on the other, it co-opted into the organization new elements that held a favorable view of the Party. The major groups falling prey to the Party were the disadvantaged and the discontented, a combination that proved to be a catalyst for a massive revolt.

In a politicized society such as China, the only way to redress grievances is through political action. Especially during the Cultural Revolution, in which everyone was compelled to take part as either an attacker or a target, it is not surprising that the discontented groups challenged the pre-emptive moves of the Party organization as a distortion of Mao's goals. In fact, the editorials of the news media constantly cautioned the Chinese masses to watch out for the "black gangs" who were struggling against innocent people to save their own skins.

While the members of underprivileged social groups became the victims selected by the Party organization, the most privileged groups, the children of cadres, became the major allies of the Party organization, ironically augmenting their privileges in the Cultural Revolution that Mao had launched to narrow down the political inequalities in China. The conflict between the privileged and the underprivileged social groups continued even after the disintegration of the Party organization, creating a situation in which the most discontented members of the society tended to be the most radical revolutionaries.

157. William Gamson, *Power and Discontent* (Chicago: Dorsey Press, 1968).

# CHAPTER 3

# The Student Mobilization from the Bottom to the Top: The Rising Tension in the Red Guard Movement

As the work teams were withdrawn and the Maoist principle of allowing "free mobilization of the masses" was indelibly written into "Sixteen Articles" where it could no longer be challenged, the Chinese students organized themselves into the Red Guards, and the Cultural Revolution became a full-fledged mass movement. The freely mobilized students, however, soon split into warring factions. The conflicts revealed in part the impact of the Party organization's pre-emptive moves in the preceding stage on the latent tensions that had been accumulating for a long time. They also reflected the continuing intra-elite conflict that simply reappeared at the mass level under the new rule of "freely mobilizing the masses."

With the shift in the level of conflict, however, the mode of the ultra-elite struggle also changed. Now the Party and the Cultural Revolution Small Group, instead of confronting each other directly, competed for control of the mass organization by attempting to manipulate the range of issues constantly generated in such a large-scale mass movement. Their differences over the issues divided basically along conservative and radical lines, with each group finding supporters among the mass organizations. At the end of this stage, the Cultural Revolution Small Group's view prevailed, thus enabling the radical students hostile to the Party organization to take over the leadership of the Red Guard movement.

## The Eleventh Plenum

Mao hurriedly convened the Eleventh Plenum of the Central Committee in August to obtain official endorsement for his private views on the Cultural

Revolution. The meeting, which lasted an unusually long twelve days, was not attended by many regular Central Committee members, but was packed with "revolutionary teachers and students."[1] Nevertheless, the Maoists still encountered strong opposition: Liu Shao-ch'i reportedly denied the charges that he had erred in the preceding stage, and declared that he was not afraid of the five consequences—dismissal, expulsion, divorce by his wife, imprisonment, or being beheaded.[2] It was only after a prolonged and heated debate that Mao succeeded in getting the "Sixteen Articles" adopted with barely more than the necessary votes.[3]

While the meeting was in session, the Maoist leaders launched a kind of public relations campaign obviously designed to build up mass support for their position and to bring pressure to bear on the Party leaders. On July 29, Mao granted an interview to the "activists of the Cultural Revolution" from the various schools. Two days later, he made a surprise appearance at the International Physicists Conference—a visit that Chinese television reported with the "same exaltation as 'Christ has risen' would be said during the Orthodox Easter Celebration," to quote the words of a cynical outside observer.[4]

On August 1, Mao sent a personal letter of support for its big-character posters to the middle school attached to Tsinghua University.[5] On August 4, the Cultural Revolution Small Group organized student rallies at Tsinghua and Peking Universities to declare the rehabilitation of those students whom the work teams had attacked.[6] The next day, Mao wrote his first big-character poster, "Bombard the Headquarters," for Peking University. It read in part:

In the last fifty days or so, some leading comrades from the central down to the local levels have acted in diametrically opposite ways. Adopting the reactionary stand of the bourgeoisie, they have enforced a bourgeois dictatorship and struck down the surging movement of the great cultural revolution of the proletariat. They have stood facts on their head and juggled black and white, encircled and suppressed revolutionaries, stifled opinions differing from their own, imposed a white terror, and felt very pleased with themselves. They have puffed up the arrogance of the bourgeoisie and deflated the morale of the proletariat. How poisonous! Viewed in connection with the Right

1. The plenum was attended only by 80 out of 120 Central Committee members. Chao Ts'ung, *Wen-ko yün-tung li-ch'eng shu lüeh* (Hong Kong: Yu-lien yen-chiu-so, 1971), vol. 1, p. 383.
2. *Hung-se tsao-fan tuan,* 22 June 1967.
3. "Speech at the Closing Ceremony of the Eleventh Plenary Session," *CB,* no. 891, (8 October 1969), p. 64.
4. D. W. Fokkema, *Report from Peking: Observation of a Western Diplomat on the Cultural Revolution* (Montreal, Canada: McGill-Queen's University Press, 1972), p. 14.
5. "A Letter to the Red Guards of the Middle School Attached to Tsinghua University," *CB,* no. 891, p. 63. This Red Guard organization was later condemned as conservative. *Hung-ch'i,* 26 December 1966.
6. "Record," p. 5.

deviation in 1962 and the wrong tendency in 1964, which was "Left" in form but Right in essence, shouldn't this make one wide awake?[7]

The implication was unmistakable: the Party leaders, particularly Liu Shao-ch'i, were to be criticized.

The "Sixteen Articles" and the Communiqué of the Eleventh Plenum were made public on August 8. As a whole, the "Sixteen Articles" represented a victory of the Maoist line, but their ambiguity on several crucial points betrays the amount of compromising required among the various political groups at the top.[8] On the question of targets, they pointed out three different but interrelated groups and directed the masses to (1) "struggle against the power holders taking the capitalist road within the Party," since they spread bourgeois ideology and resisted the Cultural Revolution; (2) "criticize and repudiate the reactionary bourgeois academic authorities"; and (3) "transform education, literature, art, and all other parts of the superstructure that do not correspond to the socialist economic base."[9] The first category clearly referred to the Party leaders, the second to the "bourgeois academicians," and the third to the masses who held a bourgeois ideology.

Despite the adoption of different terms ("struggle," "criticize and repudiate," and "transform"), the document failed to enunciate clearly what the primary objective of the movement was—the question that had been the major source of conflict in the work team period. Again, different groups interpreted the "Sixteen Articles" according to their own interests. The Party leaders and conservative Red Guards tended to emphasize the second and third objectives, while the Cultural Revolution Small Group and the radical Red Guards turned the major thrust of the movement toward the first objective.

Although one article included the Party leaders among the assorted targets, other articles still recognized the leadership role of the Party organization in the movement. On the whole, the articles unequivocally criticized the Party's practice of branding the masses as "counterrevolutionary," but fell short of suggesting how to treat "counterrevolutionaries." They described the masses as the "main force," which should be trusted and relied upon, and whose initiative should be respected, and they recommended lenient treatment for the masses who had made mistakes; but they failed to spell out what to do with the ordinary students from bourgeois families. The document was particularly confusing in its delineation of the power relationship between the Cultural Revolution Committees and the Congress, which it

7. Ch'en, *Mao Papers,* p. 117. Liu Shao-ch'i later admitted that it was Mao's letter that led him to realize Mao's determination to turn the movement against the Party organization itself. "Look! The Restoration for Counterrevolution," *SCMP,* no. 4037 (9 October 1967), pp. 1-7.
8. K. H. Fan, *The Chinese Cultural Revolution* (New York: Grove Press, 1968), pp. 161-173.
9. Ibid.

recommended as an "excellent bridge to keep our Party in close contact with the masses" and the Party leadership at the various levels.

Although the "Sixteen Articles" were unclear on many crucial issues, the shift of power that the Eleventh Plenum had effectuated among the Chinese leaders and its implications were very clear. Liu Shao-ch'i was replaced by Lin Piao as vice-chairman of the Central Committee and demoted in the Party hierarchy from second to eighth place. The Politburo added twelve new members, expanding its total membership to thirty-two, and T'ao Chu (on T'eng Hsiao-p'ing's recommendation), K'ang Sheng, and Ch'en Po-ta were made members of its Standing Committee. In addition, Mao abolished the division between the first and second lines of decision-making, under which Liu Shao-ch'i had assumed authority for making daily decisions in 1958.

The reshuffle was intended to "insure the implementation of the decisions of the CCP and the Communiqué [of the Eleventh Plenum]."[10] But, despite the increase of Maoist control over the decision-making process, the Maoists obviously still had to rely on the organizational capability of the Party to carry out the ambiguously worded decision. Mao warned:

You must never take it for granted that all things written in the decision will be carried out by all Party committees and all comrades. There are always some who are unwilling to carry them out. But this time it may be better than in the past, and, moreover, this decision is guaranteed organizationally.[11]

Once the Maoists had succeeded in having their views adopted in the official document, they proceeded to practice what they had been advocating. Mao began this with an unexpected public appearance before the masses gathered to celebrate the adoption of the "Sixteen Articles." He uttered one short cryptic sentence with profound implications: "You should be concerned about the important state affairs; you should carry out the Cultural Revolution to the end."[12] Eight days later, Mao wore a Red Guard armband when he attended the first big mass rally. Although he did not speak to the rally, his very presence was enough to convince the Chinese masses that he supported the Red Guard movement.

By August 20, Red Guard activities were seen on the main streets of Peking.[13] Three days later, a *Jen-min jih-pao* editorial officially extolled the

10. "Speech at the Closing Ceremony of the Eleventh Plenary Session," *CB*, no. 891 (8 October 1969), p. 64.

11. Ibid.

12. "Speeches by Comrade Ch'i Pen-yü and Kuan Feng," *SCMMS*, no. 15 (8 May 1967), p. 7.

13. *Yomiuri*, 26 September 1966. The sudden rise of the Red Guards indicates that it was a well-organized movement at that time. One correspondent described the suddenness with which the Red Guard rose: "By August 22, only four days after their appearance at the Peking rally, uniformly dressed Red Guards chanting identical slogans were reported active in most of the major cities." *Sankei*, 28 August 1966.

Red Guards.[14] In a second big rally, on August 31, Chou En-lai announced the policy of "great exchange of experiences,"[15] the main vehicle that carried the Red Guard movement from Peking to the periphery and enabled the Maoist leaders in Peking to establish direct contact with the local student groups.

Soon the Red Guards swept all over China, propagating Mao's Thought and learning the real conditions of Chinese society, on the one hand, and digging out information on their enemies and enjoying themselves with free trips, on the other. When the transportation facilities could no longer accommodate all the Red Guards, they embarked on a "long march" on foot. By the time the sixth and last mass rally was held in Peking on November 26, a total of ten million Chinese youths had visited Peking.[16] With this sketch of the unfolding events in mind, we can return to the more concrete issues responsible for the major cleavage in the Red Guard movement.

## Political Consciousness and Class Origin

The withdrawal of the work teams removed the Party's organizational control over the movement and left the Chinese students with "unprecedented freedom." The only officially recognized guides for their actions were the Thought of Mao Tse-tung and the "Sixteen Articles." Both, however, were ambiguous on many important questions, and the most important issue of all—class line—was completely ignored by the "Sixteen Articles" and was subject to conflicting interpretations in Mao's Thought.

Class is the most crucial concept in Communist doctrine, but particularly so in the Cultural Revolution, which the Maoist leaders justified on the basis of the need for "class struggle." Unfortunately, however, class is a very illusive concept, particularly in regard to two points—namely, whether class is to be defined only in economic terms, and whether members of a class must have a subjective awareness of their identity. In other words, "Is a class a class because thinking [self-awareness] makes it so, or is a class a class purely on objective grounds?"

In the context of the Cultural Revolution, the different views on these two ambiguous points in Marxism yielded different answers to the question of who should be the targets of the movement. If class is defined only economically, as many social scientists have done,[17] the logical targets of the class

14. *JMJP*, 23 August 1966.

15. Chou En-lai announced that students were to go only to big and medium-sized cities and were not allowed to go to small *hsien* towns, rural villages, and factories. "Speech by Premier Chou on September 10," *CB*, no. 819 (10 March 1967), pp. 28-29.

16. Chao Ts'ung, *Wen-ko yün-tung li-ch'eng shu-lüeh*, vol. 1, p. 383.

17. For instance, Dahrendorf defines Marx's notion of class purely in economic terms. See

struggle would be the remnants of the bourgeois class. But if the term refers also to various social "groupings" according to a "wide variety of standards,"[18] the targets of the class struggle could well include the Party organization itself, the locus of political power in China. This second view of class allowed those without political power to attack the power holders, while invoking the doctrine of class struggle to justify their attack. If political consciousness were to be emphasized, moreover, children of bourgeois families could lay claim to "proletarian class consciousness" obtained through the study of Mao Tse-tung's Thought, and thus be participants in rather than objects of the Cultural Revolution.

Although the interpretation of class had immediate consequences for the Chinese masses, Mao's view on the issue was somewhat ambiguous. On the one hand, he exalted the class struggle and "continuing revolution," defining the Cultural Revolution as a class struggle. On the other hand, while emphasizing class consciousness and its derivative notions of "politics in command" and ideological transformation, he failed to define class.[19] Despite the lack of clarity, it seems that Mao expanded the term to include political inequality.[20]

This interpretation of Mao's notion of class makes sense in view of the otherwise ironical fact that he raised the slogan of "Never forget the class struggle" during the Tenth Plenum in 1962, when the means of production were already completely socialized. Moreover, this interpretation is in accord with the historical experience of the CCP which had necessarily relied on the peasants as a motive force, instead of on the virtually nonexistent industrial proletariat.[21] Following the CCP's rise to power, particularly during the process of agricultural collectivization, Mao learned that some peasants were vulnerable to a "tendency toward capitalism [individualism]." By 1964, Mao

Ralf Dahrendorf, *Class and Class Conflict in Industrial Society* (Stanford, Calif.: Stanford University Press, 1959).

18. For this interpretation of class, see Bertell Ollman, "Marx's Use of 'Class,'" *American Journal of Sociology*, March 1968, pp. 573-580. According to Ollman, the central determinant of class is not necessarily economic position, but any kind of relative inequality if it is serious enough to create a permanent social cleavage in a given society.

19. Donald Munro deals with the problem of class consciousness and class origin from the perspective of the malleability of man. See Donald Munro, "The Malleability of Man in Chinese Marxism," *CQ*, no. 48 (October-December 1971), pp. 609-640.

20. Benjamin Schwartz, "A Personal View of Some Thought of Mao Tse-tung," in *Ideology and Politics in Contemporary China*, ed. Chalmers Johnson (Seattle: University of Washington Press, 1973), pp. 352-377. Also, for a similar interpretation, see Frederic Wakeman, *History and Will. Philosophical Perspectives of Mao Tse-tung's Thought* (Berkeley and Los Angeles: University of California Press, 1973); and John Starr, "Conceptual Foundations of Mao Tse-tung's Theory of Continuous Revolution," *Asian Survey* 11, no. 6 (June 1971), pp. 610-628.

21. For the controversy regarding the different interpretations of Marxism and Mao's rise to power in the CCP, see Benjamin Schwartz, *Chinese Communism and the Rise of Mao* (Cambridge, Mass.: Harvard Universtiy Press, 1968).

had coined the terms *"old* and *new* bourgeois and *old* and *new* rich peasants."[22] Beside these official pronouncements which indicate his political
interpretation of class, Mao showed increasing concern with the cleavage
between the privileged and the underprivileged, in spite of failing to mention
class background as even one of the five requirements for revolutionary
successors.[23] By 1965, Mao had classified the bureaucrats as a class:

> The bureaucratic class is a class sharply opposed to the working class and the poor
> and the lower-middle peasants. These people have become or are in the process of
> becoming bourgeois elements sucking the blood of workers.[24]

During the Cultural Revolution, the Maoists flatly declared: "Class is not
only an economic concept; more important, it is a political concept."[25]

Mao, as a charismatic leader with an egalitarian vision, could afford to
interpret class in such a way that it could justify his attack on the bureaucratization of the Party. The interests of the Party organization lay, on the
contrary, with a definition of class in strictly economic terms that would not
raise the perplexing question of "differential distribution of power" in a
socialist country. It was probably in this context that Liu Shao-ch'i in 1958
declared the end of class struggle, saying that the "question of who will win
in the struggle between socialism and capitalism in our country has now been
decided."[26] If this interpretation is correct, there may have been some truth
in the radicals' charge that Liu had emphasized class background as a
necessary condition in his formula—consisting sometimes of three and sometimes of four requirements—for revolutionary successors.[27] In the Cultural
Revolution, the radicals followed Mao's interpretation of class, thus turning
their attacks onto the power holders. The conservatives followed the economic

22. "On Khrushchev's Phony Communism," in *China After Mao,* ed. A. D. Barnett
(Princeton, N.J.: Princeton University Press, 1967), pp. 127-129.
23. Mao revealed his worry about the widening gap between the elite and the masses in his
interview with André Malraux: "The truth is that if the contradictions due to victory are less
painful than the old ones, luckily they are almost as deep. Humanity left to its own devices does
not necessarily re-establish capitalism, but it does re-establish inequality. The forces tending
toward the creation of new classes are powerful. Khrushchev seemed to think that a revolution is
done when a communist party seized power—as if it were merely a question of national
liberation." See André Malraux, *Anti Memoir* (New York: Rinehart and Winston, 1968), pp.
69-70. For Mao's five requirements, see *China News Analysis,* 16 October 1964, p. 3.
24. "Comment on Comrade Ch'en Cheng-jen's Report on Stay at a Selected Spot," *CB,* no.
891 (8 October 1969), p. 49.
25. "The Dictatorship of the Proletariat and That Renegade—China's Khrushchev," *PR,* no.
40 (29 September 1967), p. 10.
26. *The Eighth National Congress of the Chinese Communist Party* (Peking: Foreign
Languages Press, 1965), vol. 1, p. 37.
27. *Chung-hsüeh wen-ko,* 1 April 1967. Donald Munro suggests that Liu strictly adhered to
class origin in his "Later Revised Ten Articles" of Ssu-ch'ing, whereas Ch'en Po-ta and Kuan
Feng, members of the CRSG, emphasized the malleability of man through education even
before the CR. See Munro, "The Malleability of Man."

interpretation of class, thus attempting to turn the whole movement against the remnants of the bourgeoisie.

At a more concrete level, the debate involved several different interpretations of Mao's three criteria for class line: (1) "consider class status" *(ch'eng fen);* (2) "not solely class status"; (3) "but emphasis on performance."[28]

The first issue in dispute was the meaning of "class status." Does it refer to an individual member's status or that of one's parents? If the former, children from bourgeois families can claim a good class status for themselves; if the latter, their class status will be bad irrespective of their present political performance. Students from "bad" family backgrounds naturally insisted that Mao's formula referred to one's present status—such as student, worker, peasant, or party cadre. Students from "good" family backgrounds maintained that it referred to class origin *(ch'u sheng)*—the class status of one's parents.[29]

The second question revolved around the relative weight that should be given to "class status" and "political performance." Students from the "five red categories" put more emphasis on class status, whereas students from bad family backgrounds stressed the importance of political performance, selectively quoting from Mao to justify their view.[30]

The third controversial point concerned the actual relationship of "class status" to "political performance." Students from good families took the position that class status is significantly correlated with, although not directly determined by, one's ideology and political performance. Students from bad families skillfully exploited the logical implications of Mao Tse-tung's Thought to assert that it was education rather than class status that determines one's political stand. The students from the five red categories did not completely deny the efficacy of Mao's Thought in educating the bourgeoisie, but they insisted that family influences are more important than those of society as a whole. Students from bad family backgrounds maintained that the influences of society surpass those of the family; hence, even persons not belonging to the five red categories could grow up with a proper political consciousness because they had been brought up in a socialist country and exposed to a proletarian education.[31]

Thus, students with bad family backgrounds argued for the malleability of man and the efficacy of Mao Tse-tung's Thought to establish their own qualifications for taking part in the Cultural Revolution. They further suggested that the class struggle in the Cultural Revolution was qualitatively

28. *Hung-wei-ping pao,* 8 December 1966.
29. For the conservative's view, see *Tung-feng pao,* 26 December 1966, and for the radical's view, see *Chih-pa ch'un-lai pao,* 22 March 1967.
30. "Selected Big Character Posters of Tsinghua," *SCMMS,* no. 20 (18 March 1967), p. 17.
31. "What the Commotion of the United Action Committee Has Explained," *SCMPS,* no. 183 (16 May 1967), pp. 14-24.

different from the class struggle of the past by frequently using such terms as "class struggle in socialism" and "new bourgeois," and they implied that present, not past, social position was the major determinant of class. Hence, the Party leaders and the children of cadres enjoying privileges in the new society could be subsumed under the bourgeois class category. The children of cadres, of course, stuck to the economic definition of "class."

A couplet that was first heard in late July 1966, and which gained currency from the beginning of August, when the Eleventh Plenum was in session, epitomized the views of cadre offspring: "If one's father is revolutionary his son is a hero, and if one's father is reactionary his son is a bad egg."[32] Although the couplet's ideological and political implications seemed inconsequential on the surface, its implications supported the arguments that the Cultural Revolution should be aimed at the "bourgeois academicians," that its participants should be restricted only to the students of the "five red categories," and that the students from "bad" family backgrounds should not have the right to take part in the movement.

By mid-August, the correctness of the couplet was widely debated, but its influence was so rampant that even that debate was limited to students from the "five red categories." It became customary for a would-be participant to first describe his class background when he was about to speak on the issue.[33]

It seems that the couplet, with its implied class line, originated spontaneously in the mass movement and was then exploited by the Party leaders for their own purposes. The local students throughout China, upon hearing of the formation of the Red Guards in Peking, wanted to organize their own Red Guard groups, but did not know how to proceed. After much debate, they decided that the organization should be made up of students from revolutionary family backgrounds.[34] Since P'eng Chen was being publicly criticized at the time for his excessive emphasis on "performance," it is likely that some students—especially the middle school students who were ignorant of the real issues in the Cultural Revolution and of the logical implications of the couplet—mistakenly believed that the couplet truly reflected Mao's class line.

In any case, the proponents of the couplet apparently failed to note that the work teams had also interpreted Mao's class line in the manner suggested by the couplet in order to keep the targets of the whole mass movement outside the Party organization. Moreover, the Party organization, although it did not actively propagate the couplet, responded favorably to it.[35] The Party

32. "Record," p. 34; *Ping-t'uan chan-pao,* 26 November 1966.
33. *Ping-tuan chan-pao,* 26 November 1966.
34. Ch'u Ko, *Luan-shih hsün-yü* (Hong Kong: Chung-pao chou-k'an, 1969), p. 3.
35. For the views of Teng Hsiao-p'ing, T'ao Chu, and T'an Chen-lin, see "Speeches and Statements Alleged to Have Been Made by Chinese Central Leaders," *CB,* no. 819 (10 March

leaders' speeches resounded with its basic premises, which were consistent with the organizational interests of the Party.

Although the confusing situation and their own political naiveté misled some students into subscribing to the couplet's message, other students quite consciously supported it because it served their group interests. The children of cadres enthusiastically propagated the couplet to the children of workers and peasants, even though it was strictly applicable only to three of the five red categories: the revolutionary cadres, the revolutionary martyrs, and the revolutionary soldiers. At that time, before the revolutionary quality of their parents had been questioned, the couplet provided a powerful justification for their bid to lead the movement. But as the Party leaders—the "revolutionaries" in the couplet—became the target of the movement, it became untenable to argue that the children of cadres were heroes by virtue of their parents' position.

In contrast to the Party leaders' subtle support for the couplet, the Maoist leaders denounced it as a distortion of Mao's class line. In fact, the couplet contradicted Mao's view of "class." Time and again, Mao had expressed his concern about the privileges enjoyed by the children of high-ranking cadres.[36] Moreover, long before the Cultural Revolution, Ch'en Po-ta and Kuan Feng, two influential members of the Cultural Revolution Small Group, had explicitly stressed the malleability of man through education and ideological reform.[37] There are also no indications that the Maoist leaders had ever intended to classify the students along class lines in the Cultural Revolution; to the contrary, the official policy that all college students should visit Peking—announced at the end of August—suggests the opposite.

When Chiang Ch'ing met on August 6, 1966, with the "Red Flag" group of the middle school attached to Peking University—the first Red Guard organization composed of the children of cadres—she urged the students to take Mao's five requirements for revolutionary successors as the basis for distinguishing class line. She also traced the origin of the couplet back to a Peking opera that was under attack at that time.[38]

On a separate occasion, Chiang Ch'ing and Ch'en Po-ta suggested that the couplet should be changed to read: "If one's father is a revolutionary his son tries hard to be a hero, and if one's father is a reactionary his son should rebel."[39] Not surprisingly, students with "bad" class origins welcomed the

---

1967), pp. 1-84, and "T'an Chen-lin's Black Words," *SCMPS*, no. 238 (8 November 1968), pp. 8-11.

36. "Mao's Talk with Wang Hai jung and His Nephew," *JPRS*, no. 52,029 (21 December 1970), pp. 34-35.

37. Munro, "The Malleability of Man," *CQ*, no. 48, pp. 609-640.

38. "Speech of Comrade Chiang Ch'ing to Red Flag Combat Corps on August 6," *Shou-chang chiang-hua*, vol. 3 (unpaged).

39. "A Talk by Comrade Chiang Ch'ing to the Red Guard Fighters on August 6, 1966," *CB*, no. 830 (26 June 1967), pp. 24-25.

Cultural Revolution Small Group's position, which gave them the right to revolt. Later they claimed that the original couplet represented a "feudalistic hereditary blood theory" or a "theory of natural redness."[40]

As the proponents of the couplet resisted the objections raised against it, the Cultural Revolution Small Group extended its criticism to those children of cadres who used the couplet to justify their claim to the leadership of the Red Guard movement. By early September, Ch'en Po-ta openly suggested that the children of high-ranking cadres should relinquish their leadership to the ordinary students.[41] The children of cadres interpreted this as a scheme to replace them with students loyal to the Cultural Revolution Small Group. Instead of faithfully carrying out the spirit of the suggestion, they "merely resigned from their posts and designated those with the firmest class backgrounds to replace them."[42] In response to their evasive tactic, the Cultural Revolution Small Group escalated its criticism, denouncing them as revisionist Red Guards:

Among you Red Guards there are genuine Red Guards and revisionist Red Guards. . . . If you want to become Red Guards, you must become genuine ones. . . . Red Guards of Mao Tse-tung's Thought and not revisionist ones following a bourgeois counterrevolutionary [line]. The Red Guards following the counterrevolutionary revisionist line are spurious.[43]

The children of cadres responded that the Cultural Revolution Small Group was "instigating the masses to struggle against the masses," the same charge that the Maoist leaders had made against the Party leaders during the work team period.

Although the official news media rarely dealt directly with the issue, they endeavored to balance class status and political performance:

Is it possible for these young people and teenagers [with bad class backgrounds] to take the revolutionary road? Proletarians, being dialectical materialists, believe that the world can be transformed and so can man himself. . . . Since elements of the exploiting classes may be transformed, their children must all the more be treated separately. Therefore, in dealing with young people and teenagers from families of exploiting classes, it is necessary not only to see how much they have been influenced by the ideas of the exploiting classes, but also to see how they may be transformed with the help of Mao Tse-tung's Thought and the guidance of the Party. It is wrong to

40. *Ping-t'uan chan-pao,* 26 November 1966.
41. "Ch'en Po-ta's Speech at Political Consultative Auditorium," *JPRS,* no. 40,974 (10 May 1967), pp. 9-13. Ch'en visited the middle school attached to Peking Normal University on July 4 and advised Liu Shao-ch'i's daughter to relinquish her leadership. Liu P'ing-p'ing challenged Ch'en by organizing a rally of 3,000 students to debate with Ch'en. *Ping-t'uan chan-pao,* 27 April 1967.
42. "General Summary for the CR in the Past Two Months," *Issues and Studies* 7, no. 2 (November 1970): 71-78.
43. "Ch'en Po-ta's Speech at Political Consultative Auditorium," *JPRS,* no. 40,974 (10 May 1967), pp. 9-13.

regard them as having been born dark [black] and unchangeable. While one cannot choose one's family, one certainly can choose the road he wants to take.[44]

Later, Lin Piao rendered his authoritative judgment on the controversial issue:

Status [*ch'eng fen*] in the class line is not [the same as] class origin [*ch'u sheng*]. For example, you are workers, you are students, and all of you can be the main force of the revolution. Of course, not every worker is a revolutionary. Therefore, there is also emphasis on one's performance. As Chiang Ch'ing said, "[We must] see the individual's standpoint." There is no relation between standpoint and class origin. Revolutionary comrades should bridge the gulf. When the Cultural Revolution began, that gulf divided the youth, causing them to stand at the opposite end of the Milky Way, and causing the early death of the movement. . . . We consider that whether one is superior to another or not lies not in his class origin, nor in his personality, nor in his age, but in his performance and his upholding of Mao Tse-tung's Thought. . . . Not every person from a good background is better in performance than persons from bad family backgrounds. In the five requirements made by Chairman Mao himself, there is not one word about class origin.[45]

Mao endorsed Lin Piao's view on the class line:

A person's class origin [*ch'u sheng*] should be distinguished from his performance, which is more important than his class origin. It is wrong to assume that class status is everything. The crux of the problem is whether you adhere to your original class stand or alter your class stand.[46]

The issue of class line, however, remained troublesome even for the Maoist leaders. Its nature was such that both the interpretations and the applications of the concept tended toward the extremes: class background was either completely disregarded, or it was emphasized to the exclusion of every other factor.

Over the course of the movement, the relative emphases on class origin and political performance in the official line changed, according to the particular stage it was in. When the pendulum swung in the radical direction—when the Cultural Revolution Small Group was on the ascendancy—political consciousness took precedence over class origin, the "ultra-leftist tendency" emerged, and the view that emphasized political consciousness in complete disregard of class status designated the privileged class of the moment as the target of the "class struggle":

The latent but the biggest and most realistic danger in the task of [carrying out] the Chinese revolution is the wholesale restoration of capitalism in China. The most

44. "Correctly Solve the Question of Origin for Those Born of Exploiting Class Families," *SCMM*, no. 599 (6 January 1967), pp. 30-32.

45. *Wen-ko t'ung-hsin*, 11 December 1967.

46. "Chairman Mao's Latest 18-Point Instruction," *Tzu-liao chuan-chi*, 15 May 1968.

important symptom, as well as cause, is this: privileged strata are being formed and developed.[47]

To the ultra-leftists, "privileged class" referred to the Party cadres and their descendants who monopolized political power. To them, the relationship between "the privileged persons and their social base, on the one hand, and the broad mass of laboring people, on the other hand, has become an antagonistic class conflict."[48] This extreme leftist view naturally led to questioning the achievements of the original Red Guards:

The original Red Guards justified their privileges by using the "theory of natural redness," and obtained public recognition. Some of them surrendered to the theory, willing to be slaves. Others welcomed the theory, and became a new aristocracy. The theory provided the hotbed for the emergence and continuing existence of the privileged class.[49]

Once the question of a privileged class was openly discussed, it was bound to raise broader questions with far-reaching ramifications. Emboldened by the open attack on the power holders, some radicals questioned the legitimacy and achievement of the CCP with such declarations as "Ninety-five percent of the Party members should be struck down"; "The thesis of re-evaluating the past [*ch'ung-hsin p'ing-chia lun*] should be followed"; and "The past rightists were not rightists."[50]

On the question of class line and political performance, the left extremists went so far as to claim that "anyone who had been put into jail and oppressed [by the work teams] was a leftist."[51] Moreover, they held that role *(chih-wu)* should be distinguished from personal status *(shen-fen)*, so that even those who had served the Kuomintang would not necessarily have a "bad" personal status.[52]

In the eyes of the conservatives, such an extreme view was a sure sign that the "ultra-leftists" were really rightists attempting a "bourgeois reversal" and "class revenge" against the proletariat. They accused their opponents of pursuing a policy of "relying on the children of bourgeois intellectuals to unite with the children of workers and peasants to isolate and attack the children of revolutionary cadres."[53] Even the Cultural Revolution Small Group, not to mention Mao, could not tolerate such an extreme view, which could raise doubts about the very legitimacy of the regime and its achievements over the past seventeen years and make a mockery of the whole Communist doctrine of "class." Thus, the official policy shifted again to an emphasis on "class status" to restore a better balance between "class status" and "political performance."

47. *Chih-pa ch'un-lai pao,* 9 April 1967.
48. *Hsin ssu-chung,* 17 May 1967.
49. *Chih-pa ch'un-lai pao,* 9 April 1967.
50. *Tung-fang-hung pao,* 22 March 1967.
51. *Pei-ching fu-lun,* April 1967.
52. *Chieh-fang pao,* March 1968.
53. *Shou-tu feng-lei,* 28 February 1967.

Instantly, the pendulum swung in the other direction, and the radicals themselves were compelled to make self-criticisms for having accepted some " 'black categories' who have civil rights but have not been well reformed, and some historical counterrevolutionaries and people from bad family backgrounds who have not clearly limited the influence of their families."[54]

When the Cultural Revolution entered this final stage, the PLA led a "campaign to rectify the class ranks," and students from "bad" families were again attacked. Mao's switch on the issue of class origin versus political consciousness made many radicals feel that they had been used by the Maoist leaders for political purposes and then left to the mercy of the PLA. Thus, as the campaign began, many Red Guards with "bad" family backgrounds escaped to Hong Kong.

Clearly, the conflict over class origin versus political performance was not an empty ideological dispute, but a real political issue involving the basic interests of the various social groups. Those from bourgeois and other "bad" families saw an opportunity in the political definition of "class" to enhance their political position, while the economic interpretation of "class" served the political interests of the children of cadres. The latter argued that (1) if students from "good" family backgrounds behaved properly, it was an expression of class feeling; (2) if they behaved improperly, it was a case of good people making mistakes; (3) if students from "bad" family backgrounds behaved correctly, it reflected their political ambitions; and (4) if they behaved incorrectly, it was a demonstration of their true class feelings (opposition to the proletariat).[55] In any case, the children of workers and peasants, who belonged to the lowest strata of society in both pre- and post-revolutionary China, were sought after by both groups as the most reliable allies.

On the whole, then, the students with "bad" family backgrounds displayed more revolutionary enthusiasm and a true 'rebel spirit," whereas the children of cadres protected the Party leaders and thus stood on the conservative side. Nonetheless, for obvious political reasons, the radicals and the Cultural Revolution Small Group were not willing to admit directly that many of the radicals came from bourgeois family backgrounds. For instance, when Ch'en Po-ta was asked how to purify the class ranks, he bluntly replied: "You do not have to accept only [big revolutionaries]."[56] On another occasion, Ch'en simply refused to answer the question of why there were so many students with bourgeois backgrounds in the radical organizations.[57]

54. *Hung-ch'i*, 21 January 1967.
55. *Chingkangshan*, 23 March 1967.
56. *Hung-se tsao-fan pao*, 9 February 1967.
57. "Gist of Forum Comrade Ch'en Po-ta with Revolutionary Faculty and Students of Middle School," *JPRS*, no. 41,446 (19 June 1967), pp. 32-37.

The Issue of Educational Reform

At first glance, it seems paradoxical that the students from bourgeois families should become the radicals, particularly since Mao had consistently charged that the Chinese educational system favored these students. The irony disappears, however, on closer examination of the actual social position of these students in the broad context of Chinese society in general, and during the Cultural Revolution in particular. First, in comparison with such truly radical issues as the seizure of power, educational reform was a moderate and secondary issue. Second, the Party organization's defensive maneuver of turning the Cultural Revolution against the economically defined "bourgeois class" further antagonized the "bourgeois students," thus contributing to their radicalism. Third, the children of cadres, as well as the students from bourgeois families, had benefited from the pre-Cultural Revolution educational policy that simultaneously stressed "redness" and expertise."

With the merger of "power holders" and "bourgeois authorities" in the school administrations, there was also an over-representation of children from both bourgeois and cadre families. What material there is on the relative educational opportunities for the three groups of Chinese students—the children of the working class, the bourgeois class, and the cadres—supports this conclusion.

Table 1 reveals a decrease in 1961-62 in total student enrollment, as well as in the proportion of the students from the "proletarian class" (here "proletarian class" includes the children of cadres). These figures suggest that retrenchment in the educational field—characterized by the closing down of many irregular schools, a shift of emphasis to quality education, and the subsequent curtailment of total student enrollment—narrowed educational opportunity mainly for the students of the "proletarian class." However, the change would not have drastically affected the educational opportunities for members of the "proletarian class," because of the absolute limit in total educational opportunity (estimated at from 1.5 percent to 1.75 percent of the college-age population).

In 1962-63, however, if the 67 percent figure in Table 1 is reliable, a new downward trend for the students of bourgeois family background appeared. The increase of students from the "proletarian class" (from 40 to 67 percent) would have meant a drastic reduction in educational opportunity for students from bourgeois family backgrounds because the size of the college-age population from the bourgeois class was small in comparison with that from the non-bourgeois family backgrounds. In other words, because of the size differences of the two groups, a small change in the total percentage of representation from both groups tended to affect the educational opportunities for the smaller group—the students from the bourgeois class—more

Table 1. *Students of "Proletarian Class Backgrounds" (Including Cadres) as a Percentage of Total College Enrollment***

| Years | Total college enrollment | Percentage of students from the "proletarian class" |
|---|---|---|
| 1951–52 | 153,000 | 19 |
| 1952–53 | 191,000 | 20 |
| 1953–54 | 212,000 | 22 |
| 1954–55 | 253,000 | — |
| 1955–56 | 288,000 | 29 |
| 1956–57 | 403,000 | 34 |
| 1957–58 | 441,000 | 36 |
| 1958–59 | 660,000 | 48 |
| 1959–60 | 810,000 | 50 |
| 1960–61 | 955,000 | — |
| 1961–62 | 819,000 | |
| 1962-63 | — | 67 |

60 at Peking University*
40 at Peking University*
*Source:* Chūkyo sōgō yōran [Comprehensive Guide to China] (Tokyo: Naikaku Chosashitsu, 1967), p. 717.

*The only information available on the percentage of student enrollment from the proletariat for these years is from *Current Scene* (vol. 4, no. 19, p. 11), which states that 61% of the 1960 class entering the Geophysics Department of the Peking University came from the proletarian class, but only 40% of the 1962 class was from the proletariat. Another Japanese source reports that, in 1966, 52% of the total student population of Peking University were children of proletarian origin. Suganuma Mashahisa, *Chūgoku no bunka daikakumei* [Chinese Great Cultural Revolution] (Tokyo: Sanichi shobo, 1967), p. 41. Although the data are too incomplete to show a conclusive trend, the figures we do have, and the simple fact that official figures are not available for the 1960-1962 period, seem to indicate that, for a brief period immediately after the Great Leap Forward, the government encountered obstacles in its efforts to improve educational opportunities for the students from the proletarian class.

seriously. The only way to escape from a zero-sum game, which pitted the students from bourgeois families against those from the "proletarian class," was to increase the total enrollment. But, as various sources report, total college enrollment failed to register any significant increase after 1960.

Even though students from bourgeois families enjoyed some advantages (when policy emphasized academic achievements) over the students from the "proletarian class," the benefits were enjoyed by only a small portion of the college-age youth from bourgeois family backgrounds (estimated at from 3 to

7 percent of the college-age bourgeois population). In addition, there were other kinds of discrimination that seemed to outweigh their small advantage in education. Students from bourgeois families claimed that they were discriminated against in job opportunities, in admission to the PLA, in some important positions, and in some institutions of higher learning. They complained that they were treated as "born criminals."[58]

According to a refugee report, discrimination against the students from bourgeois families permeated ordinary life.[59] For instance, if a student of bourgeois background made a mistake in school life, it was treated as a serious political issue. The Cultural Revolution gave these students the opportunity to express their various discontents and to hold the Party organization responsible for their hardships. One way to overcome discrimination and prejudice was to become ultra-active or ideologically correct in the Cultural Revolution, following the prudent rule of "Better to be on the Left than on the Right."

As the relative fortunes of the students from bourgeois family backgrounds and from proletarian class backgrounds rose and fell according to the changes in policy at the Center, the lot of a subgroup within the body of students from "proletarian class" backgrounds appeared to improve steadily. This subgroup included the children of cadres and army personnel. Tables 2, 3, and 4 show that the majority of students in the three different kinds of elite schools were actually the offspring of cadres.[60] Moreover, Table 3 indicates that their lot was improving, and Table 4 shows that at a special boarding school for the children of cadres, students from cadre families occupied the absolute majority, while children from bourgeois families were thoroughly discriminated against.

Although students from both bourgeois and cadre family backgrounds were over-represented in the academic field, they were there for different reasons. The former group enjoyed advantages because of their academic achievements (expertise), and the latter because of their political qualifications (redness). Although the "red and expert" slogan was originally intended to describe the qualifications of a single student, in practice it broke

58. *Chung-hsüeh wen-ko pao,* 21 February 1967.
59. *Far Eastern Economic Review,* 29 April 1972, p. 29.
60. By elite school I refer here to three different types of school. One type is the boarding school for the children of cadres, of which there were about thirty in Peking at the time of the CR. This kind of school was initiated before 1949 to take care of the education of the cadres' children at the time when the Party cadres were not paid salaries. However, such schools expanded in spite of the government instruction in 1959 to abolish them. One Red Guard newspaper claimed that two-thirds of the thirty boarding schools were established after 1955, the year when a salary system was established for the cadres *(Ch'un-lei,* 13 April 1967). The second type of elite school consisted of middle schools attached to various universities. The third type of elite school was made up of the schools selected as models for the special educational experiments. The Party concentrated its financial and manpower support on these experimental schools, which started in 1961.

Table 2. *Class Backgrounds of Senior Middle School Graduates from the No. 101 Middle School*[a]

|  | Worker family | Peasant family | Cadres and army men | Others[b] |
|---|---|---|---|---|
| 1961[c] | 7.74% | 6.89% | 45.10% | 45.42% |
| 1962 | 3.57% | 8.21% | 42.80% | 45.42% |

*Source:* "Whom Are Such Schools Meant for," *SCMPS,* no. 200 (31 August 1967), p. 30.

[a]No. 101 Middle School is considered an experimental school.

[b]This information is reported by a radical who used the term "others" instead of "bourgeois family background."

[c]Total of this row exceeds 100%.

Table 3. *Class Backgrounds of Students in the Middle School Attached to Peking University*

|  | Worker family | Cadre family | Other | Total |
|---|---|---|---|---|
| 1957 | 145* (27.6%) | 2* (0.5%) | (71.9%) | 100 (100%) |
| 1965 | 9%* | 33%* | 68%* | 100% |

*Source:* This table is constructed from facts given in "United Action Committeee Is Necessary Product of Revisionist Educational Line." *SCMPS,* no. 200 (31 August 1967), p. 24.

*These numbers are given in the newspaper.

Table 4. *Class Backgrounds of a Freshman Class in Kwang-ya Boarding School in Kwangtung*

| Workers | Poor and lower-middle peasants | Cadres | Office workers | Landlords |
|---|---|---|---|---|
| 44 (16.3%) | 10 (3.7%) | 202 (73.3%) | 19 (6.7%) | 0 |

*Source: Kwang-ya 8..31.* March 1968.

into two components, each of which worked to the advantage of different social groups.

Political qualification—what Munro has called the "token loophole"—mainly benefited the children of cadres, rather than of peasants and workers, and discriminated against the children of the bourgeoisie.[61] Thus, it seems that students from bourgeois families owed their educational advantages to their academic achievements, in spite of their bad class backgrounds, while children of cadres owed as much to their "redness" as to their academic achievements. Yet, the single most privileged group in all of China prior to the Cultural Revolution were the children of cadres; and their advantages in educational opportunity were not offset by the negative factors (such as downward mobility or political discrimination) that counteracted whatever advantages the bourgeois students enjoyed in the educational field. Thus, during the Cultural Revolution the central issue in educational reform was which group enjoyed undue advantages, the children of the bourgeoisie and the children of cadres each pointing their fingers at the other.

In the spring of 1966, when the official news media launched the attack on the "bourgeois academicians," the school Party committees, although they approached the issue within the organizational framework, precluded student participation and dealt only with insignificant problems such as teaching materials, the curriculum, and study hours of Mao Tse-tung's Thought. Nevertheless, they still displayed an enthusiasm for educational reform that they had lacked on other political issues.[62] The Party organization maintained its enthusiasm during the work team period, sometimes specifically portraying the Cultural Revolution as an educational reform.

On June 13, 1966, the Party made a decision to change the admission policy of the colleges and to postpone enrollments for 1966 for half a year.[63] Liu Shao-ch'i set up a study group, which he ordered to prepare an immediate "proposal for educational reform in higher, middle, and primary schools."[64] By the middle of July, the Ministry of Education completed a "Circular on Entrance Examinations" and planned for an early reopening of the middle schools.

Having lost the initiative in educational reform to the Party organization, the Cultural Revolution Small Group conspicuously neglected the issue in their public speeches. When one Maoist cadre was asked in August whether there was any relationship between the current movement and educational reform, he answered: "Concerning the question of educational reform, the

61. Donald Munro, "Egalitarian Ideal and Educational Fact in Communist China," in *China: Management of a Revolutionary Society,* ed. John M. Lindbeck (Seattle: Washington University Press, 1971), pp. 256-301.
62. For instance, see *Hsin kang-yüan,* 3 June 1967.
63. *JMJP,* 13 June 1966.
64. "Record," pp. 26-28.

Center is in the process of drawing up a scheme, and, for the time being, the schools, instead of considering the question of educational reform, must seize power and dig out revisionism."[65]

The first student articles on educational reform appeared in the *Jen-min jih-pao* of July 18, five days after the official publication of the Party's educational reform plan. Their content gives no evidence that their criticisms were aimed at the Party organization. Although they criticized the existing educational system for emphasizing academic achievement over political qualification, they assigned sole responsibility for the mistaken educational policy to the "bourgeois academicians" and urged the Party organization to strengthen its authority over the educational field: "If [the Party] definitely wants to admit some students to the colleges, then [we] ask the Party itself to select [the students] directly from the high school graduates. We owe everything to the Party and the people, and we will do whatever the Party instructs us to do without any discussion."[66]

The most comprehensive critique of the existing entrance examinations was known as "the twenty-one-point criticism."[67] Despite its name, it centered on two main points: the "bourgeois educational line" benefited students with "bad" family backgrounds the most; and more weight should be given to class background.[68] Thereafter, the attack on "bourgeois academicians" and the demand for more weight to "redness" were the two major themes most frequently found in student criticisms of the educational system. These two threads of criticism, most forcefully advanced by the children of cadres in the elite schools, were helpful to the Party organization's effort to turn the spearhead of the whole mass movement away from themselves and onto the "bourgeois academicians."

To the students from bourgeois families, however, it was a supreme irony that the children of cadres—who, at the expense of workers' and peasants' children, benefited most from the Party's interpretation of "redness"—were asking for still more weight to be given to "redness" and were working to shift responsibility for the mistaken educational policy from the Party organization to the "bourgeois academicians."

As the Cultural Revolution became a full-fledged conflict between the Maoist leaders and the Party organization, and the theory of "class origin" came under attack, the students from "bad" family backgrounds advanced their own criticisms of the educational policy, which were substantially different from those of the children of cadres. They concentrated their attack on the "revisionist educational line" exemplified by the system of elite

65. "The Wrong Must Be Redressed," *SCMPS*, no. 161 (17 January 1967), pp. 3-12.
66. *JMJP*, 18 June 1966.
67. *News from Chinese Regional Radio Station*, no. 162 (23 June 1966), pp. 14-16.
68. Ibid.

schools. According to their charges, the elite schools "not only left the children of workers and peasants outside the school gates, but also decided which cadre children would get into which boarding school according to the official ranks of their parents."[69] The system contributed to the creation of "privileged strata by advocating special privileges [for the children of cadres] and inculcating [them] with privilege-thought [*t'e-ch'üan ssu-hsiang*]."[70]

To substantiate their points, the students from "bad" backgrounds amassed a large amount of material that reveals some interesting data: the elite schools had 20 square meters of space per person, whereas ordinary schools had only 3.5 square meters per person; building costs per unit were 260 yuan for an elite school, and only 35 yuan for an ordinary school.[71] Besides these favorable environmental conditions, the radicals contended, the children of high-ranking cadres enjoyed a wide range of privileges: they could freely choose their ideal university; when they tired of one, they were free to apply for transfer to another; and they were specially treated when they entered special state training institutions, which were closed to the children of the former exploiting classes, and which admitted only a very few children of the workers and peasants.[72]

But despite the counterattacks of the radicals on the privileges enjoyed by the children of cadres, the issue of educational reform in the Cultural Revolution worked in favor of the conservatives, as we shall see. Consequently, it was always conservative Red Guards who stressed the importance of educational reform as though this were the primary issue of the Cultural Revolution. Thus, when educational reform did become the primary issue of the Cultural Revolution, it signaled that the movement was entering a moderate phase in which the conservatives would dominate and the radicals would suffer setbacks.

## The Original Conservative Red Guards

The withdrawal of the work teams neither healed the dissension among the students nor completely eliminated the influence of the Party organization on the campuses. It simply shifted the power from the work teams to the pro-work-team students entrenched in the school Cultural Revolution committees or the preparatory committees that the work teams had helped organize before their withdrawal.[73] In turn, the Cultural Revolution committees and the preparatory committees helped organize the Red Guards.

69. *Ch'un-lei,* 13 April 1967; *Hsin ssu-chung,* 17 May 1967.
70. Ibid.
71. "Smash the Evil Product of Liu Shao-ch'i's Counterrevolutionary Revisionist Line on Education," *JPRS,* no, 41,514 (22 June 1967), pp. 1-9.
72. *Chung-hsüeh wen-ko pao,* 10 February 1967.
73. After organizing the school Cultural Revolution committees with the students loyal to

In Peking, the Cultural Revolution committees selected representatives of each academic class—mostly from the children of cadres—who in turn recruited the Red Guard members.[74] In localities where the school Party committees or the regional Party committees were still functioning, they screened candidates and organized Red Guard groups.[75] This "top-to-bottom" organization produced unified, school-wide Red Guard groups, such as the Red Guards of the Peking Aviation Institute and the Red Guard Headquarters of Tsinghua University. .

Theoretically, a school Cultural Revolution committee was separate from the school Red Guard organization. The committee was the official representative body, while the Red Guards formed a mass organization without official status. Since, however, there was only one Red Guard organization in each school at that time, and since the student activists—mostly Party members, CYL members, and the children of cadres—held the positions of leadership in both organizations, the two were indistinguishable in reality.[76] At Tsinghua University, for example, Ho P'eng-fei and Liu T'ao were in charge of the school Cultural Revolution preparatory committee, and Liu Ch'u-feng, daughter of the Chairman of the Chinese Federation of Trade Unions, Liu Ning-i, headed the Tsinghua Red Guard Headquarters.[77] Both organizations cooperated very closely.

The membership of the Red Guards was originally restricted to students from the "five red categories." The class origin requirements were so rigid that anyone with an "impure" close relative was refused admission or subsequently ousted if a "bad element" was discovered among his family members.[78] Owing to such strict requirements on class background, only about 15 to 35 percent of the student population originally belonged to the Red Guards. For example, only 256 (20 percent) of 1,300 students in the middle school attached to Tsinghua University, and 150 (14 percent) of 1,300 students in the Peking Second Girls' Middle School participated in the first Red Guard organizations.[79]

Subscribing to the rampant couplet and its implications on the "theory of

---

themselves, the work teams advocated the slogans "The school CR committees lead everything" and "The school Party committee should accept the leader of the school CR committee."

74. *Daily Summary of Japanese Press,* 12 October 1966.

75. Wang Chao-t'ien, *Red Guard Talks His Own Story* (Taipei: Asian People's Anti-Communist League, 1967), p. 17.

76. The leadership was selected by the work teams from Party members who "were bound with many conventions and subjected greatly to the influence of black gang Party committees." *Hung-ch'i,* 26 December 1966.

77. "Liu Shao-ch'i's Daughter Writes to Expose Her Father," *CB,* no. 821 (16 March 1967), pp. 1-25.

78. Ch'u Ko, *Luan-shih hsün-yü,* (n. 34 above), pp. 6-7.

79. *DSJP,* 1-3 October 1966, pp. 5, 30-31. Also, a radical Red Guard newspaper complained that only one quarter of the students were qualified to be the Red Guard. *Chung-hsüeh wen-ko pao,* 21 February 1967.

class origin," the Red Guards declared that they had a right to be Red Guards because they were the children of the "five red categories." An article written by the Red Guards of the Peking Aviation Institute and carried in the *Kuang-ming jih-pao* exemplified their view:

What makes us Chairman Mao's Red Guards? It is due to the fact that we are the sons of workers, poor and lower-middle peasants, revolutionary cadres, revolutionary army cadres, and revolutionary martyrs. . . . Who created history? Who pushed society toward progress. . . ? Who conquered the world? Our five-red-categories parents have done these things.[80]

At best, the Red Guards treated students outside the "five red categories" with contempt, and, at worst, made them the targets of the movement. Considering the right to revolt a privilege reserved to students from the "five red categories," they declared: "Our principle is to allow only leftists to revolt, and not to allow the rightists to turn over the world. Unfair? Uncomfortable? There can be no fairness with you [students from 'bad' family backgrounds]."[81] To the Red Guards, allowing students from outside the "five red categories" to join their organization would be "combining two into one."[82]

When these first Red Guards went to the various provinces, they wore the military uniforms of their parents and, like "imperial commissioners," showed an "arrogant and authoritative attitude" toward the local students.[83] Nevertheless, the local students admired them as model Red Guards and looked forward to receiving suggestions on how to organize and carry out the Cultural Revolution. According to one former Red Guard from Canton, they came to Canton around the end of August and ordered the leader of each Red Guard unit to recheck the class status of individual members and expel those with "bad" class backgrounds.[84] Furthermore, the provincial Party leaders supported the Red Guards' interpretation of class line.[85]

In addition to educational reform, a major component of the movement at this stage was the campaign against the "four olds"—old customs, old habits, old culture, and old thinking. The "theory of class origin" was particularly compatible with the campaign against the "four olds," since the "four olds" were mainly associated with the old feudal or bourgeois classes that were not related to the Party organization in any way. Conversely, the participants were exclusively limited to the students from the "five red categories." As one observer remarked, "Every day the Red Guards were

80. *KMJP*, 26 August 1966; *JMJP*, 29 August 1966.
81. *KMJP*, 26 August 1966.
82. "Combining two into one" refers to compromise, in contrast to Mao's "dividing one into two," which stands for struggle.
83. Ch'u Ko, *Luan-shih hsün-yü*, pp. 3-10.
84. Ibid.
85. *Hung-wei pao*, 9 September 1966.

busy destroying four olds and establishing four news. Other people? They had nothing to do all day; they played table tennis, read novels; they were excluded from the movement."[86]

Later, when the Red Guards found themselves lagging behind in the campaign against the power holders, they liked to boast of their achievements in the campaign against the "four olds." The radicals were critical even of these achievements:

You confined us inside the campuses and put us in private jails. But, although we were unable to rush into society and into the streets to destroy the big "four olds," you destroyed only small four olds and protected the big four olds—[you] protected the Liu and Teng headquarters and the reactionary line of the bourgeoisie.[87]

In fact, despite the widely publicized revolutionary activities of the original Red Guards, they did not revolt against the most formidable object: the Party organization. Rather, they followed the lead of the Party organization, sharing a common interest in associating the Cultural Revolution with educational reform and the campaign against the "four olds." In fact, it was the Party organization, not the Red Guards, that initiated the campaign against the "four olds."[88]

Politically, the Red Guards demanded the establishment of Mao's absolute authority, but their decrees were often formalistic. They dictated that every public building should put up Mao's portrait and writings; that all libraries should discard any books that contravened Mao's Thought; that any publishing company should cease putting out these "poisonous weeds"; and that the study of Mao's Thought should be routinized.[89] Calling for the "strengthening of the proletarian dictatorship," they urged the ban of all other political parties and the removal of Sung Ch'ing-ling from her vice-chairmanship of the People's Republic of China. They attacked anything even slightly related to bourgeois culture: they cut off long hair on the street, burned books which they considered to be at odds with Mao's Thought, destroyed art treasures, and so forth.

In the field of economics, they advocated a radical egalitarianism, focusing their attack mainly on the economically well-to-do groups. They clamored for nationalization of all industrial enterprises, abolition of bank interest for deposited money, eviction of landlords from their houses so that the workers could move in, tightening of the commune system, and an end to private agricultural plots.[90]

86. *Ping-t'uan chan-pao*, 26 November 1966.
87. *Chung-hsüeh lun-tan*, 6 April 1967.
88. For instance, see *JMJP*, 8 June 1966.
89. For the activities of the initial Red Guards, see "One Hundred Examples of Destroying Old and Establishing New" (handbill).
90. "Final notice" of Ch'ih-wei-tui of the middle school attached to K'ang Ta; "Revolutionary Appeal," 21 August 1966.

Interestingly, despite their militancy, none of their orders raised the question of unequal distribution of power or touched upon the "structural legitimacy" of the Party organization. On the contrary, they ordered that "old cadres, old revolutionaries should not be tested by the masses, and should not be attacked in the high tide of the Great Proletarian Cultural Revolution."[91]

The Red Guards directed their attacks specifically against the so-called "social dregs." They raided the houses of the bourgeoisie—such as teachers, professional people, capitalists, and rightists—but prohibited any raids on cadres' houses. They issued several urgent notices to the effect that people from the "four black categories" (landlords, rich peasants, counterrevolutionaries, and bad elements), as well as anyone who had been fired from his job or disciplined by his organization, should go to labor camps, and they urged the Peking Municipal Party Committee to take proper and effective measures to implement these orders.

At the same time, they assailed those who had left their posts in rural areas to come to Peking to look for jobs, and ordered them to return to their original communes.[92] They warned students who did not belong to the "five red categories" not to come to Peking to file complaints about their local Party committees, declaring that the "red capital" was not the place for "sons of bitches." To enforce their restrictions, they set up inspection stations at the Peking railway stations to check the class backgrounds of incoming students from the provinces. Moreover, they forced people from the "four black categories" to carry signs on their chests specifying their class backgrounds, and they made them leave the city for rural areas. To further increase their pressure, they forbade restaurants and hospitals to serve the "class enemy."[93] One Red Guard refugee reported that the Peking railway stations were crowded with people from the "four black categories" waiting, under the supervision of the Red Guards, for trains to the rural areas.[94]

The Red Guards adhered scrupulously to the "theory of class origin" and traced genealogies back to grandfathers and remote relatives to determine what one's origin was.[95] Their extreme view of "class origin," combined with

91. This was the first order of the United Action Committee. *Tung-feng pao,* 26 January 1967.

92. "Urgent Notice" published by East Is Red of the Second Middle School on 26 August 1966.

93. "Red Guard Handbill," *SCMPS,* no. 157 (2 November 1966), pp. 28-31. Stanley Karnow reported that "seven kinds of blacks" were banned from riding buses, entering restaurants, attending the cinema, and even strolling through the parks. Stanley Karnow, *Mao and China: From Revolution to Revolution* (New York: Viking Press, 1972), p. 214.

94. Ch'u Ko, *Luan-shih hsün-yü,* pp. 8-9.

95. An urgent order reads: "Some of your grandfathers served in the police force of Manchukuo, which the people have long suppressed. Some of your fathers were members of Kuomintang's San-min chu-i Youth Corps or were Kuomintang officials, who have not been

their childish ignorance and self-conscious awareness of their privileged position, produced some absurd episodes. For example, they took over the Peking Ballet School because all the students there were from bourgeois families and therefore not qualified to lead the Cultural Revolution in the school.[96] In other schools, the Red Guards posted lists that specified the class background of all the students, and then stipulated that the students from "good" family backgrounds should enter the classroom through the front door, while the students from "bad" family backgrounds should enter through the back door.[97] In some cases, the Red Guards cut the hair of teachers from "bad" family backgrounds so that they could be easily identified.[98] At the Peking Bethune Blood Donation Station, Red Guards issued an urgent notice declaring that people from the "four black elements" could not donate blood because their blood lacked revolutionary character.[99]

The Red Guards also organized "manual labor teams" on the basis of class background. To determine class backgrounds, they either seized personnel dossiers or compelled the paralyzed school Party committees to hand over their confidential records.[100] Consequently, most of the targets were teachers, low-ranking cadres, and even fellow students. One Red Guard source reported that those who were put into "labor teams" included "landlords, capitalists, and riffraff *(liu-mang)*, as well as so-called student 'black gangs.'"[101] At the Kwangtung Pearl River Film Studio, the twenty-two-member "labor team" organized by the Red Guards was composed of "non-Party artists and ordinary intellectuals" and only one Party member.[102]

On the whole, the attitudes of the Red Guards were arrogant, authoritarian, and coercive, reflecting a mentality that went with their privilege and high position in the society. Advancing the slogan "Long Live the Proletarian Uprising," they subjected the "class enemy" to physical abuse and torture in their private jails and torture rooms. The "red terror" against the bourgeois

deprived of the right to vote and are being reformed under supervision. Some of you have the family background of capitalists; your relatives (uncles) had spent a number of years in the People's prison, and some of your uncles were historically counterrevolutionaries. Some of your fathers have been ferreted out as members of the black gangs." "Urgent Order by Five Red Category Students of Hungchiang Municipal No. 2 Middle School," *SCMPS*, no. 157 (2 November 1966), p. 30.

96. Hayashi Michinori, *Boku no Pekin ryugaku,* (Tokyo: Kodausha, 1972), p. 27.

97. *Chung-hsüeh wen-ko pao,* 2 February 1967.

98. Hai Feng, *Hai Feng wen-hua ko-ming chi-hsu* (Hong Kong: Chung-pao chou-k'an, 1969), p. 25.

99. *Current Scene* 5, no. 9 (31 May 1967): 2.

100. *T'i-yü chan-pao,* 6 May 1967. *JMJP* reported that the conservatives used the great exchange of experience to collect materials on revolutionary rebels. *JMJP,* 16 January 1967.

101. *Hung-chün chan-pao,* 8 March 1967.

102. Wang Ch'ao, *Kuang-chou tien-ying-chieh te tsao-fan-che* (Hong Kong: Chung-pao chou-k'an, 1969), p. 44.

intellectuals reached its peak in late August, when the Red Guards maliciously broke the fingers of Yeh Chien-ying's son-in-law, a famous pianist.[103] Not surprisingly, the "rebels" from outside the "five red categories" later denounced these activities of the Red Guards: "They encircled and beat the revolutionary masses and disturbed the civil order on the pretext of sweeping out the four olds and dragging out *'liu-mang.'* "[104]

The most prominent and notorious of the early Red Guard organizations was the Hsi-ch'eng Inspection Team, organized at the middle school attached to Peking Normal University by the Red Guards who had taken part in the big rally of August 18.[105] As its name Inspection Team suggests, it was an elite Red Guard organization—the police of the Red Guards—with the proclaimed purpose of imposing discipline on fellow Red Guards. According to one source, membership was limited to the children of high-ranking cadres above grade thirteen.[106] The leaders of the teams included Kung T'an, the daughter of Hsu Ming, Deputy Secretary General of the State Council; a son of Hung Hu, deputy director of the Staff Office of Petroleum; a son of Liang Chien, deputy director of the Work Department; a daughter of Yü Ch'iu-li, acting vice-premier in charge of industry and transportation; and a son of Ch'en I, vice-premier in charge of Foreign Affairs.

All Red Guard organizations drew their membership mainly from the elite schools, such as the First, Second, Fourth, Sixth, Eighty-First, and One-Hundred-and-First Middle Schools and those attached to the various universities.[107] Of these schools, the middle school attached to People's University, in which 70 percent of the student body were the children of cadres, produced the most members.[108]

At the university level, the Red Guards formed the First Headquarters and the Second Headquarters. The latter was the counterpart of the Hsi-ch'eng Inspection Team, organized to police the activities of the Red Guards themselves. Though information on the membership of both headquarters is not available, they seem to have been organized by the Red Guards from the students at the various colleges, and operated in the name of and as representatives of their schools (such as the Red Guard Headquarters of the Industrial Engineering Institute).

The leaders of both headquarters were students who had been activists

103. Ma Ssu-ts'ung, *T'ao-wang-chü* (Hong Kong: Tzu-lien ch'u-pan-she, 1967), p. 14. This story seems untrue, because the pianist performed in Tokyo after the Cultural Revolution.

104. *Ch'un-lei,* 6 May 1967.

105. Besides the Hsi-ch'eng Inspection Team, there were Tung-ch'eng and Chung-nan-hai Inspection Teams.

106. "What the Commotion of the United Action Committee Has Explained," *SCMPS,* no. 183 (16 May 1967), p. 14-24. Some of the children of cadres reportedly advanced the slogan "The children of revolutionary cadres and revolutionary army men, be united" and "Let children of cadres take over power."

107. *Chiao-kung chan-pao,* 11 February 1967.

108. *DR,* 17 October 1967, pp. CCC7.

prior to the Cultural Revolution—such as Party and CYL members and children of cadres. They "had not suffered repression at the hands of the work teams . . . [and hence] did not realize the real danger of the bourgeois reactionary line pursued by the Party organization."[109] Their organization chart reflected the top-to-bottom style of organization: headquarters, company, platoon, and small group.

By mid-September, the First and Second Headquarters had succeeded in establishing a kind of unified control over the Red Guard movement and began to send out the Red Guards to the provinces in an organized way. As a whole, the headquarters maintained an amicable relationship with the Red Guards of the middle schools and dominated the Red Guard movement until they encountered resistance from the radical students' Third Headquarters.

Among the original leaders of the Red Guards, the most outspoken and controversial was T'an Li-fu, the chairman of the Cultural Revolution preparatory committee of the Peking Industrial Engineering Institute and the son of Deputy Procurator T'an Cheng-wen. He bluntly insisted that the couplet was an accurate expression of the Party's class line and vigorously defended the work teams by saying that the students had no reason to be happy when the cadres of the CCP made mistakes. Even when the Cultural Revolution Small Group criticized him and forced him to step down, he declared, "We have power in our hands. I dare to rebuke the people, and dare to reveal my intestines [inner thinking], and I will step down like a proletarian."[110] His pronouncements, known as "T'an Li-fu's Speeches," laid down the original ideological foundation for the Red Guards.

Although they were later purged as revisionist Red Guards, for a time the original Red Guards enjoyed the spotlight in the major newspapers and the support of the Peking leaders. They were accorded the special privilege of standing beside Mao and pinning on his Red Guard armband at the August 18 mass rally in Tienanmen. Many children of cadres from the elite middle schools were given the honor of mounting the platform and the important job of guarding and maintaining order at the rally.[111] Even Lin Piao consented to be the commander-in-chief of the Hsi-ch'eng Inspection Team, and Chou En-lai agreed to be the chief of staff.[112]

As the movement expanded to touch on the issue of the power holders and

109. *Hung-ch'i,* 26 December 1966.

110. *Hung-wei ping,* 16 November 1966. On the other hand, T'an concentrated his attack on capitalists. "You capitalist blood-suckers, who collect interest . . . and who continue to exploit and conspire to restore capitalism, we warn you to apply to the government to stop interest payment within three days."

111. *KMJP,* 18 August 1966. The Red Flag Combat Team of the middle school attached to Peking Normal University had as many as thirty-nine members on the platform of the rally. The Red Guards of the middle school attached to Peking Steel College were given the important job of guarding the platform.

112. Twenty-seven members of Hsi-ch'eng Inspection Team mounted the platform in the second big rally. *KMJP,* 9 September 1966.

the existing political order, the class background of the Red Guards ceased being an asset and became a liability. Although they could display enthusiasm in the campaign against the "four olds," they found themselves under conflicting pressures in the campaign against the power holders, as they had to choose between following the Maoist leaders or protecting their own parents. One radical Red Guard newspaper sarcastically pointed out the dilemma of the original Red Guards in the changed situation. It suggested that they were afraid the revolutionary masses would drag out the old cadres, because they did not want to see their parents exposed as "black gangs," and they did not want to become "sons of power holders taking the capitalist road within the Party."[113]

Understandably, some of the original Red Guards resisted the expansion of the political targets. The Hsi-ch'eng Inspection Team became a paramilitary organization defending the government ministries from the attacks of the radical Red Guards. Later, students from "bad" family backgrounds categorically denounced the conservatism of the original Red Guards in pursuing the "bourgeois reactionary line" of the Party organization:

Generally speaking, the Red Guard organizations established earliest in the various schools followed the pattern of the old work teams and the old revolutionary committees. Among them were a handfull of responsible persons, who were deeply saturated with T'an's characteristics and who implemented the bourgeois reactionary line.[114]

Many of the original Red Guards were bewildered by the charges. "Why," they asked, "are the Party and CYL members in our colleges mostly on the conservative side?" "How can it be possible that the sons of cadres, who constituted the creative and vital forces of the revolutionary organizations in the middle schools, are conservative?"[115] Their protests, however, were in vain. Not only were their organizations disbanded and their orientation discredited, but their leaders were arrested and put into jail. These included Sung P'ing-p'ing, who once proudly pinned the Red Guard armband on Mao and who changed her name to Sung Yao-wu at Mao's suggestion, and P'eng Meng-hsiao, whose name was prominently featured in the *Jen-min jih pao* as the leader of the Red Guards.[116]

113. *Chih-pa ch'un-lai pao,* 22 March 1967.
114. *Shou-tu hung-wei-ping chan-pao,* 10 February 1967.
115. *Hsiang-chiang p'ing-lun,* February 1967.
116. P'eng was the leader of Hung Ch'i Combat Team of the middle school attached to Peking University. Mao talked with him for twenty minutes. *Chung-hsüeh lun-tan,* 6 April 1967. Even the first Red Guard of the middle school attached to Tsinghua University to which Mao had sent his letter was denounced as conservative. "Have not the little army of the middle school attached to Tsinghua University, who wrote 'Long Live the Revolutionary Rebellion Spirit,' turned into the active promoters of Liu's line, extinguishing the fire and supporting the monarchy everywhere and declaring that they would wipe out the Red Guards of Tsinghua University Chingkangshan." *Hung-ch'i,* 26 December 1966. Chiang Ch'ing tried to explain the

In light of the abrupt downfall of the original Red Guards, why did Mao and the Cultural Revolution Small Group acquiesce in their active mobilization during the early stage of the movement? One possible answer is that they did not yet intend to launch a frontal assault on the Party organization. Nevertheless, as the Party organization, in order to evade the crucial issue of power holders, exploited rather than corrected the erroneous line and slogans, Mao foresaw a magnification of the inherent evils in bureaucratic organizations with a monopoly of political power and proceeded to attack the Party organization. An alternative answer may be that the Maoist leaders used the privileged student groups to arouse public opinion in preparation for a general attack on the Party organization. Probably the true answer lies somewhere in between.

Mao's concern with revolutionary ideology and his dissatisfaction with the existing educational system that gave undue advantages to the children from bourgeois families may have led him to acquiese in the mobilization of the "five red categories" as the dominant groups in the Red Guard movement. In the process of mobilizing these social groups, however, the children of cadres, rather than the children of workers and poor and lower-middle peasants, came to occupy the main leadership positions in the schools.[117] The dominance of the children of cadres and their tendency to use the simplistic class line to protect their vested interests came into conflict with Mao's concern about the trend toward restratification of the Chinese society. As Mao himself conceded, when the students were fully mobilized, all kinds of contradictions in Chinese society were laid bare. In the children from "bad" family backgrounds who aired the injustices of the "theory of class origin," Mao found a powerful new political force against the Party leaders, who in his eyes had been responsible for the mistaken line of the Red Guards.

## The Radical Underdogs

Initially, the withdrawal of the work teams had raised the expectations of the students who had fallen victim to the work teams. With some justification, they had hoped to remove the ignominious labels placed on them as "counterrevolutionaries" and "rightists," and they had expected to play an

change in the attitude of the CRSG toward the children of cadres to the military leaders whose children were probably involved in the early Red Guard organizations. "When I found out that a certain Red Guard, who had been appointed a leader by the former Municipal Party Committee, had now changed so much in his attitude, I was completely astonished. I wholeheartedly wanted to persuade him as much as possible during our conference. But the Red Guard refused to yield." "To Make a New Contribution for the People," *Issues and Studies* 6, no. 10 (July 1970): 82-91.

117. *Ping-t'uan chan-pao,* 27 April 1967; *Pei-ching p'ing-lun,* April 1967.

important role in the mass movement. But, contrary to their expectations, the conservative students, who had opposed the radicals and supported the work teams, took over the leadership of the movement and continued to follow the earlier line with their simplistic "theory of class origin." Although it was officially declared that the work teams had committed serious mistakes and that those who had been attacked by the work teams should be rehabilitated, rehabilitation was not automatic, because it was still felt that some victims had been genuine rightists or counterrevolutionaries. Thus, the authority for such decisions fell to the school Cultural Revolution committees, which were understandably reluctant to rehabilitate the victims of the work teams.

As the Tsinghua radicals complained, "Despite the fact that Premier Chou repeatedly vindicated K'uai [Ta-fu] and others, the preparatory committee and 'Red Guard Headquarters' of Tsinghua repressed and discriminated against him, and hit at the revolutionary minority."[118] Thus, the work team victims found that they had not actually achieved any substantive gains. They did not have any voice in the school Cultural Revolution committees, and they were still victimized by the prevalent class line and the campaign against the "four olds." They began, therefore, to organize their own groups and challenge the school Cultural Revolution committees.

There is no doubt that the students who had been branded as "rightists" and attacked by the work teams and their fellow students would not have re-emerged without Mao's personal intervention. Therefore, unlike the conservative Red Guards, the admiration they felt toward Mao was an expression of their very genuine and personal gratitude. This, combined with the well-known tendency toward exaggeration in Chinese writing style, produced many an emotional phrase and sentence, such as: "Our minds bend toward Peking where Chairman Mao lives." Or: "Just as we are living in the most difficult of times, we see a picture of you with our eyes filling with tears, and our determination becomes all the more firm. Just as we are being persecuted the most, we read works by you and our whole bodies are filled with an inexhaustible energy."[119]

Although the radicals, thanks to Mao, escaped the fate of being labeled counterrevolutionaries, their questionable class backgrounds were a handicap to them in the campaign against the "four olds." Therefore, they turned their energy and attention to the issue of the work teams. Attack on the work teams actually had a double advantage for them: it was one sure way of proving their innocence; and it helped to divert the thrust of the movement away from the "four olds" and the "theory of class origin." Moreover, it was

118. *Chingkangshan,* 17 March 1967. Moreover, many of the victims of the work teams were barred from taking part in the August 18 big mass rally. *JMJP,* 13 April 1967.
119. *Chingkangshan,* 26 December 1966.

the issue on which the school Cultural Revolution committees were most vulnerable: in some cases these committees had actually prepared farewell parties for the departing work teams.[120] Thus, the radicals promoted a thorough struggle against the work teams, as though this were the central issue of the whole mass movement.

The school preparatory committees outwardly agreed to criticism of the work teams because it was the official policy, but their actual criticism was moderate and brief and was carried out with the consent of the work teams. Then they sought to turn the movement against the school Party committees, which they claimed were the "power holders taking the capitalist road within the Party organization." In an attempt to discredit the radicals, the Cultural Revolution committee of the Geology Institute even renewed the debate on the "anti-interference campaign." Later, the conservative Red Guards of the Peking Aviation Institute conceded:

[When] the work teams spread poison, most of us actively participated in suppressing the opinions of the revolutionary masses and in practicing a reactionary line. When the work teams were withdrawing, we did not criticize their mistaken orientation and line but praised their achievements, even to the extent of launching a large-scale movement to collect signatures. When the work teams were withdrawn, we continued to protect the reactionary school Cultural Revolution preparatory committees.[121]

The debate over the work team issue polarized the Chinese students into two groups. At Tsinghua University, the students split into the "August 8 Group," which wanted to make the issue of the work teams the major objective of the student movement, and the "August 9 Group," which was organized by the school Cultural Revolution preparatory committee and insisted on redirecting the student movement against the school Party committee.[122] The anti-work-team force was still a minority.[123] In K'uai Ta-fu's own class, the students were divided into a seventeen-member majority group that supported moderate criticism of the work teams, and an eleven-member minority group that wanted thorough criticism of the work teams. The

120. *Tung-fang-hung pao*, 24 October 1967.
121. *Hung-ch'i*, 7 January 1967.
122. *Hung-se tsao-fan*, 15 January 1967.
123. The radical minority asked: "Why are there these different points of view regarding the work teams? Why do some comrades of this 'majority faction' firmly believe in the work teams and oppose the students posting big-character posters against the work teams? Most of those comrades have the mistaken thought that believing in the work team is believing in the Party and that opposing the work team is opposing the Central Party and Chairman Mao." *Hung-wei-ping*, 24 October 1967. The radicals also challenged the preparatory Cultural Revolution Committees: "Why are there different points of view concerning the college's revolutionary committees? Why do some comrades of this majority faction so carelessly embrace the revolutionary party committee [Cultural Revolutionary Committee] and say that the revolutionary committee was produced democratically? Most of the comrades also have the mistaken thought that the revolutionary committee represents the majority and that following the majority is [always] right." *Hung-wei-ping*, 24 October 1967.

students of the Peking Construction Institute split over the work team issue into a 1,000-member majority faction and a 200-member minority faction.[124]

Nonetheless, from this minority anti-work-team force emerged the radical Red Guard organizations, which adopted the term "rebels" to distinguish themselves from the original Red Guards. At Tsinghua University, the "August 8 Group" tightened its organizational structure and adopted the new name Tsinghua Mao's Thought Red Guards, and K'uai Ta-fu organized the die-hard radicals into the Tsinghua Chingkangshan.[125] At the Geology Institute, the students opposed to the work teams organized themselves on August 17 into the East Is Red group. Since the radical organizations emerged spontaneously over the various issues and in a "bottom-to-top" fashion, their organizational structures were more decentralized and conducive to factional struggle.

With the establishment of their own organizations, the radicals renewed their attacks on the work teams. Chou En-lai personally ordered the self-criticism of Yeh Lin, the head of the Tsinghua work team, and also of the Tsinghua preparatory Cultural Revolution committee for its mistaken view on the work team issue.[126] The move, however, did not satisfy the radical students, who clung to the work team issue in an obvious effort to strike down the Party leaders responsible for sending out the teams in the first place. As time went on, the radicals became bolder in their demands. Soon they wanted to drag out the work team leaders for the mass struggle and keep the former work team members in their schools so that they could "attack them until they sink."

When the work teams, after making their self-criticisms, refused to comply with the demands of a "minority," the radicals chased them back to their original ministries. The Red Flag group of the Peking Aviation Institute staged a twenty-eight-day sit-in demonstration in front of the Scientific and Technological Commission for National Defense, demanding a direct interview with Chao Ju-chang, the head of the work team at their school. The chairman of the Commission, Nieh Jung-chen, refused to permit Chao to negotiate with the radicals. Only after Ch'en Po-ta intervened on behalf of the radicals by signing a guarantee that he would ensure Chao's safety, did Chao come out and sign an agreement with the radicals to the effect that "he would come the moment he was called."[127] The East Is Red radical group at the Peking Geology Institute staged a demonstration in front of the ministry

124. "Liu Shao-ch'i's Four Speeches," *Union Research Service* 41, nos. 8 and 9 (26 and 30 April 1968): 97-116.
125. *Chingkangshan*, 22 December 1966.
126. "Premier Chou En-lai Speaks at the Tsinghua University on 22 August 1966," *JPRS*, no. 41,313 (8 July 1967), pp. 14-21.
127. *Hung-ch'i*, 7 January 1967.

of Geology, asking for an interview with the head of that work team, but the majority faction at the school, the Struggle-Criticism-Transformation Fighting Group, denounced the demonstration and physically attacked the radicals.[128]

The political implications of the work team issue were profound. The radicals' demand for thorough criticism of the work teams was bound to raise the question of who was responsible for sending them out, which ultimately led to Liu Shao-ch'i himself. Particularly in Tsinghua, the work team issue was directly related to Liu Shao-ch'i's wife, Wang Kuang-mei, who was an official member and an unofficial leader of the work team. The Tsinghua radicals, led by K'uai Ta-fu, collected information on Wang's activities and, on August 19, 1966, put up a big-character poster entitled "Wang Kuang-mei is the number one pickpocket in Tsinghua."[129]

The conservative students, however, perceived the move as an attack on Liu Shao-ch'i and rushed to Wang's defense. T'an Chen-lin succinctly expressed their views: "In campaigning against the work teams, the Tsinghua students are actually attacking Wang Kuang-mei. To attack Wang is actually to attack Liu."[130] Denouncing the attack on Wang as an attempt on the part of the "rightists" to obtain a reversal of the earlier verdict against them, the Tsinghua preparatory committee, led by Ho P'eng-tei, declared the imposition of a "proletarian dictatorship" to "prevent a rightist take-over."[131]

Accusing the radicals of engaging in counterrevolutionary activities to split the Central Committee, a crime that deserved "a thousand cuts and a thousand deaths," the conservative students began the "red terror." William Hinton vividly describes the conservatives' dominance of the Tsinghua campus:

Outsiders were ordered to leave the campus, and a curfew was imposed. Lest there remain any doubt in people's minds about the intention of the loyalists, posters went up announcing a "red terror." Squads went around looking for anti-Liu posters. If any were found, they were photographed and then torn down. If any student protested, or entered a debate on the issues, he was driven away with the slogan "Reactionaries have no right to speak." Anyone passing by on the roads or walks was searched for notes and posters in an attempt to prevent any new counter-opinions from going up on the walls and reed mats.[132]

The situation in other schools was similar. The conservatives even threatened to arrest the members of the radical organizations as "rightists." Thus,

128. *Tung-fang-hung pao*, 24 October 1967.
129. "Record," p. 18.
130. "Gangster Speeches of T'an Chen-lin," *SCMPS*, no. 178 (24 April 1968), pp. 2-34.
131. William Hinton, *Hundred Day War* (New York: Monthly Review Press, 1972), p. 75.
132. Ibid.

the radicals, who had once been suppressed by the work teams, were still being suppressed, even after the work teams had been officially criticized and withdrawn.

Was the radicals' demand for thorough criticism of the work teams spontaneous or manipulated? An examination of the situation suggests that both elements were present. The radicals had good reasons of their own to continue their attacks on the work teams. At the Peking Second Girls' Middle School, one student, whose hair had been cut during the work team period, hid her short hair with a towel and led the attack on the work teams. A former Red Guard also claimed that they acted spontaneously:

Our victory, at a much later date, resulted from the fact that the work team members turned out to be followers of Liu Shao-ch'i. But we did not act on Mao's orders at the beginning. After we won, we merely followed the trends by saying that we had also used Mao's Thought in our resolute struggle, and in saying so we gained further favor from the Party [i.e., the Cultural Revolution Small Group].[133]

In fact, the radicals were not in conflict with the official position, not to mention the stand of the Cultural Revolution Small Group. Since early July, the Cultural Revolution Small Group had been openly and unequivocally denouncing the work teams with ever-increasing intensity.[134] The news media were also encouraging criticism of the work teams.[135] Thus, the attacks on the work teams seem to have been partially spontaneous and partially manipulated.

Still, a persistent question remains: Is it likely that the Chinese students would have criticized Wang Kuang-mei, the wife of the President, without any specific instructions from the top? Although there is no evidence available to support the contention that the Cultural Revolution Small Group specifically instigated the radicals' attack on Wang, there can be little doubt that it was behind the attack. It certainly did not hide its critical attitude toward Liu Shao-ch'i. Even Ch'en Po-ta declared that, although he was against putting up wall posters criticizing Liu, the students could write such posters and send them to him by mail or in person.[136] By revealing its hostility toward Liu and by leaking evidence on the conflict at the top (the Chinese students had already noticed the demotion of Liu in the order of names appearing in the *Jen-min jih-pao*), the Cultural Revolution Small Group encouraged the radicals in their attack on Wang. Once the students began their attack, the Small Group endorsed their action.

A unified radical organization gradually emerged from the disorganized

133. *New York Times,* 14 January 1970.
134. For the remarks of the CRSG on the work team issue, see *Shou-chang chiang-hua,* vol. 3 (unpaged).
135. For instance, see *KMJP,* 11 August 1966.
136. *Shou-chang chiang-hua,* vol. 3 (unpaged).

anti-work-team forces scattered throughout the various colleges. On September 10, some four thousand members of the "oppressed revolutionary minority" set up the Third Headquarters as the "great alliance of rebels."[137] Once the radicals had their own unified organization, their conflict with the conservatives grew deeper and sharper; it added group competition and power struggles to the already complicated conflict structure. Threatened by the rapidly rising power of the aggressive Third Headquarters, the conservative majority intensified their discrimination against the minority and denied them all the materials and equipment necessary for their Red Guard activities.[138]

Since they were a minority within the schools, the radicals needed outside support more than the conservatives. However, their only support came from the Cultural Revolution Small Group, a top-level authority that did not control the middle-level echelons of the Party organization. The Small Group expressed its frustration in its efforts to support the radical organizations: "The Central Committee dispatched a communication saying that the Third Headquarters is entitled to equal material treatment. The Cultural Revolution Small Group said so. Premier Chou said so also; but that was no use. Don't think that whatever the Central Committee says will be carried out."[139]

By this stage, the split among the Chinese students—based on the cleavages in their class origins, reinforced by the political issue of the work teams, and supported and perpetuated by the divided elite—had become so deep that only a prolonged struggle could decide the outcome. Neither Mao, nor the Cultural Revolution Small Group, nor the PLA could resolve the various issues without favoring or alienating one group or the other. After this stage, the Great Proletarian Cultural Revolution was marked by the cyclical rise and fall of each group, despite Mao's continuous efforts to mitigate the conflict and obtain the best from both.

## The Party Organization

August and September of 1966 was a time of uncertainty during which the final fate of the Party organization was being decided. At that time, the Party's central organs—except the Party Center, the term used to refer loosely to the Maoist group in Peking—had already ceased to function as effective governing bodies. Yet, individual Party leaders (such as Teng

137. *Shou-tu hung-wei ping* (middle school), 7 February 1967. When the Third Headquarters was first established, the threat from the conservatives was so enormous that the Peking Garrison Command guarded the office of the Third Headquarters. *JMJP,* 29 April 1967.

138. *JMJP,* 15 January 1967.

139. "Chang Ch'un-ch'iao's Speech to the Revolutionary Students from Fukien," *JPRS,* no. 40,974 (10 May 1967), pp. 26-31.

Hsiao-p'ing, T'ao Chu, and Wang Jen-chung) were still active. Compelled by Mao's urging them to go to the masses and learn from them, they made many public appearances, not as representatives of the Party, but as individuals presenting their personal views.[140] The local Party organizations, however, had not yet experienced any reshuffling or open attacks from the students. Although cut off from the upper-level leadership and left alone to handle the student revolt, they still at least maintained their organizational capability.

Although its structural legitimacy had been seriously undermined, the Party organization still officially expected to play two irreconcilable roles imposed on it by the Eleventh Plenum—that of leader *and* target of the movement. Naturally, it proved to be impossible for the Party organization to lead the movement to attack itself. Understandably, the Party organization showed much more interest in survival than in revolutionizing itself.

Prevented from directly manipulating the masses by the principle of allowing "free mobilization of the masses," the Party organization utilized its influence, which penetrated deeply throughout Chinese society, to support those social groups that shared a common interest with it in maintaining the political status quo. Naturally, it supported the majority faction of the conservative Red Guards on all the controversial issues. By this means, the Party leaders succeeded, to some extent, in confining the Red Guard movement outside the Party organization.

When the Maoist leaders discovered that the Party organization could still divert the issues away from itself, even under the rule of "freely mobilizing the masses," they again changed the rules of the game by making it clear that the "power holders" were the main target. Although the behavior of the various members of the Party organization during this period became less uniform and increasingly complex, a careful examination of the numerous speeches by Party leaders suggests that there was some coordination of the organization's positions regarding the various issues.

First, the Party leaders were consistently evasive on the crucial issue of the major target: they never mentioned "power holders" as often or as clearly as the "Sixteen Articles" had. The most unequivocal statement came from Teng Hsiao-p'ing, who characterized the Cultural Revolution as (1) a struggle against the capitalist roaders; (2) a criticism of reactionary academic authorities; and (3) an educational reform.[141] Teng did, however, use the

---

140. For the speeches of the Party leaders, see "Speeches and Statements Alleged to Have Been Made by Chinese Central Leaders," *CB*, no. 819 (10 March 1967), pp. 1-84; "Speeches and Statements Made by Chinese Communist Leaders in July through September 1966," *CB*, no. 830 (26 June 1967), pp. 1-47; "Collection of Speeches by Central Leaders," *SCMMS*, no. 16 (5 June 1967), pp. 1-35.

141. Ibid.

term "power holders" to refer to the school Party committees, which were already under attack.

The Party leaders also insisted on a moderate method of struggle. Urging the students to engage in a brief period of criticism of the school Party committees and then to reorganize them, Liu Shao-ch'i, in his last public speech, recommended immediate free Party-member elections for the Party leadership group and the opening up of Party meetings to the public.[142] Clearly, Liu was still thinking of the mass movement within the framework of the Party leadership, at a time when the Maoists were advocating the establishment of a new power structure: the Cultural Revolution committees. Moreover, Liu openly defended the conservative Red Guards who had supported the legitimacy of the Party: "[The radicals] said that you defended the emperor. What emperor are you defending? How can it be said that you defended the emperor when you defended a Party general branch secretary or a Party committee member?"[143]

The Party leaders reluctantly agreed that the work teams had made mistakes. Nevertheless, they insisted that the students should accept the self-criticism of the work teams and return to the original target: the "black gangs" of the school Party committees. This Party view was strikingly similar to the views held by the conservative Red Guards and the school Cultural Revolution committees. Understandably, the radicals denounced the Party leaders' suggestion as a "sinister attempt to divert the major target from the question of the two lines that Chairman Mao raised in his big-character posters as early as August 5."[144]

The issue most advantageous to the Party leaders was the question of class line. Exploiting the delicate complexity associated with the class issue (even the Maoist leaders could not define their position unequivocally), the Party leaders subtly supported the simplistic view of the "theory of class origin" and its implication that only persons from the "five red categories" were qualified to be Red Guards. T'ao Chu said that "if emphasis is put on performance, it is a source of revisionism."[145] And T'an Chen-lin declared: "All the Red Guards belong to the five red categories. . . . Only those belonging to the five red categories are allowed to join the Red Guards. The first thing to do is to overhaul the Red Guards. One method is to screen the Red Guards and see whether they belong to the five red categories."[146]

When Ch'en Po-ta denounced the Party organization's manipulation of

---

142. "Liu Shao-ch'i's Four Speeches," *URS* 41, nos. 8 and 9 (26 and 30 April 1968): 97-116.
143. Ibid.
144. *Tung-fang-hung pao*, 24 October 1967.
145. "Comrade T'ao Chu's Speech at the CCP Central Committee Propaganda Department," *CB*, no. 819 (10 March 1967), pp. 11-15.
146. "Gangster Speech of T'an Chen-lin," *SCMPS*, no. 178 (24 April 1967), pp. 29-34.

the class background issue, there was widespread feeling among the Party leaders that Ch'en was wrong.[147] The Party leaders, on the other hand, enthusiastically endorsed T'an Li-fu's views on class. It was even alleged that the Peking Municipal Party Committee reprinted and distributed more copies of T'an's speeches than of the "Sixteen Articles."[148] When the radicals rose up to criticize T'an, the Peking Party Committee encouraged him, via telephone, to endure the criticism.[149]

In the rising conflict between the conservative and the radical Red Guards, the Party leaders in effect supported the conservative majority by stressing unity, order, discipline, and majority rule in the Red Guard movement. T'an Chen-lin argued: "The school Party committees should put faith in the majority, dare to exercise leadership, and unite with 90 percent of the people to work on the minority. . . . Disciplinary teams must maintain the revolutionary order."[150] And Teng Hsiao-p'ing insisted: "If there are two detachments, they must be combined. If that is a principle, can the five red categories who are the Red Guards unite together? How can this be called combining two into one?"[151]

The Party leaders' recommendation for unifying the students was a free election on the basis of proportional representation of the various factions in the leadership positions—a method obviously advantageous to the conservative majority. To the Maoist leaders, however, an election was a formalistic solution to the serious dilemma created by the situation in which the minority held the correct view. Even such a moderate as Chou En-lai acknowledged the dilemma when he revealed that the Center was considering setting up administrative organs in the schools which would take an impartial attitude toward the majority and the minority: "At present, different factions in various schools are permitted to operate. Forced mergers are impossible. Have not [the Red Guard organizations] at Peking University, which were at one time amalgamated, split again?"[152]

The local Party leaders, who had not yet undergone the trauma of the student attack, were more frank than the top-level leaders in registering their disagreement with the Maoist policy. One provincial Party leader flatly stated that the major tasks of the Red Guards were "maintaining civil order, safeguarding state property, guarding schools, preventing fights, and seriously studying Mao Tse-tung's Thought."[153] The local Party leaders actively

147. "A Bundle of Poisonous Arrows," *SCMP*, no. 4112 (6 February 1968), pp. 4-5.
148. "Record,"*JPRS*, no. 42,349, p. 138.
149. *Chung-hsüeh wen-ko pao*, 11 April 1967.
150. "Gangster Speech of T'an Chen-lin," pp. 29-30.
151. "Teng Hsiao-p'ing and Li Fu-ch'un Meet Teachers and Students from International College," *CB*, no. 819 (10 March 1967), pp. 68-78.
152. *Shou-chang chiang-hua*, vol. 3 (unpaged).
153. *Hung-se tsao-fan-che*, 15 January 1967.

organized their own Red Guards and drew on local sentiment to ward off the threats from the more radial Peking Red Guards. They first mobilized the workers through the labor unions into *Ch'ih wei tui* (teams to guard the public safety) for the proclaimed purpose of maintaining civil order, and then reported the workers' views to the Center as though they represented the spontaneous feelings of the masses. One inner-Party communication to the Center reads:

At the present time, there are comparatively strong reactions among the workers, peasants, soldiers, and revolutionary cadres. They ask: "How is it possible that the Party Center and Chairman Mao only want intellectuals?" Some current developments have precipitated this kind of view among them.[154]

Soon the workers who were mobilized by the local Party organizations clashed with the radical students. The Center issued strongly worded orders forbidding the local leaders to pit the workers against the Red Guards.[155] The local leaders, nevertheless, continued to suppress the rebels, while dressing up their complaints as the words of the masses and sending these to the Center. A report prepared by the Kiangsi Provincial Party Committee filed the following inner-Party communication to the Center:

Currently, the nationwide flow of students has created confusion in the whole transportation plan, and put all the Party committees above the *hsien* into disorder (the problems on the *hsien* level are resolved). For nearly one month, the provincial and municipal [Party committees] have fundamentally come to a standstill and been unable to work.

The current work method is to push aside the workers, peasants, and soldiers, and to trust only students, on the assumption that all students are revolutionary and all Party committee secretaries at every level have become the targets of the revolution. Furthermore, if one is a bit slow in supporting this, he becomes a counterrevolutionary or is struck down. This makes empty words of the sentence that the workers, peasants, and soldiers are the main body [of the movement].

The above-mentioned work method cannot be found in any page of Chairman Mao's writings. We sincerely feel that, if it continues, this will not only influence normal development of the movement, but also greatly influence the prestige of the Party Center and Chairman Mao. Seeing that some students do not talk reasonably, that, at present, they treat us like enemies, the workers, peasants, and soldiers question, with tears in their eyes, whether the Party has that kind of policy or not.[156]

Judging the behavior of the Party organization by Maoist standards, it was undoubtedly characterized by conservatism, evasion, inertia, and, most of all, "waving the Red Flag to oppose the Red Flag." At the same time, Mao's intentions for the Cultural Revolution were becoming increasingly clear,

154. *Hung-se tsao-fan-che,* 9 February 1967.
155. *CCP Documents of the Great Proletarian Cultural Revolution: 1966-1967* (Hong Kong: Union Research Institute, 1968), p. 77.
156. *Hung-se tsao-fan-che,* 9 February 1967.

despite some ambiguities in policy pronouncements. The Party organization, however, continued to distort Mao's will, using whatever power it had left to moderate the movement and preserve its own organizational integrity.

## The Cultural Revolution Small Group

With the removal of the "liaison personnel" which the work teams had left on the campuses, the Party organization's last official linkage with the students was severed, and the Cultural Revolution Small Group freely moved in to fill the leadership vacuum in the schools. Its members made frequent appearances among the students, seeking their opinions, transmitting instructions and policies from the Center, and most important, providing authoritative judgments on the issues in dispute.

Unlike the work teams—which had operated as units representing the Party organization and had often intervened in such concrete matters as how and when to organize public debates and who should make speeches—the members of the Small Group worked on an individual basis, directly representing Mao's line and laying down broad ideological guidelines rather than specific regulations for the movement. Their leadership style was open and straightforward; their ideological stand was radical; and the tone of their speeches was inflammatory.[157] Their behavior—which undoubtedly symbolized the true revolutionary spirit of Mao's Thought to the radicals—was regarded as recklessly seditious and irresponsible by their opponents.

Their basic leadership technique was to manipulate the issues. They consistently took a radical stand on all ambiguous points in the official policies and on all issues arising from the movement. Consequently, they consistently supported the positions taken by the radical Red Guard organizations. As early as August 1966, Chiang Ch'ing had unequivocally pointed to the power holders as the main target.[158] In their numerous speeches, the other members of the Small Group continued their efforts to make the "power holders taking the capitalist road within the Party" the main target of the movement, employing increasingly severe terms, such as "revisionist

157. K'ang Sheng said: "Do not fear chaos. Chaos and order are the unity of opposites. Without chaos there can be no order. Without persecution, how would you know the difficulty of revolution." "Chiang Ch'ing's Speech at the Normal University," *JPRS*, no. 41,313 (8 June 1967), p. 5. It was possible for the CRSG to follow the Maoist line of leadership, probably because of their proximity to Mao and their commitment to Mao's Thought, whereas the work teams could not practice the correct leadership, because they pursued a line that departed from what Mao expected. The CRSG used its proximity to Mao effectively. When the students asked Chiang Ch'ing why Mao did not come out to read the big-character posters, Chiang Ch'ing replied: "As far as I know, he has not come out. But he goes over every slip and every suggestion you send in. Haven't you seen that my bag is full of them?"

158. "A Talk by Comrade Chiang Ch'ing to Red Flag Fighters on August 6, 1966," *CB*, no. 830 (26 June 1967), pp. 24-25.

line," to criticize the Party leaders. For example, in an article broadcast by the Peking Central Broadcast Station, Ch'en Po-ta warned that the old cadres, having lost their past heroic qualities, were now unable to sacrifice their personal interests and were on the verge of becoming revisionist. He urged them to endeavor to maintain their old qualities; otherwise, they would be eliminated in the Cultural Revolution.[159]

The Small Group also persisted in challenging the "structural legitimacy" of the Party organization in the name of Mao Tse-tung's Thought. In face-to-face meetings with the students, the members of the Small Group specifically put Mao above the Party: "Leadership by the Party is mainly the political and ideological leadership of Mao Tse-tung's Thought. It is not specifically the leadership of a certain person or a certain organization. If this Party follows Chairman Mao's revolutionary line, it represents leadership by the Party, and vice versa."[160]

To make the point that the Party could not use "structural legitimacy" to protect the "power holders," Mao himself rewrote an editorial in issue number eleven (1966) of *Hung ch'i* (Red Flag) to insert two sentences: "What we accept is the leadership of the Party Central Committee headed by Chairman Mao. We must not unconditionally accept erroneous leadership that endangers the revolution, but should resolutely resist It."[161] The Small Group also put the masses above "structural legitimacy" by demanding that all the Party units should accept mass supervision and criticism, and should refrain from retaliating against the masses.[162]

While demolishing the "structural legitimacy" of the Party organization, the Small Group vigorously attempted to build up its own legitimacy. For example, it supported the correctness of the slogan "All power to the Cultural Revolution committees." Ch'en Po-ta insisted:

Some comrades have asked: If the Cultural Revolution committees are given all the power, would that not mean that the leadership of the Party could be done away with? Is the person asking this question a member of a black gang? Those who oppose this slogan are not necessarily revolutionary, and those who advocate this slogan are not counterrevolutionary. This slogan is a revolutionary and not a counterrevolutionary one.[163]

As the Cultural Revolution spread from the schools to the society in general, and as its targets expanded from the school Party committees to

159. *Chin-jih ta-lu,* 1 September 1966.

160. *Hung-se tsao-fan-che,* 26 December 1966.

161. "Record," pp. 8-21.

162. Ch'en also declared that the reason why the Communist Party member is good is because "he trusts the masses, relies on them, becomes one with them, and unites with them. Once he is alienated from the masses, he is not good any more." "Comrade Ch'en Po-ta's Speech at the Peking University," *JPRS,* no. 40,974 (10 May 1967), p. 2.

163. "Speech by Comrade Ch'en Po-ta at the Broadcast Institute on August 4," *CB,* no. 839 (26 June 1967), pp. 3-10.

other Party and government organs, the authority of the Small Group expanded, and it began to interfere directly in the work of Party and government organs. Ch'en Po-ta ordered the officials in the government ministries to go out and meet the students. The Small Group canceled the Propaganda Department's planned commemoration for Lu Hsun and organized a mass rally instead. And the Small Group's power expanded even to the PLA. Yeh Chien-ying declared: "The Cultural Revolution group will exercise leadership as long as the movement lasts. After the conclusion of the Cultural Revolution (the Military Affairs Commission will study how long it should last), the leading body of the Party will be elected and revolutionary leadership brought into being."[164]

The Small Group took an equally radical and unequivocal position on specific issues. During his fourth visit to Peking University, Ch'en Po-ta openly declared that the "attitude toward the work teams"—that is, *opposition* to the work teams—was a "matter of class struggle," and that "the June 18 incident at Peita was a revolutionary action."[165] Later, Ch'en specifically tied the school Cultural Revolution preparatory committees to the work teams: "Although the work teams have been withdrawn, they have been replaced with other forms, such as the Cultural Revolution preparatory committees."[166] As early as July 28, K'ang Sheng suggested to the students that they disregard the candidates nominated by the work teams for the school Cultural Revolution committees.[167]

On the matter of majority versus minority, Chiang Ch'ing argued that "it is necessary to see who has grasped the truth of Marxism-Leninism and the Thought of Mao Tse-tung, and who is genuinely carrying out the correct line of Chairman Mao."[168] Hsieh Fu-chih further elaborated the position of the Small Group: "Most in the minority faction are opposed to the work teams. The majority supported the work teams. In regard to the work teams, the minority holds the truth. I am in support of the minority. It is also on this premise that we [the Small Group] support the minority."[169]

At first, the members of the Small Group contacted the students as a whole, but as the students divided into conservatives and radicals they met

164. "Yeh Chien-ying's Speech at the CR Rally of All Army Academies and Schools," *CB*, no. 819 (10 March 1967), pp. 60-64.

165. "Record," p. 29. Ch'en Po-ta and Wang Li visited K'uai Ta-fu as early as July 15, 1966. "We Are the Irreconcilable Enemy of the Liu-Teng Line," *JPRS*, no. 42,073 (3 August 1967), pp. 29-35.

166. "Ch'en Po-ta's Speech at Political Consultative Auditorium," *JPRS*, no. 40,974 (10 May 1967), pp. 14-18.

167. *Shou-chang chiang-hua*, vol. 3 (unpaged).

168. "Chiang Ch'ing Speaks at Peking CR Rally on Literary Art Works," *SCMP*, no. 3836 (8 December 1966), pp. 5-9.

169. "Vice-Premier Hsieh Fu-chih's Seven Viewpoints," *JPRS*, no. 40,391 (24 March 1967), pp. 4-10.

more frequently with the radicals. They also granted interviews to local students from "bad" family backgrounds who had come to Peking to file their complaints (the group that the original Red Guards had denounced as "bad eggs"), and they encouraged these students to continue their fight. As to the divisive issue of class line, Wang Li insisted:

There is no reason why we should not unite with them. Besides, we propose that, in the schools, teachers and students should not be divided into five red categories and five black categories. Such classification and terms should be avoided. . . . How should we classify those born into different families, who are of different class status in the cities? On the other hand, the children of cadres cannot belong to the five red categories.[170]

On all controversial issues, the Small Group sided with the radicals against the conservative students, justifying their position with the authority of Mao. Although it is difficult to determine whether the Small Group supported the radicals because they opposed the Party organization or because their ideological line was correct, it is clear that each found a strong ally in the other. Despite the fluctuations in the fortunes of each group, the basic alliance between the Small Group and the radicals continued throughout the Cultural Revolution.

## Summary

Among the changes that the Eleventh Plenum effectuated, the shift in power from the Party organization to the Small Group, and the adoption of "free mobilization of the masses" as the basic guideline for the movement, are the most significant. With the Party organization's basic orientation and primary organizational format (the work teams) repudiated, and with its "structural legitimacy" undermined, the Small Group first took over the leadership of the movement and then gradually aggrandized its own power. The rise of the Small Group, plus the firm establishment of the principle of "free mass mobilization," ushered the Cultural Revolution into a new stage characterized by the "politics of manipulation."

As the loci of gravity of Chinese politics shifted from the elite to the masses, and as the spontaneity, initiative, and interests of the masses played an increasingly important role, the intra-elite conflict changed from an inner-Party struggle to an open competition in which both the Small Group and the Party organization actively manipulated the interests of various social groups in order to achieve control over the mass organizations. Thus, it seems that the "politics of manipulation" took place when the elite, having

170. "Speeches of Kuan Feng, Wang Li, and Ch'i Pen-yü," *SCMMS*, no. 15 (8 May 1967), p. 14.

reached a stalemate in their intra-elite conflict, actively sought to draw the masses into the political process, using official ideology to justify the mass involvement.

The masses had scarcely achieved free mobilization when the long-suppressed latent tensions in Chinese society rose to the surface. To further complicate matters, the newly surfaced conflicts merged with numerous other controversies that such large-scale mass movements constantly generate. The latent class tension became intertwined with the crucial question of how to distinguish the targets from the participants in the mass movement. This in turn developed into a theoretical Marxian controversy over whether "class origin" or "political consciousness" determines "class."

Sometimes Mao watched the rising conflict in the Red Guard movement with philosophical detachment: "All classes continue to assert themselves. As the law governing class struggle is not to be changed by the subjective will of man, what cannot be organized as an alliance would quickly disintegrate after it has been artificially organized. It thus becomes necessary to delay the tempo of the organization."[171] Mao, however, did not admit his disappointment over the consequences of the policy of "free mobilization of the masses." Contrary to his expectations, the sudden bottom-to-top mobilization of the Chinese masses, who were highly politicized but had been barred from articulating their interests for so long, had not resolved the existing conflicts but had generated many additional ones.

As the controversial issues continued to arise and debates became heated, even the hitherto apathetic students were drawn into the movement on either the conservative or the radical side. Once both sides had their own organizations, the members of each group developed a personal stake in the outcome of the confrontation and a loyalty to their own group, thus adding the element of power struggle to the factional struggle. When the multiple and overlapping sources of conflict became subsumed under the dichotomized positions of "radical" and "conservative," they further intensified the conflict between the two groups.

The manipulation by the elite groups also contributed to the deepening conflict in the Red Guard movement. The Small Group, whose political interests lay in expanding the targets to include the power holders, supported the radicals in the controversies, such as those over political performance versus class origin, and minority versus majority rule. The Party leaders, whose interests dictated that the targets be contained outside the Party organization, supported the conservatives' positions in stressing class origin, majority rule, and unity and discipline in the Red Guard movement.

171. "A Talk by Chairman Mao to Foreign Visitors," *SCMP*, no. 4200 (18 June 1968), pp. 1-7.

Thus, there emerged a vertical cleavage between the Small Group and the radical Red Guards, on the one hand, and the Party organization and the conservative Red Guards, on the other, which cut across the horizontal division between the elite and the masses. The radical Red Guards were the underdogs at this stage, but they successfully managed to challenge the conservative majority as the official line on the controversial issues gradually swung in their direction.

# CHAPTER 4

# The Rise of the Radical Red Guards

In the beginning of October 1966, almost exactly one year after Mao had initiated the criticism of Wu Han, the Red Guard movement entered a new radical stage, signaling the end of the campaign against the "four olds" and the opening of the campaign against the "bourgeois reactionary line" and the "power holders." This represented a victory for the radical line of the "revolutionary rebels" and the Cultural Revolution Small Group over the moderate line of the conservative majority and the Party leaders. The radical Red Guards, however, capitalized on their initial victory to launch a general offensive on the conservative Red Guards and turn the whole Red Guard movement against the Party leaders. When the radicals, with the help of the Small Group, succeeded in taking over the leadership of the Red Guard movement in December 1966, they were ready to push the Cultural Revolution into a stage of power seizure.

## The Upsurge of the Radicals

The initial impetus for these changes came from the Peking leaders—Mao, Lin Piao, Chou En-lai, and the Cultural Revolution Small Group—who, by the October National Day, seem to have reached some sort of agreement to redress the grievances of the radical Red Guards, if not to redirect the whole movement against the power holders. In a series of speeches, official instructions, and newspaper editorials, they unequivocally enunciated official positions in support of the radicals in the controversies concerning (1) the main targets; (2) the relationship between the Party organization and Mao Tse-tung's Thought; (3) the relationship between class origin and political performance; and (4) the rehabilitation of those attacked by the work teams.

110

First, in a departure from its previous practice, the *Jen-min jih-pao* of October 1 editorially condemned the powerful forces opposing the Cultural Revolution and manipulating the Red Guards.[1] The editorial of *Hung ch'i,* No. 8 (which was made public on October 3), called for the masses to "criticize and repudiate the bourgeois reactionary line."[2] Later, the "bourgeois reactionary line" was further defined as "the line which opposes the mass line, and opposes the attempts of the masses to educate and liberate themselves" by diverting the major targets from the power holders to the masses.[3] This mistaken line was attributed to the "Party committees, the work teams, and, after the withdrawal of the work teams, the delegates that the work teams hand-picked."[4]

Second, characterizing the Cultural Revolution as a "new stage in the struggle between the classes," *Hung ch'i,* for the first time in the official news media, identified the main target as the "power holders taking the capitalist road within the Party."[5]

Third, the Peking leaders made it plain that the "structural legitimacy" of any organization was subordinate to the authority of Mao Tse-tung's Thought. The Military Affairs Commission issued a directive on October 5 stating:

Whenever erroneous words and deeds that run counter to Mao Tse-tung's Thought and the general and specific policies of the Military Affairs Commission of the Central Committee are encountered—irrespective of who the persons involved are and what posts they are holding, irrespective of what time and in what place, and irrespective of whether the persons involved are directly led by you or not—all comrades must dare to struggle and consciously defend the Thought of Mao Tse-tung in general and the specific policies of the Central Committee and the Military Affairs Commission.[6]

The order, in effect, implied that any individual had the right to decide whether or not any instruction coming from the high command was in accordance with Mao's Thought. By inference, it meant that the command structure of the People's Liberation Army did not necessarily guarantee immunity from criticism. Although this theme had been more or less explicitly advanced in the past, never before had it been presented with such clarity and emphasis.

The fourth question that the Center resolved in favor of the radicals was the issue of "class line." Even Chou En-lai, who initially had endeavored to

1. *JMJP,* 1 October 1967.
2. "Forward Along the High Road of the Mao Tse-tung's Thought," *PR,* no. 41 (1 October 1966), pp. 15-18.
3. *Shou-chang chiang hua,* vol. 3 (unpaged).
4. *KMJP,* 4 November 1966.
5. "Forward Along the High Road of the Mao Tse-tung's Thought," pp. 1-18.
6. *CCP Documents of the Great Proletarian Cultural Revolution* (Hong Kong: Union Research Institute, 1968), p. 94.

maintain a balance between "class origin" and "political performance," instructed the students in October to discontinue using the term "black categories."[7] Ch'en Po-ta was particularly severe on the "theory of natural redness":

As a matter of fact, this is a reactionary bloodline theory of the exploiting class. The philosophy of the landlord class—like father, like son—is thoroughly anti-Marxism-Leninism, and anti-Mao's Thought. . . . Those who come from a worker background do not necessarily represent the interests of the working class. . . . Those people who want the students to accept the concepts of "being born red," "being born black," . . . and those who create and spread such ideas want to create confusion, poison the youth, and deny the fact that one has to keep reforming oneself during the revolutionary process.[8]

Mao appeared to agree with Ch'en, even though his comment on the problem was vague: "Some of the students do not have good backgrounds, but do we all have good backgrounds?"[9] The official condemnation of the "theory of natural redness" removed the last psychological inhibition on the part of the students with questionable family backgrounds, and according to a Red Guard source, "revolutionary organizations sprang up like bamboo sprouts after the spring rain."[10]

Fifth, the issues revolving around the "black materials" and the rehabilitation of the stigmatized students were also resolved in favor of the radicals. On October 5, the MAC again took the initiative in ordering a thorough rehabilitation of the so-called "rightists" and destruction in public of all the black materials.[11] Interpreting the MAC's order as applying to all universities and colleges, Chou En-lai defined the "black materials" broadly so as to include (1) materials classifying the students into rightists, middle roaders, and leftists; (2) the self-examinations made under the pressure of the work teams; (3) the work teams' reports incriminating anti-work-team students; (4) the notes prepared by the work teams; and (5) the records of the conferences organized by the work teams.[12] The justification for this was that the destruction was needed to mend the split in the Red Guard movement.[13]

The public destruction of such broadly defined materials was not acceptable to the conservative Red Guards or the Party leaders. As noted, the

7. *Shou-chang chiang-hua*, vol. 3 (unpaged).
8. "General Summary for the CR in the Past Two Months," *Issues and Studies* 7, no. 2 (November 1970): 71-78.
9. "Speeches at a Work Conference of Central Committee," *CB*, no. 891 (8 October 1969), p. 72.
10. *Chih-pa ch'un-lai pao*, 4 April 1967.
11. *CCP Documents of the GPCR*, pp. 89-91.
12. "Central Government Leaders' Speeches at Oath-taking Meeting of Revolutionary Teachers and Students," *JPRS*, no. 40,974 (10 May 1967), p. 20; "Speeches by Premier Chou at Oath-taking Rally," *SCMMS*, no. 15 (8 May 1967), pp. 1-3.
13. *CCP Document of the GPCR*, p. 103.

conservative Red Guards had been refusing to destroy the black materials, despite the repeated suggestions of the Maoist leaders. Particularly unacceptable was the condition that the destruction be made with the participation of the masses. Actually, this was tantamount to requesting the Party leaders to give self-incriminating evidence to the prosecutor. On the other hand, the black materials were of great strategic importance to the radicals: capturing these materials not only would eliminate undesirable personal records which their opponents might use for retaliation in the future but also would enable the radicals to identify informers working for the Party organization and thus prove to the public that the Party organization "suppressed the innocent masses." For this reason, the Party committees attempted to evade the order by hiding the black materials among the Party's classified files. In response, however, the radicals, under the pretext of seizing black materials, forcefully seized the Party's confidential materials.

The Cultural Revolution Small Group tended to tolerate the excessive actions of the radicals while denouncing the Party's practice of collecting secret information on the students:

Some people, upon discovering the shortcomings or mistakes of others, would not discuss these things with the people directly in order to help them, and would not make suggestions in a reasonable and constructive manner . . . at various meetings. [Instead,] they would record every such erroneous thought and deed in minute detail to be used in secretive reporting against these persons. This is clearly inconsistent with the Thought of Mao Tse-tung. Where can you find this stipulated by Chairman Mao in his plans for building and strengthening the Party?[14]

The official clarification of the five controversial issues gained immediate and enthusiastic applause from the radical Red Guards (who called it "a spiritual atomic bomb") and numbed the conservative Red Guards.[15] Bewildered and angered by the shift of the official line that amounted to a wholesale repudiation of their own orientation, the conservative Red Guards went to the editorial offices of *Hung ch'i, Jen-min jih-pao,* and the Liaison Office of the Central Committee of the CCP. Their ostensible purpose was to get some explanation of the new situation, but their true intention was to register their dissatisfaction. They raised very specific questions about what "the bourgeois reactionary line" and "the power holders taking the capitalist road within the Party" meant, and why the Maoist leaders had not objected at the time when the work teams were dispatched.[16]

14. "Record of Discussion between Comrade Ch'i Pen-yü and Leadership of Original Capital Higher Education Red Guard General Headquarters," *JPRS,* no. 40,349 (22 March 1967), p. 68.

15. *Tung-fang-hung,* 16 November 1967.

16. "What Is the Essential Reason for Reactionary Thinking," *JPRS,* no. 40,391 (24 March 1967); *Hung-wei-ping,* 25 November 1966.

Not surprisingly, they were given a cold reception and the unsympathetic reply that the whole premise under which they had been operating was wrong. When they challenged the editorial of *Hung ch'i*, No. 13, Lin Chieh defended it by invoking Mao's authority: "The editorial of this issue was written in accordance with the instructions of Chairman Mao and his close comrade-in-arms, Comrade Lin Piao."[17] When the conservative Red Guards protested the sudden escalation of the targets to include the power holders, they were told:

[Since] the Party organization resisted orders, failed to implement orders, the Party Central Committee published the editorial, directing the principal offensive forces of the Cultural Revolution against the power holders taking the capitalist road.[18]

In contrast to the disappointment of the conservatives, the radical groups, who also went to the various government organs, were greatly encouraged.[19] The clarification of the official line reaffirmed the correctness of what the radicals had been fighting for. Their problematic class backgrounds, their excessive tactics, their challenge to organizational principles, and the subsequent disorder and chaos were secondary problems. More important was the question of whether or not one followed the correct line of the proletarian headquarters—that is to say, criticizing the bourgeois reactionary line and turning the movement against the "power holders." The "bourgeois reactionary revisionist line" was the line that had suppressed the radical minority Red Guards. T'an Li-fu's speeches were officially denounced as "reactionary poisonous weeds" representing the mistaken line of the Party organization.

On October 6, with the blessing of Chou En-lai, the members of the Cultural Revolution Small Group, and Yang Ch'eng-wu, the Acting Chief of Staff of the PLA, the "suppressed minority" led by the Third Headquarters organized an "Oath-Taking Rally to Open Fire at the Reactionary Bourgeois Line." It was a momentous rally for the radicals, who had been "suppressed" by the work teams and then victimized even after the withdrawal of the work teams. Students who had been labeled as "counterrevolutionaries" and even barred from taking part in the big August 18 rally now occupied the presidium of a mass rally for the first time. Many participants cried when Chang Ch'un-ch'iao read the instructions of the MAC regarding their rehabilitation.[20] Chiang Ch'ing highly praised the "suppressed minority" for

17. "Speech by Lin Chieh on October 3 at Reception Given at the Red Flag Editorial Department," *SCMMP*, no. 16 (15 June 1967), p. 10. At that time there was a rumor that Kuan Feng and Lin Chieh wrote the articles in the Geology Institute and Peking Normal University. *Shou-chang chiang-hua*, vol. 3 (unpaged).

18. "A Visit to the Reception Room of the CRSG of the CCP, CC by College of Petroleum," *CB*, no. 819 (10 March 1969), pp. 79-84.

19. "Interview with Central State Council Joint Liaison Station of Central Communist Party," *JPRS*, no. 40,974 (10 May 1967), p. 39.

20. "Chang Ch'un-ch'iao's Speech to the Revolutionary Students from Fukien," *JPRS*, no. 40,974 (10 May 1967), p. 26.

having persisted in the correct line in spite of the insurmountable hardship. Endorsing Chiang Ch'ing's speech as the official view, Chou En-lai promised that the proceedings of the rally, recorded on tape, would be sent to all the campuses as a guideline for the Red Guard movement.[21]

The campaign against the bourgeois reactionary line provided the radicals with an excellent opportunity to unleash their accumulated resentment and hostility directly against the Party leaders. To criticize "the bourgeois reactionary line" meant to give a free hand to the students in selecting targets, since nearly all the Party leaders had implemented the policy of the Party organization. The choice for the radicals was not whom they were going to attack but whom they were going to exempt from attack. Understandably, the radicals readily expanded the scope of the targets.

On October 9, Chou En-lai announced the Central Committee's decision to have Wang Kuang-mei present a written self-examination to the Tsinghua students.[22] Rejecting the written self-examination, the Tsinghua radicals asked for official permission to subject Wang Kuang-mei to a public confrontation and staged a sit-in demonstration for that demand in front of the Chungnanhai, the Central Committee building.[23] It was at this time that the first few big-character posters criticizing Liu and Wang appeared in the streets of Peking, although they were covered over by other posters as soon as they appeared.[24]

On October 12, the Third Headquarters initiated an attach on Li Hsüeh-feng, the head of the new Peking Party Committee that had supported the First and Second Headquarters. The attack on the "bourgeois reactionary line" also inevitably led to the various ministers and vice-ministers, who had sent out the work teams and then had relied on the conservative Red Guards to ward off the radicals' challenge.[25]

With the radicalization of the official line, the Cultural Revolution Small Group pledged their unconditional support to the radical organizations while criticizing the conservative organizations. This marked a departure from the Small Group's previously circumscribed support of the radicals, which had been implicit rather than explicit, general rather than specific, ideological rather than organizational, and justified on the grounds that the minority should be given the same rights as the majority.

For instance, Ch'i Pen-yü and Kuan Feng publicly declared: "We lean toward the Red Flag group [of the Peking Aviation Institute] and the East Is Red group [of the Geology Institute], because their direction is relatively

21. "Premier Chou's Speech at the National Rally of Teachers and Students to Pledge Fierce Attack on Bourgeois Reactionary Line on 6 October," *JPRS*, no. 40,391 (24 March 1967), pp. 11-13.
22. "Record," pp. 40.
23. William Hinton, *Hundred Day War* (New York: Monthly Review Press, 1972), p. 101.
24. *DSJP*, 26-28 November 1966.
25. *DSJP*, 24 October 1966, pp. 8, 15.

correct and they see the mistaken line more clearly."[26] Chou En-lai changed his previously neutral attitude toward the conservative organizations and specifically supported the Third Headquarters. Even those Party leaders who were known as ardent supporters of the majority faction and the school Cultural Revolution preparatory committees shifted their support to the rebel faction led by the Third Headquarters.[27] From this time on, the names of the radical Red Guard organizations replaced those of the original Red Guard organizations in the public news media.

The shifting of the Peking leaders' support to the radical Red Guards entailed a change in the communication pattern between the elite and the masses: regular communication channels developed between the radical Red Guards and the Cultural Revolution Small Group, whereas the contact between the conservative Red Guards and the Small Group diminished rapidly. Even such a moderate as Chou En-lai now turned his back on the conservative Red Guards. When he was asked by the Second Headquarters to attend its rally, Chou first simply sent his taped speech of the October 6 rally, and then, when he finally granted an interview to the conservative Red Guards after several refusals, he bluntly criticized the leadership of the First and Second Headquarters:

You are hoodwinked and influenced by them [the Party committees]. Get rid of their influence and rectify yourselves. Those who are influenced most deeply are you, the so-called majority faction, who supported the work teams, sometimes the revolutionary committees, and sometimes the leadership of the [original] Red Guards.[28]

To the conservatives' complaint that they were being attacked by the minority faction in the Geology Institute, he commented, "You have suppressed them long enough, so they might well suppress you."[29]

Taking advantage of the favorable political mood, the radical students, at that time scattered in numerous organizations in all of the schools, proceeded to unify their forces. At Tsinghua University, K'uai Ta-fu's Tsinghua Red Guards merged with the Tsinghua Mao's Thought Red Guards (the August 8 Headquarters) and with the Temporary Headquarters of Mao's Thought Red Guards to form the Tsinghua Chingkangshan Combat Corps.[30] Calling for the disbanding of any organization guilty of one of five "protections"—protection of the school Party committees, the work teams, the preparatory committees, the Party branches, or oneself[31]—the unified

26. "Speeches by Ch'i Pen-yü and Kuan Feng," *SCMPS*, no. 15 (8 May 1967), pp. 7-10. Thus, the conservatives complained that "the CRSG supports the Third Headquarters alone, and it regards the Third Headquarters as synonymous with itself."
27. "Abstract of T'ao Lu-chia's Speech," *JPRS*, no. 40,974 (10 May 1967), p. 36.
28. *Shou-chang chiang-hua*, vol. 3 (unpaged).
29. Ibid.
30. *Chingkangshan*, 22 December 1966.
31. *Hung-ch'i*, 10 January 1967.

radical forces moved to take over the leadership from the school Cultural Revolution committees and the original Red Guard organizations by occupying their offices and then seizing black materials and propaganda equipment.

After seizing the leadership of their own schools, the radicals gave assistance to weak radical forces at other schools. For example, on October 22, 1966, two thousand Tsinghua students under the command of K'uai Ta-fu raided the Agricultural University and installed the radicals in the school leadership.[32] Once the fortune of the conservatives declined, many members of the conservative organizations surrendered to the radicals, thus further vitiating the strength of the conservative Red Guards.[33]

As noted, the conservative Red Guards first resisted the new radical line, but then tried to accommodate to the changed situation by making formalistic self-criticisms. The leadership of the First Headquarters held a mass rally to "rectify the influence of the bourgeois reactionary line on the First Headquarters."[34] This belated move to atone for their mistakes, however, was not accepted by the radicals. On October 22, the dissenting groups, led by the Chingkangshan group of Peking Normal University, revolted against their own leadership and reorganized the First Headquarters, announcing that the original leadership had carried out the bourgeois reactionary line.[35] The new leadership replaced the class background requirement for Red Guard membership with the political requirement of "following Mao Tsetung's Thought in word and deed."[36] They also invalidated the Red Guard certificates issued before this time and abolished all the liaison offices sent out to the various areas.

Following the revolt of the First Headquarters, the Red Flag group of the Peking Aviation Institute revolted on November 7 against the leadership of the Second Headquarters, seizing the official seal and the official newspaper, *Tung-fang-hung*. The rebels accused the original leadership of following the bourgeois reactionary line and pledged their loyalty to Mao:

Its [the new leadership's] sacred duty is to preserve at all costs the proletarian revolutionary line of Chairman Mao, to thoroughly criticize the reactionary bourgeois line, and to liberate the revolutionary masses deceived by this line.[37]

32. Hinton, *Hundred Day War*, p. 103.

33. For the revolt in the Broadcasting Institute, see "Notice of Change in Offical Designation of the Red Guard," *JPRS*, no. 40,274 (15 March 1967), p. 5. For the revolt in the Peking Mining Institute, see *Hung-wei-ping*, 25 November 1966.

34. *Tung-fang-hung*, 25 November 1966.

35. *Hung-wei-ping*, 26 October 1966; 8 November 1966.

36. Ibid.

37. "Former Red Guard Headquarters of Peiping Universities and Colleges Is Denounced by the Newly Formed Revolutionary Rebel Liaison Station," *JPRS*, no. 40,387 (24 March 1967), pp. 1-10. "The Second Declaration," *JPRS*, no. 40,274 (15 March 1967), pp. 1-10.

The original leadership issued a declaration that the revolt was illegal and then took the case to Ch'i Pen-yü, who, not surprisingly, chided them and expressed his support for the revolt.[38] Enraged by Ch'i Pen-yü, the ousted leaders published "A Letter to the People of the Whole Nation," which denounced the Cultural Revolution Small Group as the backstage boss of the revolt:

> Certain persons turned about, linked with the minority and attacked the majority. . . . They made no inquiry, but suppressed one group, attacked another, and consciously and unconsciously caused the masses to struggle against the masses.[39]

The internal revolts within the two headquarters aided the shift of power from the conservatives to the radicals, as well as from student members of the Party and of the Chinese Youth League to the non-member students. It also represented a shift of power from the First and Second Headquarters to the Third Headquarters.

Following the rise of the radicals in the colleges, the leadership of the middle schools shifted from the Hsi-ch'eng Inspection Team to the Ping Tuan Headquarters, which the Cultural Revolution Small Group helped to organize. However, the middle-school Red Guards, the main force in the campaign against the "four olds," lost their leading role to the college Red Guards, who thereafter dominated the Red Guard movement. The radicals' battle cry for seizing power from their fellow students and from the school Cultural Revolution committees gradually expanded to include seizing power from the school Party committees and the area Party committees and finally culminated in the "January Power Seizure."

## The October Work Conference and the Rising Conflict between the Cultural Revolution Small Group and the PLA

While the criticism of the "bourgeois reactionary line" was gathering momentum, Mao convened the October Work Conference, attended by the central leaders as well as by "responsible comrades from the various regional, principal, and municipal Party committees."[40] To be sure, there was no shortage of problems for the leaders to debate in such a high-level meeting. Some of the problems, as Mao acknowledged, might involve the simple question of how to operationalize the "Sixteen Articles" in the face of the

---

38. "Record of Discussion between Comrade Ch'i Pen-yü and Leadership of Original Capital High Education Red Guard General Headquarters," *JPRS*, no. 40,341 (22 March 1967), pp. 60-68; "Conversation Between Ch'i Pen-yü and Revolutionaries of Red Guards of Colleges and Schools in the Capital," *JPRS*, no. 40,476 (31 March 1967), pp. 17-28.

39. *Tung-fang-hung*, 9 December 1967.

40. *Chung-kung wen-hua ta ko-ming chung-yao wen-chien hui-pien* (Taipei: Chung-kung Yen-chiu, 1973), p. 202.

increasing complexity of the movement, and such a question could be resolved easily by discussion and clarification at the meeting.[41] A more serious question was how to pacify the increasing resentment of the various political groups toward the Maoist leaders. At that time, not only the Party organization but also the whole ruling structure—including the government functionaries and the PLA leaders—felt threatened by the radicalization of the Red Guard movement.

After the collapse of the central Party organs, the precarious task of leading the mass movement against the ruling structure passed down to the local Party leaders. The pressure on them was extremely heavy. Even the conservative Peking Red Guards acted more boldly in matters where they did not have any special interests to protect. Worse still, by October 1966, the Peking radicals began to dispatch their own liaison groups in order to redirect the whole movement to the local Party leaders.

As a protest against the aggravated situation, the local broadcast stations ceased covering the activities of the Red Guards. In light of such confusion and growing resentment on the part of the various political groups, it seems likely that Mao called for the meeting so as to persuade the various political groups to form a consensus about the Cultural Revolution.

The Central Committee work conference, which lasted seventeen days instead of the originally planned three days, appears to have been a stormy one. In Mao's own words, "at the first stage, the speeches made were not so normal, but later the meeting proceeded relatively smoothly."[42] At first, Lin Shao-ch'i and Teng Hsiao-p'ing reportedly refused to acknowledge their mistakes with such stubbornness that Ch'en Po-ta complained of Teng: "To talk with Teng Hsiao-p'ing is more difficult than to put a ladder against Heaven."[43] Li Ching-ch'üan and Lu Jen declared that they not only did not understand the Cultural Revolution now, but would never understand it even after their return to their provinces.[44]

Judging from the available material on the conference, it seems to have covered four major questions, from each of which a different coalition

41. Mao observed in the conference: "Some people said: 'The principle had been adopted, but the concrete problems could not be handled properly.' At first I did not see why the concrete problems could not be dealt with properly after the problems of principle had been clarified. Now it seems there is an element in what these people said." "Speeches at a Work Conference of the Central Committee," *CB*, no. 819 (8 October 1969), pp. 75-77.

42. Ibid.

43. Edward E. Rice, *Mao's Way* (Berkeley and Los Angeles: University of California Press, 1972), p. 251. The other indication that the conference faced a deadlock was reflected in the October 16 big rally. The Chinese leaders arrived late at the rally where the Red Guards had been waiting a long time, and instead of the usual procedure of mounting the rostrum and delivering speeches, they just rode by the rally in several cars. Then the disappointed Red Guards were dismissed without any explanation.

44. "Chao Tzu-yang's Coordination of Three Powers Aimed at Usurping Party Power," *SCMP*, no. 4112 (6 February 1968), p. 4.

emerged. With regard to the first question of the "bourgeois reactionary line," Mao, Lin Piao, Chou En-lai, and the Cultural Revolution Small Group appear to have agreed that some Party leaders had misled the Red Guard movement for the sake of their own self-defense, and that the victims of the mistaken line should be reinstated.[45] The strong political coalition behind the charge, supported by its factual validity, forced Liu and Teng to concede that their "mistakes" during the "fifty days of red terror" had had far-reaching consequences on the Red Guard movement thereafter. Teng blamed himself for the mistakes made by his subordinates:

It is necessary to thoroughly criticize and repudiate the mistakes made by the two of us [Liu and Teng] and eliminate the influence of the mistaken line we represented. This is because we are not only fully responsible for what happened before the eleventh plenary session, but also for the different mistakes committed by people in various places and departments after the eleventh plenary session as a result of the influence of the mistaken line we represented.[46]

On the second question of the extent to which Liu and Teng should be castigated for their share of mistakes, apparently the Cultural Revolution Small Group and Lin Piao split from Chou En-lai and the local Party leaders, leaving Mao in between. Attributing the mistakes as much to Liu Shao-ch'i himself as to the dispersion of the central leadership caused by the division of the first and second lines of command that Liu had created in 1957, Mao nevertheless showed leniency toward Liu:

Some comrades say the mistakes are not deliberate ones, they are made because of muddle-headedness. They are therefore forgivable. [We] cannot shift all the blame to comrade [Liu] Shao-ch'i and comrade [Teng] Hsiao-p'ing. They are to be blamed, [but] so is the Center [as a whole]. The Center has not done its job. Because of lack of time and energy, [I] have not prepared [the answers] to the new problems. Political and ideological work which has not been done properly will be improved after these seventeen days of conference.[47]

Chou En-lai interrupted Mao's speech to make the following statement: "Everything will be well if [mistakes] are corrected, views are unanimous, and all are united. Liu and Teng must be allowed to make revolution and rectify themselves."[48] Lin Piao, however, denounced Liu and Teng by name

45. "General Summary," *Issues and Studies,* November 1970, pp. 71-78.
46. "Teng Hsiao-p'ing's Self-criticism at the Work Conference of the CCP Central Committee on October 23, 1966," *Issues and Studies,* September 1970, pp. 84-90.
47. "Speech at a Work Conference of the Central Committee," *CB,* no. 891 (8 October 1969), pp. 75-77. While implying in this statement that Liu Shao-ch'i's problems were forgivable and belonged within the organizational framework, Mao was eager to make public the mistaken line pursued by Liu. Mao ordered the publication and distribution of Ch'en Po-ta's speech, which, though it did not criticize Liu by name, was full of criticism of the tactics used by the Party committees.
48. Ibid.

as initiators of the "bourgeois reactionary line."[49] According to one source, Lin even charged that Liu was involved in P'eng Chen's alleged "coup d'état."[50] If Mao, the supreme leader, did not want to alienate Chou and the local Party leaders by taking an extreme partisan view toward Liu, it was obviously in Lin Piao's personal interest to demolish Liu's prestige as thoroughly as possible and to purge other top Party leaders who might challenge his authority.

On the third question, concerning the extent to which the local Party leaders should be held liable for the "bourgeois reactionary line," Lin seemed to lean toward moderation:

The mistaken line of the Cultural Revolution was initiated by Liu and Teng. Much of the mistake lies in the line's execution. The comrades are very concerned about this. Of course, this must be treated analytically. Initiators and executors must be differentiated. The general estimate is that most of the comrades have unconsciously or unintentionally opposed Chairman Mao's line. It is mostly a problem of recognition, not an anti-Party, antisocialist, or anti-Mao problem.[51]

Lin's conciliatory gesture was consistent with his political interests: after he stepped into Liu's shoes, his political interests lay in taking over the existing local Party machinery and consolidating his control over it, rather than attacking it with the Red Guards, over whom he lacked any viable leverage. His newly acquired role of successor to the supreme leader required moderation in order to command allegiance from the various political groups. Furthermore, he could not afford to ignore the PLA leaders who began to feel the devastating impact of the Red Guard movement on the organizational interests of the PLA.

If Lin Piao found it politically wise to seek the support of the local Party leaders while attacking only those in a position high enough to challenge his authority, the Cultural Revolution Small Group, which lacked any institutional power base, had nothing to lose by directing the spearhead of the Red Guard movement toward the central and local Party leaders. Ch'en Po-ta warned:

Some of our comrades consider themselves as senior revolutionaries. They are typical bureaucrats; they have forgotten all about their own revolutionary histories. They possess all the traits of bureaucraticism, gloominess, daintiness, and arrogance, all of which have been criticized by Chairman Mao. . . . All they wanted was to use the supreme prestige of Chairman Mao and the Party to mobilize the masses to protect themselves.[52]

49. "Lin Piao's Address at the CCP Central Committee Work Conference," *Issues and Studies* 6, no. 1 (October 1969); 101-105; no. 2 (November 1969): 93-99.
50. Rice, *Mao's Way,* p. 236.
51. "Lin Piao's Address," *Issues and Studies,* no. 1 and no. 2 (1969).
52. "General Summary for the CR," *Issues and Studies,* November 1970, pp. 71-78.

What course the Cultural Revolution would take next was unclear from the available speeches of the leaders. The ambiguity surrounding this question might be due, in part, to the conference's fictitious assumption that the principles set forth in the Sixteen Articles were still effective at the time, despite the radicalization of the Red Guard movement. The participants' conscious avoidance of this question, which was too sensitive to every political group and too complicated to be defined in simple terms, may have clouded its resolution. However, as ambiguous as the leaders' attitudes were on this important question, a close comparison of Ch'en Po-ta's and Lin Piao's speeches reveals two different views of the Cultural Revolution: Lin stresses "revolutionizing one's ideology" as the main task of the movement, while Ch'en stresses "struggling against the power holders."

In a lengthy speech mostly devoted to a general discussion of the theoretical relationship between economics, politics, and ideology, Lin Piao defined the Cultural Revolution as "a revolution in the ideological sphere" and then justified this by citing his previous thesis that bourgeois ideology in the superstructure could bring about a restoration of capitalism even in a socialist country.[53] According to Lin, once the Cultural Revolution was defined as "revolutionizing one's ideology, demolishing private interests, and establishing public interests," then it could be related to the study of Mao's Thought.

Lin praised the Red Guards, without mentioning the confrontation of two antagonistic lines among them. In contrast, Ch'en Po-ta emphatically underscored the thesis of a two-line struggle:

The struggle of lines within the Party is a reflection of the class struggle in the society. The wrong lines have their social base. The main thing is that the mistaken bourgeois line has a market within the Party, and there is a small group of muddle-headed people whose world outlook has not yet been properly transformed.[54]

Ch'en added that "the struggle between the two lines is still continuing, and will be repeated many times."[55]

The difference between the two views was subtle, but its implications for the future course of the mass movement were profound. The campaign against the "four olds" and the attack on the "bourgeois academicians" could be more easily justified by Lin Piao's view than Ch'en's. If the main

53. "Lin Piao's Speech," *Issues and Studies* 6, no. 2, pp. 93-99.
54. "General Summary for the CR," *Issues and Studies,* November 1970, pp. 71-78. According to Edward Rice, "Lin Piao had emerged from the conference under something of a cloud. He did not address a rally held on November 3. But pictures taken at a subsequential rally of November 11 show Mao Tse-tung flanked by Ch'en Po-ta and Chou En-lai, rather than Lin Piao at his side, and for about five months thereafter Lin Piao made no public appearances of note." Rice, *Mao's Way,* p. 264.
55. Ibid.

objective is "revolutionizing ideology," then the target should not necessarily be the Party leaders, but could include the masses. Everyone, regardless of whether he is a cadre or an ordinary citizen, has something to rectify. However, if the Cultural Revolution is regarded as a "class struggle between two lines," then the main target should be the "power holders taking the capitalist road within the Party." The consequences of the first view would be to employ a moderate method of criticism and self-criticism combined with the study of Mao's Thought, whereas the thesis of a two-line struggle would tend to justify a violent approach.

After this period, there was a continuing tension between the two views all through the Cultural Revolution. The conservative Red Guards tended to stress "revolutionizing one's ideology," while the radical Red Guards tended to stress the "class struggle between the two lines." Whenever the Cultural Revolution entered a moderate stage, the PLA's view became dominant. That is, when the PLA exercised strong leadership over the movement, it tended to portray the Cultural Revolution as "revolutionizing ideology," and emphasized the unity of the Red Guards by stressing the importance of criticism and self-criticism of both the conservatives and the radicals. For instance, when the Cultural Revolution entered a moderate stage in the autumn of 1967, the themes of "revolutionizing one's ideology, destroying private interests, and establishing public interests," which Lin Piao advanced again in his public speech of October 1967, gained currency. On the other hand, the Cultural Revolution Small Group seldom emphasized this point, and the radicals even considered it the main instrument by which the PLA suppressed them.

Meanwhile, after the October Work Conference, the official news media tended to portray the Cultural Revolution as a mass campaign to "revolutionize one's ideology." Following Lin Piao's declaration that "Chairman Mao is the greatest talent [genius] in the present era, [and of a calibre] that appears only once in several thousand years in China,"[56] and following his instruction to "raise the study of Chairman Mao's writings to a new stage,"[57] all the major newspapers gave full coverage in October and November to the campaign to study Mao's Thought and to emulate the PLA.[58]

56. *JMJP*, 17 December 1967.
57. Ibid., 10 October 1967.
58. During the entire month of November, the *JMJP* prominently featured the exhortation to study Mao's thoughts in order to achieve ideological transformation, and praise for the PLA's success in studying Mao's thought. The *CFCP* carried only five major editorials from October 1 to December 22, all of which portrayed the Cultural Revolution as "revolutionizing ideology" rather than as a struggle against the power holders. The *Hung-wei-ping* (former *Yang-ch'eng wan-pao*) primarily propagated "revolutionizing ideology," giving prominent features to the PLA's experiences of studying Mao's thought. It is interesting to note that Chung Han-hua, the political commissar who revolted against the CRSG in the Wuhan incident, contributed a long

The catchword was "Push the mass movement of living study and living application of Mao Tse-tung's Thought to a new stage," and the official "motto *(tso yu ming)* of the revolution" was the "three old articles"[59]—a theme which was moderate and harmless in the context of the Red Guard movement at that moment. Also conspicuous in the news media was the effort to build up Lin Piao's image as Mao's close comrade-in-arms and student. With the advantage of hindsight, it can be said that Lin Piao engaged in the political campaign to consolidate his newly acquired authority.

Finding their interests identical to those of Lin Piao—the other option being to follow the radical line of the Cultural Revolution Small Group—the local Party leaders displayed genuine enthusiasm for the slogan of "revolutionizing one's ideology" through the study of Mao's Thought. For example, the Kwangtung Provincial Party Committee, under the influence of T'ao Chu, distinguished itself by prominently propagating stories about the successes of the PLA, and by organizing the Congress for Activists for the Study of Mao's Thought.[60] Rewarded by the Party committees with the honors of "five good laborers, five good office-workers, five good soldiers, and five good militia," the activists were apt to defend rather than challenge the local Party leaders. In brief, the campaign to study Mao's Thought represented a masterful political move which benefited Lin Piao, while at the same time providing the local Party leaders with a means to divert the mass movement from themselves.

By underscoring the moderate view of the Cultural Revolution, and by carrying reports irrelevant to the Red Guard movement at the very time that the violent confrontations between the radicals and the conservatives were taking place almost everywhere, the news media not only lost their former role of leading the mass movement, but also failed to address themselves to the real and meaningful issues of the movement. *Hung ch'i* was the only exception to this. Obviously reflecting the view of the Cultural Revolution Small Group, it still continued to carry provocative articles dealing with concrete problems arising from the conflict between the radicals and the conservatives. The editorial of issue No. 14, which provided a verbatim account of Ch'en's speech at the Work Conference, encouraged the masses to concentrate on criticizing and repudiating the bourgeois reactionary line and attacking the power holders, and also warned the power holders themselves to make their self-examinations to the masses.[61]

---

article, "Respond Firmly to the Call of Lin Piao, Push the Movement in Living Study and Living Application to the New Stage." *Hung-wei-ping,* 25 November 1966.

59. The three old articles refer to "Serve the People" "In Memory of Norman Bethune," and "The Foolish Old Man Who Removed the Mountains."

60. *Hung-wei-ping,* 3 October 1966.

61. "Victory for the Proletarian Revolutionary Line Represented by Chairman Mao," *PR,* no. 45 (4 November 1966), pp. 6-7.

In November, the radical Red Guards, now taking their line solely from the Cultural Revolution Small Group rather than the news media, intensified the campaign to criticize the "bourgeois reactionary line," thus putting increasingly heavy pressure on all the ruling structures. It was during this period that the big-character posters denouncing Liu and Teng as the "heads of the bourgeois reactionary line" appeared on the streets of Peking, and the Red Guards began to broadcast the slogan that "Liu and Teng are the representatives of the bourgeois reactionary line."[62]

The Peking University Hsin Peita, which for the first time published articles criticizing Liu and Teng by name, was raided by the conservatives. Nonetheless, as the radicals' power grew, they frequently resorted to violent means themselves, such as forced entry into government buildings, sit-in demonstrations, and violent political meetings. They stormed into the compound of the Ministry of National Defense,[63] and even attempted a forced entry into the Chung-nan Hai, prompting T'ao Chu to order the big doors of the building to be kept closed.[64]

Having become more assertive and independent, the Red Guards not only clashed with low-ranking officials such as the personnel of the reception centers, who could neither meet their demands nor promptly provide satisfactory answers for them, but also displayed disrespect for the top leaders other than those of the Cultural Revolution Small Group.[65] Their already tense relationship with the PLA deteriorated further, as the radicals tried to enter the PLA compounds searching for black materials.[66]

## The "December Black Winds"

In the early part of December, the conservative Red Guards launched their last organized counterattacks on the radical Red Guards and the Cultural Revolution Small Group, thus creating what was called the "December Black Winds." The middle-school conservatives pooled their forces into the "United Action Committee," which mainly consisted of former members of the now defunct Hsi-ch'eng Inspection Team, and issued a communique declaring that "the *new* bourgeois reactionary line . . . is the greatest menace in the current movement."[67]

62. Chao Ts'ung, *Wen-ko yün-tung li-ch'eng shu-lüeh* (Hong Kong: Yu-lien yen-chiu-so, 1971), vol. 1, pp. 373-374.

63. "Instructions Given by Ch'en Po-ta," *SCMMS*, no. 16 (5 June 1967), p. 22.

64. "Speech Delivered by T'ao Chu, Li Fu-ch'un, Ch'en I, and T'an Chen-lin at a Small Auditorium of Chung-nan-hai," *SCMMS*, no. 16 (5 June 1967), pp. 25-31.

65. Ibid.

66. The conservatives charged that the radicals killed three PLA members. Regardless of the validity of the charge, the mere fact that the conservatives made this kind of charge indicates the bad relationship between the PLA and the radicals. "Record," p. 56.

67. Ibid., pp. 58-62.

The conservative Red Guards of the Peking Aviation Institute went on the attack in "Three Questions to the Cultural Revolution Small Group," and later in "Again Questioning the Cultural Revolution Small Group."[68] The conservatives of the Peking Forestry College organized public debates on the Small Group and put up big-character posters which proclaimed: "Look what line the Cultural Revolution Small Group carried out in the Great Proletarian Cultural Revolution!"[69] The Tsinghua campus was covered with many anti-Small Group big-character posters, one of which, entitled "An Open Letter to Chairman Mao," contended that "after October 3, the movement in Peking committed mistakes in line and direction."[70] Various streets of Peking were decorated with anti-Small Group slogans, such as: "The Cultural Revolution Small Group implemented the ultra-leftist line"; and "Let's kick out the Cultural Revolution Small Group and promote the Cultural Revolution by ourselves!"[71]

The conservatives criticized the Small Group on the grounds that the latter (1) was not elected according to the principles of the Sixteen Articles; (2) had instigated the masses to struggle against the masses by supporting only the Third Headquarters; and (3) under the pretext of criticizing the "bourgeois reactionary line," had actually attacked not the bourgeoisie but rather students whose parents were workers, peasants, revolutionary cadres, soliders, and martyrs.[72]

As shown in the last criticism, the conservatives still regarded "class origin" as the major factor for determining targets. On the other hand, they defended themselves by pointing to their good class background. "How was it possible," they asked, "to say that those who rose up first, bearing deep class hatred against the class enemy, did not defend the revolutionary line of Chairman Mao?"[73] Some of their big-character posters were explicit in emphasizing class background: "Lin Piao came from a bankrupt petty bourgeois family, and was a beggar in his youth. How can he be our leader?"[74]

In the eyes of the radicals, whatever justification the conservatives might draw on to attack the Small Group, their attacks were indicative of their opposition to directing the movement against the power holders, and thus, regardless of whether they were actually controlled by the power holders or not, objectively they were defending the interests of the power holders.

68. *Hung-wei-ping,* 13 December 1967.
69. Ibid.
70. "Record," pp. 48-60.
71. *Hung-wei-ping,* 13 December 1966.
72. *Hung-wei-ping pao,* 22 December 1966.
73. Ibid.
74. *Chung-kung yen-chiu* 3, no. 9 (September 1969), p. 27.

The conservatives' counterattack backfired, only inviting further retaliation from the radicals and the members of the Small Group, who had the Peking Public Security Office arrest the leaders of the conservative Red Guards. A member of the United Action Committee bitterly complained:

In the city of Peking, there is white terrorism, and the Third Headquarters is indiscriminately grabbing people, and many innocent school friends have been thrown into jail, simply because their views differ from those of the Third Headquarters. The Public Security Ministry also is arresting people. . . . I feel deep doubts about Chiang Ch'ing. She says things which are incomprehensible and make others feel dissatisfied.[75]

On December 12, the radicals raided P'eng Chen's house and, with the consent of the Small Group, subjected P'eng Chen, Lu Ting-yi, Lo Jui-ch'ing, and Yang Shang-k'un to a public struggle meeting. The editorial of *Hung ch'i*, No. 15 (made public on December 13), encouraged the "revolutionary rebels" to "seize new victory," while denouncing those "resisting the criticism of the bourgeois reactionary line" and "manipulating the mass organization of the students and workers against the revolutionary leftists," and then "sitting on top of the mountain to watch the tigers fight."[76] It declared that "what target the spearhead of the struggle is directed against is a cardinal matter of right and wrong."[77] The Third Headquarters, "encouraged and delighted" by the editorial, organized the "National Rally of Revolutionaries in Peking to Defend Chairman Mao's Revolutionary Line and to Strive for a New Victory." At this rally, Chiang Ch'ing hinted for the first time at the need for seizing power:

The reason that the faction in power is taking the capitalist road, and those who stubbornly uphold the bourgeois reactionary line can continue to perpetuate so many bad things, such as manhandling and killing others, is that they remain in power. As the faction in power, they still hold some power. For this reason, we must destroy them.[78]

On December 25, three thousand Tsinghua students paraded through the streets of Peking denouncing Liu and Teng. On the next day, Mao's birthday, Liu and Teng's October 25 self-criticisms were made public in the big-character posters.

Among the most significant developments in December was the downfall of T'ao Chu, fourth-ranking member in the Chinese political hierarchy. In a way, T'ao Chu's brief career in Peking graphically illustrates the dilemma faced by many other Party leaders in the Cultural Revolution. Having been

75. *Mainichi*, 6 February 1967.
76. "Seize New Victory," *PR*, no. 51 (16 December 1966), pp. 5-7.
77. Ibid.
78. "Record," p. 62.

promoted, in May 1966, to the head of the Propaganda Department of the Central Committee and the Ministry of Education and Culture, he not only took part in making decisions to send out the work teams, but also supervised the operation of the work teams in the organs under his jurisdiction.

As the head of a governmental ministry that had more intellectuals than any other government organ, he could not avoid involvement in the controversy over whether "bourgeois aeademicians" or "black gangs" should be targeted by the work teams. For instance, when a work team attacked Wu Ch'uan-ch'i, a close associate of Kuan Feng in the Department of Philosophy and Social Science of the Chinese Academy of Science, he took an equivocal stand: "I hope that when you debate the problem of Wu, you do not expand the problems to Kuan Feng. Kuan Feng is a firm leftist whom the Center and the Central Propaganda Department trust."[79]

When the official policy changed, T'ao Chu had to lead the criticism of the work teams. However, his role as head of the Propaganda Department, plus his close association with the work teams, hampered his unequivocal support of the dissenters in his organs, even if he had wanted to lend such support. Moreover, he had another problem to handle: in order to protect his regional power base in Kwangtung, he had to maintain close contact with the local Party leaders of the Central South Regional Bureau and the Kwangtung Provincial Party Committees.[80] He tried to resolve the dilemma by keeping the Cultural Revolution within manageable boundaries, that is, by keeping the scope of the targets as narrow as possible and directing attacks outside the Party organization.

T'ao Chu earnestly supported the original Red Guards and their positions on the various controversial issues and enthusiastically promoted the campaign to study Mao's Thought. Meanwhile, he consistently opposed the public attack on Liu and Teng as late as early December.[81] This led him into conflict with the Small Group, even though he was one of their advisers. Ch'en Po-ta complained that T'ao Chu "never consulted [with us] on the various problems of the Cultural Revolution," and Chiang Ch'ing charged that "he arbitrarily made decisions behind the back of the Cultural Revolution Small Group."[82] Thus, the Small Group could not push the Cultural Revolution into the stage of power seizure without first purging T'ao Chu, the last spokesman for the interests of the Party organization.

The Red Guard newspapers portray the mass criticisms of T'ao Chu as spontaneous. In October, a Shanghai student wrote the Small Group a letter denouncing T'ao Chu's previous writings as "poisonous weeds of anti-Mao Tse-tung's Thought."[83] The dissenters in the Ministry of Education and

79. *P'i T'ao chan-pao,* 4 March 1967.
80. *Hung-se pao-tung,* 27 February 1967.
81. *P'i T'ao chan-pao,* 26 April 1967.
82. *Huo-chü pao,* January 1967.
83. *Kang pa-i chan-pao,* February 1968.

Culture put up big-character posters criticizing him in November.[84] T'ao Chu gave up his previous opposition and openly denounced Liu and Teng at the end of December. But the radical Red Guards, led by the Chingkangshan group of Peking Normal University, organized the Committee to Criticize T'ao Chu—which in the history of the Cultural Revolution was the most radical and most closely associated with the Small Group, and was later denounced as "ultra-leftist."[85] The Committee, together with demobilized soldiers and contract workers, staged a violent demonstration at Chung-nan-hai on January 4. Chou En-lai dissuaded them from dragging T'ao Chu from his office, but Ch'en Po-ta encouraged them. "You did a very good job," he said. "I support you very much. Thank you."[86]

Now, with the downfall of the last spokesman for the Party organization, the Small Group was ready to usher the Red Guard movement into the stage of power seizure. This would not have been possible, however, without the support of the workers.

## The Radical Workers

As was the case with the students, the workers were initially mobilized by the existing leadership for carefully selected issues and roles. When the Cultural Revolution intensified, they rose up in revolt more spontaneously, but their revolt came later than that of the students, and the students precipitated the workers' revolt. This is because the workers were less politically sensitive and more inhibited against revolt than the students. Moreover, the Maoist leaders were reluctant to mobilize them freely, lest this would disrupt the Chinese economy. Also unlike the students, who were interested in "power," the workers were more interested in "money." As a whole, the workers were more moderate than the students in ideological orientation, and the influence of the radical workers was very weak relative to that of the conservatives. Therefore, the Cultural Revolution Small Group relied more heavily on the students than the workers, and the conservative mass organizations often complained that the Small Group only trusted the petty intellectuals, disregarding the working class.

Like the student radicals, the radical workers endeavored to turn their movement squarely on the Party leaders, notwithstanding the sometimes subtle and sometimes ruthless retaliation by the power holders. When their rebellion was officially endorsed as a "revolutionary action" and the boundary between the campus and the factory was finally removed, the radical workers allied themselves with the radical students, thus completing the

84. *Shou-tu hung-wei-ping,* 6 January 1967.
85. For the committee, see its publication, *P'i T'ao chan-pao.*
86. *Huo-chü pao,* January 1967; *Shou-tu hung-wei-ping,* 6 January 1967.

basic division between radicals and conservatives throughout the entire society. Moderate as they had been, however, once the workers were freely mobilized, they proved to be much more powerful than the students. It was only when they finally revolted and their movement merged with the Red Guard movement that the Cultural Revolution entered the stage of power seizure.

Who were the radical workers? Did they have any discernible characteristics? Given the fact that only a minority of the workers revolted in the name of Mao's "proletarian line," the radical workers had to be those who saw their group interests lying in a positive response to the official call for criticizing the "bourgeois reactionary line." Obviously, they were disadvantaged workers with various specific grievances. This, however, does not mean that the Maoist leaders launched the public criticism of the "bourgeois revisionist line" in order to mobilize the discontented workers, or that the discontented workers faithfully followed the Maoist leaders' wishes. Rather, it seems that the Maoist leaders criticized the "bourgeois revisionist line" for ideological reasons, and the discontented workers made use of this to seek redress of their grievances. Certainly, there were both spontaneity and manipulation in the workers' revolt.

The discontented workers consisted of four primary groups: contract and temporary workers; workers in the part-study and part-work program; apprentice and unskilled workers in the large factories, and individual laborers; and workers from small factories.

*Contract and Temporary Workers:*

In contrast to permanent workers, whose welfare fell within the responsibility of the enterprise, contract and temporary workers were hired on a seasonal basis. "Rotation workers," supplied by the rural communes according to contracts signed with the enterprises, would work for several years— usually three to seven—and then return to their original communes when the contracts expired. By the time of the Cultural Revolution, the total number of contract workers reached about ten million, and in some businesses the contract workers comprised more than 95 percent of the total work force.[87]

In spite of the ideological justification that the system was designed to narrow the differences between the rural and urban areas, the system was primarily aimed at reducing labor costs. As the average age of the permanent workers increased, the enterprises were squeezed by the increasing cost of retirement pensions. The system also lessened the state's responsibility for supplying grain to urban workers by sending the temporary workers back to the rural communes when there was no work to be done.[88] One more

87. *K'o-chi chan-pao,* March 1967.
88. Maeda Sumino, "The CR and the Economy of Mainland China," *Asia Quarterly,* April 1969, pp. 46-72.

advantage for the enterprises was that the system maintained strong leverage over the workers by retaining the right to hire and fire according to performance. When someone opposed the idea of giving such enormous power over the workers to the enterprises, Liu was reported to have said: "[We] must destroy the idea of the iron [rice] bowl. . . . [The idea that] workers can be hired but cannot be fired exists nowhere in the world. Workers can be fired in the Soviet Union and Eastern Europe."[89]

From the contract workers' point of view, the system was obviously "antisocialistic." Economically the contract workers were paid lower wages than the permanent workers. In addition, the contract and temporary workers were not eligible for fringe benefits, such as medicare, accident insurance, job security, retirement pensions, sick leave, and so forth.[90] In contrast even to the capitalist market system, in which the law of supply and demand generally sets up the wage and the labor unions protect the interests of the workers vis-à-vis the owners, in a socialist economy in which the management is strongly motivated toward profit there is no such mechanism to protect the interests of contract workers. The absolute power regarding contractual conditions for hiring rested in the hands of the enterprise. The contract workers complained:

In that kind of "negotiation" [between an enterprise and a worker], "Party A" arbitrarily advances some conditions, asking "the hired" to sign the "contract." Since "Party A" has the right to fire "Party B" during the effective date of the contract, "Party B" cannot raise any "complaints" or "demands." An "agreement" that does not recognize the right to raise any complaints or demands basically takes away the right to work from the contract workers.[91]

In some places, the management asked for monthly renewals of the contract in order to strengthen their position vis-à-vis the contract workers. Furthermore, the permanent workers had vested rights in the factory, while the contract workers did not. Consequently, the contract workers argued:

The system of contract and temporary workers divides the workers into two strata, creating differences, disintegrating the ranks of the workers, eliminating revolutionary enthusiasm, and obstructing the development of the productive forces in the society.[92]

The system also discriminated against the contract workers politically, denying them participation in political activities in the Cultural Revolution. When the Cultural Revolution reached the industrial enterprises and created tensions, the factory management laid off the contract workers and sent them back to the rural areas, thus intensifying their discontents.[93]

89. *Lao-tung chan-pao*, 3 February 1968.       90. *Shou-tu hung-wei-ping*, 10 January 1967.
91. *Lao-tung chan-pao*, 3 February 1968.       92. Ibid.
93. Ibid.

As we have noted, the original Red Guards were critical of the system of contracted work. When the Party organization's economic policy was openly criticized as "putting profit in command" or "money in command," naturally the contract and temporary workers rose to attack the Party committees. They charged:

[The power holders insist that] the contract and temporary workers are the cheapest and most mobile labor force. "Most mobile" because the enterprise can conveniently gather the contract and temporary workers according to the needs of production, and can fire them when they are not necessary without inviting the protests of the contracted workers. "Cheapest" because the system can maximize profit by paying the contract and temporary workers wages below the average. This is management's method of "profit in command" and "money in command" that the power holders taking the capitalist road like most.[94]

### Workers in the Part-Study and Part-Work Program

Another dissenting group was the Chinese workers (or students) in the "half-study and half-work" program. In concept, the system was designed to bridge the gap between school learning and practical training, combining theory with practice. A more practical goal that the system intended to achieve was to increase the educational opportunities for disadvantaged students by covering their educational expenses with the students' labor contribution to the factories. However, the students of the program neither enjoyed the special treatment reserved for the students of the regular schools nor received the economic rewards of the regular workers. Moreover, considering the factory-managed schools from the standpoint of the factory management and the permanent workers, the system put an unnecessary financial burden on the factories.

Factory management can be motivated to run a school attached to their factory well only when the whole rationale of managing the factory is defined in terms of its broad contribution to society. But when the performance of the factory is evaluated by its "profitability" and "efficient management," the intended goals of the half-work and half-study program are transformed into a source of cheap labor power for maximum production.[95] Once Liu Shao-ch'i's educational and economic lines were attacked, the students in the part-work and part-study program revolted, charging that the enterprises were exploiting them as a source of cheap labor (some of them were fourteen or

94. "Black Materials on Liu Shao-Ch'i in the Temporary and Contract Work System," published by Revolutionary Rebel Teams of Ministry of Labor *Hung-wei-ping tzu-liao hui-pien* (Center for Chinese Research Materials), pp. 5352-5354.

95. *JMJP,* 18 January 1967; *Kang-ta chan-pao,* 1 April 1967; 13 May 1967; *Fang-yü t'e-k'an,* May 1968; *11.19 chan-pao,* 12 May 1967; "Premier Chou's Speech at Mass Rally Attended by Revolutionary Teachers and Students of Part-work Part-study Schools," *SCMMS,* no. 16 (5 June 1967), pp. 17-20.

fifteen years old), and were suppressing them as "anti-Party" and "riffraff" when they revolted at the initial stage of the Cultural Revolution.

*Unskilled and Apprentice Workers and Individual Labor:*

The cleavage between the radical and conservative workers emerged along the division between unskilled and apprentice workers, on the one hand, and skilled workers, on the other. While the unskilled and apprentice workers joined the radical faction, the conservative workers' organizations contained more skilled workers, master workers, and model workers.

For instance, the backbone of the Shanghai Scarlet Red Guards consisted of skilled and technical workers, so if they left their work posts production was brought to a standstill.[96] In the Canton Railway Bureau, the conservative organization known as Spring Thunder consisted of some 10,000 railway cadres, train engineers, and skilled workers, whereas 50,000 "railway coolies" organized the radical organization, the Canton Railway Workers' Headquarters.[97] The pedicab drivers of Canton joined the radical August 1 Combat Corps.

After observing that the Canton Ti-tsung ("conservative organization") consisted mainly of mechanics, Chou En-lai attributed the serious conflict between the radical and conservative workers in Canton to the deep-rooted conflict between the unskilled laborers *(tsa-kung)* and the technical workers *(chi-chieh-kung).*[98] One of the major reasons for the PLA's support of the conservative workers was that these workers were the "backbone" of production.

Like the unskilled workers, the apprentice workers revolted against the Party committees and consequently were subjected to suppression. Most of them fought in the Cultural Revolution on the radical side. Their grievances were so strong that Chou En-lai promised to change the apprentice system to the half-work and half-study program.[99]

The removal of the Party's control also gave rise to various occupational groups, such as organizations of blind men, drivers, bus conductors, pedicab drivers, cooks, and alumni associations of universities and colleges.[100] In Shanghai, private peddlers organized the Revolutionary Rebel General Headquarters of Individual Labor. They sponsored a "meeting of pouring out bitterness," crying that the individual peddler was the worst off in the

96. *JMJP*, 23 January 1967.
97. "Factionalism in Kwangtung: Comments of a Disillusioned Canton 'Radical.'" (Interview with a former Red Guard).
98. *Hung-se tsao-fan-che,* 12 October 1967.
99. "Premier Chou's Speech at Mass Rally Attended by Revolutionary Teachers and Students of Part-work, Part-study School," *SCMMS,* no. 16 (5 June 1967), pp. 17-20. Also see, *Honan 27 chan-pao,* 1 June 1967; *Ko-ming kung-jen chan-pao,* 12 January 1967.
100. *Chieh-fang jih-pao,* 8 March 1967.

new society."[101] Then they switched the attack to the tax officials, demanding: (1) "the supply plan of materials must be decided democratically, and the state should not interfere with it"; (2) "commodities in great demand must be given first to privately owned businesses, then to collectively owned businesses, and lastly to state-owned businesses"; (3) "the business tax must be based on self-appraisal, not on collective appraisal or the decision of the tax officials"; and (4) "taxes must be reduced at times of hardship, and the amounts should be decided by ourselves."[102]

*Workers from Small Handicraft Factories*

Related to the split between the skilled and unskilled workers was the division between the big state-owned factories and the small handicraft factories. For example, of 270 workers in a small factory under the jurisdiction of the handicraft department of Harbin Municipality, 170 workers (63 percent) belonged to the radical organization, whereas twelve of seventeen Party members belonged to the conservatives.[103] In contrast to the dominance of the radicals in the small handicraft factories, the conservative organizations were strong in the big factories in the Canton area. (See Table 5.)

Although not sufficient proof by itself, the fact that the conservatives very often used the names of the big factories seems to indicate that they were strong there. The Harbin conservatives, for instance, claimed that they represented workers of sixteen state-owned factories in Harbin.[104] When the conflict between the unskilled laborers in the small factories and the skilled workers in the big factories developed into armed conflict, it took the form of territorial fighting in Canton: the conservatives in the suburban areas, where many new big factories were concentrated, tried to blockade the radicals controlling downtown Canton.[105]

In addition to the sociological and economic factors that contributed to the dissatisfaction of the unskilled and individual laborers and workers in the handicraft workshops, a political factor contributed to their radicalism. In general, the political control in small factories was weaker than in larger factories. For example, the above-mentioned handicraft factories in Harbin had 18 Party members out of 270 workers (6.7 percent), whereas in the big factories, according to Barry Richman, Party membership ran to about 10 to 15 percent.[106]

101. *Chieh-fang jih-pao,* 7 March 1967.
102. Ibid.
103. *JMJP,* 15 February 1967. In Canton a small factory with 600 workers is reported to be a stronghold of the radicals. *515 chan-pao,* 29 September 1967.
104. *Tung-feng chan-pao,* 9 December 1967.
105. *Hung-se pao-tung,* 22 August 1967.
106. *JMJP,* 15 February 1967; Barry M. Richman, *Industrial Society in China,* (New York: Random House, 1968), p. 762.

Table 5. *Ratio of Radical and Conservative Workers in*
*Kwangtung Big Industries (%)***

|  | Total workers | Militia department | Political department | Middle-level cadres | Basic-level cadres |
|---|---|---|---|---|---|
|  | EW/RF | EW/RF | EW/RF | EW/RF | EW/RF |
| Canton Heavy Duty Plan | 75/25 | 100/0 | 100/0 | 50/50 | 55/45 |
| Canton Iron and Steel Works | 70/30 | 100/0 | 90/10 | 100/0 | 80/20 |
| Canton Paper Mill | 54/46 | 100/0 | 79/21 | 67/33 | 73/27 |
| Canton Shipbuilding Yard | 79/21 | 100/0 | 94/6 | — | — |
| Canton Nitrogenous Fertilizer Plant | 69/31 | 100/0 | — | 50/50 | 80/20 |
| Whampao Shipbuilding Yard | 62/38 | 100/0 | 93/7 | 100/0 | 77/23 |
| Canton Cement Plant | 75/25 | 50/50 | 90/10 | 60/40 | 89/11 |
| Canton Municipal Electric Supply Company | 75/25 | 100/0 | 94/6 | 100/0 | 84/16 |
| Canton Municipal Water Supply Company | 70/30 | 100/0 | 94/6 | 83/17 | 67/33 |
| Canton Satin and Hemp Mill | — | 100/0 | 79/21 | — | — |

EW = East Wind Faction (conservative)
RF = Red Flag Faction (radical)
   *Source: Kuang-chou kung-jen,* no. 34 (in SCMP, no. 4208), and no. 38. These figures were
compiled by the radicals, and if there is any bias, it would be against East Wind.

Also, in the small handicraft factories, the influence of the political
department, the militia department, and the labor union was weaker than in
the big factories. In the big factories, the three organizations served as
transmission belts for the Party committees' sponsored mobilization and
continued to protect the Party organization. The Kwangtung Provincial
Party Committee, for instance, used the labor unions to mobilize workers in
the factories and to oppose the closing down of the *Yang ch'eng wan-pao* in
December 1960.

The political and militia departments were closely related to the PLA even
before the Cultural Revolution. Political departments were established in
1962 in imitation of the control system used in the PLA to insure Party
control, and in many cases were staffed with PLA personnel. Militia departments were under the joint control of the factory Party committees and the

PLA. When the PLA moved into the Cultural Revolution, taking over responsibility from the Party committees and exercising it in the form of military control committees, it naturally relied on these departments, whose members could claim mass status even though they were close to the locus of power in the factories. As a result, the radical workers complained:

In the Cultural Revolution, all the important members of the political department and all the important political and functional cadres of the Party and mass organizations were the high-ranking staff of a certain organization [the East Wind] of every factory, and they manipulated and split the working class for the power holders taking the capitalist road in the Party.[107]

*Other Characteristics of the Radicals:*

The available data on the workers' social background is sparser than the data on the students' social background. However, in the Kwangtung Pearl River Film Studio, it was reported that the radicals consisted of workers from bourgeois, petty bourgeois, overseas Chinese, small landlord, and rich peasant backgrounds.[108] The radical organization of the Harbin handicraft factory discussed above was reputed to be composed of workers from "bad" family backgrounds, and the organization itself admitted that it included seventy-five workers who were politically "most backward."[109]

Although it is open to dispute whether the workers from bourgeois backgrounds constituted the most disadvantaged groups among the Chinese workers, what appears to be conclusive is that workers located outside the locus of power formed the radical groups. The radicals in the Harbin automobile factory described their own position in the factory in the following way:

All those who joined the Red Rebel Corps were those workers called "bad eggs," and they were suppressed by the power holders taking the capitalist road. They were not given any rights beside the right to work. But those who joined the conservative organization, except for the hoodwinked masses, were the ones favored by the power holders. . . . From the beginning, the Red Rebel Corps firmly directed the attack against the small handful of power holders within the Party.[110]

It seems that those workers who could not get along with the Party committees joined the radical faction. According to a conservative charge,

107. *Kuang-chou kung-jen,* no. 34 (n.d.). The model workers and "master" workers tended to join the conservative organizations. "Model Workers Should Stand at the Forefront of the GPCR," *Hung ch'i,* no. 2 (16 January 1967), p. 44; *Hung-se tsao-fan pao,* 25 January 1967. The radicals denounced the model workers as "worker aristocracy." *Hung-se tsao-fan pao,* 25 January 1967.
108. Wang Ch'ao, *Kwangtung tien-ying-chieh te tsao-fan-che,* (Hong Kong: Chung-pao chou-kan, 1969), p. 16.
109. *JMJP,* 15 February 1967.
110. *JMJP,* 19 February 1967.

only 800 out of 45,000 workers joined the radical faction (Bombard faction) in the Harbin First Weapons Factory, and 450 persons (51.8 percent) out of 800 radicals had "various problems" *(ke chung wen ti).*[111] The leadership of the radical faction consisted of seven persons: the former Party first secretary who was purged in the Socialist Education Movement; one worker who was attacked as a rightist in 1957; two temporary workers; one engineer who came from a capitalist family; one office worker who was criticized in the Socialist Education Movement; and one worker who was without any "problem."

In contrast, the leadership of the conservative faction included fifty-four Party members and seven CYL members.[112] Understandably, the radicals supported only twenty-four cadres, all of whom had been maligned in the Socialist Education Movement, while attacking 81 percent of the foremen and most of the Party cadres.[113] It seems likely that the radicals concentrated their attacks on the Party cadres rather than on management.

In terms of age, the radical organizations tended to contain younger members than the conservative groups. Younger workers were generally apprentices, unskilled laborers, and contract workers. The average age of the four hundred contract workers in one factory is reported to have been twenty-four, whereas the average age of the Canton Ti-tsung was thirty or more.[114] As the Chinese society had consolidated its revolutionary gains, the Party had become bureaucratized, filling the leadership positions with the older age groups. Thus, the younger age groups of workers found themselves in an increasingly disadvantageous position in competition for jobs and promotions. Emphasis on skill and expertise reinforced the seniority system that discriminated against the younger age groups. In addition to this narrowing upward mobility for the younger age groups, idealism, the effects of the shared socialization process, and the subjective factors that Mannheim has characterized as common "historical experience" probably also contributed to the radicalism of the younger Chinese workers.

The revolt of the discontented workers started in earnest in early December when the contract and temporary workers formed their own organization, the Rebel Headquarters of the Nationwide Red Workers, and collectively bargained with the Ministry of Labor to redress their grievances. Initially, the Ministry of Labor agreed that the revolt was a revolutionary action and the workers' demands legitimate, but later the Ministry revoked its concessions. Consequently, the contract and temporary workers took their case to the Cultural Revolution Small Group.

111. *Tung-feng chan-pao,* 17 October 1967.
112. Ibid.
113. Ibid.
114. *Lao-tung chan-pao,* 3 February 1968; "Factionalism in Kwangtung: Comments of a Disillusioned Canton 'Radical.' " (Interview with a former Red Guard).

Denouncing the contract worker system as Liu Shao-ch'i's scheme "to save wages as in the capitalist system," the Small Group supported the workers' revolt against the system and encouraged them to revolt against the Federation of Labor Unions.[115] At the meeting, Chiang Ch'ing ordered the Labor Minister and the General Secretary of Labor Unions to issue the following instructions: (1) all the contract and temporary workers should be allowed to participate in the Cultural Revolution, and they should not be discriminated against; and (2) those workers who were fired after June 1, 1966, should be allowed to return to their original units, and their salaries should be paid retroactively.[116]

The principal issue at this time was "rampant economism," which was officially defined as

economic bribery to corrupt the revolutionary will of the masses in order to direct the political struggle of the masses to the road of capitalism. That is to say, it wants the proletariat to struggle for a small increase of wages and better welfare, to pay one-sided attention to temporary interests at the expense of long-term fundamental interests of the proletariat, and to neglect the political struggle for realizing socialism and communism.[117]

To be sure, the Party organization was responsible for economism. When the Party leader in industry came under attack, and their methods of mobilizing the conservative workers were openly denounced, they made unconditional concessions to the grievances of the workers by abandoning whatever responsibility they had had. Subscribing to the idea that "economic problems can be set free, and the wage scale can be attacked,"[118] the Party leadership suddenly changed course from its excessive concern with production to an excessive concern with the economic well-being of the workers. A Red Guard newspaper charged:

Those power holders taking the capitalist road and doggedly sticking to the bourgeois reactionary line toyed with the various tactics to undermine the guideline: "Grasp the revolution and stimulate production." At the beginning of the campaign, in the name of grasping production, they repressed the revolutionary masses. Now, at a time when the masses are breaking through the various barriers created by them and rising in rebellion, again in the name of showing concern for people's livelihood and improving their livelihood, they are providing material incentives and corroding the revolutionary will of the workers by means of revisionist tactics such as additional wages and amnesties.[119]

115. "The Record of the CRSG's Interview with the Representatives of the National Red Labor Corps," 26 December 1966.
116. Ibid.
117. "Oppose Economism and Smash the Latest Counterattack by the Bourgeois Reactionary Line," *Hung ch'i*, no. 2 (16 January 1967), pp. 19-21.
118. Ibid.
119. *Hung-se tsao-fan-che*, 21 February 1967.

This charge is partially valid; but the Maoists' tactics had also contributed to the economism. In contrast to Lenin's warning that the workers' movement, when left alone, would go toward trade unionism, the Maoists displayed an almost mystical faith in the political consciousness of the workers, and therefore demanded their free mobilization. Not surprisingly, the freely mobilized workers raised economic demands. In addition, the Cultural Revolution Small Group manipulated the grievances of the workers for its own purposes, particularly the grievances of the disadvantaged groups. The factory Party leaders went one step further than the Small Group by inciting the discontented workers to raise specific economic demands and then making concessions to those demands.

Whoever was primarily responsible for the rise of economism, it paralyzed the Chinese economy and plunged the entire society into chaos. In the communes, the peasants divided among themselves the "communal reserves, public accumulations, and funds earmarked for next year's production."[120] In the factories, the wages and grades were raised, and back wages, bonuses, and sometimes even back bonuses were paid.[121] The Party committees freely distributed travel expenses so that the workers could go wherever they wanted. Seventy thousand workers left their work posts in the Ta-ch'ing oil field to exchange their revolutionary experiences.[122] High-ranking cadres also left their work posts, putting away technical data and specifications.

Particularly susceptible to economism were the apprentice workers. According to one report, the Number Three Steel Mill of Shanghai paid each apprentice worker three months' wages in advance, plus 250 yuan in cash, and encouraged them to go out for revolutionary exchanges.[123] As each side pinned the blame for economism on the other, the conservative and the radical workers staged strikes and counter-strikes, thereby bringing transportation, water, and electrical services to a halt.

The rise of economism and the resultant paralysis of the Chinese economy left Mao with only two options: to step up the attack on the Party organization or to capitulate to the pressure of the Party organization by restoring its leadership. Confronted with this difficult choice, Mao chose the former course, pushing the Cultural Revolution one step closer to power seizure. As a countermeasure to economism, he removed the boundaries between the students and the workers and used the students, who were less susceptible to economism, to dissuade the workers from raising economic demands. In so doing, Mao turned the pressure on him to his own advantage, like a brilliant commanding general.

120. *JMJP,* 19 January 1967; 27 January 1967.
121. *JMJP,* 14 January 1967.
122. *Tsu kuo,* no. 70 (January 1967), p. 3.
123. "Money Cannot Divert the Revolutionary Will," *Hung ch'i,* no. 2 (16 January 1967), p. 34.

# CHAPTER 5

# The January Power Seizure

Undoubtedly, the January Power Seizure was a unique event not only in Chinese political history but also in the history of mankind, for in this period a so-called totalitarian regime governing a quarter of the world's population ordered its people to seize power from itself for the sake of revolution. The January Power Seizure was the most daring undertaking Mao ever attempted, whether or not he really intended to let the power remain in the hands of the masses.

Most of the Party members, government leaders, and cadres—who had previously wielded enormous political power and been admired even outside of China for their ability to exercise this power—submitted themselves to the judgment of the masses without putting up much open resistance to Mao, although they devised all kinds of ingenious means to survive the storm. For the masses themselves, who had been widely credited with being submissive to authority (whether because of their cultural tradition or the strict regimentation that the regime imposed), it was a drastic moment as they rose up to seize power in their own hands.

During this turbulent period, all the Chinese leaders—except Mao and Lin Piao—came under open criticism. Aside from Liu Shao-ch'i and Teng Hsiao-p'ing, the fates of T'ao Chu and Wang Jen-chung were sealed, and all the regional and provincial Party leaders were attacked. Many top PLA leaders, such as Chu Teh, Ho Lung, and Yeh Chien-ying, were publicly denounced by the mass organizations. Among the government officials, Ch'en I, Nieh Jung-chen, Li Hsien-nien, Li Fu-ch'un, T'an Chen-lin, Yü Ch'iu-li, and almost all the other ministers were attacked by the radicals. Even Chou En-lai was attacked, in one instance by a fifteen-foot-long big-character poster put up on Tienanmen Square. Nor was the Cultural Revolution Small Group spared from public criticism: the conservative mass organizations opposed the radical policies of the Small Group; the moderates were confused over the Small Group's "calling for this and that"; and the radicals resented manipulation of the mass organizations by any elite group.

Relative to the prestige and power of the other political groups, however, those of the Small Group reached an all-time high in January. It even publicly defended Chou En-lai from mass attack, after which Chou took a subservient attitude by extolling the Small Group as the "Chief of Staff" of Mao's proletarian headquarters, and by referring condescendingly to the State Council as a mere administrative branch.[1] In a public speech on January 10, Ch'en Po-ta rendered authoritative but summary judgment on the publicly attacked government officials, denouncing T'ao Chu, Lü Cheng-ts'ao (the Minister of Railways), and Liu Chih-chien (the head of the All Army Cultural Revolution Small Group). At the end of his speech, he arrogantly asked Chou En-lai whether he had any more persons to protect.[2]

Yet, the January Power Seizure cost the Cultural Revolution Small Group its internal cohesion. Among its members, K'ang Sheng, Hsieh Fu-chih, and Chang Ch'un-ch'iao displayed moderation—the first two probably because of their close ties with the Establishment, and the third because of his newly acquired task of governing Shanghai. Kuan Feng and Wang Li reportedly derided Hsieh Fu-chih as a man "for compromise and mixing."[3] Ch'en Po-ta was compelled to deny the rumor that the Small Group had split up and compromised its ideological principles for political gains.[4]

How did such an extraordinary event take place? Was it spontaneous or manipulated? No doubt there were both elements. The inherent dynamics of the student movement provided the background for the eventual power seizure. The Maoist leaders manipulated the already explosive situation by removing the boundaries between the workers and the students. The 1967 New Year editorials of *Jen-min jih-pao* and *Hung ch'i* called for the "worker-peasants" to "boldly launch the struggle and to overthrow power holders in factories, mines, and rural areas," and declared "the integration of revolutionary intellectuals with worker-peasant masses an objective law."[5] Once the workers joined the students in revolt, the masses became powerful enough to push the Cultural Revolution into the stage of power seizure. Thus, as Mao observed, "the intellectuals and the broad masses of young students started the criticism and repudiation of the bourgeois reactionary line, but the workers accomplished the January Power Seizure."[6]

1. Chao Ts'ung, *Wen-ko yün-tung li-ch'eng shu-lüeh* (Hong Kong: Yu-lien yen-chiu-so, 1974), vol. 2, p. 454.
2. Ibid., p. 446.
3. *Tung-feng p'ing-lun*, March 1968.
4. *Hsin pei-ta*, 29 February 1967.
5. *JMJP*, 1 January 1967.
6. "A Talk by Chairman Mao to Foreign Visitors," *SCMP*, no. 4200 (18 June 1968), pp. 1-6.

Following "the law of revolutionary development," Mao allowed the maximum possible freedom to the masses in January while he searched for a workable formula of power seizure. His strategy was first to let events take their own course and then to select a "model" which he could adopt as official policy and give back to the masses to follow. The January Power Seizure therefore proceeded without much guidance from the Center. The few restraints that the Center imposed in January were primarily intended to maintain a minimum of civil order.

Exempted from attack, the PLA was given the task of safeguarding broadcast stations, confidential state materials, prisons, warehouses, harbors, bridges, and civilian aviation facilities.[7] The public security organs were ordered to watch out for criminal activities and proven counterrevolutionaries,[8] and the masses were warned against economism.[9] Except for these few controls, the masses were completely free during January of 1967 to take whatever measures necessary for the seizure of power. That the Chinese political system survived such a strenuous test seems to indicate its viability and strength, even though the scheme of the power seizure did not work out as its planners had wanted.

Since the January Power Seizure took place all over China at all levels of the government and the Party, it is impossible to discuss all its aspects here. Therefore, we will limit our discussion to the following three points: the Shanghai power seizure that ignited the power seizures in other areas; the emerging differences between Chou En-lai and the Cultural Revolution Small Group over the concrete strategy of power seizure; and why and in what sense the January Power Seizure failed.

## The Shanghai Power Seizure

The power seizure in Shanghai derived from and was the culmination of the confrontation between the conservative Scarlet Red Guards and the radical Workers' General Headquarters.[10] In the last days of December, the Scarlet Red Guards successfully pressured the Shanghai Party Committee into signing its eight-point demands. However, the Committee soon revoked the agreement because of vehement condemnation by the radicals. Outraged by the cancellation, the Scarlet Red Guards staged a protest demonstration, but the radicals physically assaulted them.

7. *Chung-kung wen-hua ta ko-ming chung-yao wen-chien hui-pien* (Taipei: Chung-kung Yen-chiu, 1973), p. 89.

8. Ibid., pp. 59-63.

9. *CCP Documents of the Great Proletarian Cultural Revolution* (Hong Kong: Union Research Institute, 1968), pp. 173-174.

10. For the Shanghai Red Guard and Worker movement leading up to the January Power Seizure, see Neal Hunter, *Shanghai Journal* (New York: Praeger, 1969).

On December 31, the Scarlet Red Guards set off for Peking to file their complaints with the leaders of the Center. Again, the radicals intercepted them, this time in Kunshan, a small town thirty miles from Shanghai, and forced them to return to Shanghai. This clash between the two large workers' organizations (each claimed half a million members) resulted in economic chaos and dislocation. "The Municipal Party Committee had been paralyzed. Many factories, including vital industrial plants, had stopped production. . . . The piers and railway stations were immobilized, causing dislocation."[11]

Meanwhile, the rebel faction of the Shanghai *Wen-hui-pao* sent their delegate to Peking and obtained Chou's approval of their plan to take over control of the newspaper. On January 5, after seizing the newspaper, the rebels published "The Letter to the People of the Whole Municipality" under the names of eleven revolutionary rebel organizations.[12] Denouncing the conservative mass organizations as "pawns" of the handful of power holders and as the "initiators" of economic chaos in Shanghai, the "Letter" demanded that the Scarlet Red Guards return to their work posts for production. The next day, the Shanghai rebels held a mass rally to denounce the Shanghai Party Committee and requested the Central Committee of the CCP to reorganize the Party Committee completely.[13]

The Peking leadership at first hesitated to endorse the seizure of the *Wen-hui-pao*, but Mao intervened personally in support of the rebels.[14] On January 9, the *Jen-min jih-pao* reprinted the "Letter" with its own note of endorsement. Calling for a "vigorous counteroffensive upon the bourgeois reactionary line," the note urged the cadres to revolt and other areas to follow the lead of Shanghai.[15] This endorsement finally removed the distinction between the authority of the government and that of the mass organizations and convinced the latter that they could exercise the authority hitherto reserved solely for the Party committees.

On January 9, encouraged by the support of the Center, thirty-two Shanghai rebel organizations published an "Urgent Notice" suggesting ten concrete measures to fight economic chaos in Shanghai.[16] Among their recommendations were the freezing of wages, retrieval of the funds provided for the exchange of experience, and punishment for violations of the measures. The tone of the "Urgent Notice" sounded more like a government order than an

11. *Kuang-ying hung-ch'i*, 23 November 1967.
12. *Wen-hui-pao*, 5 January 1967.
13. Hunter, *Shanghai Journal*, p. 218.
14. Chao Ts'ung *Wen-ko yün-tung li-ch'eng shu-lüeh*, vol. 2, p. 452; "Speech at a Meeting of the Cultural Revolution Group under the Central Committee," *CB*, no. 892 (21 October 1969), pp. 47-48. *Tsao-fan*, 15 January 1967.
15. *JMJP*, 9 January 1967.
16. *Wen-hui-pao*, 9 January 1967.

appeal to a rival mass organization. This time, the response from the Center came even faster than before. On January 11, the *Jen-min jih-pao* widely publicized greetings from the Central Committee of the CCP, the State Council, the Military Affairs Commission, and the Cultural Revolution Small Group, which praised the action of the Shanghai rebels as a brilliant example for the working classes.[17]

On January 9, when the Center expressed its approval of the "Letter," the rebel workers took over the Control Office of the Shanghai Railway Bureau and proceeded to put the railway system into action. Workers with some technical experience were placed to supervise the technical personnel, the train conductors were sought out and persuaded to return to work, and students were mobilized to man the ticket booths and entry points to the train platforms.[18] The report of a Hsin-Hua News Agency correspondent graphically describes the composition of the rebel workers and their spontaneous effort to reopen the railway system:

The establishment of a new revolutionary order required an enormous amount of organization, and this was all done by those who had formerly been looked down upon as "nobodies," such as train conductors, engine drivers, switchmen, signal men, and ticket inspectors. The leaders of the railway rebel organization are ordinary bench-workers, who were branded as "counterrevolutionary" for writing the first posters to expose the Party people in authority in the factory.[19]

When the Center sanctioned the "Urgent Notice" on January 11, the rebels expanded their power seizure to take over the whole Shanghai Railway Bureau, and soon the railway system began to move again.[20]

The power seizure followed similar patterns in other fields: the rebel workers organized various production committees that simply took over the functions of management. In the Shanghai docks, thousands of student volunteers helped the rebel workers to unload the cargo, sometimes working sixteen- to twenty-four-hour shifts. To coordinate the city-wide economic activities the rebels set up the "Fire Line Committee," which consisted of fifty members nominated by the workers in various factories, the municipal economic bureau, and the universities.[21] The Committee functioned as the highest decision-making organ for the Shanghai economy, concentrating its efforts on restoring economic order and production.

On January 14, *Wen-hui-pao* for the first time used the term "power

    17. *JMJP*, 12 January 1967.
    18. NCNA, 9 February 1967; *JMJP*, 15 January 1967.
    19. "On the Power Seizure of Proletarian Revolutionaries," *Hung ch'i*, no. 3 (1 February 1967), pp. 13-18.
    20. NCNA, 9 February 1967; *JMJP*, 15 January 1967.
    21. NCNA, 10 February 1967.

seizure" in the context of encouraging the workers to take over control of factories for production.[22] By that time, the rebels were already parading the Party leaders at the various levels through the streets, and what was left of the city administration was completely crippled. Thus, the workers' take-over of the factories led to the de facto power seizure of the Shanghai Municipality. Chang Ch'un-ch'iao confirmed that the combined effects of the workers' spontaneous initiative and the Center's post facto support of their action led the Shanghai Cultural Revolution to the power seizure:

In the early stage of the "seizure of power" in Shanghai, we never thought of the "capture of power," nor did we use the words "January Revolution." . . . We just proceeded in the main from the Party spirit with no thought of factionalism. This is because we saw with our own eyes the stoppage of work in the industrial plants, and the piers were in such a state of paralysis that foreign vessels entering Shanghai harbor were unable to load or unload cargos. . . . We submitted a report to the Center . . . and Chairman Mao endorsed our actions, telling us that the "seizure of power" was wholly necessary and correct. This is how we came to use the term "seizure of power," as suggested by Chairman Mao.[23]

Probably deeply impressed by the Shanghai workers' movement, the Center finally adopted power seizure as an official policy on January 22.[24] On February 5, thirty-eight Shanghai rebel groups under the leadership of Chang Ch'un-ch'iao announced the formation of the Shanghai People's Commune with a steering committee as its highest organ. Aside from Chang Ch'un-ch'iao and Yao Wen-yuan, the committee was dominated by repre-sentatives of the mass organizations: five representatives for the workers, two each for the peasants and the PLA, and one each for the Red Guards and the revolutionary cadres.[25] When the Shanghai People's Commune changed its name to the Shanghai Revolutionary Committee, on February 24, power shifted back to the cadres and the PLA. The new leadership consisted of five representatives of the revolutionary cadres, six representatives of the PLA, and only one representative (Wang Hung-wen) of the mass organizations.[26]

Thereafter Chang Ch'un-ch'iao handled the delicate task of rebuilding the new power structure, using a mixed method of coercion and persuasion. He could afford to use coercion because he controlled the Workers' General Headquarters, the largest mass organization in Shanghai, through his loyal lieutenant Wang Hung-wen (a middle-level cadre from the Shanghai Seven-teenth Textile Mill). *Wen-hui-pao* served as his loyal propaganda machine.

22. *Wen-hui-pao*, 14 January 1967.
23. *Kuang-ying hung-ch'i*, 23 November 1967.
24. *JMJP*, 22 January 1967.
25. Chao Ts'ung, *Wen-ko yün-tung li-ch'eng shu-lüeh*, vol. 2, p. 505. Also see *Wen-hui-pao*, 5, 6, and 7 February 1967.
26. Chao Ts'ung, p. 511.

The new Shanghai leadership headed by Chang Ch'un-ch'iao and Yao Wen-yuan survived numerous challenges, thus making Shanghai the most successful case of power seizure.

Nevertheless, Chang Ch'un-ch'iao had his share of political opponents in Shanghai. Opposition to him came not from the conservatives but from the radicals who had supported him up to January 1967. The anti-Chang forces in Shanghai consisted of three groups: (1) the Revolutionary Committee, a student organization that had collaborated closely with the Workers' General Headquarters to bring down the Shanghai Party Committee; (2) the Workers' Second Regiment and the Workers' Third Headquarters, the two splinter groups of the Workers' General Headquarters; and (3) the Red Flag Army, the demobilized soldiers' organization, which merged with the Workers' Second Regiment and the Workers' Third Headquarters when the Center disbanded the nationwide organization of the Red Flag Army. These three groups were well-known rebel organizations whose contribution to bringing down the Shanghai conservative forces was readily acknowledged by their critics.[27]

There is not enough data to positively ascertain why these three groups challenged Chang Ch'un-ch'iao. However, it is very likely that the following three factors, separately or together, engendered the split between Chang and his former allies. First, there was the element of power struggle and ideological difference. Some rebels justifiably felt that Chang was unfair in assuming the powers of the former Shanghai Party Committee, which they had brought down. Or they might have seriously believed the Cultural Revolution Small Group's rhetoric that it was the masses who were going to seize the power. Whatever their motivation, some rebels rejected Chang on the ground that he was a member of the Establishment. Their distrust of Chang was further enhanced by his moderate stands on controversial issues such as the great alliance, the liberation of the cadres, and the treatment of the masses who had been "hoodwinked" by the power holders. Chang made no distinction between "those who revolted early and those who revolted later" and absorbed many former members of the Scarlet Red Guards into the Workers' General Headquarters, sometimes in high positions.[28]

This political and ideological explanation seems to be especially valid for the members of the Red Revolutionary Committee, the student anti-Chang group. Naively believing the rhetoric of the Small Group that the masses would determine the fate of the cadres, they attempted to capture Hsü Ching-hsien, the former director of the Shanghai Writers' Union, who had "suddenly changed sides" a month before and started to work as Chang's main speech-writer and propagandist. Their attempted kidnapping was

27. For the organizations opposed to Chang, see Hunter, *Shanghai Journal*, pp. 222-243.
28. Ibid., p. 265.

spoiled, however, by the direct intervention of the PLA. The outraged students renewed their challenge to Chang by organizing an "Oath-Taking Rally to Bombard Chang Ch'un-ch'iao."[29]

An equally plausible explanation for the students' rejection of Chang's leadership is that Chang and the Revolutionary Committee differed on how to treat the bourgeois intellectuals: the Red Revolutionary Committee, reportedly consisting of children of the workers, wanted to attack the bourgeois intellectuals, while Chang tried to protect them, particularly those personally close to him. Later, Chang's opponents even collected materials reportedly bearing witness to the fact that Chang had once surrendered to the Kuomintang.[30]

The second possible factor was "factionalism." Chang himself blamed factionalism for the rebels' challenge to him:

At the mention of "power seizure," we found the resultant evils of factionalism. . . . When people were subjected to oppression and branded as "counterrevolutionary," they hardly noticed these evils. But once the movement for the seizure of power came, some people became obsessed with selfishness and the "mountain stronghold mentality."[31]

Certainly, "mountaintop-ism" and a "small-group mentality" surfaced among the mass organizations that fought together against the common enemy, when the time came to distribute the spoils. Nevertheless, factionalism does not explain why Chang supported the Workers' General Headquarters over the other rebel forces, thus pushing the latter to be his opponents.

This leads us to the third possible reason: that Chang could not tolerate some rebel organizations composed of the discontented groups who attempted to have their grievances redressed. Very likely, the Second Regiment was an organization of manual laborers—"coolies"—of the Shanghai Railway Bureau.[32] If that was the case, it is not surprising that the Second Regiment did not see any hope of having their grievances redressed if Chang rose to a position of leadership and Shanghai returned to normalcy. The anti-Chang forces therefore continued to instigate the masses to struggle against the basic-level cadres and to demand the return of rusticated youth to the urban areas.

Whatever their reasons were for revolting, the anti-Chang forces formed the New Shanghai People's Commune to challenge Chang's Shanghai People's Commune, and they sent their delegation to Peking to present their

29. *Hung-se tsao-fan pao,* 4 February 1967.

30. Lynn White, "Leadership in Shanghai," in Robert Scalapino, ed., *Elites in the People's Republic of China* (University of Washington Press, Seattle, 1972), pp. 363-364.

31. *Kuang-ying hung-ch'i,* 23 November 1967.

32. *Kung-jen tsao-fan pao,* 13 March 1967.

case against Chang. Through 1967 and even early 1968, these anti-Chang forces continued to put up big-character posters denouncing Chang for spreading the doctrine of the extinction of the class struggle, for supporting capitalist and rightist elements, for attacking "revolutionaries," and for advocating an "independent kingdom in Shanghai."[33]

Despite all this, Chang managed to consolidate his power base in Shanghai. Several factors accounted for his success. First, the policies that he pursued after the January Power Seizure were quite practical. Once Chang took over the power and responsibility of governing the largest city in China, he found it unavoidable to moderate his previous revolutionary rhetoric. In order to obtain the help and cooperation of the Shanghai bureaucrats, Chang restrained the masses from attacking the low-ranking cadres and carried out the policy of "liberating the revolutionary cadres" in earnest.[34]

On the other hand, Chang refused to liberate cadres who revolted on account of their personal grudges.[35] He stood firmly against the rusticated youth and temporary and contract workers.[36] To impose a "proletarian revolutionary discipline," he did not hesitate to use the Public Security Force and the PLA against the dissenting mass organizations.[37] He handled such complicated issues as the problem of class background, rehabilitation, and the liberation of the cadres on a case-by-case basis rather than categorically. By doing so, he avoided the convulsive swing from one extreme to another that the large-scale mass movement tended to generate and stood firmly against the "bad elements" and "class enemies" who displayed "ultra-leftist" tendencies, as well as against the conservatives.

Second, although Chang suppressed his political opponents regardless of whether they were ultra-leftists or conservatives, his methods of dealing with the ultra-leftists were mild compared with those of the PLA leaders. As a well-known radical, Chang felt sympathetic toward the disadvantaged social groups. But at the same time he was aware that China's reality could not fulfill the revolutionary ideals of all the aggrieved social groups. As an intellectual engaged in the propaganda field, he knew very well the delicate dilemma posed by the issues of "class origin" and "class consciousness." For these reasons he resisted the conservatives' attempts to attack

33. Lynn White, "Leadership in Shanghai," pp. 359-360.
34. *Wen-hui-pao,* 4, 5, 9, 16, and 21 February 1967.
35. *Wen-hui-pao,* 10 February 1967.
36. *Wen-hui-pao,* 15 and 16 January 1967. *Wen-hui-pao* supported the temporary and contract workers in the struggle to abolish the system in January. *(Wen-hui-pao,* 6 January 1967). But when the Center issued an order prohibiting the formation of a contract and temporary workers organization, Shanghai moved immediately to carry out the order. (Shanghai Broadcast Station, 28 February 1967, 9:00 P.M.) For the problem of rusticated youth in Shanghai, see *Wen-hui-pao,* 18 January, 9 and 19 February 1967. *Wen-hui-pao* also attacked the "guild mentality." *Wen-hui-pao,* 11 March 1967.
37. *Wen-hui-pao,* 1 March 1967.

all the bourgeoisie, as well as the radicals' attempts to indisciminately attack all the Party cadres.

Third, Chang's credentials as a revolutionary leader during the Cultural Revolution were impressive. As a member of the old Shanghai Municipal Party Committee and as a deputy head of the Cultural Revolution Small Group, he was best qualified to lead the new Shanghai power structure. He had directed the Shanghai mass movement, at first from behind the scenes and later publicly, since his handling of the Anting incident.[38] It seems very likely that he was behind the revolt of the *Wen-hui-pao* and the Workers' General Headquarters' challenge to the Scarlet Red Guards, as well as the fight against economism.[39]

Fourth, because of his impeccable status as a key member of Mao's entourage, he could confidently expect the allegiance of the Shanghai bureaucrats and could thus balance spontaneity and discipline without fearing attack from either the conservatives or the radicals. Despite the rebels' challenge, Chang continued to enjoy Mao's support. To Mao, Chang was exercising his leadership and power correctly, especially in purging the undesirable tendencies of the radicals while utilizing their revolutionary enthusiasm for the purpose of making revolution.

In the last part of 1967, Chang and his Shanghai Revolutionary Committee were given the task of experimenting with the reconstruction of the Party organization and with the campaign to rectify class ranks. In carrying out these experiments, he again balanced two contradictory sets of considerations: enlisting the rebels into the Party organization while rehabilitating "good" Party members, and purging "bad" bourgeoisie while protecting "good" bourgeoisie.[40]

On the whole, Chang attempted to maintain a balance between revolution and production, discipline and freedom, and leadership from the top and mass spontaneity from the bottom. This might have been a shrewd, purely politically calculated tactical move. Or, like Mao, perhaps Chang was genuinely concerned with balancing revolutionary ideals with realistic politics. Whatever his true motives might have been, his policy line was quite practical and sensible. In addition, his revolutionary record in the preceding stage of the Cultural Revolution, his skillful manipulation of the Shanghai mass organizations, and his strong support from Mao enabled him to successfully carry out the January Power Seizure, thus helping him to emerge as one of the most influential political figures after the Cultural Revolution.

---

38. On November 9, 1966, Shanhai radical workers commandeered a train to go to Peking to file their complaints with the Peking leaders. Chang Ch'un-ch'iao came to Anting, where the commandeered train stopped, and signed the list of worker's demands.

39. *Kuang-ying hung-ch'i,* 23 November 1967.

40. *Wen-ko t'ung-hsin,* July 1968; *Tung-fang-hung pao,* July 1968.

Although the January Power Seizure started in Shanghai, that city was an atypical case, riper for power seizure than any other area in China. First of all, Shanghai is the largest and most industrialized city in China, with more real capitalists, bourgeoisie, and workers than any other place in China.[41] These antagonistic classes had successfully collaborated in the period of socialist transformation, and the experience had helped them to be politically mature and sophisticated.

Second, Shanghai was the stronghold of the Maoists and the most politically advanced area in China. Mao's close friend K'o Ch'ing-shih had led the Shanghai Party Committee for a long time until his death in 1965, and it was in Shanghai that the Maoist leaders had launched the Cultural Revolution by publishing Yao's criticism of Wu Han. Even the Shanghai Municipal Party Committee had steered the Cultural Revolution more skillfully than any other area Party committee. Consequently, the division between the conservative and the radical mass organizations followed not the class line of "red categories" versus "black categories" or the well-to-do versus the disadvantaged groups, but the more political line of opposition or support for the Party Committee, and this worked to the advantage of the Maoist leaders.

Third, the rebel forces were strong and were led by workers rather than students. The direct confrontation between the conservative and radical workers had completely discredited the Scarlet Red Guards, thus drastically weakening the conservative forces to such an extent that they could not regroup themselves as an organized force.

Fourth, and most important, Shanghai had readily available alternative leadership in the person of Chang Ch'un-ch'iao.

To summarize, then, despite some shortcomings in the Shanghai experience—for example, the premature adoption of the Commune formula—Shanghai was a successful case of power seizure, thanks to the strong political consciousness of the workers and the skillful leadership of Chang Ch'un-ch'iao, who combined revolutionary zeal with pragmatic calculations and maintained good relations with the Peking leaders. In a sense, one can say that the mass movement in Shanghai met the two most important requirements for success: mobilization both from "the bottom to the top" and from "the top to the bottom," the two conditions absolutely necessary for balancing revolution and order, and for harnessing the energy generated by the mass mobilization in the desired direction.

## Two Different Strategies of Power Seizure

It was inevitable for the complicated process of power seizure to raise many specific questions on which the Chinese leaders had to make decisions. The

41. Lynn White, "Leadership in Shanghai."

basic questions concerning power seizure were which organs were to be seized, which organs were to be exempted, how to proceed with the seizures, what the new power structure would be, and what policies the newly established power structure would pursue.

Although no Chinese leaders openly voiced opposition to power seizure per se, they differed among themselves when it came to devising concrete strategies. Moderate leaders, such as Chou En-lai, advocated a moderate and practical approach, whereas the Cultural Revolution Small Group advanced a radical one. The two different sets of strategies evolved from two different understandings of power seizure: Chou viewed the official policy of power seizure as basically a response to economism, while the Small Group viewed the policy almost exclusively as the inevitable continuation of the Chinese revolution. In turn, the different strategies were intimately related to the respective political interests of Chou and the Small Group.

By interpreting the power seizure as an extraordinary response to economism, which the bourgeois reactionary line had initiated, Chou could link the goal and scope of the seizure to production. He argued that "without a power seizure, it is impossible to uphold revolution and production," and that the power seizure was a "new stage of grasping revolution, stimulating production, opposing economism, opposing the shifting of problems to a higher level, and smashing the new counterattack of the bourgeois reactionary line."[42]

Though the Center sanctioned the power seizure as a countermeasure against economism, Chou conceded that it had come to have its own momentum, producing a chain reaction even in areas where economism was not serious.[43] The chain reaction, however, was exploited by the radicals, who "wanted to bombard the power holders whether or not there were any power holders."[44] The reason why the Center acquiesced in the spread of the power seizure by chain reaction was that

debate on who is a power holder takes such a long time. At present, it [the power seizure] is a chain reaction, and the trend is to proceed inevitably with [it], and the Center decided to lead the trend and support you.[45]

In contrast to Chou's view, the Small Group took the view that the Cultural Revolution had been a revolutionary class struggle aimed from the beginning at power seizure. If power seizure was the ultimate expression of the class struggle, it logically followed that the scope of the seizure should be broad, and it should be carried out thoroughly in a bottom-to-top fashion.

42. "Premier Chou's Important Speech," *SCMPS*, no. 181 (8 May 1967), pp. 11-20.
43. *Hung-se chan-pao*, 17 February 1967.
44. "Premier Chou's Talk to Revolutionary Rebels of Industrial Communication Department," *SCMPS*, no. 178 (24 April 1967), pp. 21-24.
45. Ibid.

Ch'en Po-ta compared the power seizure of the Cultural Revolution with the 1949 liberation and the Russian October Revolution:

When we entered the cities in the past [i.e., in 1949], we exercised military control, issued orders from top to bottom, and sent men to take over. Now, it is the masses who take over, and our experience is richer than that of the Paris Commune and the October Revolution. Since we have comparatively more experience, we should take over in a more satisfactory way.[46]

Ch'i Pen-yü viewed the power seizure as a mass revolt against the ruling structure:

Why do you need rules in seizing power? Forget about the grades of [cadres]. The grade system resembles the feudal society and should be destroyed. The rule that only cadres above a certain grade can take part in a conference and others below that grade cannot must be eliminated. . . . Somebody said that "those without mustaches [i.e., young people] cannot manage affairs well." That is not true. "Those without mustaches" can manage affairs very well.[47]

In contrast, Chou En-lai had stressed the importance of leadership and guidance from the top to the bottom, and he had encouraged the Party and the government cadres to exercise their leadership in the power seizure.[48] In Chou's opinion, the power seizure was not a real revolution by the proletariat against the bourgeoisie; rather, it was an exercise for a future occasion when political power might fall into the hands of the revisionists: "[It] is not an actual seizure of power by the masses. It is a practice. . . . If revisionism emerges in the future, then the masses will rise to seize power."[49]

In a sense, Chou's attitude toward the power seizure was contradictory: on the one hand, he recognized the need of the power seizure in conformity with the official policy, but, on the other hand, he was determined to minimize the social and economic disruption by tying power seizure to econonism and consequently to production. He was not concerned with whether the radicals or the conservatives seized power so long as the seizure could ensure a normalization of production. Nevertheless, his emphasis on production benefited the conservatives and the power holders rather than the radicals. The radical minority could not immediately restore order and production because of their own technical inability and the opposition of the conservatives.[50]

Chou's ambivalent and sometimes clearly conflicting attitudes toward the power seizure may have reflected his attempt to balance two contradictory considerations: the need to revolutionize the ruling structure while maintaining a certain continuity, and upholding ideological principles while seeking

46. "Ch'en Po-ta Talks to University Representatives," *JPRS,* no. 41,450 (19 June 1967), pp. 42-43.
47. *Yü-t'ien feng-lei,* 10 February 1967.
48. "Premier Chou's Important Speech," *SCMPS,* no. 181 (8 May 1967), pp. 11-20.
49. Ibid.; *Hung-se chan-pao,* 17 February 1967.
50. "Chou En-lai Talk with Railway Rebels," *JPRS,* no, 41,450 (19 June 1967), pp. 39-41.

moderate and practical methods of implementing the principles. On the other hand, the ambivalence may have been a calculated political move to protect himself and his power base in the government ministries, which were as responsible as the Party leaders for the policy of economism.

Whatever his real intention was, on the whole Chou displayed little ideological zeal, choosing to argue and explain his position in practical terms. His behavior during the Cultural Revolution was more consistent than that of any other leader, in the sense that he did not swing from one extreme to another but persistently maintained a' moderate line. That is to say, Chou maintained his moderate views even during the radical stages of the Cultural Revolution, but at the same time he readily criticized the exploitation of his moderate views by the conservatives. His speeches were more open and public and less manipulative than those of others. Even though he was criticized by the radicals, he did not show any resentment or make defensive remarks. What he advocated in January appeared to be a sound and practical solution, and there are some indications that Mao shared Chou's strategy even then.[51]

The Cultural Revolution Small Group, however, followed an extremely ideological line, completely disregarding practical considerations. They generalized the theme of power seizure from the Shanghai context and applied it to all other areas. Wang Li urged the masses to take the power in their own hands, since that was the surest way to ensure the political safety of the rebels:

If we the working class, the proletarian revolutionary rebel faction, control power, these problems [i.e., dismissal of officials, rehabilitation, and black materials] can be settled by ourselves without depending on them [the power holders]. . . . Who will be elected or who will not be elected must follow the principle of the Paris Commune. Those unfit for the positions should be removed at any time. If we had power in the hands of the proletarian class, then our comrades labeled as "counterrevolutionary" could vindicate themselves. . . . If we don't seize power and we don't hold power, the circumstances force them to rehabilitate us today, but they will revoke it in the future. Therefore, we must be concerned with the essential thing, power. When we have power, we can dispose of the black materials and the white materials by ourselves. If we don't have power, and if we don't take firmly hold of it, in the future they will reverse verdicts and collect black materials on us. Therefore, the most important and essential thing is power seizure.[52]

The Small Group also tried to strike down as many top leaders as possible by making obviously manipulative and provocative speeches and readily denouncing anyone deviating from their ideological line as "revisionists." A thorough and wholesale power seizure by the narrowly defined rebel groups was consistent with the political interests of the Small Group, which was not

51. For Mao's conversation with Chou on the power seizure, see Chao Ts'ung, *Wen-ko yüntung li-ch'eng shu-lüeh*, vol. 2, pp. 524-543.
52. *Yü-t'ien feng-lei*, 10 February 1967.

an institutionalized group and did not have a strong power base among the elite, aside from Mao and his ideology. The Small Group therefore did not display any concern over the continuity of the regime's legitimacy.

These basic differences betweeen Chou and the Small Group led them to different strategies on several points. The first difference between them concerned the units from which power was to be seized. Chou advocated seizing power from selective units, exempting those that performed vital functions in the Chinese society. On the other hand, he advocated a thorough power seizure in "those organizations which do not have any functional work *(yeh wu)*, such as the inner organs of the Party, the Chinese Woman's Association, and the Chinese Youth League."[53] For this reason, he prohibited power seizure in the Ministry of Foreign Affairs, the Ministry of Finance, and PLA units in strategic locations.[54] The other factor that he stressed as a precondition for power seizure was the extent of the mass mobilization: power seizure was to be allowed only in units where the masses were fully mobilized.[55]

These two conditions had nothing to do with whether or not a unit was led by power holders taking the capitalist road, the ideological consideration that the Small Group often applied. On the contrary, Chou insisted that "it cannot be said that the members of committees in various ministries, provinces, and cities all belong to a handful of Party people in authority taking the capitalist road, or are all die-hards persisting in the bourgeois reactionary line."[56] Chou's plan for selective power seizure was intended to make the seizure effective and workable, and to prevent its being "empty," but the implications were obvious: government ministries that performed the vital functions of the Chinese economy, and for that reason had not yet experienced a serious inner revolt, were to be exempted from the power seizure.

The Small Group, on the other hand, never attached any conditions to the power seizure. Viewing it as "the overthrow of one class by another," they advocated a thorough, wholesale, and unconditional power seizure in every important state organ:

At present, every person, every organization, every leader, every school, and every unit should all receive the test of the Cultural Revolution, allowing the people to decide whether they are bourgeois representatives or proletarian representatives. Persons who are not capable of serving the proletariat should be eliminated. Unlike our take-over of some organs at the time when we entered the cities [in 1949], at the present everything which does not fit the socialist system and proletarian dictatorship should be attacked.[57]

53. "Premier Chou Issues an Important Directive on the Question of Power Seizure," *SCMPS,* no. 174 (10 April 1967), p. 25.
54. Chou ordered the arrest of Tu Hsiang-kuang, vice-minister of the Finance Ministry, who attempted to seize the ministry in defiance of Chou's instruction. Chao Ts'ung, *Wen-ko yün-tung li-ch'eng shu-lüeh,* vol. 2, p. 538.
55. "Premier Chou Issues an Important Directive on the Question of Power Seizure."
56. "Premier Chou's Important Speech," *SCMPS,* no. 181 (8 May 1967), pp. 11-20.
57. *Hung-se tsao-fan-che,* 18 January 1967.

The second difference between Chou and the Small Group centered on the new power structure to follow the power seizure. Chou did not advocate any new structure until his formula of the revolutionary committee was officially accepted in February, because his strategy of limited power seizure did not require him to lay out a new power structure. On the other hand, the Small Group widely propagated the Paris Commune, the essence of which was a direct participatory deomocracy wherein representatives were freely elected and were subject to recall by the masses.[58] There was no room for the leadership of the Communist Party under this formula. Ch'en Po-ta and Chiang Ch'ing actually instructed the Red Flag group of the Peking Aviation Institute to organize the Peking Commune.[59] Even when the principle of the three-in-one combination began to be propagated as official policy, Wang Li, the most radical member of the Small Group, viewed the revolutionary committee as a temporary measure to be replaced by a system modeled after the Paris Commune.[60]

The third difference involved the scope of the power to be seized. Did the power seizure mean a take-over of all power exercised by the Party committees, or a more limited take-over of such powers as the authority to lead the Cultural Revolution or the right to supervise the Party committees? After distinguishing between various forms of power, Chou En-lai recommended that "first, the authority to lead the Cultural Revolution should be taken over." On another occasion, he suggested that the rebels take over only the "power to supervise" and rely on "the chiefs and those who understand the business"—a policy that Robinson called the "mass supervision and cadre work formula."[61] Chou ordered the "existing personnel of business organs who can work" to "carry on their work as usual, but under the supervision of the revolutionary mass organization."[62] On the other hand, he was critical of the Small Group's formula of complete take-over.[63] The Small Group was insisting that "all power monopolized by the bourgeoisie should be taken over,"[64] and the conflict over the issue was revealed to the masses directly when Chiang Ch'ing raised her opposition during Chou's speech.[65]

The fourth difference focused on the need to regulate the process of the power seizure. Chou wanted to have a gradual power seizure, carried out

58. For the Paris Commune, see John Bryan Starr, "Revolution in Retrospective: the Paris Commune through Chinese Eyes," *CQ*, no. 49 (January-March 1972), pp. 107-125.

59. "Ch'en Po-ta Talks to University Representatives," *JPRS*, no. 41,450 (19 June 1967), pp. 42-43.

60. *Hung-se tsao-fan-che*, 8 February 1967.

61. Thomas Robinson, "Chou En-lai and the Cultural Revolution in China," *The Cultural Revolution in China*, ed. Thomas Robinson (Berkeley and Los Angeles: University of California Press, 1971), pp. 165-312.

62. *Hung-se chih-kung*, 29 January 1967.

63. *China News Summary*, no. 154 (19 January 1967), p. A8.

64. *Hung-wei chan-pao*, 23 February 1967.

65. *T'ieh-tao hung-ch'i*, 20 January 1967.

mainly by the mass organizations of the respective units under the guidance of the Center,[66] whereas the Small Group insisted on simultaneous power seizures in the various organs with a minimum of prescriptive rules from the Center. Chou emphasized the great alliance of the masses as a prerequisite for the power seizure, but his great alliance was quite moderate in that it included a broad spectrum of mass organizations within the structure of the system *(hsi-tung)*. According to Chou, any mass organization "holding high the great red flag of Mao Tse-tung's Thought, taking the socialist road in accordance with the direction suggested by Chairman Mao, and observing the Sixteen Articles" was eligible to join the great alliance.[67]

While defining the great alliance broadly, Chou repeatedly criticized the extreme position that only narrowly defined radical organizations were entitled to join the great alliance: "Not all revolutionaries are certainly clean," and "even the sham leftists are not completely false."[68] When the radicals complained about the false power seizures made by the power holders through the conservative mass organizations, he replied: "[One] should not say in absolute terms that this one is false and that one is real. Often the appearance of a matter is not clear. It is possible to have rightists, middle roaders, and leftists in a power seizure. The problem of whether a [power seizure] is real or false should be solved through compromise."[69]

Thus, Chou avoided taking a narrow partisan view concerning the mass organizations, and he accepted power seizures based on the great alliance regardless of whether or not leftists had seized the leadership. In contrast, the Small Group regarded the great alliance not as a prerequisite for power seizure but as something which could only be achieved among the narrowly defined leftists in the process of power seizure.[70] Since they believed that the leftists could be detected only after the split among the masses themselves in the struggle for power, they argued that "the units where internal splits have not yet occurred" should undergo further splits.[71] According to the Small Group's strategy, the proven rebels would first seize power into their own hands and then, as the core leaders of the new power structure, they would recruit other organizations into the great alliance. Otherwise, the great alliance would "promote compromise, harmony, and a mixture of various heterogeneous elements."[72]

All of these differences were manifested during the short period between

66. "Premier Chou Issues an Important Directive on the Question of Power Seizure," *SCMPS*, no. 174 (10 April 1967), pp. 24-26.
67. *Hung-se chih-kung*, 29 January 1967.
68. *Hung-se chan-pao*, 17 February 1967.
69. Ibid.
70. *Pei-ching wen-i tzu-liao*, 29 January 1967.
71. *Tung-fang-hung pao*, 28 June 1967.
72. *JMJP*, 22 January 1967.

January 4 and January 22, when a *Jen-min jih-pao* editorial finally enunciated the official strategy of power seizure, while attempting to eliminate the
radical elements. On the whole, the editorial neither clarified the controversial points nor provided any clear-cut strategy for the power seizure.[73] Worse
still, *Hung ch'i,* the mouthpiece of the Small Group, continued to attack the
moderate view of the power seizure as late as January 27:

Some responsible persons, though not in the category of anti-Party and antisocialist
elements, have not effectively remolded their bourgeois world outlook. They neither
study nor mix with the masses in the course of the Great Proletarian Cultural
Revolution. Therefore, to this day, they still have a very poor understanding of this
revolution. They blindly echo the absurd charges that "you are going too far," "you
are making an awful mess of it," "your revolutionary spirit is alright, but the way you
are doing things is wrong," and so on. We would like to warn these comrades
sharply: If you go on this way, you will go from merely having a very poor understanding of the Great Proletarian Cultural Revolution to actually opposing it.[74]

## The Failure of the January Power Seizure

In Shanghai, three factors helped to carry out the power seizure successfully: (1) the well-organized and powerful rebel workers' organization, which
served as a nucleus for the other mass organizations; (2) the thorough
disintegration of the conservative workers' organization; and (3) the strong
leadership of Chang Ch'un-ch'iao backed by the Peking leaders. These
factors, however, did not exist in other areas. In some cases, the workers
were not yet fully mobilized, let alone formed into a strong, unified, rebel
worker organization. In the areas in which the rebel forces were strong, the
leadership was still in the hands of students. In provinces where direct
confrontations between the radicals and the conservatives did not occur, the
conservative forces, instead of being disintegrated and discredited, simply lay
low, waiting for the opportunity to reassert themselves.

Despite the absence of the proper conditions, the power seizure gained its
own momentum when the Center took it out of the Shanghai context and
adopted it as the official policy. Soon the euphoria of power seizure swept all
over China, and all the Party organs and government units succumbed to it.
The result was confusion and chaos.

Of the three preconditions for the success of a power seizure, the availability of alternative leadership was the most crucial. This can be seen in the
fact that in all four provinces where the revolutionary committees were
successfully established at the earliest period there was a revolt of the leading

73. Ibid.
74. "On the Power Seizure Struggle of Proletarian Revolutionaries," *Hung ch'i,* no. 3 (3
February 1967), pp. 13-17.

cadres.[75] It was Liu Ko-p'ing, a member of the Central Committee and concurrently vice-governor of the Shansi Provincial Goverment who, together with the other four high-ranking members, supported the rebel groups and hence successfully carried out the power seizure.[76] P'an Fu-sheng, the First Secretary of the Provincial Party Committee who was once purged for his opposition to Mao's Great Leap Forward, had an opportunity to prove his loyalty to Mao by leading the rebel forces against the Heilungchiang Provincial Party Committee.[77]

In Shantung, Wang Hsiao-yü, Second Secretary of the Municipal Party Committee of Tientsin, and Mao Lin, a member of the Shantung Standing Party Committee, supported the rebel forces, thus leading to the early establishment of the Shantung Provincial Revolutionary Committee.[78] In Kweichow, Li Tsai-han, Deputy Political Commissar of the Kweichow Provincial Military District, supported the rebels.[79] In brief, it seems that the revolt of the leading cadres offered a rallying point for the unification of the rebel forces, thus making it easier for the mass organizations to form a "great alliance" and "three-in-one combinations."

In areas where a revolt of the high-ranking leaders did not occur, the Party leaders and cadres were as much divided as the mass organizations, each individual supporting and seeking favor from a different mass organization in order to survive the storm. In some cases, the leaders publicly resisted the power seizure, criticizing the rebels for being "one-sided," for "going too far," and for "rejecting all the cadres."[80] In other cases, they "identified themselves with the masses," so that any attack on them would constitute an attack on the masses. The high-ranking cadres who could not claim mass status suddenly changed their stands toward the rebels by taking a conciliatory and cooperative attitude, even to the extent of dividing the power among the rebels. Consequently, the power seizure was obstructed by open resistance, by "sham power seizures," by "peaceful transfers of power," by counter-power seizures, and by constant squabbling among the various mass organizations.

There were conflicts between the workers and the students, between the conservatives and the radicals, and among the radicals themselves over the principles and procedures of power seizure, and other constantly emerging issues. The tactical collaboration between the radical mass organizations and

75. For the date of establishment of revolutionary committee, see Frederick C. Teiwes, "Provincial Politics in China," in *Management of a Revolutionary Society,* ed. John M. Lindbeck (Seattle: University of Washington Press, 1971), p. 189.

76. For the cadres who revolted with Liu Ko-p'ing, see *Communist China 1967* (Union Research Institute), p. 157.

77. *JMJP,* 11 February 1967.

78. *JMJP,* 7 February 1967.

79. For the power seizure in Kweichow, see *JMJP,* 1, 5, 6, and 23 February 1967.

80. *Kuang-ming jih-pao,* 20 January 1967.

the power holders invited attack from the conservatives, who themselves sometimes openly sided with the power holders to oppose the minority radicals. The radical mass organizations which failed to take part in the power seizure found themselves in the same boat as the conservatives against their previous allies. This added a new dimension to the already complicated rifts among the mass organizations.

The Center was partially responsible for the confusion and chaos in January because it sanctioned the power seizure but failed to lay down its basic rules. The Center completely removed all institutional, functional, organizational, and geographical divisions that compartmentalized and regulated China's social interactions, but it failed to offer specific guidelines as to who would take over whose power. Consequently, everybody wanted to seize power, claiming to be "revolutionary," and the power seizure proceeded at all levels and in all areas simultaneously: the workers seized power at the factory level, and also joined the power seizure of city, provincial, and state organs; while the students seized power in their own schools, and at the same time took part in the power seizure in the various governmental organs.

Each mass organization, claiming to be a revolutionary rebel organization, dispatched a few representatives to other units to seize power and to claim their share of power. The students from Peking participated in the power seizure in the provinces, and the students from the provinces demanded that their voices be heard in the power seizure at the government ministries in Peking. Moreover, there were no regulations governing the status of mass organizations. Competing mass organizations which could not settle their differences were engaged in seizures and counter-seizures. The pre-existing mass organizations split up when new issues arose, and new mass organizations sprang up, the proliferation of which made the work of power seizure even more chaotic. The command structure of the Red Guard organizations also crumbled: even the Third Headquarters of Peking lost control over its member units, which fought against each other for power. The liaison personnel sent by the Third Headquarters to the provinces quarreled among themselves.[81] The net result was anarchy, chaos, and increasing conflicts among the mass organizations.

To be sure, a major source of the chaos was what the Maoists called "factionalism"—infighting among the rebel organizations for power. As Ch'en Po-ta described it, "When you want to seize power and I want to seize power, it becomes a struggle among the small groups, and they forget to seize the power from the power holders taking the capitalist road. At first, one seizes power, and then those without power still want to seize power, thus creating an internal struggle."[82]

81. *Shou-tu hung-wei-ping,* 22 January 1967.
82. *Hung-se chih-kung,* 29 January 1967.

The students were much more susceptible to "factionalism" than the workers, and they were blamed for carrying it to the factories by supporting "this or that worker group." The trend toward "factionalism" is not surprising, however, given the fact that the stakes of the power seizure were so high. In addition, the Center's policy of nonintervention in the power seizures by the masses was bound to create "factionalism." On the whole, in view of the fact that Shanghai confronted these same problems, despite its ripeness for power seizure, it is not surprising that the Small Group's radical strategy could not be worked out in other areas.

In January 1967, attempts were made to seize power in ten provinces, but only one was successful (Heilungchiang). In Kwangtung, eight local mass organizations aided by nine outside mass organizations declared a seizure of power, with the cooperation of Chao Tzu-yang, the First Secretary of the Provincial Party Committee.[83] This hasty and ill-prepared power seizure provided the conservatives with ammunition to attack the radicals for collaborating with Chao. A similar pattern followed in Wuhan, when the Party Committee collaborated with the radical minority in handing over their power.[84] This power seizure was recognized neither by the Center nor by the conservative mass organizations.

The PLA later used the theme of "sham power seizures" as an excuse to suppress the radical organizations. In Kwangsi, the Kwangsi Revolutionary Rebellion Army declared a power seizure, but they were soon suppressed by the PLA.[85] The participants of the abortive power seizure later formed the core of the radical Kwangsi April 22 group, which waged a bloody struggle against the Kwangsi Proletarian Alliance Command supporting Wei Kuo-ch'ing.

In Peking, three broad coalitions of mass organizations contended for power: (1) the Metropolitan Revolutionary Rebel Faction for Winning Power, which consisted of thirty-five organizations; (2) the Preparatory Committee of the Metropolitan Rebel Faction Red Guards, composed of thirty-two organizations; and (3) the Peking Revolutionary Rebel Commune, composed of twenty-four organizations.[86]

In Chungking, the municipal Party Committee resorted to a different tactic: they collaborated with the August 15 group of Chungking University (alleged to be loyal to Li Ching-ch'üan, the First Secretary of Szechwan), handing over the seals and chops of the provincial government to the latter in

83. See page 00.
84. For the Cultural Revolution in Wuhan, see Deborah S. Davis, "The Cultural Revolution in Wuhan," in *The Cultural Revolution in the Provinces* (Harvard East Asian Monographs, no. 42), pp. 147-170.
85. Victor C. Falkenheim, "The Cultural Revolution in Kwangsi, Yenan and Fukien," *Asian Survey* 9, no. 8 (August 1967): 580-597.
86. *DSJP*, 3 February 1967.

"eight minutes."[87] This power seizure was vehemently opposed by the Liaison Office of the Peking Red Guards and Szechwan University's August 26 Combat Regiment. Nonetheless, the conservative forces under the August 15 group of Chungking University organized a great alliance, the United Revolutionary Assembly, and thereafter all the other mass organizations in Szechwan split into proponents and opponents of the January Power Seizure.

The power seizure in the government ministries was as complicated as that in the Party organs, if not more so. Despite Chou's attempt to moderate the disruptive impact of power seizure by a tactic of "combined caution, personal appeal, and repression,"[88] almost all the government ministries had experienced power seizure in January, either "genuine" or "sham." The power seizure proceeded smoothly in a ministry if only one rebel group possessed unchallengeable credentials.[89] In ministries where a leading rebel group did not emerge (as was the case in most ministries), power seizure and counter-power seizure ensued.

Complicated as the power seizure in the government ministries was, however, the several sources of conflict can be identified. First of all, there was conflict between the mass organization of a ministry and outside mass organizations. The seizure of power by an internal rebel organization was the best way to ensure the normal functioning of the ministry, but this was often challenged by the students as "sham power seizure." The second source of conflict was the complete opposite of the first: outside student organizations would take over power with little participation by the mass organization of the original unit. In this case, the power seizure was challenged by the staff and workers of the ministry. This was the case in the First Ministry of Light Industry, where the Chingkangshan group of the Light Industry Institute declared a power seizure. Third, there was conflict along hierarchical lines within a ministry: conflict between the lower- and higher-ranking cadres, and between a ministry and its subordinate enterprises. For example, when the rebel organizations of the Ministry of Coal and the Ministry of Metallurgical Industry declared a power seizure, they were challenged by rebel organizations from subordinate enterprises.

But most complicated and troublesome were the cases in which antagonistic student organizations formed alliances with divided rebel groups of a unit. This pattern usually occurred in ministries that had no production units under their jurisdiction but only academic and research units (e.g., the Ministry of Culture, the Ministry of Higher Education, and the Ministry of

87. Thomas Jay Mathews, "The Cultural Revolution in Szechwan," in *The Cultural Revolution in the Provinces*, p. 146.

88. Robinson, "Chou En-lai and the Cultural Revolution," in Robinson, ed., *The Cultural Revolution in China* (n. 61 above), pp. 165-312.

89. For the most successful case of the power seizure in the government organization, see *K'o-chi chan-pao*.

Health). In such cases, the main conflict occurred along the lines of radical versus conservatives. The Hsin Peita Commune of Peking University seized the power of the Ministry of Higher Education with the help of the Peking Commune of the ministry, but their power seizure was challenged by the Chingkangshan group of Tsinghua University and the Hung Ch'i group of the Peking Aviation Institute, which collaborated closely with the more radical Yenan Commune of the ministry.[90]

Worse still for the Small Group, the strategy of power seizure "from the bottom" encouraged the mass organizations to push for their own narrow interests. For example, the Rebel General Corps of Red Labor, which consisted of contract and temporary workers, closed down the office of the Chinese Federation of Trade Unions and issued an urgent notice on January 2, inviting the temporary and contract workers to come to Peking to "clamor for transfer of the contract workers to permanent status, and for back pay since 1958."[91]

Another prominent interest group was the rusticated youths who organized themselves into the National Revolutionary Rebel Corps of Educated Youth Going to the Mountains and the Rural Areas to Defend Truth. Yet another was the National Revolutionary Rebel Corps of Army Reclamation Fighters.[92] Ex-servicemen also organized a nationwide Red Flag Army, despite the MAC's orders to the contrary.[93] Even the peasants began to complain that they were discriminated against in favor of the cities and treated as "third-class citizens."[94]

These groups proved to be the most enthusiastic in attacking the power holders and seizing the power for themselves. Readily subscribing to the radical ideology of the Small Group, they acted as the advance guard for the radical mass organizations, frequently resorting to extremely violent means. They not only "stormed into the Chungnanhai, but also attacked other organs of the Party Central Committee, kidnapping cadres of the state at will, and encircling and attacking cadres of resident committees."[95] They appropriated the name of the Party Central Committee several times to summon rallies at Tienanmen Square.[96] The ex-servicemen reportedly used "bricks and iron" to break the doors and windows of the State Council, and forcibly ransacked its confidential offices. Admirable as their revolutionary

90. *Hsin pei-ta.* 13 April 1967.

91. *Chih-tien chiang-shan,* 9 March 1967.

92. *T'i-yü chan-pao* (n.d.).

93. One of the leaders of the "Red Flag Army" claimed to be an old subordinate of Lin Piao's, and this soon attracted many new members. *Hung-wei-ping,* 16 February 1967; *Tung-fang-hung* (2nd Hqs.), 11 February 1967; *K'o-chi chan-pao,* 1 March 1967.

94. "Quarterly Chronicle and Documents," *CQ,* no. 30 (June-August 1967), pp. 206-207.

95. *T'i-yü chan-hsien* (n.d.); *Tung-fang-hung,* 1 January 1967.

96. *Hung-wei-ping.* 16 February 1967; *Tung-fang-hung,* 11 February 1967; *K'o-chi chan-pao,* 1 March 1967.

Table 6. *Power Seizures in the Government Ministries*

| Ministry | Date of power seizure | Organizations seizing power | Opposition | Type of conflict |
|---|---|---|---|---|
| 1. Water Conservation and Electric Power | Jan. 17 | Red Guards from the Institute of Water and Electric Power | | |
| 2. Textile | Jan. 18 | The United Commanding Headquarters for Taking Over, supported by the East Is Red Group of the Geology Institute | The Chingkang-shan Group of Tsinghua | Students vs. Cadres |
| 3. Coal | Jan. 16 | The Revolutionary Rebel Liaison Office of Organs in the Coal Ministry | The East Is Red Group of the Mining Institute | Cadres vs. Students |
| 4. Metallurgy Industry | Jan. 16 | The Red Flag Group of the Steel Institute and seven other organizations | The Commanding Headquarters of the Grasp Revolution and Promote Production Group | Students vs. Workers |
| 5. First Light Industry | Jan. 14 | The Chingkang-shan Group of the Light Industry Institute and the Red Rebel Committee | | Students vs. Cadres |
| 6. Petroleum | Jan. 14 | The Ta-ch'ing Commune of the Peking Petroleum Institute and the Revolutionary Rebel United Preparatory Committee of the Petroleum Systems | The Peking Commune and the Revolutionary Rebel Temporary Alliance Committee | Moderates vs. Radicals |

Table 6 Continued.

| Ministry | Date of power seizure | Organizations seizing power | Opposition | Type of conflict |
|---|---|---|---|---|
| 7. Chemical Industry | Jan. 16 | The Rebel Corps for the Sixteen Articles of the Chemical Engineering Institute and the Temporary Committee | The Red Combat Corps and the Revolutionary Production Committee | Students vs. Cadres and Workers |
| 8. First Machine Building | Jan. 16 | The Revolutionary Alliance | | |
| 9. Building Construction | Jan. 20 | The Revolutionary Rebel Headquarters | The Red Revolutionary Rebel Alliance General Command of the Building System | Cadres vs. Workers |
| 10. Post and Telecommunication | Jan. 20 | The East Is Red Group of the Post Institute and the Workers of the Revolutionary Rebel Corps | | |
| 11. Railway | Jan. 20 | The East Is Red Commune of the Railway Ministry | The Capital Revolutionary Workers' Headquarters and 48 other units in the railroad system | Radicals vs. Conservatives |
| 12. Finance | Jan. 20 | The Revolutionary Rebel Command | | Moderates vs. Radicals |
| 13. Commerce | Jan. 19 | The Red Rebel Army and the Red Rebel Regiment | | Moderates vs. Radicals |
| 14. Allocation of Materials | Jan. 19 | The Revolutionary Rebel Corps of all organs and the Red Guards of the Economic Institute | | Moderates vs. Radicals |

Table 6 Continued.

| Ministry | Date of power seizure | Organizations seizing power | Opposition | Type of conflict |
|---|---|---|---|---|
| 15. Geology | Jan. 19 | The Revolutionary Rebel United Committee | | |
| 16. Labor | Jan. 19 | The Command Post of the Revolutionary Rebels for the Seizure of Power | The Red Guards of the Economic Institute | Cadres vs. Students |
| 17. Aquatic Products | Jan. 17 | The Red Rebels' Take-Over Committee | | Cadres vs. Students and Workers |
| 18. State Farm and Land Reclamation | Jan. 21 | The Joint Command of the National State and Land Reclamation System for the Seizure of Power | | |
| 19. Forestry | Jan. 15 | The Grasp Revolution and Promote Production Take-Over Supervisory Committee | The Red Guards of the Forestry Institute | Cadres vs. Students |
| 20. Culture | Jan. 19 | The Revolutionary Rebel Joint Committee | The East Is Red Group of the Geology Institute and the Red Flag Group of the Peking Aviation Institute | |
| 21. Higher Education | Jan. 19 | The Hsin Peita Commune of Peking University and the Peking Commune | The Chingkang-shan Group of Tsinghua University and the Yenan Commune | Moderates vs. Radicals |
| 22. Public Health | Jan. 17 | 14 organs including the Red Rebel Corps of the | The East Is Red Commune and the Revolutionary | Moderates vs. Radicals |

Table 6 Continued.

| Ministry | Date of power seizure | Organizations seizing power | Opposition | Type of conflict |
|---|---|---|---|---|
| | | Health Organs | Rebel Liaison Headquarters of the Ministry | |
| 23. Agriculture | | The Red Rebel Liaison Office of Agricultural Systems | The Revolution-ary Rebel Liaison Office | Moderates vs. Radicals |
| 24. Seventh Machinery | | The September 16 Revolutionary Rebel Corps | The September 14 Rebel Corps | Moderates vs. Radicals |
| 25. Eighth Machinery | | The East Is Red Group of the Ministry and the East Is Red Group of the Agricultural Machinery Institute | | Moderates vs. Radicals |

*Source: Communist China 1967* (Hong Kong: Union Research Institute, 1969), pp. 95-101.

zeal may have been, their obviously "bad" motivation could not be over-looked even by the Maoist leaders. These groups were first suppressed on the grounds that they had formed nationwide organizations in violation of the official ban,[97] and then were publicly denounced as "counterrevolutionaries" by the PLA and the conservative mass organizations.[98]

The January Power Seizure also confronted the Maoist leaders with some sticky questions: How far back should the repudiation of the revisionist line go? In other words, now that the power holders were being denounced as following the revisionist line, how should the past official policies associated with the purged leaders be handled? To redress their grievances, the radicals wanted to repudiate the past policies as far back as possible, sometimes going to the extreme of asking for "re-evaluation of the past seventeen years,"[99] which in effect amounted to questioning the legitimacy of the regime as a whole. The cadres who had been disciplined in past campaigns (such as the Socialist Education Movement) demanded a "reversal of the

97. *CCP Documents of the GPCR*, no. 277.
98. *Hunan hung-ch'i-chün wen-t'i chuan-k'an*, 11 and 18 December 1967.
99. *Tung-fang-hung pao*, 7 March 1967.

verdict" on the grounds that they had been framed by the same Party leaders now denounced as power holders. On the other hand, the members of the work teams of the Socialist Education Movement were indiscriminately subjected to attack.[100]

The power seizure by the masses also resulted in the ironical phenomenon of non-Party members deciding the affairs of the Party organization. For instance, after its power seizure, the Red Flag group of the Peking Aviation Institute declared that Party membership would be checked by the masses, and that the Party organs of the Institute would not enter into any organized activities without permission from Red Flag.[101]

Consequently, however ideologically desirable it might have been, the Small Group's strategy of power seizure, with its emphasis on the Paris Commune and the unlimited spontaneity of the masses without the participation of the cadres, proved to be unworkable. It was therefore inevitable that the Center adopted the more moderate strategy of Chou En-lai as the official policy.

100. *CCP Documents of the GPCR*, p. 203.
101. *Hung-ch'i*, 19 January 1967.

# CHAPTER 6

# The "February Adverse Current"

The power seizure took a drastic turn in February as official policy increasingly stressed five themes: (1) the great alliance "uniting inside and outside" as a precondition for power seizure; (2) limitation of targets to a small number of cadres; (3) lenient treatment for the erring cadres; (4) the three-in-one combination; and (5) the revolutionary committee as a new power structure. The new moderate policy was intended to make the basic idea of power seizure workable by selectively accepting the cadres into the new power structure and utilizing their leadership and organizational skills to impose control from the top on the otherwise uncontrollable mass organizations.

Consequently, February witnessed an improvement in the power position of the elite vis-à-vis that of the masses. The new policy, however, had subtler and more far-reaching consequences among the various groups contending for power. First of all, the new policy undermined the power position of the radical mass organizations while advancing the lot of the conservative forces. The moderate policy also enabled the cadres not only to survive the Cultural Revolution for the time being, but also to reassert their influence beyond what the Maoist leaders had expected. Most important, the People's Liberation Army emerged as the most influential elite group in shaping the course of the Cultural Revolution, particularly at the provincial level, whereas the Cultural Revolution Small Group lost its exclusive claim to leading the mass movement. Consequently, the moderate official policy pronounced in February gave birth to a coalition of the PLA, the cadres, and the conservative mass organizations—a coalition powerful enough to reverse whatever the January Power Seizure had achieved, thereby creating what the radicals called the February Adverse Current.

In this chapter, we will examine four aspects of the new developments: (1) the new policy's emergence; (2) the power seizures in the government ministries that illustrate the actual ramifications of the moderate policy; (3) the PLA's active involvement in the power seizure, which accelerated, if not created, the deradicalization process in February; and (4) a bird's-eye view of the Great Proletarian Cultural Revolution in the summer of 1967 up until the Wuhan incident.

## The Emergence of the Moderate Policy Line

Various components of the moderate official line evolved in February from the different experiences in different areas, and the official line only gradually formed into a coherent whole. Yet, the origin of the policy change can be traced back to Mao himself. Probably convinced by the end of January that the masses were not capable of carrying out the power seizure successfully by themselves, Mao made a series of comments backing the deradicalization process. He condemned the factionalism and violent struggle over the power seizure.[1] Obviously referring to Chiang Ch'ing's remark that "the title of chief should be smashed to pieces," Mao commented: "You have been calling them 'such and such chiefs,' and they are called 'persons on duty' or 'service personnel.' This is mere formalism. Actually, 'chiefs' are necessary. The question lies in the content."[2] More important, Mao initiated a policy of leniency toward the erring cadres by inserting the following statement into the editorial of *Hung ch'i*, No. 3:

All those [leaders] who were not anti-Party, antisocialist elements, and do not persist in their errors or refuse to correct them after repeated education, should be allowed to correct their errors and be encouraged to make amends for their crimes by good deeds.[3]

An editorial that was published in the *Jen-min jih-pao* of February 23, 1967, acknowledged for the first time the existence of Maoist cadres who, "for quite a long time in the past, waged a struggle within the Party against the handful of people taking the capitalist road."[4] Another article, entitled "On Revolutionary Discipline and Revolutionary Authority," expounded on the need for "proletarian revolutionary organizational discipline" if the power seizure was to be successful, and condemned "ultra-democracy, anarchism, liberalism, departmentalism, and a small-group mentality."[5]

1. *DR*, 1 February 1967, *Chung-kung wen-hua ta ko-ming chung-yao wen-chien hui-pien* (Taipei: Chung-kung Yen-chiu, 1973), p. 212.
2. *DR*, 7 March 1967, p. CCC13.
3. "Premier Chou's Talks to Revolutionary Rebels of Industrial and Communication Department," *SCMPS*, no. 178 (24 April 1967), p. 21.
4. "On the Power Seizure Struggle of Proletarian Revolutionaries," *Hung ch'i*, no. 3 (3 February 1967), pp. 13-17.
5. Ibid.

After the publication of the *Hung ch'i* editorial, the Heilungchiang rebels applied the formula of the three-in-one combination by cooperating with P'an Fu-sheng and the PLA leaders in seizing the power of the Provincial Party Committee.[6] The Heilungchiang experience, although incorporating the three-in-one combination, still retained some elements of the January radicalism: the main force for power seizure was still the mass organizations; and the "responsible persons within the Provincial Party Committee who carried out the correct line of Chairman Mao," and the "responsible leaders of the PLA," continued to suppress the conservative mass organizations. The idea of the Paris Commune and the theme of radical egalitarianism still persisted in the Heilungchiang experience.[7]

Mao selected the Heilungchiang experience as a model, and the *Jen-min jih-pao* widely propagated it.[8] From the Heilungchiang experience evolved the official line that "without the three-in-one combination it is impossible to obtain victory," and that the main criterion for a good cadre is "whether one supports Mao's Thought," a moderate qualification that any cadre could claim to meet. Conversely, the radicals' view that "every cadre should be struck down" came under official attack as "left in form and right in essence."[9]

In Kweichow, the second province to successfully seize power after Heilungchiang, the deradicalization had gone one step further. Here it was the cadres who played the prominent role in the power seizure. The cadres first seized the power of their respective units and then established a "temporary power seizure organ," which acted as the "commanding headquarters" by coordinating the various rebel organizations taking over the Provincial Party Committee.[10] Because of the active leadership of the cadres, Kweichow could follow the correct line of "seize power from the top, sweep away hindrance at the bottom, and shoot arrows at both sides [right and left]," thus avoiding the extremism that any bottom-to-top power seizure tended to generate. The Kweichow experience added to the official strategy of power seizure the idea of "unite inside and outside, with inside as the main force; firmly rely on the revolutionary rebel forces of the provincial and municipal Party and government organs; neither replace them nor be their master."[11]

The deradicalization process continued throughout February. *Hung ch'i*, No. 4, carried an editorial, "The Cadres Must Be Correctly Treated," which urged the masses to limit the scope of the purge to a "handful," and to adopt the policy of "curing the sickness to save the patient."[12] The reason, the

6. *JMJP*, 11 and 15 February 1967.     7. *DR*, 9 February 1967, p. DDD1.
8. *DR*, 21 February 1967, p. CCC2.     9. *DR*, 9 February 1967, p. DDD1.
10. *JMJP*, 23 February 1967.     11. Ibid.
12. Ibid.

editorial explained, was that the "leading cadres are more politically mature and have greater organizational skill and experience, so that they have the ability to hold the state power and manage functional affairs for the proletariat."

While upgrading the role of the cadres, the Center disbanded the inter-trade, interdepartmental, and intersystem mass organizations, and ended the great exchange of experience.[13] Even the emphasis on the three-in-one combination was shifted from the masses to the cadres; henceforth the cadres were going to participate in the power seizure not only as equal partners but as the leaders.[14] Yet, the PLA's participation in the three-in-one combination was limited to the provincial and municipal levels. The PLA was excluded from the three-in-one combination in the Central and government organs, which consisted of "revolutionary leading cadres, revolutionary middle-level cadres, and revolutionary masses."[15] This formula later evolved into the principle of combining old, middle-aged, and young cadres. In the industrial and mining enterprises, the three-in-one combination was formed by "revolutionary cadres, leading cadres, technicians, old workers, young workers, and representatives of militia men."[16] In the schools, instead of the revolutionary committees, the Cultural Revolution Committees were the highest power organs.

As the January radicalism was being repudiated by the new moderate official line, the top government and military leaders, objects of the mass attack in January, launched a political counterattack on the Cultural Revolution Small Group, climaxing in the work conference held in the Hai Jen Auditorium on February 16, 1967. T'an Chen-lin led the criticism of the Small Group by making an emotional remark:

I have made no mistake. I need no protection from others. Veteran cadres have been struck down. I should not have lived for sixty-five years, should not have joined the revolution, should not have joined the Party, and should not have followed Chairman Mao in making revolution for forty years.[17]

After finishing his speech, T'an tried to leave the meeting, but Ch'en I stopped him by saying: "We are going to turn this place into a mess. Don't go." Chou En-lai intervened: "You are taking too much liberty. Come back."[18] Yeh Chien-ying is reported to have broken his finger because he pounded on his table so furiously.[19] Declaring that "the present

13. *JMJP*, 1 March 1967.
14. "Cadres Must Be Correctly Treated," *Hung ch'i*, no. 4 (1 March 1967), pp. 5-11.
15. *JMJP*, 28 February 1967.
16. Ibid.
17. "February Adverse Current," *Issues and Studies* 5, no. 12 (September 1969): 103-104.
18. Ibid.
19. Ibid.

contradiction with Liu Shao-ch'i is a contradiction among the people," Ch'en I withdrew his January self-criticism on the ground that it was made under duress.[20]

On February 17, the day following the work conference, the Central Committee and the State Council jointly issued six instructions.[21] Five of them purported to check the excessive behavior of the radicals: (1) disband the contract workers' organizations; (2) protect the security of confidential state files; (3) prohibit attacks against the work team members of the Socialist Education Movement; (4) check the activities of the rusticated youth; and (5) prohibit the Cultural Revolution in units engaged in construction work in the border areas.

Paralleling the attempt to check the power of the radicals in the power seizure, the Center proceeded to impose its control over the Cultural Revolution: in February alone, it issued nineteen notices, many of which were designed to maintain law and order.[22] The notices included orders banning the revolutionary exchange of experience, specifying the important units which should be exempted from the Cultural Revolution, and prohibiting the mass organizations from expelling Party members. Incidentally, none of these orders were issued under the name of the Cultural Revolution Small Group; instead, all of them came from the Central Committee of the CCP, or from the Military Affairs Commission, or the State Council, or a combination of these three organizations.

Finally, the idea of the Paris Commune itself was officially criticized in mid-February when the Center, reversing its previous stand that a power seizure needed only post facto approval, officially prohibited the use of the commune formula (except for Shanghai) and stipulated that any power seizure should be approved beforehand by the Center.[23] Mao personally told Chang Ch'un-ch'iao to change the name of the Shanghai People's Commune, and the city therefore changed its name to the Shanghai Municipal Revolutionary Committee on February 24.[24] At the same time, the Center barred the Red Guards from publishing unauthorized materials or the Party leaders' speeches.[25] This series of measures succeeded in restoring a semblance of order in Peking by the end of February.[26]

20. *Hung-wei chan-pao,* 8 April 1967.
21. "Directives and Notices on the CR," *SCMMS,* no. 17 (15 January 1968), pp. 49-50.
22. Ibid.
23. *Chung-kung wen-hua ta ko-ming chung-yao wen-chien hui-pien,* p. 40.
24. Neal Hunter, *Shanghai Journal* (New York: Praeger, 1969), p. 261; *DR,* 27 February 1967, p. DDD12; 7 March 1967, p. CCC14.
25. *DR,* 7 March 1967, p. CCC10; 10 March 1967, p. CCC13.
26. A Japanese correspondent reported the Peking situation at the end of February: "The storm of the Great Proletarian Cultural Revolution, which had been rising throughout China and centering on the Red Guard movement, has started to abate recently, and it is said that one

Worse still for the radicals, the masses were ordered to rectify their non-proletarian ideologies such as the "extremely harmful non-organizational viewpoint," "ultra-democratism," liberalism, subjectivism, individualism, the "military viewpoint," viewpoints advocating "materials in command," and small-group mentalities.[27] The official rationale for the rectification was that the masses would strengthen their political capability by purging themselves of these bad trends that the class enemies had instigated. However, contrary to the official rationale, the rectification worked against the radicals politically by shifting the target from the elite to the masses.[28]

This shifting was intensified because there were political groups eager to make the rectification the major task of the Cultural Revolution. Under the pretext of criticizing "leftist adventurism," "petty bourgeois fanaticism," and actions which were "left in appearance but right in essence," the conservative forces launched their attack on the radicals. The power holders also found opportunities to "discredit the achievements of the masses and regain their positions" by "lightening their [own] crimes while exaggerating the mistakes of the small soldiers."[29] Some Party authorities openly declared:

We implemented the reactionary line of suppressing the masses, but you also carried out the reactionary line of attacking cadres; we protected the handful, but you attacked the large numbers, so both are cancelled.[30]

Understandably, the radical mass organizations and the Cultural Revolution Small Group were bitter about the conservatives' exploitation of the moderate official line in order to maximize their political power and undermine the Small Group.[31] Hsieh Fu-chih observed that "the conservative forces in society attacked the left and the Cultural Revolution Small Group, taking advantage of the minor rectification and creating the adverse current."[32] The members of the Small Group, however, were not yet ready to accept their initial setback. At the end of February, Wang Li expressed the

can now again see people enjoying a walk or shopping occasionally, even in the streets of Peking, the capital city. Wall newspapers have more or less fulfilled their historic mission and are about to disappear from the stage of the political struggle." *DR*, 15 March 1967.

27. "Where Is Our Lu Hsün Corps Going?" *SCMP*, no. 3893 (7 March 1967), pp. 9-11. The military viewpoint refers to the "concentration of attention and energy on the 'rooting out of so and so' and 'overthrowing so and so.'" The "material in command" refers to some Red Guards' preoccupation with collecting secret information on the cadres. Since the CRSG actively encouraged the radicals to gather secret information to expose the power holders in the previous stage, the denunciation of this tactic was an indirect criticism of the CRSG.

28. The radical cried that "the rectification campaign suits the taste of the enemy." "Chop Off the Black Hands of P'an Tzu-nien and Wu Ch'üan-ch'i," *SCMPS*, no. 204 (22 September 1967), p. 27.

29. *JMJP*, 7 March 1967; *Tung-fang-hung pao*, 3 March 1967; 9 March 1967.

30. *JMJP*, 24 April 1967.

31. *Chin-chün pao*, 20 February 1967.

32. *Hsin-wen chan-pao*, 14 May 1967.

bitterness of the Small Group and the uncertainty of the whole Cultural Revolution in the following terms:

The three months from February through April will be extremely important. Through the struggle in the months ahead, the Cultural Revolution may take shape in the provinces and cities. . . . It can be said that the Cultural Revolution as a whole has taken some shape. However, this is not yet so in Peking, and we are unable to shoulder both revolution and production although we have seized "buildings and seals."[33]

Before following the radicals' counterattack on the "February Adverse Current," we shall first examine the impact this "Current" had on the actual power seizure in the government ministries.

## The "February Adverse Current" and the Power Seizure in the Government Ministries

In contrast to his defensive and somewhat weakened posture of January, Chou En-lai acted in February with confidence and authority: he made more frequent public appearances, expressing more forcefully his view on the various problems and freely invoking Mao's authority.[34] Undoubtedly, he derived his new confidence from the incorporation into the official policy of what he had been advocating in January. In turn, he continued his efforts to protect the minimum institutional interests of the Party bureaucrats, the government leaders, and the PLA.

By defending the institutional interests of the PLA against the Cultural Revolution Small Group's radicalism and at the same time publicly acknowledging Lin Piao's authority as the successor to Mao, Chou rendered himself invaluable to Lin Piao. Chou was also indispensable to Mao. Chou's practical strategy of power seizure served Mao's goal of revolutionizing the ruling structures while maintaining the continuity of the regime. Moreover, by keeping Chou on his right and the Small Group on his left, Mao could maximize his maneuverability in decision-making, while shielding himself from culpability when any policy worked less favorably than expected.

With renewed confidence and vigor, Chou proceeded to restore some order in the now almost defunct government. He divided the government cadres into five categories, according to the degree of seriousness of their mistakes.[35] The first category consisted of "three anti-elements, double dealers, and conspirators" who should be struck down. The second were the "handful of power holders taking the capitalist road." Chou divided this category into two sub-groups, according to their willingness to admit and rectify their

33. *DR*, 1 March 1967, p. CCC9.
34. The standard phrase used by Chou was "On behalf of our great leader Chairman Mao and his close Comrade-in-arms Lin Piao, I bring you greetings." *DR*, 3 March 1967, p. CCC1.
35. *Hung-se chan-pao*, 17 February 1967.

mistakes. Only those who "persistently refused to admit and rectify their mistakes" were to be purged. On the other hand, those who were willing to mend their mistakes, even though they were the ones who had initiated the "bourgeois reactionary line," would be saved. This group would be relieved from active duty for a probation period of three months.

The third category included those who implemented the bourgeois line. They would be allowed to discharge their ordinary duties under the supervision of the masses. The fourth category included those who implemented the bourgeois reactionary line but had already rectified their mistakes. They would be allowed to remain at their posts under supervision *(chien-tu liu-yung)*. In the fifth category were those who had not implemented the bourgeois reactionary line but had made serious mistakes. Their positions and duties would not be changed. At the end, Chou specified that only a few in the government fell into the first two categories.[36]

Chou also clarified the term "power holders" by distinguishing between the power holders and the "power holders taking the capitalist road." He argued that all "chiefs" ranking from the chief of a section to that of a ministry were power holders in their respective units but not necessarily power holders taking the capitalist road. "How to distinguish [between them]?" Chou asked. "Use the method of self-examination: |allow them| to examine themselves, revolutionize themselves, while permitting them to defend themselves."[37]

After stressing the need of leadership from the top, Chou urged his vice-premiers and ministers to exercise their leadership in the power seizure.[38] On the other hand, he ordered the mass organizations to consult him first if they wanted to drag out his ministers, and he also ordered them to allow his ministers to continue their work after criticizing them.[39] He was particularly vigorous in defending his vice-premiers, usually on the basis of their past achievements: Li Hsien-nien for his financial contribution in paying back foreign loans in the most difficult time of 1961; and Yü Ch'iu-li for his contribution to the achievements of the Ta-ch'ing oil field.[40] When a courageous radical challenged him by pointing out that his approval of the power seizure contradicted his protection of the vice-premiers, he replied that his protection of the vice-premiers and the power seizure were two different matters.[41]

Chou first implemented his moderate strategy of power seizure in the field of finance and trade, the most important sector of the Chinese economy. He

36. Ibid.
37. Ibid.
38. *Tsao-fan,* 25 February 1967; *Hung-se tsao-fan pao,* 19 February 1967.
39. Ibid.
40. *DR,* 28 March 1967, p. CCC17.
41. *Hung-se tsao-fan pao,* 19 February 1967.

and Li Hsien-nien helped the moderate forces in the system to form the Liaison Office of Rebels in the System of Finance and Trade and on January 18 personally attended a mass rally organized by the Liaison Office to fight against economism. Emphatically stating that the main task at that moment was combating economism, Chou urged those attending the rally to take hold of their work posts to the point of "blood and death," because the "system of finance is the most important front in the Cultural Revolution."[42] Then he recommended that the Liaison Office set up local branches, a suggestion that was carried out immediately.

The Liaison Office acted as the highest power organ in the field of finance and trade, and its local branches worked as the links between the central government and local government agencies.[43] Through this elaborate organizational network, Chou endeavored to carry out the normal government business and the power seizure at the same time. This effort was opposed, however, by the radical students (mainly the Peking Rebel Commune of the Peking Finance Institute) and the radical cadres (mainly the Chingkangshan group and the East Is Red group of the Finance Ministry) under the leadership of Vice-Minister Tu Hsiang-kuang. The radicals condemned the Liaison Office as conservative, while the Liaison Office accused the radicals of opposing official policy.[44]

The power seizure in the government started at a high-level Party meeting on January 16, when T'an Chen-lin and Li Hsien-nien ordered the Party Committees in the government organs to "give power to whoever wants it."[45] Immediately after this order, the Party authorities in the government approached the mass organizations on each ministry that they trusted and peacefully handed power over to them. In return, those who seized the power offered the original Party Committee members positions in the revolutionary committees. This façade of power seizure did not go unchallenged by the radicals.

On January 17, in the Ministry of Public Health, the temporary Party Committee which T'ao Chu had set up in September 1966 signed an agreement on the power seizure with the Rebel Corps of the Organs in the Ministry of Public Health.[46] Later, the Rebel Corps formed a Revolutionary

---

42. *Ts'ai-mao hung-ch'i*, 1 February 1967. On the other hand, the CRSG organized the "Headquarters of Municipal Workers, Peasants and Soldiers for Grasping Revolution and Promoting Production" in competition with Chou's organization along the functional line. "Drag Out Counterrevolutionary Ch'i Pen-yü" (pamphlet), 26 February 1968.

43. *Ts'ai-mao hung-ch'i*, 23 February 1967.

44. Actually the "Liaison Office" defended Li Hsien-nien even during the height of the radicalization in March and consequently clashed with the radical minority organizations in the system. Ibid.

45. *Hsin nung-ta*, 1 April 1967.

46. *Hung-i chan-pao*, 18 May 1967.

Committee with fourteen mass organizations, boasting a total of five thousand members. The Revolutionary Committee liberated many high-ranking cadres, including Chien Hsin-chung, the Minister of Public Health, and Sun Cheng, the head of the temporary Party Committee, both of whom had signed the agreement on the power seizure. Furthermore, Sun Cheng was made the head of the Revolutionary Committee.

Challengers to this power seizure rallied around the Liaison Headquarters of the Revolutionary Rebels.[47] Chou En-lai approached the dispute with his typical contradictory attitude. On the one hand, he criticized the temporary Party Committee for handing over power peacefully, characterizing it as a typical example of "peaceful transfer." On the other, he supported the participation of Chien Hsin-chung and Sun Cheng in the three-in-one combination because they had rectified their mistakes and should be given a new opportunity, in accordance with Mao's dictum of "criticizing the people to rectify their mistakes."[48] The radicals nevertheless continued their opposition through the summer of 1967.

In the Ministry of Petroleum, the conservative organization, led by the cadres above the "bureau chief" level, seized power after forty-five minutes of negotiation with the Party Committee.[49] Later, the organizations supporting the power seizure formed the Ta-ch'ing Commune, which included the conservative student faction of the Peking Petroleum College, while the opponents of the power seizure set up the Peking Petroleum Commune. The Ta-ch'ing Commune liberated "some cadres who implemented the bourgeois reactionary line and committed mistakes, even some serious mistakes" (e.g., K'ang Shih-en, the Acting Minister), since they believed that "most of the cadres who erred would be able to rectify their mistakes."[50] The radicals challenged the liberation, but the Ta-ch'ing Commune accused the Peking Commune of "provoking the masses to strike down all cadres, creating an antagonism between the masses and the cadres."[51]

Among the government ministries, the agricultural system underwent the most controversial power seizure, one that the radicals regarded as a "model of sham power seizure."[52] Here the radical forces were represented by the Liaison Station of the Revolutionary Rebels in the System of Agriculture and Forestry, and the conservative forces were represented by the Red Rebel Liaison Office. Only a few cadres joined the Liaison Station, and many of them had rather complicated class backgrounds and political problems. For instance, the Red Flag group of the Agricultural Ministry totaled only seventeen members (one cook, two drivers, and fourteen young staff members

47. Ibid., 23 May 1967.
48. Ibid.
49. *Ta-ch'ing kung-she,* 24 February 1967.
50. Ibid., 24 February 1967.
51. *Chingkangshan,* 18 March 1968.
52. *Chung-ta hung-ch'i,* 4 April 1968.

who had graduated in 1965), while the radicals of the Meteorology Observatory Bureau consisted mainly of those cadres who had been attacked in the initial stage of the Cultural Revolution.[53]

The leaders of the radical coalition were Ch'en Hua-lung, director of the Political Department, and Huang T'ien-hsiang, director of the Propaganda Department. They had also been attacked during the initial stage of the Cultural Revolution because, according to the radicals, they had led their departments to revolt against T'an Chen-lin.[54] These rebellious cadres were closely allied with the radical mass organizations made up of contract and temporary workers and rusticated students.

In contrast, the Red Rebels were actively supported by T'an Chen-lin, and also by Acting Minister Chiang I-chen and Ch'i Tsung-chuan, director of the General Office of the Ministry. This group was mainly composed of workers, staff, and cadres of the system, with support from some conservative student organizations such as the Red Flag group of the Agricultural Institute. When the decision to allow power seizure in the government ministries was made on January 16, the Red Rebels, through their secret communication channels, ordered their member organizations to proceed with the power seizure immediately. Within twenty-four hours, the conservative forces declared their seizure of power with the help of the Party Committees in the Weather Bureau and the Ministries of Agriculture, Agricultural Reclamation, and Aquatic Production.

The most extreme case was the power seizure of the Weather Bureau, in which the official seals were seized after twenty minutes of talks between the conservative organizations and the power holders.[55] The radicals of the Liaison Station immediately took their complaints to the Cultural Revolution Small Group, explaining the nature of the power seizure. Ch'en Po-ta commented that "the Weather Bureau was a typical sham power seizure," and "Premier Chou and Comrade K'ang Sheng replied with smiles."[56]

Nevertheless, the government leaders supported the power seizure by the Red Rebels. T'an Chen-lin reportedly congratulated the conservatives on their success: "You won victory. . . . The Premier has sent me to see you. Among the agricultural units, your condition is comparatively good, and your situation of struggle is also good."[57] The radicals were embarrassed by Chou's sympathy with the conservatives, and maintained that T'an deceived Chou, but there is clear evidence that Chou actually supported the power seizures by the conservative mass organizations. Fortunately, we have a copy of *Nung-lin chan-pao*, which was published by the conservative organizations and carried a revealing speech by Chou in his interview with the conservative

53. *Hsin nung-ta*, 24 March 1967.          54. *T'i-yü chan-pao*, 18 March 1967.
55. *Chin-chün pao*, 11 March 1967.          56. *Hsin nung-ta*, 16 March 1967.
57. Ibid., 1 April 1967.

mass organizations.[58] Since Chou seems to have been more candid and less guarded than usual in this talk, his speech will be summarized in detail.

First, Chou expressed his support of the power seizure by the conservatives, saying that "you have seized the power. . . . There will still be a struggle for the counter-power seizure. You have to fight that battle firmly." Second, he denounced the challengers of the power seizure, while encouraging the conservatives to "stand firmly on the moderate standpoint." Third, linking the power seizure to production, Chou emphatically stressed the importance of leadership in seasonal work such as agriculture. Fourth, defining the three-in-one combination as an alliance of "revolutionary leaders, revolutionary middle-level cadres, and revolutionary masses," he insisted that vice-premiers and ministers would supervise the power seizure on his behalf. Fifth, Chou was furious over the fact that non-Party-member students had expelled the Party members from the Party. Finally, he was especially critical of the radical students:

At present, [these students] do not pay any attention to study, and only like to go out and put up big-character posters and, without much preparation, open big rallies, sometimes of several thousand people. . . . The big-character posters become simple slogans. The movement has been promoted for half a year, but it cannot drift in such a way anymore.[59]

As has always been the case in any mass movement without organizational control from the top, any slight shift of official policy toward either the left or the right was voraciously exploited by the social groups favoring the new direction of the Cultural Revolution for their own political interests. Although initiated by the Center to make the January Power Seizure workable, the moderation of the power seizure encouraged the conservative forces to reassert themselves. Using the newly instituted policy to evaluate the radicals' behavior in January, the conservatives attacked the radicals in February partly to enhance their own power position and partly to retaliate for their earlier suffering.

Many of the high-ranking cadres who were attacked and dismissed by the radicals during the January Power Seizure—such as the Acting Minister of Agriculture, the Minister of Petroleum, and the Minister of Coal—were reinstated and drawn into the "three-in-one combination."[60] The Party Committee of the Finance Ministry issued a notice that "all chiefs of the various bureaus and corporations and units under the Ministry, and accountants and responsible persons who worked before January 20 should be reinstated to work, and hereafter are responsible to the Party Committee."[61]

The justification given for this was that, although these chiefs had made

58. *Nung-lin chan-pao,* 22 February 1967.     59. Ibid.
60. *Chingkangshan,* 16 March 1967.            61. *Pei-ching kung-she,* 12 April 1967.

serious mistakes, they "are not anti-Party and antisocialist elements, so they should be criticized and then included in the three-in-one combination."[62] Chou En-lai also contributed to the reinstatement by strictly enforcing his view—now adopted as a part of the official policy—that the mass organizations could only seize the leadership of the Cultural Revolution and should not seize other powers. He even ordered the arrest of Tu Hsiang-kuang, the leader of the radicals in the Ministry of Finance, on the ground that Tu had defied his order.[63]

Once reinstated, the cadres endeavored to prove their innocence by repudiating their attackers on the ground that the excessive January attack on cadres had been "class revenge by the bourgeois class" and "mistaken in orientation." Some were bold enough to declare that "we had imposed fifty days of white terror, and you imposed fifty days of terror [in January], so each one's mistake is cancelled."[64] Some rebels tried to atone for their mistakes by returning the power they had seized in January—which the power holders, however, refused to accept—and by writing a "petition for amnesty" *(ch'ing tsui shu).*[65]

The power holders obviously "were not satisfied with taking back the leadership of the movement and the supervision of business,"[66] but intended to exploit the new mood to the maximization of their political interests. They wanted to repudiate the whole idea of power seizure and to destroy the radical forces once and for all. The rebels, who just one month earlier had been praised as the bearers of the proletarian revolution, now faced a subtle but effective suppression. The material supplies to the radical factions ceased, and their meetings were stormed by the conservatives.[67]

The radical cadres faced a more severe retaliation than the radical students. In particular, the cadres in the agricultural system suffered most from the strong-handed retaliation of T'an Chen-lin, who publicly declared that, "besides a few in the schools, all the organizations that participated in the Liaison Station of the Revolutionary Rebels in the System of Agriculture and Forestry were rightist organizations."[68] The leaders of the radical cadre organizations were denounced as "pickpockets," "backstage bosses," and "counterrevolutionaries," and were arrested, photographed, and fingerprinted. Their dossiers were collected and forwarded to the Public Security Bureau for further investigation. Moreover, any local cadre organizations

62. "How Li Hsien-nien Attacks a Big Group to Protect a Handful," *SCMPS*, no. 238 (8 November 1968), pp. 22-27.
63. France News Agency from Tokyo, 23 February 1967.
64. *JMJP*, 24 April 1967.
65. *Chingkangshan*, 6 April 1967.
66. *Hsin nung-ta*, 13 March 1967; *Tung-fang-hung pao*, 3 March 1967.
67. *P'i T'an chan-pao*, 16 June 1967.
68. *Wen-i hung-ch'i*, 30 May 1967.

that had had contacts with the upper-level radical cadre organizations were branded as "reactionary." The retaliation was thorough and ruthless.

The houses of some rebels were raided and ransacked. Some rebels were kidnapped, interrogated, and forced to make confessions. Some were forced to go to a raised platform and bow their heads. Some were paraded before the public. Some cadres of rebel groups were relieved of their duties or demoted. Some truck drivers were forced to surrender the keys of their trucks. Some telephone operators were expelled from the exchange rooms. The orders, leaflets, and anonymous letters of the conservative groups were distributed everywhere, threatening and intimidating the revolutionary rebel comrades. The conservative groups also arranged the time, place, and personnel for attacks on the comrades of the rebel groups. Every conceivable device was resorted to.[69]

Although not suppressed by the power holders as openly and as directly as the radical cadres, the radical students also came under increasing pressure from the conservative student organizations. With the help of the Red Rebels, the Red Flag group of the Peking Agricultural College raided and closed down the headquarters of the East Is Red group in mid-February. The power of the school gradually passed over to the Leading Production Teams that the Red Flag group organized with the cadres whom the East Is Red group had attacked as power holders in January.

It seems that the rebel forces in the agricultural system confronted a total collapse by the end of February:

More than twenty organizations, big and small, were crushed by this adverse current. . . . There were extremely few revolutionary organizations which escaped being crushed by this adverse current. . . . [Only three student organizations survived the crush.] Even so, these three organizations were in serious difficulties. The revolutionary rebel groups in the agricultural and forestry sectors were savagely undermined and damaged.[70]

In contrast, the conservative forces, which had almost disintegrated in January, now regrouped themselves. After changing their names, some of them "directed the spearhead at the revolutionary groups, filling the role of butchers for T'an Chen-lin."[71] The suddenly changed fortunes of the rebels and the power holders were well summarized by the rebels themselves: "Those cadres who were rectified by the masses became self-evident 'leftists,' and those revolutionary big-character posters which were attacked by the power holders at the early stage of the Cultural Revolution again became poisonous weeds overnight."[72]

Alarmed by the extent of the reversal and the possible total collapse of

69. *P'i T'an chan-pao,* 16 June 1967.    70. Ibid.
71. Ibid.    72. *Hung-chan pao,* 16 March 1967.

their power bases,[73] the Cultural Revolution Small Group intervened on behalf of the student radicals. They demanded that T'an Chen-lin protect the East Is Red group and withdraw the Red Rebels from the school campuses.[74] T'an then moved to reconcile the two warring factions by declaring that both the East Is Red group and the Red Flag group of the Agricultural College were revolutionary organizations, and by instructing the Red Rebels to accept the students into the revolutionary committees of the various ministries.[75]

On March 6, Ch'i Pen-yü informed the radical groups by telephone that all the rebel organizations in the government units which had been labeled as counterrevolutionary in February were to be reinstated, and that the Center had withdrawn the provision protecting T'an, thus signaling a new reversal and a new wave of attacks on the "February Adverse Current."[76]

## The PLA and the "February Adverse Current"

Despite its numerous internal cleavages (e.g., factional affiliations, differences between reds versus experts, central leaders versus regional military commanders, and interdepartmental differences),[77] the PLA acted as a more or less unified entity in the Great Proletarian Cultural Revolution. Two basic institutional interests bound all the diverse PLA leaders. First, the PLA leaders had common interests in preserving the basic social structures of which the PLA was an integral part. Second, the PLA was a combat force which needed organizational integrity, especially hierarchical command structures, more than any Leninist Party. These two basic institutional interests defined the maximum extent to which the PLA could tolerate radicalization of the mass movement, and also defined the boundary within which the PLA could form coalitions with other political groups. The PLA

73. As T'an Chen-lin told his confidant, "the struggle [against the radicals] in the agricultural department is actually against the CRSG." It seems that among the government leaders the CRSG was openly criticized. They said that "Chiang Ch'ing has never done any mass work and has no practical experience in struggle," that "the CRSG was not amenable to Chairman Mao's criticism [and] since it dares not oppose Chairman Mao outwardly it can only exploit the T'an Chen-lin question." Chiang I-chen, acting Minister of Agriculture, even wrote a "petition to Chairman Mao on behalf of the people," asking "Does the CRSG depend on the workers and peasants or intellectuals?" "Crush T'an-Chiang-Ch'i Counterrevolutionary Clique," *SCMPS*, no. 219 (29 February 1968), pp. 6-10.

74. *Hsin nung-ta,* 1 April 1967.

75. "Shocking Counterrevolutionary Tragedy on March 13," *SCMPS*, no. 198 (16 August 1967), pp. 10-15. *Chin-chün pao,* 20 March 1967.

76. *Chin-chün pao,* 15 March 1967.

77. For the various interpretations of the PLA in the CR, see Joffe Ellis, "The Chinese Army After the CR: The Effect of Intervention," *CQ*, no. 55, July-September 1973; Harvey Nelson, "Military Forces in the Cultural Revolution," *CQ*, no. 51 (July-September 1972), pp. 444-474; William W. Whitson, *The Chinese High Command* (New York: Praeger, 1973).

could go along with the Cultural Revolution Small Group only insofar as the latter was willing to respect the PLA's two minimum interests.

As noted, the PLA took radical stands concerning the mass movement at the early stage when the two interests were not threatened. It challenged P'eng Chen's "February Outline" by producing the "Shanghai Forum," and, with its radical interpretation of "politics in command," it opened the attack on the moderate ideology of the Party. When the Red Guards appeared in the summer of 1966, the PLA provided no more than simple logistical support. But when the Cultural Revolution changed from an inner conflict within the elite to a mass conflict against the elite, the PLA reached a point from which it could not further radicalize the movement without undermining its own institutional interests. It could not support the radical mass organizations as unequivocally as the Small Group wanted, since the radicals consisted mainly of discontented social groups that were demanding a complete restructuring of the Chinese society. Nor could the PLA allow an uncontrolled mass movement within its own ranks without seriously undermining its own command structure. Moreover, it was not in Lin Piao's political interests to completely destroy the Party machinery when he became the official successor to Mao.

Thus, as noted, the PLA tried to resolve the dilemma between its rhetorical commitment to revolution and its conservative institutional interests by defining the Cultural Revolution as a mass movement for studying Mao's Thought. This attempt was again reflected in the 1967 New Year editorial of *Chieh-fang chün-pao*. In 1966 *Chieh-fang chün-pao* and *Hung ch'i* published a joint New Year editorial, but in 1967 *Chieh-fang chün-pao* published its own, while *Hung ch'i* published a joint editorial with *Jen-min jih-pao*. Moreover, in ironic contrast to *Hung ch'i* and *Jen-min jih-pao*, which called for a new victory of the Cultural Revolution, *Chieh-fang chün-pao* carried a sober and restrained editorial calling for the PLA to study Mao's Thought.[78]

When Mao's Thought was stressed as an object of study rather than as a guide for action, its relevance to the Cultural Revolution became minimal and it actually worked to calm down the revolutionary activities of the masses. Not surprisingly, Lin Chieh, one of the best-known radicals of the Cultural Revolution Small Group, contended that the masses should practice Mao's Thought, rather than study it for philosophical enlightenment:

The basic spirit of "creative study and application" as proposed by Comrade Lin Piao is to combine theory with practice. . . . "Application" means criticism, struggle, and revolution. It means daring to revolt against the small handful of inner-Party power holders who follow the capitalist road, to defeat the new counterattack of the

78. "Hold Still Higher the Great Red Banner of MTTT, Bring the Mass Movement for the Creative Study and Application of Chairman Mao's Work to a New and Higher Stage and Turn Our Army into a Genuine Great School of Mao Tse-tung's Thought," *PR*, no. 3 (13 January 1967), pp. 8-13.

bourgeois reactionary line. . . . Creative study and application of Chairman Mao's writing on the Great Proletarian Cultural Revolution means properly learning skills for struggling against the small handful of inner-Party power holders.[79]

Without naming it, Lin Chieh also criticized the PLA for its attempt to direct the Cultural Revolution to an apolitical study of Mao's Thought:

In some places, responsible persons deliberately set the study of Chairman Mao's writing and the Great Proletarian Cultural Revolution against each other. They organized meetings which were attended by a thousand people and at which applications were discussed. But they do not permit these to be associated with the Great Proletarian Cultural Revolution. On the contrary, they strike against comrades who insist that the study of Chairman Mao's writing must be associated with the Great Proletarian Cultural Revolution.[80]

In contrast to its subtle resistance to any substantive change of the political status quo, the PLA's opposition to the Cultural Revolution within its own ranks was more apparent. Like the Party organization, the PLA endeavored at the initial stage of the mass movement to preserve its own organizational integrity by stressing the importance of Party Committee leadership, organizational discipline, and the unique character of a military organization, and by directing the spearhead of the Cultural Revolution to the anti-rightist campaign. Like the civilian work teams, the PLA work teams sent to the various military academies suppressed the revolting PLA students.[81]

The Sixteen Articles gave the MAC and the General Political Department of the PLA discretion to oversee the Cultural Revolution within the PLA. Accordingly, the MAC formed the All Army Cultural Revolution Committee, with Liu Chih-chien as the deputy director of the General Political Department. During August and September of 1966, the All Army Cultural Revolution Committee continued the old policy of imposing strict control from the top on the PLA students, denying them the "four big freedoms" on the ground that the "military academies and schools had special characters."[82]

When the Red Guard movement shifted to the campaign against the "bourgeois reactionary line" in October, the MAC issued the "Urgent Notice" canceling all the previous regulations restraining the freedom of the PLA students.[83] However, the "Urgent Notice" still prohibited the mingling of the PLA personnel in the military academies with the local Red Guards, and this prohibition was effectively used against the PLA rebels. Liu Chih-chien was reported to have banned PLA personnel from reading Red Guard

79. "Living Study and Application of Chairman Mao's Writings in the CR," *Hung ch'i*, no. 2 (16 January 1967), pp. 42-43.

80. Ibid.

81. *Hsing-huo liao-yüan*, 2 February 1967.

82. Ibid.; *Tung-fang-hung*, 16 January 1967; *Chingkangshan*, 23 January 1967.

83. *CCP Documents of the Great Proletarian Cultural Revolution* (Hong Kong: Union Research Institute, 1968), p. 85.

newspapers, watching television broadcasts of political meetings, receiving Red Guard publications through the mail, or even meeting relatives who were in the Red Guards.[84] When the PLA's need to isolate itself from the Cultural Revolution became more acute in January 1966, Hu Chih, an active PLA member who was appointed president of the Hsin Hua News Agency in the autumn of 1966, tried to issue a "message to the whole army" that probably would have restricted the applicability of the Shanghai power seizure to the PLA.[85]

Despite this strenuous effort to prevent a full Cultural Revolution within the PLA, the PLA students in the military academies and schools had split into radicals and conservatives by the time of the January Power Seizure. For instance, the radical students of the PLA Literature Academy organized the First Revolutionary Commitee, while the conservative students formed the Second Revolutionary Committee.[86] Naturally, the PLA leaders supported the latter and refused the radicals' demand for a free exchange of experience with non-PLA mass organizations.

The rising tension between the PLA and the Cultural Revolution Small Group resulted in a reshuffling of the All Army Cultural Revolution Committee in January: Hsü Hsiang-chien replaced Liu Chih-chien; Chiang Ch'ing was made an adviser; and Kuan Feng, a member of the new All Army Cultural Revolution Committee, which was placed under the direct control of the MAC.[87] The Small Group expanded its influence over *Jen-min jih-pao* after Hu Chih and Tang P'ing-chu were dismissed from their posts. Mao's daughter, Li Na, who was working at *Chieh-fang chün-pao*, wrote a big-character poster on January 13 charging that, under the leadership of Liu Chih-chien, the paper had deviated in the past few months from the struggle between the two lines.[88] Shortly thereafter, *Chieh-fang chün-pao* was reorganized.[89] Right after the reorganization, the paper publicly acknowledged the existence of "a sharp and complicated" class struggle within the PLA, and recommended an all-out Cultural Revolution in the "higher-level leading organs, the military academies and schools, and the cultural and art organizations of our army."[90]

84. *Hsing-huo liao-yüan,* 27 January 1967, *DR,* 19 January 1967, p. CCC1.

85. *DR,* 20 January 1967,

86. *Hsing-huo liao-yüan,* 2 February 1967.

87. The new members were (1) head of the group: Hsü Hsiang-ch'ien; (2) advisor: Chiang Ch'ing; (3) deputy heads; Hsiao Hua, Yang Ch'eng-wu, Wang Tung-hsing, Li Man-ts'un; (4) members: Wang Hung-k'un, Yu Li-chin, Liu Hua-ch'ing, Tang P'ing-chu, Hu Chih, Yeh Ch'ün, Wang Feng, Ho Chu-en, Chang T'ao.

88. Chao Ts'ung, *Wen-ko yün-tung li-cheng shu-lüeh* (Hong Kong: Yu-lien yen-chiu-so, 1974), vol. 2, p. 467.

89. *Tsu kuo,* no. 71 (February 1970), pp. 32-36.

90. "Great Proletarian Cultural Revolution in Our Army Must Be Thoroughly Carried Out," *CFCP,* 14 January 1967, in *JMJP,* 15 January 1967.

It seems that the Cultural Revolution Small Group was eager to deepen its influence over the PLA by purging PLA leaders at the upper echelons. The next logical target was Hsiao Hua, director of the General Political Department, who, as a superior of Liu Chih-chien, was responsible for the suppression of the Cultural Revolution within the PLA. In his speech to the representatives of the military circle on January 19, Ch'en Po-ta criticized Hsiao Hua, who reportedly had insisted that "the Cultural Revolution in the Army cannot be interfered with."[91] Chiang Ch'ing also vilified him publicly: "Hsiao Hua is a gentleman but not a military man, and he has changed the Army into an army of bourgeoisie."[92] Soon the radical Red Guards raided Hsiao Hua's house.

However, the public attack on Hsiao Hua provoked instant opposition from the PLA and Chou En-lai. In a conference of nine hundred military leaders convened on January 21, Chou declared that, even though Hsiao Hua had made some mistakes, his problem was not serious and should be handled inside the MAC without interference from the masses. Chou was also critical of Ch'en Po-ta:

Comrade Ch'en Po-ta is a person who must have fully understood and practiced Mao's ideology, in view of his several decades of experience. It is inconceivable that he would have said things which would lower the prestige of the Army.[93]

After Chou's public criticism, Chiang Ch'ing, instead of denying the remark attributed to her, put the blame on those who revealed the Small Group's criticism to the masses.[94]

Some of the issue of the Cultural Revolution within the PLA was overshadowed by the PLA's new task of supporting the leftists. Recalling that the PLA had already exercised military control over the important state facilities, such as the broadcast stations and aviation facilities, since early January, Mao instructed the PLA to support the leftists in his January 22 letter to Lin Piao.[95] Lin objected to the idea because he felt that the PLA could not be trusted in all respects. Mao and Lin talked about the problem on the night of January 22,[96] but Mao insisted on his view, arguing that, "through supporting

91. *DR,* 25 January 1967, p. CCC16. Hsiao Hua was charged with resisting the CR within the PLA. He played the most active role in the Political Conference in February 1966 and was known as Lin Piao's man. *Chan wang,* no. 142 (1 January 1968), p. 20.

92. Reuter's, 20 January 1967.

93. *DR,* 25 January 1967, p. CCC16.

94. *Tsu kuo,* no. 71 (February 1970), pp. 32-36. After Chou's criticism, the Red Flag of the Peking Aviation College put up a big-character poster, alleging that "there are distortions in the statement made by comrades Ch'en and Chiang to criticize Hsiao Hua. Care should be taken, as false rumors are rampant." The Peking Third Headquarters, which had issued a public criticism of Hsiao Hua, withdrew its criticism. *Shou-tu hung-wei-ping,* 25 January 1967.

95. "Directives and Notices on the CR," *SCMMS,* no. 17 (15 January 1968), 29.

96. D. W. Fokkema, *Report from Peking: Observation of a Western Diplomat on the CR* (Montreal, Canada: McGill-Queen's University Press 1972), p. 62.

the leftists, the PLA will expose its own problems to society, and hence will be able to enhance the ideological level of our army."[97] The next day, the MAC ordered the PLA to support the leftists, to suppress the counterrevolutionary mass organizations, and not to be an "air raid shelter" for the power holders.[98]

At about this same time, Mao took steps to limit the Cultural Revolution within the PLA by ordering that "the large military areas" and "the frontier military regions, such as Tsinan, Nanking, Foochow, Canton, and Kunming Military Regions," should not all carry out the Cultural Revolution simultaneously.[99] On the basis of Mao's instruction, the MAC further expanded the number of units to be exempted from the Cultural Revolution in its order of January 28.[100] First, the order stipulated that commanders, fighters, political workers, orderlies, and medical personnel should all remain at their work posts. The exchange of revolutionary experience in the war preparation and security systems of the armed forces was also expressly prohibited. Second, the order prohibited the mass organizations from attacking the military leadership organs or confiscating military documents. Third, it left the impression that the Cultural Revolution within the PLA, if there was going to be any at all, was to be conducted under the existing leadership. Fourth, it ordered that even the armed forces units in which the Cultural Revolution had already been undertaken must use mild methods appropriate for handling contradictions among the people.

In February, the MAC further broadened the list of units to be exempted from the Cultural Revolution. These now included the navy fleet, the naval and air force schools, and the production and construction corps of the Sinkiang Military Region and other specified military districts. Even in the units in which the "four freedoms" were allowed, the power seizure was banned and a limited Cultural Revolution was to be conducted under the leadership of the Party Committee.[101]

The MAC also specifically limited the sphere in which power seizure could be carried out within the armed forces to the following units: "(1) academies and schools (exempting schools for training confidential personnel, schools specialized in pioneering techniques, flying schools, and classes and departments charged with the task of training foreign personnel); (2) literature and art groups, and physical culture detachments; (3) hospitals (limited only to the general hospitals of the PLA, the hospitals of the military services, and hospitals for training purposes); and (4) military factories (excluding those testing pioneering techniques, factories attached to naval bases, and top

97. *Huan ch'iu-chih,* 10 August 1967.
98. *CCP Documents of the GPCR,* pp. 195-197.
99. "Directives and Notices on the CR," *SCMPS,* no. 17 (15 January 1968), p. 34.
100. Ibid.
101. *CCP Documents of the GPCR,* p. 240.

secret factories)."[102] As a whole, all but a few military units were exempted from the power seizure.

With the Cultural Revolution within the PLA confined to manageable proportions, the PLA was given the additional task of providing the students with military training. The military training program had first been attempted at the end of December 1966, but was not carried out effectively, because of the Small Group's objection at that time.[103] However, on March 7, 1967, Mao renewed the program by approving an experimental training project by the Tientsin Military District.[104] Apparently the training was aimed at unifying the warring Red Guard factions.

In addition, the PLA had one more task to discharge. On March 28, when the radicals began to counterattack the "February Adverse Current," the Center ordered the PLA to support industry and agriculture. Although the meaning of this order was not specified, it clearly implied that production came before revolution.[105]

Thus, the PLA was given three supporting tasks and two military ones: it supported "leftists," industry, and agriculture, and provided military control and training. This meant that the PLA was involved in the Cultural Revolution at three different levels with three different functions: (1) it exercised military control over some localities and some Party organs and helped the leftists with the seizure of power; (2) it imposed a certain degree of discipline on the Red Guards so that they could form a great alliance at the school level; and (3) it ensured production at the basic levels of industry and agriculture.

Apparently the decision to use the PLA to achieve seemingly contradictory goals stemmed from the compromise reached among the various elite groups. Although we do not have much evidence, it is a reasonable guess that the Small Group did not oppose the policy of using the PLA to support the left in the power seizure. On the other hand, the Small Group had to agree with Chou's attempt to minimize economic disruption by using the PLA at the basic production units. Some PLA leaders might well have opposed using the PLA for the support of the left,[106] although they would not have opposed military control in principle. They also undoubtedly preferred the PLA's participation in the three-in-one combination to the alternative of supporting the leftists and giving power to them. Confronted with a choice between an

102. Ibid., p. 289.

103. "Directives and Notices on the CR," *SCMMS*, no. 17 (15 January 1968), p. 23. Chiang Ch'ing reportedly said that the military training team could only be carried out in schools where the radicals had consolidated their position.

104. *Hsin pei-chi*, 9 March 1967.

105. For instance, see *JMJP*, 19 March 1967; "See What Kind of 'United Action Committee of Capital Red Guard' It Is," *SCMP*, no. 3906 (28 March 1967), pp. 14-15; *Chingkangshan*, 15 February 1967.

106. Edward E. Rice, *Mao's Way* (Berkeley and Los Angeles: University of California Press, 1972), p. 309.

active or a passive involvement of the PLA, the PLA leaders might well have agreed to the PLA's support of the leftists in exchange for a restriction of the Cultural Revolution within the PLA.

Whatever the rationale of the PLA's involvement, once it was given such important tasks the PLA's actual behavior became the most powerful factor in shaping the course of the Cultural Revolution. Generally speaking, the PLA supported the conservative rather than the radical mass organizations for the following reasons. First, the PLA moved into the Cultural Revolution in February 1967, the period when deradicalization started. Second, as we have noted, the PLA expected to play contradictory roles: it was expected to support the left in the power seizure, while ensuring production; and simultaneously it was expected to help the left to consolidate its power, while imposing a great alliance on the students. Third, the PLA in general had maintained a good relationship with the power holders, especially with the provincial Party Committees. This good relationship was due to the organization of the PLA.

Organizationally, before the Cultural Revolution, the PLA commanders were under the regional Party Committees, and it was the usual practice to appoint the First Secretary of a regional Party Committee to be the First Political Commissar of the local PLA unit. At the level of Central Ministries, many PLA personnel were recruited for the work teams. Obviously, the lack of conflict between the PLA units and the local Party Committees kept the PLA from taking an aggressive attitude toward them. This was particularly true when there was no alternative leadership within a Party Committee. In the Party Committees where alternative leadership did exist—such as Shanghai, Shansi, Shantung, and Heilungchiang—the PLA could throw its support to the revolutionary cadres without much difficulty. But where no alternative Party leadership existed, the PLA had to select leading cadres who satisfied its own tastes as well as the demands of the leftists. However, the leftists usually supported cadres who completely disregarded the norms of the Party organization, and these cadres were often regarded as unacceptable "ambitionists" by the PLA, which preferred cadres who were at least willing to balance revolutionary zeal with organizational norms. In the eyes of the radicals, on the other hand, such cadres were the power holders who had not broken their ties with the Party Committees.

Finally, there was no reason for the PLA to support the radicals except for the order from the Center. As we have noted, the radicals' family back ground was generally "bad," their social status was low, and their grievances were many.[107] In addition, their tactics were violent, their ideology was

---

107. For instance, one of the crimes attributed to the Kwangtung August 1 Steel Combat Corps reads: "They openly agitated all those who have been criticized to rise together to seize power and reverse the verdict. They also enlisted into their organization the landlords, rich

anti-organizational, and their ultimate aim was to change the Chinese social structure in which the PLA had its own very high stakes. Worse still, the radicals considered the PLA leaders to be power holders, and had attacked the PLA units in late January and early February. In Canton, the radicals raided the PLA compounds, demanding a thorough Cultural Revolution within the PLA; and in Fukien the radicals stormed the military headquarters on two occasions, kidnapping soldiers and beating them up.[108]

Considering these factors, it is not surprising that the PLA exercised the authority granted to it by the order of January 28 to disband "counterrevolutionary organizations" by suppressing the radicals, thereby creating what the radicals later called the "March Black Winds." In Szechwan, the PLA fired at the radicals, killing and wounding many persons. In Kwangtung, the best-known radical-worker organizations were disbanded and their leaders arrested.[109] Also disbanded and suppressed were the Anhwei Revolutionary Rebel Command Headquarters and the Revolutionary Rebel Workers' Headquarters in Anhwei, the Workers' General Headquarters in Wuhan, and the Hsiang-chiang Feng-lai in Hunan.[110]

Among the many provinces, Fukien was the most interesting case, for it was this case that clearly showed that it was not only the individual military leaders but the general mood of the Peking leadership that contributed to the "March Black Winds."[111] The Fukien radicals gathered around a broad alliance of the August 29 Commune, while the conservatives, supporting Yeh Fei, First Secretary of the province, rallied under the Revolutionary Rebel Committee *(Ko tsao hui)*. In January, the August 29 Commune declared a power seizure of the provincial Party Committee, but the Center did not officially approve it. On January 26, under the leadership of the August 29 Commune, the radicals raided the "Conference of Mao's Thought Activists" and its sponsor, the Fukien Military Command. On February 11, the Fukien PLA organized a mass rally with the member organizations of the Revolutionary Rebel Committee, which denounced the January 26 raid as a "new

peasants, counterrevolutionaries, bad elements, and rightists in certain districts and hsien in Kwangtung province, with the vain attempt of counterrevolution. They carried out class retaliation and sought to reverse the verdict on five categories. . . . In places where they had power, they spread the words that they would strike down all party members, CYL members, and activists in studying Chairman Mao's work, and openly changed the verdict on the puppet army officers and five category elements. With their encouragement and support, hordes of monsters and demons got out of the cages, while landlords and capitalists stepped up to the platform to make complaints about their grievances." "The Counterrevolutionary Crimes of the August 1 Fighting Corps," *SCMP,* no. 3905 (23 March 1967), pp. 1-4.

108. Chao Ts'ung, *Wen-hua yün-tung li-ch'eng shu-lüeh* (Hong Kong: Yu-lien yen-chiu-so, 1974), vol. 2, pp. 682-698.

109. See page 230.

110. *Chung-kung wen-hua ta ko-ming chung-yao wen-chien hui-pien,* p. 146.

111. Ibid., pp. 156, 158, 233.

counterattack of the bourgeois reactionary line."[112] The Center approved the Revolutionary Rebel Committee by publishing its declaration in *Jen-min jih-pao.*[113] Obviously encouraged by the support of the Center, the Fukien PLA disbanded many organizations of the August 29 Commune and arrested several thousands of their members.[114]

When the PLA started the twenty days of military training, most of the middle-school campuses were deserted, since many students had left for an "exchange of experience" or a power seizure, and even the few remaining students were divided into various warring factions.[115] The Center therefore issued two orders at the end of February to the effect that all the students were to stop their exchange of experience and return to their respective schools to make revolution there.[116]

The military training teams from the PLA organized "meetings of accusation," "meetings of criticism," and "meetings of discussion" with the different factions. They also criticized mistaken views such as the "theory of natural redness," and they rehabilitated the victims of the "bourgeois reactionary line" to the satisfaction of the radicals. At the same time, they restrained the rehabilitated students from attacking their conservative classmates.[117] In other words, the PLA impartially criticized both conservatives and radicals for their share of mistakes, but did not actively attempt to change the existing organizational strength of either side, and so left the conflict unresolved. Consequently, whichever side held power at each middle school supported the PLA military training team, and in the colleges the radicals supported the program, since they had the upper hand there.

The PLA's task in the middle schools was more complicated than that in the colleges, for in the middle schools the "theory of natural redness" was still the hottest issue, and it was the conservative forces that constituted the majority. The radical minority insisted on a thorough criticism of the "theory of natural redness" as a precondition for the great alliance, whereas the conservatives refused to repudiate the theory earnestly.[118] As for the method of alliance, the radicals demanded that the PLA take the leftists—"those who had suffered most from the bourgeois reactionary line"—as the "core"

112. *JMJP*, 17 February 1967.
113. Ibid.
114. *Chung-kung wen-hua ta ko-ming chung-yao wen-chien hui-pien*, pp. 150-152.
115. *Tung-fang-hung pao*, 25 April 1967.
116. *CCP Documents of the GPCR*, p. 319, 343.
117. *Ta-han ta-chao*, 22 February 1967. *Tung-fang-hung pao*, 23 February 1967.
118. Even though the children of good class background made self-criticism about their mistaken view of class line, the children from the "bad" family background were suspicious of their sincerity. They said that "at the present they [conservatives] criticized the theory of 'natural redness' if they seized power. . . ." On the other hand the conservatives insisted that, although they made mistakes, still the children from "bad" families were not good enough to seize the power. *Chung-hsüeh lun-t'an*, 6 April 1967; *Tung-fang-hung pao*, 25 April 1967.

of the leadership and develop a leftist majority around them, while rejecting all "those who made mistakes" by following the "bourgeois reactionary line."[119] The conservative majority, however, called for free elections, refusing to accept the leadership of the radicals because of their "bad" family background: "In the past, we had privileged thought *(t'e ch'üan ssu-hsiang)* and suppressed our classmates from 'bad' family backgrounds. We admit that. But now it is reversed. These sons of bitches want to discriminate in reverse and suppress us."[120]

The radicals opposed free elections, since that would only give rise to the "harmonizers, compromisers, and strategists."[121] The conservatives argued that they were "hoodwinked" by the power holders but were now reformed.[122] But the radicals refused to accept that they were reformed, "since there is no room for them to be 'reborn' or to be 'reformed.' "[123] As for the criterion of being a revolutionary, the radicals insisted on looking at "the history of struggle" rather than verbal commitments, since anyone could make verbal commitments to revolution; whereas the conservatives criticized the radicals for opposing Mao's dictum of "curing the disease to save the patient," and for attacking anyone holding different opinions on the excuse of attacking the United Action Committee.[124]

In these endless squabbles between the two sides, the PLA leaned toward the conservatives, if not because of its ideological agreement with them, then because of the conservatives' support of the great alliance. When the PLA pressed for the great alliance, the Peking middle school students were divided into the April 3 and the April 4 factions, according to their opposition to or support of the military training program. The April 3 faction denounced the military training program as "rightist capitulationism," "reformism," and a "new bourgeois reactionary line," and called on the PLA members to revolt against the "power holders within the PLA."[125] For their part, the military training teams and the April 4 faction accused the April 3 faction of "splitism," "anarchism," and "sabotaging the military training and the great alliance initiated by Chairman Mao."[126]

Nevertheless, the opposition to the PLA's military training program spread to the factories, the government organs, the schools, the universities, and the

---

119. *Tung-fang-hung pao,* 25 April 1967; *Ping-tuan chan-pao,* 12 March 1967.

120. *Ping-t'uan chan-pao,* 12 March 1967.

121. Ibid., 25 March 1967.

122. Ibid., 20 May 1967.

123. Ibid., 20 March 1967.

124. Ibid., 8 May 1968.

125. Ibid., 20 May 1967; *Tung-fang-hung pao,* 6 June 1967; *Chung-hsüeh hung-wei-ping,* May 1968.

126. *Ping-t'uan chan-pao,* 20 May 1967.

colleges,[127] and the radicals began to criticize the PLA by using the slogan of "dragging out the handful of power holders in the PLA":

The handful of capitalist-roaders in the Army, taking advantage of the big plan of the three-in-one combination suggested by Mao, cultivated the conservative organizations, suppressed the revolutionary masses, reinstated the power holders who were struck down by the revolutionary masses, and in some areas carried out the revival of capitalism.[128]

The radicals' criticism of the PLA found support in the Cultural Revolution Small Group. The Small Group basically agreed to the need for military training, but at the same time charged that the PLA tended to support the conservative forces. As early as March 3, Chiang Ch'ing bluntly stated that the Peking Garrison Command had supported the United Action Committee.[129] By April 4, Chiang Ch'ing again whipped up the enthusiasm of the radicals by reproaching the PLA for suppressing them. "Asking the Communist Army to train the students was a mistake," she said.[130] Even a moderate member of the Small Group, Hsieh Fu-chih, joined in criticizing the PLA by saying that the military training program was a mistake and, if necessary, "should be suspended."[131] Yao Wen-yüan was even more blunt:

The great revolutionary alliance and the revolutionary three-in-one combination must support and strengthen the leftists. Recently, more than three hundred middle schools in Peking underwent military training, but the strength of the leftists is weak and the strength of the conservatives is comparatively strong in some schools. That trend is due to the insufficient stress on revolution in the great alliance. The great alliance is a revolutionary great alliance. The Red Guard Congress and the Workers' Congress are the representative organs of the revolutionary masses; neither are they a conference of all workers and all students, nor can they be elected by all students or all workers. . . .
In military training, the important thing is that the students [should be allowed to] resolve [conflicts] by themselves. The PLA does not have that much capability. Also the PLA needs time to understand the situation in the schools. The military training must not stand outside the great revolutionary criticism [of the bourgeois reactionary line].[132]

Later, the Small Group ordered the rehabilitation of the students who were attacked because of their "opposition to the military training" and their "opposition to the PLA."[133]

As the military training program became the hottest dispute between the radicals and the conservatives, Chou En-lai again tried to resolve the conflict

127. Ibid.
128. *Chan wang*, no. 150 (May 1968), pp. 6-9.
129. Ibid.
130. Ibid.; *Nihon keizai*, 7 April 1967.
131. *Chan wang*, May 1968, pp. 6-9.
132. *Kan chin chao*, 26 April 1967.
133. Special issue of *Hsin nung-ta*, quoted in *Fei-ch'ing nien-pao*, July 1970.

by ordering both factions to send their delegates to the Small Group to settle the controversy. Chou appeared to side with the Small Group by criticizing the PLA for promoting the "alliance of the various classes" instead of the "alliance of leftists."[134] After his criticism, *Jen-min jih-pao* carried an article criticizing the military training teams for emphasizing organizational discipline while disregarding revolutionary zeal.[135] Nevertheless, the effort to persuade the PLA to support the radicals did not work out. The PLA continued to support the conservatives in subtle ways.

## The Radicals' Counterattack and the Stalemate in the Summer of 1967

The shift of official policy back to the radical direction was first hinted at on March 10, when *Jen-min jih-pao* declared that, "within the revolutionary three-in-one combination, it is imperative to give full weight to the rule of the leaders of the revolutionary mass organizations, and never to regard them simply as the supporting cast."[136] Otherwise, it said, "there can be no revolutionary three-in-one combination, and the Great Proletarian Cultural Revolution will be negated." There was also an ominous warning to those who made use of "minor mistakes of the masses to discredit their achievements" that unless they rectified their own mistakes and "drew a clear line between themselves, on the one hand, and the power holders, on the other," they would be excluded from the three-in-one combination.[137]

Immediately after the editorial, the Peking radicals, led by the Peking Normal University Chingkangshan, launched a public criticism of T'an Chen-lin, who was highly vulnerable because of his outspoken personality and his active manipulation of the conservative mass organizations in the agricultural system.[138] Soon the Peking Red Guard Congress designated T'an as their number one enemy, and the anti-T'an campaign became a major activity of the Peking Red Guards.

The criticism of T'an was followed by an attack on all the vice-premiers—Ch'en I, Li Hsien-nien, and Yü Ch'iu-li—who were more or less responsible for the "February Adverse Current." Although Chou En-lai was not openly criticized, the attack on his vice-premiers, who carried out his policies in February, was bound to lead to Chou. In fact, many radicals were secretly preparing a future attack on Chou, and it was during this time that many

134. *Chan wang,* May 1968, pp. 6-9.
135. *JMJP,* 13 May 1967.
136. Ibid., 10 March 1967.
137. Ibid.
138. The CRSG publicly criticized T'an Chen-lin on March 10. *Pei-ching kung-she,* 14 August 1967. For the attack on Li Hsien-nien, see *Pei-ching kung-she,* 1 April 1967.

big-character posters defending Chou and condemning his critics went up in the streets of Peking.[139]

When the counterattack on the "February Adverse Current" was gathering momentum in mid-March, Mao called for separate meetings of the Politburo and the MAC to "study the present situation related to the 'reversal current,' and to discuss ways and means to overcome [it]."[140] Although information is scarce, it is possible to deduce each group's position. In the Politburo meeting, the Cultural Revolution Small Group probably pressed for the reversal of the lenient cadre policy, and for an official sanction of the Red Guards' counterattack on those perverting Mao's cadre policy.[141] Chou En-lai probably admitted that some cadres were guilty of exploiting the cadre policy to protect themselves, but argued that the exploitation should not be regarded as an "antagonistic contradiction," and could be rectified by correctly implementing the policy rather than by changing it. The PLA leaders probably argued that, although the PLA had made mistakes in supporting the leftists, those mistakes should not be used to attack the PLA.

Mao probably agreed with the majority opinions, partially because at that time he could not afford to antagonize Chou and the local PLA commanders by expanding the targets to the vice-premiers and the regional PLA commanders, and partially because the majority opinions were consistent with his strategical dictum of "uniting 95 percent to attack 5 percent."[142] Consequently, the meeting appears to have made the following compromise solutions: first, to launch a public campaign against Liu Shao-ch'i; second, to continue the policies of the great alliance, and three-in-one combination, and the revolutionary committee formula; and third, to bolster the position of the rebel mass organizations within the framework of the existing policy, and not to the extent of completely depriving the conservative mass organizations of their right to take part in the power seizure.

Liu Shao-ch'i had been attacked in the Red Guard newspapers since

139. *DR*, 1 / March 1967, p. CCC6. One of the interesting big-character posters against Chou charged that he exercised abstention on the question of dispatching work teams, thus wavering. Intentionally or unintentionally, Chou was on a foreign trip at the time when the work teams were dispatched. The content of the big character poster leads us to suspect that the information was provided to the radicals by the CRSG.
140. *DR*, 17 March 1967, p. CCC4.
141. For the conference, see *DR*, 17 March 1967, p. CCC4; 7 April 1967, p. CCC21. While the meetings were in session, Ch'i Pen-yü complained. "In connection with the problems of screening, the bourgeois power faction is attempting to take advantage of this opportunity to make counterattacks or to support the conservatives from the rear, trying to make use of all possible chance. The same can be said about the problem of great alliance and the rectification problem." *DR*, 17 March 1967, p. CCC4. A Japanese correspondent speculated that "therefore it is possible that new instructions will be issued on the method of promoting the great cultural revolution from now on, following the convening of a series of meetings." Ibid.
142. For the article defending Chou En-lai, see *Hung-wei-ping*, 30 May 1967.

December 1966, but his problem was never mentioned in the official newspapers until Ch'i Pen-yü's article, "Patriotism or National Betrayal?" was published in *Jen-min jih-pao* on March 30, 1967. The newly reorganized *Pei-ching jih-pao* opened the official attack on Liu's "Self-Cultivation" and his theory of "docile tools" on April 7, 1967.[143] Soon the public news media were filled with articles criticizing Liu, and the Tsinghua radicals were so bold as to interrogate his wife, Wang Kuang-mei, on April 6.[144]

The official campaign against Liu was undoubtedly intended to limit the targets and to unify the warring mass organizations by directing the main thrust of the movement at Liu. In particular, the charge that Liu carried out a policy of "hitting at many in order to protect a few," though partially valid, was a shrewd and timely political attempt to regain the support of the cadres by attributing the rampant anti-cadre feelings among the masses to Liu.[145]

Concurrently with the official attack on Liu, the Center moved to re-emphasize the role of the masses in the three-in-one combination and the priority of revolution over production. *Hung ch'i*, No. 5, specifically criticized those who wanted to moderate the power seizure for the sake of production.[146] The PLA was warned not to put production before revolution in its work of supporting industry.[147] Furthermore, the PLA was also instructed to apply the following specific and radical criteria to determine if an organization was leftist: first, find out how the organization was born; second, see who fought most bravely and most resolutely against those in authority who were taking the capitalist road; third, find out who followed Chairman Mao's instructions and consistently clung to the "specific policy of grasping revolution and promoting production"; fourth, see who was discriminated against and punished by those in authority who were taking the capitalist road; and fifth, find out who was capable of uniting the great majority of the masses to realize the great alliance.[148] According to these criteria, only the radicals could claim to be leftists.

While enhancing the radicals' position, the Center took measures to circumscribe the PLA's power. In April, the All Army Cultural Revolution Group was reorganized, and Hsü Hsiang-ch'ien was relieved as its head. On April 6, the MAC issued the "Ten Point Order," which prohibited the PLA from arresting the masses, disbanding mass organizations, or retaliating against those radicals who raided the PLA.[149] Simultaneously, the Center

143. *JMJP,* 10 April 1967.
144. *Current Scene* 31, no. 9 (31 May 1967): 7-8.
145. *JMJP,* 31 March 1967.
146. *JMJP,* 23 March 1967.
147. Ibid. Also see *JMJP,* 11 and 28 April 1967.
148. *JMJP,* 23 March 1967.
149. "Directives and Notices on the CR," *SCMMS,* no. 17 (15 January 1968), p. 78.

proceeded to undo the mistakes made by the local PLA commanders—that is, the Peking leaders met with the representatives of the mass organizations and with the PLA leaders from the provinces and rendered their judgment on the PLA's work. The Peking leaders condemned Chao Yung-fu, the Deputy Commander of the Tsinghai Military Region, for ordering his troops to fire at the masses.[150] They also ruled that the PLA had wrongly disbanded the mass organizations in Anhwei, Fukien, Inner Mongolia, Kwangtung, and Szechwan, and that the disbanded mass organizations should immediately be rehabilitated.[151]

In order to persuade the PLA to rectify its mistakes and to support the radical mass organizations, on the one hand, and, on the other, to restrain the radical mass organizations from retaliating against the PLA, an ambiguous slogan was devised telling everyone to "love the people and support the Army." However, the mere coining of the slogan did not resolve the conflicts, which were deeply rooted. The Cultural Revolution Small Group and the PLA differed on the slogan's interpretation—the PLA stressing the part about supporting the army, and the Small Group stressing the part about loving the people.

If the Cultural Revolution had undergone a cyclical change from the radical phase of January—with its strategic priority on rooting out the vested interests in Chinese society through a power seizure controlled from the bottom—to the moderate phase in February—with its emphasis on checking disruption and conflicts that the January Power Seizure had created these two strategic goals were pursued simultaneously after April and until July. In other words, the Center tried to combine the revolutionary momentum of January and the pragmatism of February without the two tendencies undermining each other. As a result, with regard to such crucial issues as the power relationships among the mass organizations, the PLA, and the cadres, and the conflict between the conservative and radical mass organizations, the official positions were very ambiguous, at best.

Power seizure and "ideological transformation" were simultaneously emphasized as the major tasks of the movement. The masses were encouraged to seize power, and at the same time were told to limit their activities within their respective units. In order to moderate the power seizure, the Center even revived the ambiguous slogan of "struggle, criticism, and transformation of each unit"—a slogan that had earlier been denounced on the ground that it had been coined by the power holders to sabotage the Cultural Revolution in the autumn of 1966.

The Center also endeavored to form great alliances, three-in-one combinations, and revolutionary committees without giving up its effort to strengthen

150. *Chung-kung wen-hua ta ko-ming chung-yao wen-chien hui-pien,* p. 157.
151. Ibid., pp. 149-166.

the position of the mass organizations within the three-in-one combinations. They insisted that the masses were to determine the good cadres, while at the same time urging the masses to liberate all those cadres whose mistakes were due not to their opposition to the Party or Mao's Thought but to a lack of proper understanding of the Cultural Revolution, deception by the power holders, or personality shortcomings. The Center readily conceded that the masses tended to make many mistakes as they changed from a position of oppression to one of exercising power, but the Center still demanded that the cadres respect the authority of the mass organizations.

However, the most crucial point remaining unclear in the official policy was the relationship between the radical and conservative mass organizations. Here again, the Center pursued contradictory goals by trying to give the upper hand to the radicals without disbanding the conservative mass organizations, so as to form a great alliance which would be as large as possible. The Center defined the conflict between the conservative and radical mass organizations as a contradiction among the people, but continued to stress a revolutionary great alliance with "leftists" at the core.[152] At the request of Chou En-lai, Mao even ordered the release of the United Action Committee members who had been arrested in December 1966.[153]

Despite the Center's intervention on behalf of the disbanded radical mass organizations, the official strategy of balancing revolution and order hurt the radicals, whose efforts to regain the dominant position they had held during the January Power Seizure could not be realized without a wholesale radicalization of the official policy. Even the official call to concentrate the spearhead of the mass movement against Liu Shao-ch'i, a dead tiger by that time, served the interests of the conservatives. The main issue dividing the conservatives and the radicals was no longer Liu but the government leaders and the PLA. The conservatives were therefore quite willing to concentrate their attack on Liu so as to check the expansion of the targets and to prove their revolutionary enthusiasm; whereas the radicals, whose main concern was to seize the power of the government and the PLA in their own hands, denounced the conservatives' attack on Liu as "criticizing 'Self-Cultivation' in the fashion of self-cultivation."[154] This meant that, in the eyes of the radicals, the conservatives were displaying a "slave mentality" by attacking only the officially sanctioned targets.

On the whole, the attempt to achieve these contradictory goals simultaneously was as ineffective as the earlier attempt to achieve them in sequence. The radicals and the conservatives both readily justified their own positions by quoting selective elements from the official policy. The conservatives

152. *JMJP*, 21 April 1967; 18 June 1968.
153. *Ping-t'uan chan-pao*, 21 April 1967, *Sankei*, 29 April 1967.
154. *Ping-t'uan chan-pao*, 27 April 1967.

accused the radicals of sabotaging the official policy of the great alliance and the three-in-one combination, and of being guilty of split-ism, anarchism, and factionalism. They also denounced the radicals for using "the demarcation lines between the 'masses,' the 'ordinary cadres,' and the 'leading cadres' as a criterion for revolution and counter-revolution."[155]

The radicals rejoined that it was the conservatives who "distorted the policy of the revolutionary three-in-one combination, used the three-in-one combination to promote compromise, . . . and brought back the power holders by fishing in muddy waters, usurping the fruit of the Great Proletarian Cultural Revolution, and carrying out the counterrevolutionary restoration."[156] Another radical criticism was clearly directed against the PLA, "who used their legitimate authority *(chih-ch'üan)* to propagate the theory of harmony, confused the demarcation line between the revolutionary rebels and the conservatives, and hit at the revolutionary rebels."[157]

To complicate matters further, each side knew perfectly well that its stand was supported by some members of the divided elite. The Small Group continued to reveal its preoccupation with power seizure rather than with the ideological transformation of the mass organizations. Chiang Ch'ing interpreted the relationship between the two:

The struggle, criticism, and transformation within each unit does not contradict the criticism of the power holders taking the capitalist road in the Party organization, and both can be unified. . . . One should not divert the struggle against the handful of power holders in the Party.[158]

Hsieh Fu-chih warned against exploiting the moderate official policy:

In early April, the Peking Municipality started the big criticism and big demonstrations. That is the main direction. But the conservative forces again became active, exploiting the main direction: they took the rebels as the major targets; they did not aim at the main direction or at the important persons, nor at the big right and big wrong. Naturally, we should not be tricked. At present, the main direction is to criticize in a big way, to struggle in a big way, and to form alliances in a big way. Without the great criticism and a big struggle, the great alliance is impossible. . . . Only through a great criticism and a big struggle can the big alliance be realized, and the revolutionary three-in-one combination is only possible where there is a big alliance.[159]

In contrast, the conservatives stressed criticism and struggle within each unit, justifying their position with Lin Piao's remark that "we should make ourselves the object of revolution. . . . If one does not revolutionize oneself, the revolution cannot proceed smoothly."[160]

The burden of reconciling these two divergent positions was passed on to

155. *Ts'ai-mao hung-ch'i,* 23 February 1967.      156. *Pei-ching kung-she,* 14 March 1967.
157. *Tung-fang-hung pao,* 6 June 1967.            158. *Ping-t'uan chan-pao,* 21 April 1967.
159. *Hsin-wen chan-pao,* 14 May 1967.             160. *JMJP,* 10 July 1967.

the PLA, which now was given the responsibility and authority to carry out the ambiguous policies. From April onward, the PLA outwardly conceded that it had supported the conservatives. However, it was one thing to admit mistakes under pressure from the Center, and another thing to support the radicals. As the Party leaders had done, the PLA developed many ingenious tactics to passively resist the pressure from the Center and to discriminate against the radicals. The self-criticism of the Fukien Military Region made in April 1968, one year after the Center had pointed out its mistakes, graphically illustrates the attitude of the PLA toward the radical mass organizations:

> After the Center pointed out our mistakes, we still did not understand the nature, seriousness, and danger of our mistakes. . . . We did not do our best to carry out the Premier's six-point instruction on the problem of January 26 and February 7. After the Center delivered a ten-point opinion on the Fukien problem [on April 30, 1967], we should have promptly rectified the mistakes, but we misunderstood the Center's support as a [sign] of forgiving our mistakes. Since our understanding of important instructions by the Premier, Comrade Ch'en Po-ta, and the Cultural Revolution Small Group was not deep, instead of promptly and sincerely carrying out [the instructions], we dragged out the work of making self-examinations and rehabilitations. Some arrested people were not released until the end of July. We thought that there was some resistance at the bottom of the rehabilitations and releases, but actually the resistance first rested with us.
>
> After rehabilitation . . . we still had some ideological and emotional reservations. In words we treated equally two factions of mass organizations respectively represented by the August 29 Commune and the Revolutionary Reform Committee, but in deeds we patronized one faction and neglected the other. We were enthusiastic toward one faction and cold toward the other, thus leading to the confrontation between the two factions. Because our determination was not high and our Party character was not strong, we failed to educate the troops by making a penetrating self-examination; nor did we make ourselves the models for our troops by rectifying our mistaken actions. Consequently, some subdistricts, militia departments, and other units made mistakes in the work of supporting leftists, and rectification was not made quickly. Our leadership must bear responsibility for the problems which occurred at the lower levels.[161]

This long quotation clearly shows that the PLA had continued to discriminate against the radicals in subtle ways. The same was true of the government leaders. The government leaders were willing to admit their mistakes, to accept the radicals as "revolutionary rebels," and to allow them to criticize the "February Adverse Current," but they were unwilling to support the radicals or to share power in a meaningful way with them. Nor did they give up their support of the conservative mass organizations. Throughout the summer, the radicals held mass rallies denouncing the "February Adverse Current" and its instigators, the vice-premiers and the ministers. But all the

161. *Chung-kung wen-hua ta ko-ming chung-yao wen-chien hui-pien,* p. 160.

vice-premiers survived, and their mass organizations also survived, so that the radicals gained nothing in terms of power.[162]

The masterful evasive tactics of the PLA and the government leaders reinforced the radicals' determination to seize power in their own hands, but they could not achieve their goal unless the official policy shifted back to the radical power seizure of January. This was impossible because of the stalemate between the Cultural Revolution Small Group and the moderate group at the elite level.

According to the rules of the game at that moment, the attacks on the "February Adverse Current" and on the vice-premiers were officially tolerated and even sanctioned, whereas any public attack on Chou En-lai was prohibited, although he was ultimately responsible for the "February Adverse Current." The PLA's suppression of the radicals in March was officially criticized, and the masses were allowed to criticize the PLA, but an open attack on the PLA was prohibited,[163] despite its continuing discrimination against the radicals. Also, any open challenge to the official policy was strictly prohibited. These rules bound the elite more strictly than the masses; hence only the masses could break the stalemate.

Soon the rules gave rise to the tactic of attacking the lower-level leaders of each elite group and holding them responsible for the actions of the group. The radicals attacked the local PLA leaders as if they were solely responsible for the actions of the PLA, even though the radicals well knew that they only carried out the instructions of the MAC.[164] On the other hand, the MAC evaded its responsibility for the behavior of the local military commanders. When the Honan radicals complained to Hsiao Hua about the Honan military leaders, he replied that "the local PLA leaders did not ask for instructions from the MAC. But, naturally, as their superior, the MAC has responsibility, and I, as a member of the MAC, am also responsible."[165] The attacks on insignificant members of each elite group were obviously the first move against the political groups themselves—that is, the PLA, the government leaders, or the Cultural Revolution Small Group.

---

162. Even T'an survived the CR. When the radicals attacked him, he ordered his followers to "fight your battle and I will fight mine," and made arrangements whereby "the leaders went underground and engaged in secret activities, and the workers moved to the first line." "Crush T'an-Chiang-Ch'i's Counterrevolutionary Clique," *SCMPS*, no. 219 (29 February 1968), pp. 6-10.

163. Chiang Ch'ing publicly declared that "anyone who has an opinion about the PLA can write big-character posters and small-character posters and present them to the pertinent person, the upper level, and even to the Center, but they should not turn the spearhead against the PLA." *Ping-t'uan chan-pao*, 21 April 1967.

164. *Chih-tien chiang-shan*, 23 April 1967; *Tung-fang-hung*, 17 April 1967; *Hung-ting pao*, 20 May 1967.

165. *Honan 27 chan-pao*, 5 June 1967.

Next, the rules of the game gave birth to a secret, factional, and conspiratorial organization that directed the mass movement against officially prohibited targets. Unable to challenge the official policy or to attack Chou Enlai and the PLA publicly, Kuan Feng, Wang Li, and Ch'i Pen-yü organized the May 16 Group with persons they trusted, and used it to lead the mass movement in the direction they wanted.[166] Among forty-four persons identified as leaders of the May 16 Group, twenty-two worked in the news media, ten were cadres in the United Front Work Department, nine came from various government ministries, and three were affiliated with the Academy of Social Science. Ten were also members or staff of the Cultural Revolution Small Group. Most of them were well-educated intellectuals, probably with bourgeois class backgrounds. Their ultra-leftist ideology coincided with their political interests. As intellectuals without much power prior to the Cultural Revolution, they saw an opportunity to reach powerful positions through a thorough power seizure from the bottom to the top.

This group "manipulated and provoked" the radicals to attack Chou Enlai in Peking and the local PLA commanders in the provinces. According to the charges of their opponents, they contributed articles to the Red Guard newspapers demanding a complete overthrow of the power holders, and they sent out information-gathering agents to the government ministries disguised as correspondents for *Hung ch'i,* which provided them with the necessary credentials.[167] Ch'i Pen-yü, Kuan Feng, and Wang Li frankly told reliable friends in the group what they could not say publicly. Ch'i advised T'an Hou-lan, the leader of the Peking Normal University Chingkangshan, that "Yü Ch'iu-li, Li Hsien-nien, and Ch'en I must first be unhorsed," but Li Fu-ch'un should not be attacked for a while.[168]

When the May 16 Notice was made public, the May 16 Group explicitly turned the spearhead against Chou En-lai by advancing the slogan that "the current struggle is one between the new Cultural Revolution Group and the old government."[169] It is necessary, they said, to drag out the person "who has stood guarantee for the greatest number of people. . . . Now that Liu Shao-ch'i and Teng Hsiao-p'ing have fallen, Chou has become the general representative of all reactionary forces in China."[170]

The May 16 Group also dispatched their agents to the provinces to collect materials incriminating the PLA and to establish contact with the local

166. For "May 16 Corps," see Barry Burton, "The Cultural Revolution's Ultra-left Conspiracy: The May 16 Groups," *Asian Survey* 11, no. 11 (November 1971): 1029-1053.

167. *Ko-ming hsüeh-sheng lien-ho ch'i-lai yin-lan fan-ko-ming ying-mao tso-chi "5.16" he ping-tuan.* (Red Guard Monograph.)

168. *Wen-ko feng-yun,* March 1968.

169. *Ko-ming hsüeh-sheng lien-ho . . .*(Red Guard monograph).

170. Burton, "The Cultural Revolution's Ultra-left Conspiracy," *Asian Survey,* November 1971, pp. 1029-1053.

radicals. In Kwangtung, they set up the Committee to Criticize T'ao Chu, which acted as the commanding headquarters of the Kwangtung radical forces and directed the radicals' attack on the PLA. The factional activities of the Cultural Revolution Small Group also provoked the PLA's passive resistance to the Center. The PLA defended itself by instigating the conservative mass organizations to raid and attack the radical mass organizations. Instead of resolving their differences at the policy-making level, the manipulation of the mass organizations by the Small Group and the PLA resulted in increasingly violent confrontations between the radicals and the conservatives. The high point of the violence came when the conservatives kidnapped Hsieh Fu-chih and Wang Li in Wuhan.[171]

171. See Chapter 8 for the Wuhan incident.

# CHAPTER 7

# Patterns of Alliance in the Red Guard Movement from January to July 1967

In the preceding two chapters, we have examined the shifting official policy lines from January to July of 1967 mainly on the basis of the behavior of the elite. This chapter will analyze the behavior of the Red Guards during the same period. Our purpose is to identify the basic conflicts in the Red Guard movement and relate them to the divided elite groups.

This chapter consists of four sections. The first section identifies the types of Red Guard organizations. The second section presents a brief discussion of the five major Peking Red Guard organizations that played important roles not only in Peking but also in the nationwide Cultural Revolution. Their cleavages and coalitions are examined in the third section. The fourth section presents an account of the main cleavages and coalitions in the Kwangtung Red Guard movement. Despite its own unique features, the Kwangtung case exemplifies fairly well what happened in the other provinces and clearly shows the factional linkage between the mass organizations and the divided Maoist elites.

## The Types of Red Guard Organizations

In the initial stage of the Cultural Revolution, the Red Guards were not tightly unified groups. Their organization was more like a loose association of individuals sharing similar views on particular issues. The membership of each Red Guard organization underwent constant changes: those individuals who disagreed with their organization on particular issues withdrew from it and joined others or formed dissenting organizations. In other words, a large number of Red Guard organizations emerged, split, merged with others, and disappeared.

Nonetheless, as the movement continued, both the leaders and the ordinary members of each organization gradually developed their loyalty to the group, and their personal interests became tied with the fate of the organization. By the middle of 1967, the membership of each Red Guard organization was stabilized, and each organization came to have its own life, thus making it possible for outside observers to use the Red Guard organizations as units for analysis.

It is extremely difficult to classify all the Red Guard organizations, because their size varied widely—from a few persons in a small organization to half a million in the largest. However, all the Red Guard organizations can be roughly classified into five types, according to their level of inclusiveness, irrespective of their names.

1. The basic and most important organization was the Red Guard unit at each school—such as the Hsin Peita Commune of Peking University, the Chingkangshan of Tsinghua University, and the Chingkangshan of Peking Normal University. With its membership limited to the students, faculty, cadres, and workers at its own school, this type of organization possessed a maximum degree of independence and autonomy in its actions and its ideological orientation. Generally, the Red Guard organizations referred to in the literature on the Cultural Revolution are those at this level.

Workers seldom formed organizations whose membership was restricted to any particular factory. Instead, they tended to form organizations with memberships drawn from many factories in similar functional fields. Thus, their basic organizational unit corresponded to the Headquarters (the second type of student organization).

Invariably, such organizations claimed to represent all the Red Guards of a given school or unit, even though there was rarely only one Red Guard organization in a school. Even such nationally known organizations as the Hsin Peita Commune of Peking University and the Chingkangshan of Tsinghua University were opposed by minority factions in their schools (respectively by the Chingkangshan and the April 14 Group). Usually, the dominant Red Guard organization of each school set up the school revolutionary committee. For example, at Peking University, the Hsin Peita Commune formed the school revolutionary committee, and at the Peking Aviation Institute it was set up by the Red Flag group.

In theory, the school revolutionary committee was distinguishable from the Red Guard organization, but, in reality, they were inseparable. Thus, a challenge by the minority faction to the majority faction meant challenging the school revolutionary committee. In some schools in which the students were divided into two factions of equal strength, the revolutionary committee could be established only after a prolonged struggle. This was the case at Tsinghua University.

2. Above the school level, there was a coalition of the various basic-level Red Guard organizations, generally known as the Headquarters. In Peking, there were three Headquarters: the First Headquarters, the Second Headquarters, and the Third Headquarters. The United Action Committee of the Peking middle schools might also be classified as a Headquarters. In Kwangtung, there were the New First Headquarters, the Third Headquarters, and the Red Headquarters of the student radicals; and the New Red Headquarters of the student conservatives. The Workers organizations, such as the Red Headquarters, the District Headquarters, and the August 1 Combat Corps in Kwangtung could also be considered varieties of Headquarters.

The Headquarters format represented the initial effort to establish a unified Red Guard command structure, but the effort failed because of the ever-increasing numbers of Red Guard organizations and the internal conflicts that this created within the Headquarters. Eventually, the Headquarters lost its significance as a commanding structure, and dissolved completely when the Red Guard Congresses were established.

3. Between the Headquarters and the basic units there were many Liaison Offices, which were short-term alliances among the basic Red Guard organizations. The members of the alliance tended to share common interests and a common ideological orientation, and thus took similar views and actions on specific issues. For instance, the members of the Committee to Criticize Liu Shao-ch'i included many moderate Red Guards from the Heaven faction (see below), because Liu was an officially sanctioned target; while the Committee to Criticize T'an Chen-lin tended to attract radicals from the Earth faction, because T'an was not an officially sanctioned target.[1] The best-known liaison organization was the Committee to Criticize T'ao Chu, which was made up of radical Red Guards drawn mostly from the Earth faction in Peking and the Red Flag faction in Kwangtung. It worked as a front organization for the Cultural Revolution Small Group and later developed into the May 16 Corps.

4. Above the level of the Headquarters, there was the "factional alliance," into which the various basic organizations and Headquarters of a given area were divided. The Peking Red Guards were divided into the Heaven and the Earth factions; the Kwangtung mass organizations into the East Wind and the Red Flag factions; and the Heilungchiang mass organizations into the Bombard and the Commanding Headquarters factions.[2] The factional alliances included middle school Red Guards, worker Red Guards, and cadre mass organizations on both sides, but in some cases—for example, in Heilungchiang—one faction was dominated by the students and the other by the workers.

1. For the two Peking factions, see page 259.
2. *Tung-feng chan-pao,* 9 October 1967; *Harbin feng-lei,* 15 December 1967.

Although in almost all areas the mass organizations were split into two warring factions, the factions were not an officially recognized format of the mass organizations. Only a few factions published a Red Guard newspaper under their factional names.[3] Nonetheless, conflict at the factional level constituted one of the basic cleavages in the Cultural Revolution. Hence it is not an exaggeration to say that one cannot comprehend the Cultural Revolution without understanding the conflict at this factional level.

5. At the lowest level, there were the sub-units below the basic Red Guard organizations. The Tienanmen Column, the Mao's Thought Column, the East Is Red Column, and the Chung-nan-hai column were all semi-autonomous units under the Tsinghua University Chingkangshan. Although such sub-units were part of the basic Red Guard organization and were usually formed from an academic class or department, some of them were quite assertive in their dealings with their basic organization.

In a few cases, sub-units supported the basic unit of another school in opposition to the basic unit of their own school. For example, the April 14 Committee of the Peking Rebel Commune at the Central Finance Institute cooperated with the Hsin Peita in opposing its mother unit over the issue of attacking Li Hsien-nien. The Ta-ch'ing Commune of the Peking Petroleum Institute belonged to the Heaven faction, but its sub-unit, the Chingkangshan Column of the Ta-ch'ing Commune, belonged to the Earth faction. The East Is Red group at the Peking Mining Institute was a Heaven faction, but its sub-unit, the Thorough Revolution Column, supported the Earth faction.

When such a rebellious sub-unit grew strong enough, it challenged and competed with its basic unit for representation of its school. Then there would be two strong Red Guard organizations at a single school. For example, various forces at Peking University united to form the Chingkangshan, which challenged the Hsin Peita Commune. A similar development occurred at Tsinghua University.

With Red Guard structures as loose as those indicated above, conflicts tended to spill over from one level into another. A discontented sub-unit of any basic organization could always find support from a Red Guard organization outside its school. Conversely, a conflict between the basic units of two schools could readily be transposed to the factional level. For instance, a conflict between the Geology Institute and Peking University quickly became a conflict between the Earth and the Heaven factions, involving all the Red Guard organizations in Peking. Conflict between two basic factions could also obliterate divisions among the Headquarters. For instance, the Hsin Peita Commune sought support from the members of the First Headquarters to counterattack the rising influence of the Geology Institute in the Third

---

3. For instance, see *Erh-ch'i chan-pao* in Honan and *Hsi-chiang nu-t'ao* in Kwangsi.

Headquarters. This loose organizational structure indicates that the Chinese students were free to form their own organizations in the Great Proletarian Cultural Revolution.

The Center simultaneously attempted to unify the various Red Guard organizations at two levels: at the school level, through the military training teams; and at the municipal or provincial level, by organizing the Red Guard Congresses. The middle school-students, the college students, and the workers were separated from each other and organized into their own Red Guard Congresses, supposedly the highest commanding structures of the mass organizations. These Congresses, however, were not as effective as had been expected, since they were organized before the great alliances were established at the school level. Consequently, some schools had two representatives at their Red Guard Congress, and some representatives were challenged by rival organizations in their respective schools. Although this method of organizing the Red Guard Congresses from the top down was advantageous for control from the Center, it could not build up consensus and give the Red Guard Congresses the necessary legitimacy. Thus the factional struggle continued.

## The Five Major Red Guard Organizations

### *The Hsin Peita Commune of Peking University*

One of the best known and most influential Red Guard organizations, the Hsin Peita Commune of Peking University, followed a comparatively cautious and moderate line. This was due to the peculiar role of its leader, Nieh Yuan-tzu, who dominated the Cultural Revolution at Peking University after her big-character poster of May 25, 1966. Following Lu P'ing's purge on June 2, 1966, Nieh's main concern was to restore order and to rebuild a new power structure, rather than to destroy the old school Party Committee. Her comparatively high position as a lecturer and a Party cadre at the departmental level also made her less eager than young students to strike down all the power holders.[4] Possibly Nieh was even supported by the work teams.[5] At least, she became Chairman of the Peking University Cultural Revolution

---

4. Nieh frequently visited Wang Jen-chung. "Liu Shao-ch'i's Daughter Writes to Expose Her Father," *CB*, no. 821 (16 March 1967), pp. 1-25.

5. There is no positive evidence showing Nieh's close relationship with the work team. But the fact that we have no report on the conflict between Nieh and the work team at the Peking University during June and July 1966, despite an abundance of such reports at other schools, seems to suggest a good relationship. It is further known that she was not involved in the now famous "June 18 incident." Nieh made a public criticism of the work team, but only on July 19, one day after Mao's return to Peking and three days before Ch'en Po-ta's and Chiang Ch'ing's first visit to the University. "K'ang Sheng's Speech on July 28," *CB*, no. 891 (3 October 1967), pp. 1-3.

Preparatory Committee on July 18, when the influence of the work teams was still strong. Her authority was underlined when she retained her position in September, a time when leaders of many other Preparatory Committees were losing their posts.

Nonetheless, the radical surge of October placed Nieh and the Hsin Peita Commune in a delicate position: because of their close association with the work teams, they could not easily denounce policies of the "Fifty Days" period; nor could they repudiate the class basis of the original Peking University Red Guards, because of their close association with these Red Guards.[6] In fact, other students challenged Nieh and the Hsin Peita Commune in November, when the original Red Guard organizations were generally coming under increasing pressure from the more radical second generation of Red Guards. Denouncing Nieh as the successor of Chang Ch'eng-hsien (the head of the Peking University work team), some Philosophy Department students called for free mobilization of the students.[7] However, Neih and the Hsin Peita Commune survived the challenge, thus becoming the only Red Guard group which achieved prominence during the work team period and maintained power through the radical developments of October 1966.

The February moderation in the official line reduced the radical pressure. Neih and the Hsin Peita Commune hounded such opponents as Yang Ke-ming, an original signer of the May 25 *ta-tzu-pao* (big-character poster), and Kung Feng, Vice-Chairman of the Cultural Revolution Committee.[8] Further, at this time the Hsin Peita Commune amalgamated all the moderates of Peking University under the Hsin Peita banner. This included a large number of cadres who participated in the 1964 effort to remove Lu P'ing.[9] In fact, with the approval of the Hsin Peita Commune, these cadres dominated the reorganized Standing Committee of the Peking University Red Guards.[10]

The cadres' continued pre-eminence angered the radical students, who had expected a thorough power seizure by the students.[11] The Hsin Peita Commune defended the newly liberated cadres and labeled their opponents

6. For instance, see "The Cultural Revolution at Peking University," *JPRS*, no. 43,416 (22 November 1967), pp. 1-45.
7. The anti-Nieh force was led by her comrade Yang Ke-ming, one of the seven members who signed the first big-character poster of the CR. He was the principal teacher *(pan-chu-jen)* of the second-year class in the philosophy department, and it was the students of that class who pioneered the attack on Nieh. *Hsin pei-ta*, 4 March 1967; *Shou-tu hung-wei-ping*, 25 January 1967; *Pei-ching hung ch'i chan-pao*, 2 November 1967.
8. *Hsin pei-ta*, 17 February 1967.
9. Ibid., 14 March 1967.
10. Out of sixteen standing committee members, six were cadres and teachers, six were students, and one was staff. Nijima Atsuyashi, *Proletarian Kaikyu daikakumei*, p. 207; Suganuma Mashahisa, *Chugoku no bunka daikakumei* (Tokyo: Sanichi shobo, 1967), p. 44.
11. *Hsin pei-ta*, 9 May 1967; 16 May 1967.

"ultra-leftists."[12] At the same time, the Hsin Peita Commune forged relations with conservative mass organizations in the ministries and the PLA.

With the March counterattack on the "February Adverse Current," the Hsin Peita Commune was again on the defensive. Opponents of Nieh and the Hsin Peita Commune formed the Peking University Chingkangshan as part of the Peking Earth faction, and ironically this organization gained the support of the professors. For example, Chou P'ei-yüan was so involved with the Chingkangshan that the Hsin Peita Commune considered him its main leader. From February 1967 until the middle of 1968, the Chingkangshan defended professors and attacked Party cadres, while the Hsin Peita Commune supported cadres and vilified professors.[13]

### The Chingkangshan of Tsinghua University

In contrast to Peking University, where the cadres played the key role, the students were the main force at Tsinghua from the beginning. The many children of top-ranking cadres at Tsinghua—including Liu Shao-ch'i's daughter, Liu T'ao; Ho Lung's son, Ho P'eng-fei; and Liu Ning-i's daughter, Liu Ch'u-feng—cooperated with the work teams and formed the original Red Guards when the work teams were withdrawn in July. By that time, the work teams had branded eight hundred students and cadres as counterrevolutionary, and these people were subsequently outside the mainstream of the student movement until October.

In August, the Tsinghua students split over the record of the work teams.[14] Those who felt that the work teams should be criticized formed the August 8 faction. Pitted against them was the Cultural Revolution Preparatory Committee of Tsinghua University (established by Liu T'ao and Ho P'eng-fei with the work teams' support), which mobilized the pro-work-team students into the August 9 faction. The radicalization of the official policy in the autumn of 1966 eventually helped the work teams' critics and victims, who gained leadership of the school under K'uai Ta-fu.

By December 1966, K'uai had succeeded in merging his diverse supporters into the Chingkangshan and in closing down the conservative Tsinghua Red Guards.[15] Thereafter, he dominated the Tsinghua campus until he confronted a new coalition of challengers in April 1967. K'uai detested Liu Shao-ch'i and Wang Kuang-mei, for they had led the campaign against him in July. In return, K'uai was particularly instrumental in bringing Wang and Liu down. Chiang Ch'ing visited the Tsinghua campus on December 31, and

12. Ibid., 11 January 1967.
13. Ibid., 9 May 1967.
14. For the detailed discussion of conflict, see page 85; 94-95.
15. *Chingkanshan*, 1 December 1966.

four days later the Tsinghua students "captured" Wang by a trick and subjected her to public interrogation, in defiance of Chou's orders.[16]

Although K'uai had close links with the Cultural Revolution Small Group, he remained an independent force. Unlike Nieh Yüan-tzu at Peking University, who displayed sensitivity to the power relations at the top and was open to compromise, K'uai tenaciously adhered to his beliefs. Resenting elite manipulation of Red Guard organizations, he urged the Red Guards to be their own masters and not to blindly obey directives from the Center.[17] He even denounced the submissive attitude of his close allies in the Red Flag group at the Peking Aviation Institute and participated in the Team to Investigate Kang Sheng.[18]

Understandably, K'uai and the Chingkangshan were critical of the February deradicalization. The Chingkangshan newspaper carried seven installments of "A Discussion on Revolutionaries," which systematically expounded the radical formula of power seizure.[19] The Chingkangshan scorned the great alliance as a policy of "combining two into one," and viewed the three-in-one combination as "capitulation" to the power holders.[20] It accused other Red Guard organizations willing to follow the moderate official line of being "rightists" and "compromisers." And it remained militantly hostile toward Party cadres, bourgeois intellectuals, and students who had once belonged to the August 9 faction.[21] In stressing that behavior during the Cultural Revolution rather than class background was the primary criterion for judging revolutionary fervor, K'uai contended that only those who defied the work teams were qualified for leadership positions.

As leader of the Chingkangshan, K'uai was a strict disciplinarian and rejected anyone who disagreed with him as a "Trotskyite."[22] K'uai's extremely radical ideological line and his inflexible attitude alienated many students, who gradually formed a united opposition. In April, when the Chingkangshan tried to establish the school Revolutionary Committee, K'uai's opponents formed the April 14 Group, led by cadres such as Lo Chung-ch'i, deputy head of the Propaganda Department of the former Party Committee; Wen Hsueh-ming, deputy head of the United Front Department; and Li Kang, deputy chief of the former Party Committee General Office.[23] The anti-K'uai coalition included former members of both the

16. Ibid., 11 January 1967.
17. Ibid., 1 December 1966.
18. *Tung-fang-hung pao*, 31 January 1967; *Hsin pei-ta*, 23 January 1967.
19. *Chingkangshan*, 1 December 1966.
20. Ibid., 9 February 197 .
21. Ibid., 1 and 9 February 1967.
22. Ibid., 9 February 1967; 19 March 1967.
23. "What Is April 14?" *SCMPS*, no. 234, (6 September 1968), p. 5. *Chingkangshan*, 28 December 1967.

August 8 and the August 9 factions. The April 14 Group was more flexible in adjusting to the changing political situation, but was conciliatory toward K'uai as well. This, plus its submissive loyalty to the Cultural Revolution Small Group, helped the April 14 Group to join the Earth faction and to develop close ties with the Small Group.

### The Red Flag Group of the Peking Aviation Institute

The Peking Aviation Institute was a semimilitary institute under the jurisdiction of the National Scientific Defense Commission. As was the case with other schools, a work team was sent to this school, and the students became divided over the issue of the work team.[24] The conservative students, headed by the August 8 Combat Team, established the school Cultural Revolution Preparatory Committee with the help of the work team. The anti-work-team students organized the Red Flag group, and became the dominant Red Guard organization in the school when the work teams were officially repudiated. Initially, Red Flag was a member of the Second Headquarters, but in November 1966 it revolted and thereafter operated independently.

Despite its anti-work-team stand, Red Flag took a rather moderate and flexible posture toward the various issues in 1967. For instance, it advocated lenient treatment for the erring cadres, while criticizing in strong terms "the wrong tendency of some persons [who] want to blindly strike down every cadre, as though there were not one good cadre among the power holders."[25] The group was equally generous to the former conservative Red Guards, "who were hoodwinked and readily realized their mistakes, and truly returned to Chairman Mao's line."[26] Even when the "February Adverse Current" came under official attack, Red Flag issued a regulation calling on the students to adopt the correct "method of first examining and then helping even those who made serious mistakes."[27] As late as March 28, the group publicly declared that, "generally speaking, the present stage is for checking the leftism rather than the rightism that some comrades talk about."[28]

With regard to the issue of class line, Red Flag called for a balance between class origin and political performance. In practice, however, it often criticized the extreme leftist views that (1) "all minorities are revolutionaries"; (2) "all those who were imprisoned, suppressed by the power holders, or took part in the January Power Seizure are leftists"; and (3) "any persons talking about class origin are conservatives."[29] Thanks to its moderate orientation, Red Flag was able to establish the school Revolutionary

24. *Hung-ch'i,* 21 March 1967.          25. Ibid., 28 February 1967; 8 March 1967.
26. Ibid.                                27. Ibid., 28 March 1967.
28. Ibid., 28 March 1967.                29. Ibid., 18 February 1967.

Committee on May 12, 1967, without much trouble, and gained the support of the government bureaucrats and the PLA leaders.[30]

## The East Is Red Faction of the Geology Institute

A unique feature of the Cultural Revolution in the Geology Institute was the close cooperation of the radical students with rebellious cadre teachers. When a 300-member work team headed by the Vice-Minister of Geology labeled some professors "counterrevolutionary teachers" and gave them to the students to attack, some rebellious students defended the teachers by "establishing contact with and holding meetings with them, in spite of potential threats from the conservative faction."[31] Li Kuei, a member of the Standing Committee of the school Party, supported the anti-work-team students. Consequently, Li and thirteen other cadres were branded as anti-Party elements by the work team.[32]

Later, when the work team was withdrawn, the entire student body split over the work team issue into the Struggle-Criticism-Transformation Combat Team—the majority faction which defended the work team—and the East Is Red minority faction, which attacked the work team. East Is Red pursued the work team to the Ministry of Geology, where they staged a sit-in demonstration.[33] Yü Ch'iu-li, who replaced Po I-po as the vice-premier in charge of the industrial and transportation system, mobilized the Hsi Ch'eng Inspection Team to break up the demonstration.[34] (Yü's daughter, incidentally, was one of the leaders of this Inspection Team.)

During this uncertain period, East Is Red solidified its ties with the professors. In order to do ideological work and to dispel their teachers' worries, East Is Red visited the teachers' houses and wrote them letters. In the struggle against the power holders in the Party, East Is Red shared hardships with the revolutionary teachers and consolidated comradeship with them.[35] As the conservative Red Guards collapsed in the autumn of 1966, East Is Red became the school's majority faction.

East Is Red, which had a particularly close relationship with Wang Li and Kuan Feng, was the most radical and active group of the five major Red Guard organizations. It was a founding member of the Third Headquarters, although it clashed with the more moderate members of the Headquarters. East Is Red's first leader, Chu Ch'eng-wu (who was later identified as a

30. The Standing Committee was composed of nine students, two cadres, and one teacher. *Hung-ch'i*, 21 May 1967.

31. Ibid., 6 June 1967.

32. Ibid., 17 and 23 February 1967; 3 March 1967.

33. *Chin-chün pao*, 1 April 1967; *Tung-fang-hung pao*, 15 March 1967.

34. Ibid.

35. *Tung-fang-hung pao*, 15 March 1967.

member of the May 16 Group), stepped down under pressure from the Hsin Peita Commune because of his involvement in anti-K'ang Sheng activities. However, Wang Ta-pin, who succeeded Chu, continued to pursue the radical line.

During February, East Is Red stubbornly resisted the moderate official line. For instance, at no time from February 15 to March 3 did its newspaper, *Tung-fang-hung-pao,* carry any articles genuinely supporting the deradicalization policies. Instead, the paper constantly warned against the danger of false power seizure and readily denounced the moderate Red Guard organizations as representatives of the bourgeoisie. It advocated a "thorough revolution," which meant "striking down firmly, thoroughly, cleanly, and wholly the handful of power holders taking the capitalist road."[36] Its view of the great alliance was equally militant:

Alliance for the sake of alliance, alliance without class standpoint, without principle, without the initial alliance [of the radicals], is not alliance but confusion. . . . The core of alliance is struggle. Make alliances for struggle, and through struggle make alliances.[37]

On the other hand, East Is Red liberated the school president, Kao Yüan-kuei, and continued to advocate close cooperation with the teachers: "The teachers should go to the students and be united with the students. The unity of the teachers and students is a vital blow to the power holders."[38] On the question of responsibility for the wrong educational policy in the schools, East Is Red pinned the blame on the power holders rather than on the professors.[39] In March 1967, East Is Red led the radicals of the various specialized colleges and institutes (which were mainly under the jurisdiction of government ministries) against the "February Adverse Current" and the government bureaucrats.

The combination of a lenient policy toward the teachers and the cadres and a radical policy toward the power holders was an extremely shrewd program that broadened East Is Red's power base. Unlike Peking and Tsinghua Universities, the dissenters in the Geology Institute were weak and insignificant. As we shall see later, it was not until March 1968—when the fortunes of the radicals were at a low ebb—that the weak dissenting group posed a real threat to the dominance of East Is Red.[40] The dissenters demanded a free election, on the ground that East Is Red did not represent all the students of the school. Retorting that only revolutionaries had a political right to vote, and that it would hold on to the power seized and not concede even an inch to the conservatives, East Is Red managed to survive the challenge.[41]

36. Ibid., 15 March 1967.     37. Ibid., 25 March 1967; 16 April 1967.
38. Ibid., 6 June 1967.       39. Ibid., 11 April 1967; 2 June 1967.
40. Ibid.                     41. Ibid.

### The Chingkangshan of Peking Normal University

This group is comparatively unknown, although the vice-president of the school was P'eng Teh-huai's wife. In June 1966, T'an Hou-lan led the anti-work-team movement at Peking Normal University, and was met by a physical attack organized by the work team. The balance of power shifted in T'an's favor after the visit of the Cultural Revolution Small Group on July 29. At that time, T'an was declared to be a revolutionary, and thereafter she appeared to be in firm control of the Cultural Revolution at the University.[42] She was known to be the leader of the October revolt of the First Head-quarters, and she was also personally close to Lin Chieh, a Peking Normal University graduate who was working for *Hung ch'i* magazine. The Ching-kangshan opposed the moderate official line of February, and led the coun-terattack on the "February Adverse Current."

Besides the five major Red Guard organizations described above, a few more Red Guard organizations require a brief discussion because of their roles in the Peking Cultural Revolution. The Red Guard organization which initially dominated People's University was the August 18 faction, which also was a founding member of the First Headquarters.[43] At first, the August 18 faction agreed with its work team's verdict that the president of the school, Kuo Ying-ch'iu, was a good cadre, and this view was supported by T'ao Chu. When it became fashionable to criticize the work teams, however, the August 18 faction organized an anti-Kuo struggle, which those students who had opposed the work team from the beginning considered a "feint struggle."

During the January Power Seizure, the conservatives organized themselves into the Three Red Banners and allied themselves with the Heaven faction; while the New People's University Commune allied itself with the Earth faction. During the "February Adverse Current," the Three Red Banners launched a violent attack on the New People's University Commune, thus gaining the upper hand in the school.[44]

In contrast to the situation at People's University, at the Steel Institute the president, Kao I-sheng, was attacked by the Institute's work team and committed suicide in July 1966. The students at the Institute were divided into anti-Kao and pro-Kao factions: the anti-Kao students organized the New Steel Institute Commune and dominated the school; while the pro-Kao students formed the Yenan Combat Team with the support of Fu Ying, the school's Party Committee member and political department head. The Steel

42. The dissenting group known as "Rebel Corp" wanted first to have a great alliance according to class and department and then to form the CR committee. The Chingkangshan denounced it as an attempt to nullify the superiority of the leftists. *Chingkangshan*, 28 March 1967.

43. For the CR in the People's University, see *Hsin jen-ta* and *Jen-ta san-hung*.

44. *DR*, 1 March 1967.

Commune belonged to the Heaven faction, whereas the Yenan Combat Team joined the Earth faction.[45]

Also deeply involved in the Peking factional struggle was the Department of Social Science and Philosophy at the Academy of Science.[46] The radical organization there, the Red Guard Regiment, was led by Wu Ch'uan-ch'i and P'an Tzu-nien, who were personally close to Kuan Feng and Wang Li.[47] With the help of the Cultural Revolution Small Group, the Red Guard Regiment took over the power of the department in January and ruthlessly suppressed its opponent, the Red Guard Headquarters.

Acting as an unofficial spokesman for the Small Group, the Red Guard Regiment's newspaper, *Chin-chün pao,* openly challenged the moderate official line in February 1967 and, as early as February 23, pledged to "hit back at those who held the Cultural Revolution Small Group responsible for the minor mistakes of the Red Guards."[48] All of its complaints were taken up by *Hung ch'i,* No. 5, which heralded the counterattack on the "February Adverse Current." In March, *Chin-chün pao* attacked all the vice-premiers. Consequently, the conservative forces of Peking concentrated their attacks on the Red Guard Regiment as the first step toward undermining the Cultural Revolution Small Group.

## Cleavages and Coalitions among the Peking Red Guards

The five major Red Guard organizations were officially acknowledged rebel groups, and with the possible exception of Nieh's group, all of them owed their survival and their rise to prominence to the support of the Cultural Revolution Small Group. None of them was as conservative as the conservative Red Guard organizations in the provinces. Nevertheless, the five major organizations were divided into two major factions in 1967: the Hsin Peita Commune, the Tsinghua University Chingkangshan, and the Red Flag group were the leaders of the Heaven faction, a name derived from the Peking Aviation Institute; while the East Is Red group and Peking Normal University's Chingkangshan led the Earth faction, a name derived from the Geology Institute.

Although the divisions between the Earth and Heaven factions were very clear, we do not have enough information to ascertain the origin of these alliances. The only available data point to several partial conflicts—for example, the conflict between the Earth faction and the Red Flag group of the Peking Aviation Institute, and the conflict between the Earth faction and

45. For the CR in the Steel Institute, see *Hsin kang-yüan.*

46. For the CR in the Department of Social Science, see *Chin-chün pao.*

47. P'an was the secretary of the Party Committee in the Department of Social Science and Philosophy. Wang was the acting editor of the *Study of Philosophy.*

48. *Chin-chün pao,* 23 February 1967.

Table 7. *The Members of the Heaven and Earth Factions*

| *The Members of the Heaven Faction* |
| --- |

The Twenty-seventh Combat Corps of the National Palace
The Ta-ch'ing Petroleum Commune of the Peking Petroleum Institute
The Red Flag Battalion of the Peking Foreign Language Institute
The Three Red Banners Group of People's University
The Kang Ta Commune of the Nationality Institute
The January Storm Group of the Chemical Engineering Institute
The East Is Red Group of the Mining Institute ,
The Red Flag Group of the Peking Aviation Institute
The Hsin Peita Commune of Peking University
The East Is Red Group of the Peking Foreign Trade Institute
The Core Group of 88 of the Central Finance Institute

| *The Members of the Earth Faction* |
| --- |

The East Is Red Group of the Peking Geology Institute
The New People's University Commune of People's University
The Red Flag Rebel Corps of the Foreign Language Institute
The Chingkangshan Group of Peking Normal University
The Red Flag Group of the Agricultural Machinery Institute
The Politics and Law Commune of the Peking Political Science and Law Institute
The East Is Red Group of the Peking Postal Institute
The East Is Red Group of the Peking Forestry Institute
The East Is Red Group of the Peking Agricultural College
The East Is Red Group of the Peking Science and Techological Institute
The Rebel Corps of the Peking Commercial Institute
The Thorough Revolution Corps of the East Is Red Group of the Peking Mining Institute
The Red Guard Headquarters of the Chingkangshan Group of the Peking Music Institute
The East Is Red Group of the Peking Industrial Institute
The August 1 Combat Corps of the Peking Construction College
The East Is Red Group of the Nationality Institute
The Peking Commune of the Peking Petroleum Institute
The 729 Corps of the Peking Light Industry Institute
The East Is Red Group of the Peking Foreign Language Institute
The East Is Red Group of the Peking Hydro-Electricity Institute
The East Is Red Group of the Peking Teachers Institute
The East Is Red Group of the Peking Mathematics Institute
The East Is Red Group of the Peking Economics Institute
The New East Is Red Group of the Peking Foreign Trade Institute
The Maoism Commune of the Peking Movie Institute
The August 18 Red Guard Headquarters of the Peking Medical School
The Red Flag Commune of the Peking School of Chinese Medicine

the Hsin Peita Commune. I will therefore first present the partial conflicts as revealed in the Red Guard newspapers, and then interpret them to shed some light on the question of why these factions were divided.

After the anarchism of the January Power Seizure in which the Peking Red Guard organizations clashed with one another, these organizations were formed into the Red Guard Congress, dismantling the three Headquarters, which were already powerless in any case. When the Preparatory Committee was formed on January 22, the Earth faction dominated the seven-member core group with a four-member majority. However, when the Tsinghua Chingkangshan and the Peking University Hsin Peita Commune joined the core group, the Heaven faction expanded its strength from three to a five-member majority over the four-member minority of the Earth faction.[49] Moreover, by the time the Red Guard Congress was officially inaugurated on February 22, the Heaven faction dominated the five-member Standing Committee by occupying three seats as well as the chairmanship.[50] The Earth faction opposed Nieh's appointment as chairman on the ground that she was not a student, but their objection was overruled.

A more concrete issue over which the Earth and Heaven factions clashed was the power seizure in the United Front Department of the Central Committee. During the January Power Seizure, the radicals of the Department, who were mostly intellectuals from bourgeois families,[51] raided the Department in cooperation with the Red Flag Army and the Hsiang Chiang Feng Lei (the two most radical organizations, composed mainly of contract workers and demobilized soldiers), and removed ninety boxes of documents on the Political Consultative Conference.[52] The conservative organizations, such as the Red Guard Headquarters of the Department of Social Science and Philosophy and the Kang Ta Commune of the Nationality Institute, opposed the seizure of the documents because they were state secrets.[53] However, the Cultural Revolution Small Group used the Peking Public Security Bureau to arrest the leaders of the conservative mass organizations. But when the Red Flag Army and the Hsiang Chiang Feng Lei were declared counterrevolutionary organizations and the radicals came under attack in February, the conservative organizations, aided by the Hsin Peita Commune and the Capital Headquarters of the Revolutionary Rebel Workers, tried to recapture power from the radicals in the Department.[54]

As the movement returned to radicalization in March, the East Is Red group of the Geology Institute and the Red Guard Regiment of the Department of Social Science and Philosophy investigated the situation in the United Front Department and collected materials incriminating the conservative mass organizations. The Hsin Peita Commune and other conservative

49. Seven-member core groups were the Red Flag of the Peking Aviation Institute, the Red Flag of the Light Industry Institute, the East Is Red of the Mining Institute, East Is Red of the Geology Institute, East Is Red of the Forest Institute, East Is Red of Agricultural Machine Institute, and Chingkangshan of the Peking Normal University. *Chingkangshan,* 20 February 1967.

50. The five major Red Guard organizations were the standing committee members.

51. Twenty-one out of twenty-eight radicals in the department came from the exploiting class, and most of them were middle-ranking cadres at the bureau level. *Kang-ta,* 15 June 1967.

52. *Kang-ta,* 15 June 1967; *Hsin pei-ta,* 13 April 1967.

53. Ibid.

54. *8.8 chan-pao,* 13 March 1967.

organizations retaliated by raiding the offices of the Earth faction and seizing the materials collected there. On April 4, the Hsin Peita Commune organized a meeting to "Thoroughly Criticize the Counterrevolutionary Line of Liu and Teng in the Nationality Works." Disparaging the meeting as a "sham" one, the Earth faction stormed the meeting, thus creating a violent physical confrontation between the two factions.[55]

The Red Guard Congress issued an order for a cease-fire between the two groups. The Earth faction disregarded the order, insisting that Nieh and K'uai did not have the authority to issue it. On April 11, the Earth faction marched onto the Peking University campus shouting slogans such as "Drag out Neih Yüan-tzu!" "Peking University is conservative!" "Disband the Red Guard Congress and resto re the Third Headquarters!" and "How did Nieh become Chairman of the Red Guard Congress?"[56] In response to the raid, the Hsin Peita Commune mobilized its supporters in a 10,000-man rally to show its determination to fight against the Earth faction. At the rally, Sung Feng-i, the vice-chairman of the Hsin Peita Revolutionary Committee, openly denounced the Earth faction as "ultra-leftists," and implicated Hsieh Fu-chih as the backstage boss of the Earth faction.[57]

Immediately following this incident, the Heaven faction launched a public relations campaign to castigate the Earth faction. The *Shou-tu hung-wei-ping*, the Peking Red Guard Congress's official organ controlled by the Heaven faction, vilified the Earth faction as anarchists opposing the Red Guard Congress and urged the Red Guards to "oppose anarchism in a big way and in the biggest way."[58] The East Is Red group of the Geology Institute immediately responded to the charge by publishing an article entitled "Where Is the *Shou-tu hung-wei-ping* Going?"[59] This article accused the *Shou-tu hung-wei-ping* and some leaders of the Red Guard Congress of attempting to unify the conservatives and the revolutionaries and urged the "true leftists" to take over the leadership of the Red Guard Congress.[60]

Meanwhile, the Peking Revolutionary Committee was organized with Hsieh Fu-chih as chairman. Reflecting the radical mood of that time, the Revolutionary Committee was dominated by the leaders of the mass organizations: of thirty-three Standing Committee members, twenty were the representatives of mass organizations, six were military men, and seven were cadres. Although there is no direct evidence, it seems certain that the leaders

55. For the Earth faction units involved in the incident, see *Tung-fang-hung pao*, 25 April 1967.
56. *Hsin pei-ta*, 13 April 1967.
57. Ibid.; *Tung-fang-hung pao*, 25 April 1967.
58. *Shou-tu hung-wei-ping*, 18 April 1967.
59. *Tung-fang-hung-pao*, 25 April 1967.
60. Ibid., 25 April 1967.

of the mass organizations were close to the Cultural Revolution Small Group. After the purge of Wang Li and Kuan Feng, the Heaven faction publicly charged that Chou Ch'ing-fang, a follower of Wang Li and Kuan Feng, appropriated the important position of Secretary General of the Peking Revolutionary Committee and exercised enormous power.[61] Of fourteen members in the college section of the Revolutionary Committee, eight belonged to the Earth faction and six to the Heaven faction.[62]

Thus, despite its dominance of the Peking Red Guard Congress, the Heaven faction failed to outnumber the Earth faction in the Peking Revolutionary Committee. As a result, the Heaven faction supported the Red Guard Congress while challenging the Peking Revolutionary Committee, whereas the Earth faction challenged the Red Guard Congress while defending the Peking Revolutionary Committee. The Earth faction charged that the Heaven faction "actively cultivated some conservative forces, turning the spearhead against the Peking Revolutionary Committee, the firm revolutionary leftists, and Vice-Premier Hsieh, and actively cut down the foundation of the Peking Revolutionary Committee."[63] On the other hand, the Hsin Peita Commune criticized the Earth faction for following an extreme leftist trend and collaborating with the conservative forces to challenge the Red Guard Congress.[64] Interestingly, both factions charged each other with "servility" to either the Red Guard Congress or the Peking Revolutionary Committee.[65]

The Heaven faction and the Earth faction also clashed over the issue of the *Pei-ching jih-pao*. The Red Flag group of the Peking Aviation Institute was deeply involved in this conflict. Red Flag took over the *Pei-ching jih-pao* in January, but their moderate line created strong resentment among the radicals, particularly the Peking Normal University Chingkangshan, which blocked the distribution of the newspaper through the mails.[66] After this incident, the *Pei-ching jih-pao* was suspended until the establishment of the Peking Revolutionary Committee.

On April 2, the *Pei-ching jih-pao* resumed publication as the official organ of the Peking Revolutionary Committee. This time, it was dominated by the Peking Normal University Chingkangshan and the radical intellectuals close to the Cultural Revolution Small Group. Soon the *Pei-ching jih-pao* began to publish radical articles, such as "Strike Down the Theory of Docile Tools" and "Study the Great Document [of the May 16 Notice] to Protect the Proletarian Dictatorship."[67] Red Flag struck back by publishing "For

61. *Tung-ch'eng feng-pao,* 10 November 1967.
62. *Hung-se tsao-fan che,* 13 May 1967.
63. *Tung-fang-hung pao,* 19 March 1967.
64. *Hsin pei-ta,* 6 May 1967.
65. *Hsin pei-ta,* 6 May 1967; *Hung-ch'i,* 23 May 1967; *Tung-fang-hung pao,* 19 May 1967.
66. *Hung-ch'i,* 18 February 1967.
67. *Tung-fang-hung pao,* 18 April 1967. *Chingkangshan,* 8 June 1967. After Wang Li and

Whom Does the *Pei-ching jih-pao* Speak These Days?"[68] This article charged that the *"Pei-ching jih-pao,* in cooperation with the black hands in the society, supported one faction, struck at the other faction, and actively created and expanded division among the left."[69] The Earth faction interpreted this criticism as an attack on the Peking Revolutionary Committee and its chairman, Hsieh Fu-chih.[70]

At the same time, the power struggle over the leadership of the Red Guard Congress continued. On May 12, the Heaven faction gathered its members and produced a position paper, "Some Opinions Regarding the Situation at Universities and Colleges in the Capital," in the *Shou-tu hung-wei-ping.*[71] Reiterating its moderate position regarding poewr seizure, cadre policy, and the need for a unified leadership in the Peking Red Guard movement, the article charged the Earth faction with "anarchism and splitism," which were helpful only to the "bourgeois reactionaries."[72] The Heaven faction also admitted to the Red Guard Congress the Nationality Institute Kang Ta Commune a group which the Earth faction strongly condemned as conservative.[73]

In response to the Heaven faction's charges, the Earth faction immediately convened a meeting of its member organizations and published the "Summary of the Meeting Regarding the Present Situation."[74] This report reaffirmed the Earth faction's radical views: (1) that the great alliance should be achieved in the process of struggle; (2) that the predominance of the mass organizations in three-in-one combinations should be maintained; (3) that there should be further divisions among the Peking Red Guards; and (4) that the conservatives should not exploit the principle of the three-in-one combination in order to reverse the achievements of the Red Guards. At the same time, the Earth faction physically seized the *Shou-tu hung-wei-ping* and set up a new propaganda team and editorial board with the East Is Red group of the Geology Institute as the head of both departments.[75] The Earth faction admitted eighteen minority organizations to the Red Guard Congress and reorganized the Standing Committee of the Congress by occupying thirteen of its fifteen seats.[76]

Kuan Feng's purge, they were publicly accused of having transformed *Pei-ching jih-pao* into a factional newspaper.

68. *Hung-ch'i,* 30 May 1967; 3 June 1967; *Hung-ch'i t'i-yü chan-pao,* 3 June 1967.

69. Ibid.

70. Ch'i Pen-yü defended the *Pei-ching jih-pao. Tung-fang-hung pao,* 18 April 1967; 9 June 1967. *Chingkangshan,* 8 June 1967.

71. *Pei-ching tsao-fan kung-she,* 26 May 1967.

72. Ibid.

73. Ibid.

74. *Tung-fang-hung pao,* 19 May 1967.

75. *Tung-fang-hung,* 15 June 1967.

76. For those admitted to the Red Guard Congress, see *Tung-fang-hung,* 2 June 1967. *Shou-tu hung-wei-ping,* 11 June 1967.

The Heaven faction challenged the legality of the Earth faction's actions on the grounds that neither their three members in the five-member organizational section (Nieh, K'uai, and Han) nor their five members in the nine-member core group had taken part in the decision.[77] The Earth faction, however, defended its actions, contending that the decisions were made in accordance with the instructions of the Cultural Revolution Small Group and the Peking Revolutionary Committee.[78] Understandably, the Heaven faction resented the Small Group's support of the Earth faction and so "attempted to put up a big-character poster, to turn the spearhead against *Hung ch'i* magazine headed by Comrade Ch'en Po-ta, and to split the Cultural Revolution Small Group."[79] After this incident, the Red Guard Congress ceased to play any significant role in the Peking Red Guard movement, although it continued to exist under the control of the Earth faction.

What we have so far examined suggests that the conflicts between the two factions were power struggles, especially over control of the Peking Red Guard Congress and the Peking Revolutionary Committee. The thesis of power struggle, however, fails to explain why some Red Guard organizations joined the Heaven faction and others joined the Earth faction. Were there any discernible characteristics shared by all the members of each faction? In other words, what were the basic differences between the two factions? In the remainder of this section, we will examine sociological, ideological, and personal factors, the combined effect of which appears to have been responsible for the formation of the two factions in Peking.

*Sociological Factors*

The cleavage between the Earth and Heaven factions generally ran along the division between prestigious and less prestigious schools: the Heaven faction included the more prestigious schools, while the members of the Earth faction came from numerous but less prestigious institutes. When the Red Guard Congress was organized, the coalition of prestigious schools (Tsinghua University, Peking University, and the Peking Aviation Institute) gained hegemony over the less prestigious schools (Peking Normal University and the Geology Institute), which wanted to extend the membership of the Red Guard Congress to various small institutes so as to broaden their power base in the Congress. The sociological cleavage, however, does not explain why the student body of a given school was divided into the Earth and Heaven factions.

*Ideological Factors*

Consistent with our general thesis that the lower strata in Chinese society

77. *Shou-tu hung-wei-ping,* 11 June 1967.
78. Ibid.
79. Ibid.

tended to be radical in the Cultural Revolution, the Earth faction—composed of Red Guards from less prestigious schools—was certainly more radical in its general orientation than the Heaven faction. As noted earlier, the East Is Red group of the Geology Institute and the Chingkangshan of Peking Normal University took more radical postures than the Hsin Peita Commune or the Red Flag group of the Peking Aviation Institute. (The Chingkangshan of Tsinghua University was an exception to the following discussion, and hence is treated separately.) Most members of the Earth faction explicitly or implicitly raised their opposition to the moderate official line of February, insisting on a thorough power seizure by the narrowly defined leftists. In fact, it was the Earth faction that initiated the counterattack on the "February Adverse Current."

Undoubtedly, the Cultural Revolution Small Group sympathized with the Earth faction. It was the practice of the Small Group to support the radicals from the lower strata of Chinese society. In addition, the Small Group actively endorsed the criticism of the "February Adverse Current." Thus, although it is not clear whether the Earth faction initiated the counterattack on the "February Adverse Current" for its own political interests or at the prompting of the Small Group, obviously the political interests of the Small Group coincided with those of the Earth faction. Moreover, the fact that the radical members of the Small Group, through the May 16 Corps, attempted to manipulate the Earth faction to attack Chou En-lai further bespeaks the close cooperation between them.

In contrast, the Heaven faction followed a moderate line. Most of its members responded favorably to the February moderation. The Earth faction denounced some members of the Heaven faction, especially the Hsin Peita Commune, as a "new conservative faction," but the Heaven faction never used such terms for its opponents. Even Chiang Ch'ing is reported to have commented that the movement at Peking University was not "excessive but moderate,"[80] and the Hsin Peita Commune made a self-criticism for following the "mild" line in February 1967.

Some members of the Heaven faction also opposed the counterattack on the "February Adverse Current," and publicly defended Li Hsien-nien and Yü Ch'iu-li.[81] The Earth faction privately grumbled that Chou En-lai was a backstage boss of Nieh Yüan-tzu and the Hsin Peita Commune.[82] The members of the Heaven faction—such as the Red Flag group of the Peking

---

80. *Hsin pei-ta,* 14 March 1967.

81. *Pei-ching tsao-fan kung-she,* 15 March 1967.

82. *Tung-fang-hung* (National Economic Planning Commission), 13 November 1967. The May 16 Corps argued that "according to our understanding, the May 16 Circular was published to drag out Chou," *Hung chan-pao,* 30 May 1967. They also charged Chou with "formulating and implementing the bourgeois reactionary line and inciting the masses to struggle against the masses." The radicals also revealed that "Comrades Ch'en Po-ta, Chiang Ch'ing, and Ch'i Pen-yü are collecting the materials on Chou En-lai." *Hung-wei-pao,* 30 March 1967.

Aviation Institute, the Kang Ta Commune of the Nationality Institute, and the Red Flag group of the Peking Foreign Language Institute—publicly warned the Earth faction that Chou En-lai should not be attacked.[83]

On the other hand, there are good reasons to believe that the Heaven faction was antagonistic to the Small Group's manipulation, or at least less amenable to it than the Earth faction was. First of all, the well-known Red Guard leaders from the prestigious schools were less likely to lean one-sidedly toward the Small Group. With their nationwide reputations as leaders of the most powerful Red Guard organizations, Nieh, K'uai, and Han had easy access to top figures such as Chou En-lai. As an experienced cadre, Nieh may have known that it was not in her political interest to be identified closely with the Small Group. For his part, K'uai Ta-fu may well have resented the Small Group's manipulation because of his ideological belief that the masses should lead the Cultural Revolution without interference from the elite. Moreover, when Wang Li and Kuan Feng were later purged, it was the Heaven faction that led the public criticism and implicated the Earth faction in the May 16 Corps conspiracy.[84]

The Heaven and Earth factions also differed over the question of how to treat the "bourgeois authorities." Since the work teams had attempted to divert attention from the power holders by attacking the "bourgeois authorities," the conservative trend was to stress the "bourgeois authorities" as the main target, while the radical trend was to emphasize the power holders. Related to this controversy was the question of whether a cadre should be evaluated by his entire record of the past seventeen years or by his political behavior during the "fifty days" of the work teams. This question was also a part of the broader controversy of class origin versus political consciousness. Almost by definition, the "bourgeois authorities" came from "bad" family backgrounds, whereas the "power holders" belonged to the five red categories. Again, the trend was that the conservatives stressed class origin and "seventeen years," while the radicals emphasized political consciousness and one's political behavior during the "fifty days." The Heaven faction followed the conservative trends, while the Earth faction followed the radical ones.

As noted earlier, the East Is Red group of the Geology Institute had maintained a good relationship with the academic faculty of its school, whereas Nieh's major rival at Peking University was Professor Chou Pei-yüan.[85] The Three Red Banners group of People's University reportedly declared that "about a thousand of our teachers have problems and two hundred have

83. *Hung-ch'i,* 28 March 1968.
84. *Hsin pei-ta,* 6 December 1967; *Chang-ch'eng,* 3 December 1967; *Min-yüan tung-fang-hung,* 29 November 1967.
85. The Hsin Peita commune charged that Chingkangshan "benefited the bourgeois authority by all means." *Hsin pei-ta,* 21 October 1967; 22 November 1967.

serious problems."[86] On the other hand, its opponent, the New People's University Commune, was led by the deputy head of the philosophy department, Hsiao Chien, whom the Small Group specifically supported.[87]

*Personal Factors*

Besides the common ideological orientatoin and political interests, the Earth faction was linked to the Cultural Revolution Small Group by personal ties. Lin Chieh was known to be close to the Peking Normal University Chingkangshan, and Wang Li and Kuan Feng, despite their seemingly cordial relationship with the Heaven faction, were on much more intimate terms with the Earth faction. Moreover, many of Wang Li's and Kuan Feng's personal friends were the active leaders of the Earth faction or closely associated with it. Later, they emerged as key members of the May 16 Corps, which apparently acted as an intermediary between the radical members of the Small Group and the Earth faction. Also, all the radical cadres of the government ministries who challenged the Vice-Premiers in defiance of Chou's orders were members of the May 16 Corps and closely related to the Earth faction.[88]

Among these intellectual radicals, the most controversial were P'an Tzu-nien and Wu Ch'uan-ch'i, the leaders of the Red Guard Regiment of the Department of Social Science and Philosophy.[89] These two belonged to a group of intellectuals with "bad" family backgrounds who had even written some articles critical of Mao's Thought prior to the Cultural Revolution, though they stood on the correct side during the Cultural Revolution. To further complicate matters, they were close friends of Wang Li and Kuan Feng, at whose instruction they challenged Wu Han in April 1966.[90] Despite their instant change, however, the work teams attacked them as "bourgeois authorities" in the summer of 1966. The Earth faction regarded them as revolutionary because of their correct political behavior during the "fifty days," whereas the Heaven faction denounced them as political opportunists who "pretended to revolt" only to save their own skins.[91] Both sides justified their positions by selectively stressing either class origin or political consciousness, bourgeois authorities or power holders, and motivation or action.

In addition to these personal and ideological reasons, there was a good political reason for the Small Group to take a lenient attitude toward the

86. *Hsin jen-ta*, 8 May 1967.
87. Ibid., 9 December 1967.
88. They included Lo Feng, editor of *Economic News*, Liu Cheng, deputy chief of Regional Bureau of the State Council, Ch'en Ta-lun, deputy chief of Research Office of Economic Planning Office, etc. *Tung-ch'eng feng-pao*, 7 December 1967.
89. *Chingkangshan*, 28 December 1967. *Hsin pei-ta*, 9 May 1967.
90. For Kuan Feng's and Wang Li's involvement in the CR of the Department, see *Yeh-chan-pao*, no date.
91. *Chingkangshan*, 3 June 1967.

bourgeois intellectuals. By April 1967, the Small Group had secured control over the Propaganda Department, and Ministry of Culture, the Ministry of Education, the Hsin Hua News Agency, and other organs in the fields of literature and art—exactly the areas in which the intellectuals were concentrated.[92] In exercising control, the Small Group had to rely on some cadres in the various units, and understandably they relied on intellectuals whom they personally trusted.

The Heaven faction disregarded the Small Group's special position in the cultural and propaganda fields and insisted on a thorough power seizure there. The faction argued:

In the past seventeen years, the bourgeois class has imposed its dictatorship over the proletarian class in the fields of literature and art. At this moment, the leadership of some units and departments of literature and art, newspapers, and publications are again being seized by the representatives of the bourgeois class. These people are extremely afraid that the masses will expose and criticize them.[93]

With this justification, the Heaven faction attacked those who had worked closely with Chiang Ch'ing for the reform of the Peking Opera prior to the Cultural Revolution.[94] In the Hsin Hua News Agency, they attacked Yang Hsiao-nung, a member of the Standing Committee of the Hsin Hua Revolutionary Committee, who was apparently supported by the Small Group.[95] Ch'en Po-ta was compelled to issue a warning to the members of the Heaven faction not to interfere with the Small Group in the agency.[96] The Heaven faction viewed this instruction as the Small Group's interference with the mass movement in order to protect its personal friends and to defend its factional power base.

The Heaven faction advanced the slogan of thoroughly destroying the "three olds"—that is, the old Propaganda Department, the old Peking Party Committee, and the old Ministry of Culture—and incited the workers to seize the power in these fields. They also called for the destruction of the "three highs and three famous."[97] The Heaven faction even coined the slogan "Select targets and friends according to one's salary scale."[98] Ironically, even though it started the Great Proletarian Cultural Revolution by challenging the establishment in the cultural fields, the Small Group now found itself defending the professionals. Ch'i Pen-yü warned that the "three highs and

92. *Hung-se hsüan-chuan-p'ing,* 10 May 1967.
93. *Hung-ch'i,* 30 May 1967; 3 June 1967.
94. *Wen-i hung-ch'i,* 25 April 1967.
95. *Hsin-hua chan-pao,* 7 June 1967.
96. *Hsin-wen chan-pao,* 3 May 1967.
97. "Three highs" refers to high wages, loyalty, and treatment. "Three famous" refers to famous writers, directors, and actors.
98. *Kung-nung-ping tien-ying,* 3 April 1967, 1 May 1967.

three famous" should be analyzed case by case and reminded the students that they might someday be the "three highs and three famous" themselves.[99]

The Earth faction publicly opposed the slogans on the grounds that they (1) diverted the attack from the power holders; (2) failed to take into account the fact that some of the "three highs and three famous" fought in the Cultural Revolution on the revolutionaries' side; and (3) tended to "turn the spearhead downward" to insignificant intellectuals "possessing ordinary bourgeois academic views," while evading the question of the power holders "who invented and carried out the policy of the three highs and three famous."[100]

Nonetheless, the Heaven faction continued its attack on the intellectuals by stressing their bad motivation: "Since the Cultural Revolution, some freaks and monsters in the fields of literature and art jumped out and even infiltrated the ranks of the revolutionary rebels by exploiting the occasion of criticizing the bourgeois reactionary line."[101] The Earth faction rejoined that the Heaven faction was shooting at "ordinary cadres in the fields of literature and art who made insignificant mistakes in words and action, starred in some bad dramas and movies, or had written some bad works."[102]

The preceding discussion indicates that the Earth faction was close to the Small Group and was antagonistic to Chou En-lai and the PLA. The relationship between the Heaven faction and Chou, however, was obscure. Despite all the reasons for Chou to support the Heaven faction, there is no definite evidence that he actively exploited the factional struggles of the Peking Red Guards to undermine the Small Group. This seems to indicate that Chou used the Heaven faction to defend his own power position in the government ministries, but did not ally himself with it to the extent of forming a secret alliance against the Small Group. Chou's cautious approach might have reflected his fair attitude toward both factions, or the approach might have been due to his shrewd political calculation that too close an involvement with the Heaven faction was risky at that moment, since the relationship among Chou, the PLA, and the Small Group was not yet settled. The Heaven faction had maintained a good relationshp with the PLA, and was in a position to move closer either to the PLA or to Chou.[103]

The Tsinghua Chingkangshan poses some difficulty for the thesis of

99. *Wen-i chun-pao,* 5 May 1967.
100. *Wen hua chan pao,* 5 May 1967.
101. *Chuan-chu chan pao,* 9 December 1967.
102. *Wan-chiang-hung,* 7 June 1967.
103. For instance, the Earth faction collaborated with the radical faction in the PLA schools, the Bombard faction, and there are ample indications that they attacked the PLA. For instance, see *Hsin pei-ta,* 25 April 1967. *Tung-ch'ing feng po,* 7 December 1967.

vertical cleavage, although it does not completely invalidate it. The Ching-kangshan basically belonged to the Heaven faction, despite its radical ideological orientation.[104] However, its affiliation with the Heaven faction was rather weak. It acted more or less independently of the Heaven faction, and its relationship with the other members of the faction was very complicated. In January, the Chingkangshan clashed not only with Nieh of the Hsin Peita Commune but also with the Red Flag group of the Peking Aviation Institute. Within the Heaven faction, the Chingkangshan formed a more radical sub-group with Red Flag, and also with the East Is Red unit of the Physical Science Institute.

Another sub-group was formed around the Hsin Peita Commune, the Three Red Banners of People's University, the Kang Ta Commune of the Nationality Institute, and the New Steel Institute—the more conservative Red Guard organizations from schools where the students were divided into two warring factions of equal strength. Unlike the Hsin Peita Commune, the Tsinghua Chingkangshan was never charged by the Earth faction with conservatism. The Earth faction tried to win over the Chingkangshan to its side, even when the former was engaged in a serious power struggle with the Heaven faction over the control of the Red Guard Congress. The main reason for K'uai's joining the Heaven faction therefore seems to have been political: he joined in reaction to the Earth faction's support of the April 14 Group, which challenged his leadership at the Tsinghua campus.

In brief, then, the political behavior of the Peking Red Guard organizations was as complicated as that of any political force in China. Certainly, each Red Guard unit endeavored to realize its own ideology, to maximize its own power position, and to articulate its own group interests, which usually —though not always—went together. Each unit pursued these goals, however, within limits set by external factors. The units had to at least pretend to conform to the official ideology and policy at any given moment, for to do otherwise was to invite criticism from the rival faction. When the official line converged with their goals, the Red Guard organizations earnestly supported it. When there was a divergence, however, they resisted, but only so subtly that the resistance would not create the impression of challenging the official line.

The political behavior of each Red Guard unit must also be understood in the context of group rivalry, although the rivalry occurred within the constraints of the official lines and the relationships with the elite groups. Thus, on some occasions each side attempted to eliminate the other as a viable Red Guard unit, but on other occasions they competed to outdo each other with

104. William Hinton, *Hundred Day War*, (New York: Monthly Review Press, 1972), pp. 145-154.

regard to certain issues on which the official line was firmly established. For instance, the two factions at Tsinghua University attacked each other over the issue of good and bad cadres, but they competed with each other in attacking Liu Shao-ch'i, in order to prove their revolutionary zeal.[105]

Another factor influencing the political behavior of the Red Guard units was their relationship with the elite. Broadly speaking, the radicals were more assertive in their relationship with the elite, whereas the conservatives were more submissive. As the cleavages among the Maoist leaders were revealed to the public, each Red Guard organization developed special ties with the Small Group, or the PLA, or Chou En-lai, or with any elite group that showed sympathy to its group interests. Some Red Guard organizations endeavored to maintain good relationships with all the elite groups. This could not work for long, however, since the changes in the power positions of the elite groups and in the official line eventually led each Red Guard organization to be identified more closely with one elite group or the other. Thus, by mid-1967, all the divided Red Guards and the elite groups formed a veritical division, cutting across the horizontal split between the elite and the masses.

## The Kwangtung Red Guard Movement

The Kwangtung Provincial Party Committee did not act differently from other provincial Party committees during the "fifty days." It dispatched the work teams and carried out the "bourgeois reactionary line" of suppressing the rebellious students and protecting the lower-level Party committees.[106] In August 1966, the Committee organized the Red Guards from the five red categories, and these original Red Guards diverted the spearhead of the mass movement against those from bourgeois class backgrounds, whether they were cadres or ordinary students.[107]

Nonetheless, the Kwangtung Party Committee was more successful than other Party committees in coping with the rapidly changing political situation in the autumn of 1966. This success was largely due to T'ao Chu, who continued to informally advise the Kwangtung Party Committee even after being promoted to Peking in June 1966. (As the Director of the Propaganda Department and Adviser to the Cultural Revolution Small Group, he was for a while ranked fourth in the hierarchy of the Peking leadership.)[108]

105. Ibid.
106. For instance, see *Chung-ta hung-ch'i*, 30 April 1967; *Kung-an hung-ch'i*, 31 October 1967; *Hung-se pao-tung*, 27 February 1967; *P'i T'ao chan-pao*, 14 March 1967; *Kuang-chou jih-pao hung-ch'i*, 11 July 1967.
107. *Hung-wei-ping*, 18 September 1966; *Kuang-chi hung-ch'i*, January 1968.
108. *Hung-se pao-tung*, 27 February 1967.

When the Cultural Revolution took a radical turn in October 1966, the Kwangtung Provincial Party Committee, on the instruction of T'ao Chu, decided to "switch its support to the rebel faction." Chao Tzu-yang, the First Party Secretary, made a public self-criticism on behalf of the entire Provincial Party Committee.[109] But the Party authorities continued to maintain a close relationship with the original conservative Red Guards that they had helped to organize in the preceding stage.

The Party Committee instructed the conservatives to restrain themselves from challenging the radicals and to accept the "switch of direction" imposed by Peking. In order to avoid an open clash with the radicals, the conservatives dispersed their forces by going to other areas under the pretext of exchanging experience and helping the peasants to fight the drought that was plaguing a part of Kwangtung province at that time. In some cases, the conservative Red Guards were willing to admit their mistakes and to disband their organizations voluntarily.[110] Thus, the switch of direction in October 1966 took place without entailing the complete destruction of the conservative forces in Kwangtung. The conservative forces simply lay low, waiting for the proper opportunity to reassert themselves.

Successful as the Kwangtung Party Committee was in surviving the official criticism of the bourgeois reactionary line, it could not survive the downfall of T'ao Chu. In November, T'ao Chu was criticized and subsequently lost his control over the Peking Red Guards coming to Kwangtung. The new batch of radical Red Guards from Peking were hostile to T'ao Chu, and came to Kwangtung for the purpose or redirecting the Red Guard movement against the Provincial Party Committee. Armed with notebooks and tape recorders, they visited the cadres throughout Canton, encouraging them to rebel against T'ao Chu, and gathering information that could be used in an all-out campaign to mobilize public opinion against him.[111] Not surprisingly, the Peking Red Guards found that those cadres who had been attacked by the work teams in the *Kuang-chou jih-pao* (the official organ of the Canton Party Committee) and the *Yang-ch'eng wan-pao* (the official organ of the Kwangtung Provincial Party Committee) were willing to cooperate with them against T'ao Chu and the Kwangtung Party Committee.

Following the shutdown of the *Liberation Daily* in Shanghai, the rebel forces in Kwangtung called for the shutdown of the *Yang-ch'eng wan-pao*.[112]

109. "True Face of T'ao Chu," *SCMM*, no. 574 (1 May 1967), pp. 20-27.

110. Wang Ch'ao, *Kuang-chou tien-ying-chieh te tsao-fan-che* (Hong Kong: Chung-pao chou-k'an, 1969), p. 49.

111. Ezra Vogel, *Canton Under Communism* (Cambridge: Harvard University Press, 1969), p. 328.

112. For the paper's response to the CR, see *Hung-wei-ping*, 1 September 1966–22 December 1966.

This demand posed a dilemma for the Kwangtung Party leaders, for closing down the newspaper meant acknowledging that their official organ made mistakes, but opposing the demand meant alienating the radical students, forcing a direct confrontation with them. The provincial leadership at first pursued a double-edged policy: they negotiated with the radicals for closing down the paper, while mobilizing the workers from the big factories to oppose the shutdown.[113] Nevertheless, when T'ao Chu telephoned the Kwangtung leaders and ordered them not to oppose the rebels, they yielded to the demands of the radicals and persuaded the conservatives to go along with this tactical decision.[114] Thus, a dangerous confrontation between the radical and conservative forces was averted, and both sides preserved their political strength.

## The January 22 Power Seizure

As soon as the power seizure became the official policy, the Kwangtung radicals were instructed by the Cultural Revolution Small Group to carry it out.[115] Although some rebel groups opposed an immediate power seizure on the grounds that Kwangtung was not yet ripe for one, the Red Flag group of Chungshan University, with the help of eight other rebel organizations inside Kwangtung and nine organizations outside the province, declared the power seizure of the provincial government on January 22, 1967.[116]

The Kwangtung Provincial Party Committee cooperated with the power seizure. When the rebels informed Chao Tzu-yang that they wanted to seize the power of the provincial government organs, he ordered the Kwangtung Provincial Party Committee to hand over the "three seals of the committee."[117] However, Lin Li-ming, the secretary in charge of the seals, refused to hand them over without the Center's approval. He telephoned Peking, but did not get any definitive answer.[118] Later, Chao Tzu-yang himself handed over the seals to the rebels.

After seizing power, the rebels drew thirty more organizations onto their side in order to create the appearance of a great alliance. They established

113. "True Face of T'ao Chu," *SCMM*, 1 May 1967, pp. 20-27; *Kuang-chou hung-wei pao i-chou-nien chuan-k'an*, 13 December 1967.

114. Ibid.

115. "Upsetting Heaven and Earth in a Heroic Manner," *SCMP*, no. 3921 (18 April 1967), pp. 9-17. Though the content is not known, in light of the fact that the Center probably decided to formally sanction the power seizure on January 22, which was published in a January 23 editorial, it is very likely that the instruction ordered the Red Flag faction to proceed with the power seizure.

116. *Hung-se pao-tung*, 27 February 1967.

117. *Kuang-chou hung-ch'i*, 10 February 1967.

118. Ibid. It is interesting that Lin Li-ming, who opposed the handing over of the power to the minority radicals, was later supported by the East Wind as a revolutionary cadre. *Hung-se pao-tung*, 27 February 1967.

the Provincial Joint Revolutionary Rebel Committee (PJRRC), which exercised its power through an Executive Committee and the General Service Groups, which in turn supervised the work of the Provincial Party Committee. Under this formula, all the "original working personnel" worked as usual. Thus, all that the radicals had actually seized were the empty seals, and their power seizure did not produce any substantive changes.[119]

The problems of the January 22 power seizure were so serious that even the Small Group, which had instigated the action, could not openly support it. First, the units participating in the power seizure were so few that it could not by any criteria be legitimized. The only cadre group that genuinely supported the power seizure were the "provincialists," those native Kwangtung cadres related to Fang Fang and Ku Ta-tsun who were purged or rectified by T'ao Chu prior to the Cultural Revolution.[120] But they were not acceptable to the Peking leaders.[121] The error became more apparent when, in February 1967, the official policy of power seizure changed from the "Paris Commune" formula to the "Revolutionary Committee" formula.

Furthermore, the January 22 power seizure was peaceful.[122] Whatever the reason for the cooperation of the Party Committee, the peaceful transfer of power spoiled Mao's conception of what power seizure should entail. Moreover, since one of the most important factors for successful power seizure was the availability of an alternative leadership among the Party Committee members, the radicals, as a minority without the support of cadres within the Party organization, had no choice but to rely on the former Party Committee in order to exercise power as effectively as possible. Consequently, all the members of the Party Committee, including Chao Tzu-yang, continued to perform their functions, though under the supervision of the radicals.[123] Thus, the only change made by the power seizure was that "one additional procedure [approval by the Red Guards of Party Committee actions] is required."[124]

It was over this ill-prepared and poorly executed maneuver that a heated controversy emerged, which was eventually to split the Kwangtung mass organizations into two factions. The first consisted of conservatives who

119. *Kuang-chou hung-wei-ping,* 10 February 1967.
120. *Yeh chan-pao,* March 1968. For a systematic discussion of provincialism, see Hai Feng, *An Account of the CR in the Canton Area* (Hong Kong: Union Research Institute, 1971), pp. 125-131.
121. *Yeh-chan-pao,* March 1968.
122. *Wen-ko p'ing-lun,* January 1968; *Kuang-chou hung-wei-ping,* 10 February 1967; *Hung-se pao-tung,* 27 February 1967.
123. *Hsiao-ping,* 25 February 1967. Some conservatives charged that the radicals even failed to seize the seals physically. Chao Tzu-yang is reported to have said, "Don't allow them to take away the seals, and let them use the seals under supervision." *Kuang-chou hung-wei-ping,* 10 February 1967.
124. *Kuang-chou hung-wei-ping,* 10 February 1967.

Table 8. *Political Factions in Kwangtung Province*

---

*The Red Flag Faction*

---

A. Moderate
1. The Red Flag group of the organs directly under the Provincial Committee: 4,000 to 5,000 low-ranking cadres of the government organs.
2. The Red Flag Workers: an organization of 20,000 inter-industrial workers.
3. The New First Headquarters: a student organization led by the East Is Red group of Chungshan Medical School.
4. The Third Headquarters: a student organization led by the Red Flag group of the South-Central Engineering Institute and the Physical Education students.
B. Radical
1. The Red Flag group and the August 31 group of Chungshan University. These were the main leaders of the Red Flag faction, and formed the Red Headquarters within the Red Rebels of the South-Central Forestry Institute.
2. The August 1 Combat Corps: 160,000 members, of which roughly 40% were demobilized soldiers, 40% were workers, and 20% were middle school students.
3. The Young Intellectuals to the Countryside Rebellion Headquarters: 120,000 youths from communes in the Canton area and from as far away as Hainan Island.
4. The Canton Fighting Corps: 40,000 middle school students between the ages of 14 and 18. It was organized by the Cultural Revolution Small Group as the commanding headquarters of the Red Flag faction and was later accused of being the Kwangtung branch of the May 16 Corps.
5. The Red Headquarters of Middle School Teachers: 60,000 to 70,000 middle school teachers.
6. The Canton Railway Workers' Headquarters: 50,000 coolies.
7. The East Is Red Group of the Kwangtung Pearl River Film Studio: one of the most active members of the Red Flag faction and closely related to the Cultural Revolution Small Group. It led the Red Headquarters of the government organs
8. The Central-South Liaison Headquarters: the middle-level cadre organization closely associated with the Cultural Revolution Small Group.
9. Besides these organizations, the Red Flag faction included the Workers' Revolutionary Alliance; the Friendship Association of Red Peasants; the Red Headquarters of the Canton Municipal Organs; the New Public Security Office; the Red Headquarters of Art and Literature; and the Red Headquarters of Literature and Physical Science of the PLA.

---

*The East Wind Faction*

---

1. The Canton Area General Headquarters (Ti Tsung): 100,000 state factory workers whose average age was at least 30.
2. The Red General Headquarters (Hung Tsung): 800,000 state factory workers.
3. The Ism Red Guards: 40,000 middle school students ranging from the age of 14 to 18, many of whom were the children of the Party and military cadres. Its leaders included the son of the Deputy Commander of the Canton Military Region; the son of the head of Spring Thunder; and the daughter of Tseng Sheng (the Mayor of Canton).
4. The Canton Suburban Area Poor and Middle Peasants' United Command: 800,000 militia members from communes surrounding Canton.
5. The Red First Headquarters: 6,000 to 7,000 Physical Education students.
6. The United Headquarters of Provincial Organs: 4,000 to 5,000 middle-ranking provincial and municipal cadres who fought to protect their positions.
7. Spring Thunder: 10,000 or more railway cadres and skilled workers.
8. Besides these groups, East Wind also included the Revolutionary Committee of Chungshan University; the New District Headquarters; the New East Is Red group of the Kwangtung Pearl River Film Studio; the Tsung-yi Commune of Canton Municipal Organs; the East Is Red group of the Provincial Party Committee; and the Allied Headquarters of Public Security.

---

opposed the power seizure because they had not taken part in it and did not share political ascendancy afterwards. The second was composed of radicals who supported it because they had staged it and acquired authority as a result of it.

The Kwangtung PLA initially took a neutral position toward the January 22 power seizure, neither supporting nor opposing the PJRRC. But when the Military Control Commission was imposed on Kwangtung, the PLA was bound to clash with the Red Flag faction, which claimed to be the legitimate ruler of the province. The first open clash between the Red Flag faction and the Kwangtung PLA took place when the core units of the Red Flag faction (the Chungshan University Red Flag group, the Pearl River Film Studio East Is Red group, and the August 1 Combat Corps) gathered one hundred thousand persons and raided the Kwangtung Military Command compound on February 8, 1967.[125] The rebels demanded that the PLA leaders rehabilitate those PLA radicals who had been branded as "counterrevolutionaries" at the early stage of the Cultural Revolution. Their true intention, however, was to seize the PLA's power. Later, the various sources of the East Wind faction charged that the Cultural Revolution Small Group instigated the raid, and this charge seems quite valid.[126]

### The Rise of the East Wind Faction from February to April 1967

As the official policy became moderate in February, the PJRRC confronted increasing difficulties in maintaining its power. By mid-February, ordinary living staples were in short supply in the Kwangtung market, and the economy as a whole was in disarray.[127] Worse still, the provincialist leaders, having realized that the PLA was going to be the real locus of power and that the conservative mass organizations were growing powerful, took a cooler attitude toward the PJRRC. Under mounting public criticism, the PJRRC suspended Chao Tzu-yang and Ou Meng-chüeh, and named Yin Lin-p'ing (who later proved to be a provincialist) as the provincial governor.[128]

In contrast, the PLA gradually aggrandized its own power by stepping into the power vacuum through the Military Control Commission, and it used its increased power to discriminate against the Red Flag faction and pro–Red Flag cadres. This discrimination was in part intentional, but it also stemmed from the PLA's efforts to restore order and production—for which purpose the Military Control Commission had been imposed.

For production, the PLA had to rely on the existing governing structures and personnel. The first thing that the Military Control Commission did was

125. For the Red Flag's clash with the PLA, see *Kuang-chou jih-pao,* 24 January 1967; *1.25 chan-pao,* 3 April 1967.
126. *Kuang-chou hung-wei-ping,* 28 August 1968; *T'i-yü chan-pao,* 18 March 1968.
127. *Wen-ko p'ing-lun,* January 1968.
128. Ibid., January 1968.

to organize a three-level cadre conference along the lines of the hierarchical structure of the Party organization at the provincial level.[129] In these meetings, the PLA defined the restoration of civil order and production as the most urgent tasks of the moment.[130] The PLA also assured the cadres of their safety if they cooperated with the Military Control Commission, and criticized those cadres who took a position of "fearing, complaining, shrinking, and pushing aside responsibility," a widespread attitude among the cadres during the confusion of the power seizure.[131]

Although it is not known how the PLA selected the cadres participating in the three-level cadre meetings, it is obvious that they were selected by the existing leadership structure with the help of the mass organizations sympathetic to that leadership. One cadre organization that the Military Control Commission relied on for information and materials necessary for screening the cadres was composed of three hundred cadres from the *ch'u* level and above, the "working personnel of the Cultural Revolution Office" whom the old Provincial Party Committee regarded as "loyal and reliable."[132] Those cadres who supported the PJRRC not only were excluded, but were also criticized for their failure to "stand firmly by their standpoint" and for "being used by the class enemy."[133] The PLA organized the Kwangtung Provincial Production Headquarters, whose members were drawn exclusively from the conservative workers who were the "backbone of production."[134] The conservative forces were thus unified under the Kwangtung Provincial Production Headquarters, and the radical forces were unified under the PJRRC.

In the beginning of March, the PLA started to pressure the Red Flag faction directly. The public campaign to discredit the PJRRC started with an anonymous letter from a PLA soldier (though the radicals contended that the author was a high-ranking PLA leader). The letter, which was published in the *Nan-fang jih-pao,* stated that the "PLA did not, does not, and will not support the PJRRC."[135] Soon after this, the PLA ordered the arrest of the six top PJRRC leaders.[136] Then the Hsin Peita's Liaison Office to Kwangtung published an article which denounced the January 22 power seizure as a

129. *News From Chinese Provincial Radio Stations,* no. 197 (9 March 1967), pp. M1-M17.
130. Ibid.
131. Ibid.
132. *Wen-ko p'ing-lun,* January 1968.
133. *CNS,* no. 161 (15 March 1967), p. 2. The Kwangtung PLA admitted that it excluded the members of PJRRC from the Provincial Production Headquarters. *Tzu-liao chuan-chi,* 17 November 1967.
134. *News From Chinese Provincial Radio Station,* 9 March 1967, pp. M1-M24.
135. *Nan-fang jih-pao* was the official organ of the provincial party committee and functioned as spokesman of the East Wind, while *Kuang-chou jih-pao,* the official organ of the Canton Municipal Party Committee, was seized by the Red Flag and became a mouthpiece of the radicals.
136. *China News Items from the Press,* no. 160 (9 March 1967), pp. 7-8.

factional maneuver.[137] The PLA distributed six million copies of the article, and thus effectively undermined the PJRRC's claim that the Peking leadership supported its power seizure. To be sure, the radicals launched their own propaganda campaign to defend their power seizure. However, they could not match the propaganda campaign of the conservatives, who, thanks to the support of the PLA, could sometimes even use airplanes to drop handbills.

At the same time, the Kwangtung PLA dissolved the August 1 Combat Corps and the Kwangtung Film Studio East Is Red group as "counterrevolutionary and illegal organizations," and intimidated other organizations belonging to the Red Flag faction by investigating and collecting information on their activities.[138] According to one source, more than three thousand persons were arrested, and more than sixteen thousand persons were registered as members of "reactionary organizations."[139] Even those who were not arrested or registered were subjected to various recriminations: they were attacked at the mass meetings, forced to confess their crimes, and even dismissed from their jobs.[140] In some cases, not only the workers of the Red Flag faction but also their families were discriminated against. As a result, the Red Flag faction nearly disintegrated. Even though it was not officially disbanded, the Workers' Revolutionary Alliance saw its membership decline from thirty thousand at the time of the January Power Seizure to three thousand at the end of March.[141]

Although the students did not meet as harsh a fate as that of the radical workers or cadres, they were also subjected to various harassments and discriminations: they were investigated, and each one was forced to make a self-criticism and to write a "letter asking for amnesty." In carrying out their policy favorable to the conservatives, the military training teams relied on the East Wind faction to help suppress the Red Flag faction.[142] The East Wind faction dug out and collected information necessary for the PLA to condemn the Red Flag faction, and at the same time seized the power from the various Red Flag member organizations.

After turning the balance of power between the East Wind and Red Flag factions in the former's favor, the PLA proceeded to establish revolutionary committees which were dominated by the conservative mass organizations. One of the most conspicuous examples of this type of revolutionary committee was at the Kwangtung Railway Bureau, which the Kwangtung PLA widely propagated as a model. Originally, the radical Revolutionary Rebel

137. *Chung-hsüeh hung-wei-ping,* May 1968.
138. *Kung-yeh ta-tao hung-ch'i,* July 1968.
139. *Kang pa-i,* 5 October 1967.
140. Ibid.
141. Hai Feng, *An Account of the CR in the Canton Area,* p. 155.
142. Gordon Bennet and Ronald Montaperto, *Red Guard* (New York: Doubleday, 1971), pp. 166-180. Wang Ch'ao, *Kuang-chou tien-ying-chieh te tsao-fan-che,* p. 96.

Committee of the Kwangtung Railway Bureau consisted of unskilled workers, who declared a power seizure on January 23, 1967. When the Military Control Commission was imposed, however, the PLA reactivated the Spring Thunder group, the conservative mass organization controlled by the cadres of the bureau's political department.

With the PLA's support, Spring Thunder expanded its membership from seventy persons to thirteen thousand and set up a new Revolutionary Committee.[143] This new committee consisted of two representatives from the mass organizations, seven high-ranking cadres (including the bureau chiefs) who actively suppressed the rebels at the early stage of the Cultural Revolution, and two military representatives who had maintained a close relationship with the former bureau Party Committee even before the Cultural Revolution.[144] Thus, as was the case in Peking, the Kwangtung rebels, who were once glorified as the main force of the Cultural Revolution, faced a possible complete collapse by the end of March 1967.

### Stalemate—The Summer of 1967

By the beginning of April, the impact of the counterattack on the "February Adverse Current" was being felt in Kwangtung. Thus, the PLA resorted to its usual practice of selectively complying with the official policy as the line again became increasingly radical. For instance, when *Hung ch'i*, No. 5, heralded the official attack on Liu Shao-ch'i as well as the attack on those who exploited the "three-in-one combination to suppress the revolutionaries," the Kwangtung PLA responded only to the call for criticizing Liu, while remaining silent on the second target.[145] On the other hand, the Kwangtung radicals responded enthusiastically to the criticism of the "February Adverse Current," while showing little interest in criticizing Liu. Encouraged by the new official line, Red Flag launched a large-scale propaganda campaign to boost their morale. There was a rumor that Chiang Ch'ing herself would come to Kwangtung to punish the PLA.

In fact, the Peking leaders did interfere directly with the Kwangtung Cultural Revolution on behalf of the radicals. First, Kang Sheng secretly visited Kwangtung and "talked with the PLA leaders."[146] He probably criticized the PLA leaders for supporting the conservatives and demanded that they support the Red Flag faction. Then, Chou En-lai came to Kwangtung and held an open meeting with the leaders of both factions.[147] His

143. Hai Feng, *An Account of the CR in the Canton Area*, pp. 113-114.
144. *Kuang t'ieh tsung-su*, 15 July 1967.
145. *China News Items from the Press*, no. 165 (13 April 1967), p. 6.
146. Wang Ch'ao, *Kuang-chou tien-ying-chieh te tsao-fan-che*, p. 105.
147. Ibid., p. 106.

speech to the meeting was typical of his talks, which were characterized by compromise and pragmatism.[148]

On the one hand, Chou declared that the Red Flag faction was a revolutionary organization, and he specifically ordered the rehabilitation of the East Is Red group of the Pearl River Film Studio. He conceded that the Red Flag faction had made mistakes in the January 22 power seizure, but he insisted that the mistakes were not errors of orientation. On the other hand, he declared that the District Headquarters and the Red Headquarters were "inclined toward conservatism" *(ta men chih pu kuo yu kuo pien yu pao pa le)*, even though they were not "old conservatives" *(lao pao)*, as the Red Flag faction charged. Finally, he acknowledged that the Kwangtung PLA had made mistakes, but he still urged Red Flag not to attack it.

Because of the pressure from the Peking leaders, the Kwangtung PLA changed its stand during May and June from one that was pro–East Wind to one of neutrality.[149] The Canton Radio Station, which was under the PLA's control, began to report the activities of the Red Flag faction, and PLA personnel appeared at Red Flag's mass meetings. Even Huang Yung-sheng made frequent appearances at the Red Flag meetings, where he admitted, at least verbally, his earlier mistake of neglecting the Red Flag faction.[150]

The Kwangtung PLA, however, still resisted the complete rehabilitation of the East Is Red group of the Pearl River Film Studio. It issued a notice which reinstated East Is Red, but it still refused to acknowledge that it had been a mistake to dissolve that mass organization. Furthermore, the PLA released those arrested, not with a notice of reinstatement, but with a "Notice of Release," which read: "X has gone through re-education, and since he has realized his mistakes, has produced a self-criticism, and has behaved well, he is released."[151] On the other hand, the PLA continued to maintain a good relationship with the East Wind faction, which it regarded as a revolutionary mass organization.

As lukewarm as the PLA's support was, it helped improve Red Flag's lot. According to one observer, Red Flag emerged "suddenly from a humble status to an honorable position."[152] Conversely, East Wind lost the predominance it had had in March, and it also suffered many defections in its ranks. The defectors set up their own organizations, which retained their former names simply prefaced by "new"—for example, the New District

148. Hai Feng, *An Account of the CR in the Canton Area,* pp. 121-124; *Chung-ta chan-pao,* 1 March 1967.

149. For the PLA's view of its own records, see *Hung-se pao-tung,* 8 July 1967. For Mao's comments on the Kwangtung PLA, see Hai Feng, *An Account of the CR in the Canton Area,* p. 124.

150. *Liu-yueh t'ien-ping,* 29 June 1967.

151. Wang Ch'ao, *Kung-chou tien-ying-chieh teh tsao-fan-che,* p. 115.

152. Bennett and Montaperto, *Red Guard,* p. 185.

Headquarters.[153] However, these organizations did not cross over the factional cleavage, but remained in East Wind's camp—which indicates that rather than being a genuine revolt, the establishment of new organizations was a defensive measure for East Wind to prepare its retreat.

The confrontation between the two factions, which were well matched in strength, continued during the summer of 1967. The Red Flag faction, now officially recognized as a revolutionary rebel organization, tried to regain the dominant position that it had enjoyed in January; whereas the East Wind faction made a desperate effort to maintain the edge which it had gained in March.

The power struggle between the two factions was epitomized by two issues. The first issue was the characterization of the Kwangtung Cultural Revolution in March. Red Flag called this period the "March Black Wind," while East Wind regarded March as a period when the "East Wind was prevailing over the West Wind."[154] Had the thesis of a "March Black Wind" been accepted, it would have justified the complete reversal of what the PLA had done in March (including the rise of the East Wind faction); whereas the thesis of the "East Wind prevailing over the West Wind" effectively precluded that reversal.

The second issue concerned the question of the August 1 Combat Corps. Unlike the case of the East Is Red group of the Pearl River Film Studio, the PLA had good reason to disband the August 1 Combat Corps, for the Corps consisted of discontented workers, and its attack on the Party organization could well be considered "class revenge."[155] Moreover, it had a close relationship with nationwide organizations that the MAC had declared to be counterrevolutionary (e.g., the Red Flag Army and the Hsiang Chiang Feng Lei). Therefore, neither Chou nor the Kwangtung PLA was ready to reinstate this organization. From the viewpoint of the Kwangtung radicals, however, the reinstatement of the August 1 Combat Corps was crucial for tipping the balance of power between the two factions in their favor. For the same reason, the East Wind faction violently opposed the rehabilitation.[156]

The PLA issued the "May 20th Notice," the "May 30th Notice," and the "June 22nd Explanation," stating that it was impossible to reverse the verdict because the decision was "approved by the central authority," and accusing the radicals of disrupting "normal operations and democracy."[157] However, insisting that the disbanding of the Corps had been unknown to the

153. Hai Feng, *An Account of the CR in the Canton Area*, p. 115.
154. "Ten Major Differences," *URS* 50, nos. 11 and 12 (February 1968): 166-180.
155. "The Counterrevolutionary Crimes of the August 1 Fighting Corps," *SCMP*, no. 3905 (23 March 1967), pp. 1-4. For a defense of the August 1 Fighting Corps, see *Hung-se pao-tung*, 7 August 1967, and *Tung-fang-hung* (Kwangtung), 17 November 1967.
156. *Nan-fang jih-pao*, 9 July 1967.
157. *Hung-se pao-tung*, July 8; *33 chan-pao*, 28 June 1967.

Cultural Revolution Small Group, the Red Flag faction pressured the PLA for the Corps' rehabilitation by organizing a mass rally and sit-in hunger strikes.[158] In the end, in defiance of the Kwangtung PLA's orders, Red Flag took the matter into its own hands by organizing a mass rally that declared the rehabilitation of the Corps.[159] This incident further strained the relationship between Red Flag and the PLA and brought the PLA closer to the East Wind faction, which publicly declared its unconditional loyalty to the PLA.

The summer of 1967 was a most difficult time for the PLA. Forced to do so by the Peking leaders, the PLA admitted its mistake in suppressing the revolutionary rebels, but it still refused to support the Red Flag faction wholeheartedly. It had no desire to completely repudiate what it had done in March, nor did it want to suppress the East Wind faction, as the Red Flag faction so fervently desired. Trapped between the Center's pressure and its own preferences, the PLA took an equivocal attitude toward Red Flag. It supported Red Flag in words, while supporting East Wind in deeds. At the best of times, it attempted to maintain a good relationship with both factions. Consequently, the PLA lost its effectiveness as a force unifying the warring factions.

When the PLA abandoned its active attempt to bring the warring factions together, the two sides confronted each other without restraint, employing increasingly violent means. Each side attempted to consolidate its own camp by merging its member organizations. Red Flag's radical students established the Preparatory Committee of the Kwangtung Red Guard Congress as their unified command structure.[160] They abolished the various headquarters (e.g., the New First Headquarters, the Third Headquarters, and the Red Headquarters), and put their equipment and treasures at the command of the Preparatory Committee. The radical workers also further unified themselves into the Kwangtung Workers' Revolutionary Alliance (Kung Ko Lien). On the other hand, the conservative student organizations formed the Red Guard Congress of the Kwangtung Institutes of Higher Learning, while the conservative workers established the Workers' Revolutionary Committee (Kung Ko Hui).[161]

The series of armed struggles began with East Wind's attack on Red Flag on July 19, the same day that the Wuhan Incident occurred (see Chapter 8). In view of the fact that East Wind maintained close contact with the Wuhan conservatives, the armed struggle in the summer of 1967 could be regarded as a calculated move on the part of the conservative forces to pressure the Center to moderate the official line.

158. Ibid. *Kwangtung tung-fang-hung*, 11 July 1968.
159. *San-chün lien-wei chan-pao*, 18 September 1968.
160. *Hsin nan-fang*, 1 July 1967; *Kuang i hung-ch'i*, 1 October 1967.
161. *Nan-fang jih-pao*, 9 July 1967.

## Summary

With the assistance of T'ao Chu in Peking, the Kwangtung Party Committee led the Kwangtung Red Guard movement so skillfully that the masses did not split into conservatives and radicals until the January 22 power seizure. The delayed split helped the conservative forces to preserve their strength during the radical phases of the mass movement and to reassert themselves during the moderate phases. Because of this, the conservatives and radicals confronted each other with full strength, although each one's fortunes rose or fell at each stage of the movement. The structure of the conflict in Kwangtung thus resembled a "bi-polar" system, to use the terminology of international politics, although there was not a leading mass organization (or "super power") around which the members of each faction were united.

This "bi-polar" conflict structure had some interesting characteristics. First, the main cleavage took place along the clear-cut ideological line of conservative versus radical: East Wind tried to maintain the status quo as much as possible, and Red Flag attempted to change it with just as much determination. Neither recognized the other as a legitimate revolutionary mass organization, nor did the Center recognize either as such until September 1967, when it finally granted this status to East Wind. At one time, the Kwangtung PLA branded some Red Flag members as counterrevolutionaries and disbanded their organizations. At no time, however, did the Cultural Revolution Small Group publicly regard East Wind as a revolutionary organization.

Second, the division between the two factions was so complete that there was no neutral organization in between. Unlike those in Peking, the Kwangtung workers and cadres were all divided into radicals and conservatives, siding respectively with either Red Flag or East Wind. In general, the radical forces were strong among the students, whereas the conservative forces were strong among the workers. This clear-cut division between the two factions was maintained on all the issues. This was in sharp contrast with the Peking factional structure, in which the dividing line between the Earth and Heaven factions was hazier as some member organizations took a selective position on various issues, holding a conservative or a radical view according to the issue in question. Consequently, Kwangtung experienced more violence than Peking.

Third, in contrast to the localized conflict in Peking (in which only some members of both factions were involved in any given conflict), the conflict structure of the Kwangtung Red Guards was "total," in the sense that all members of both factions were usually involved in any given conflict. In other words, the member organizations of each faction were more tightly integrated in Kwangtung than in Peking. In Peking, each faction sought the support of a particular organization of the opposite faction, and member organizations of both factions could sometimes take a joint stand on certain issues. For instance, the Earth faction tried to buy off the Tsinghua Ching-kangshan, thus isolating the Hsin Peita. However, in the Kwangtung "bi-polar" system, each faction, instead of trying to win over the opposite faction's member organizations, tried to destroy them. Member organizations from both factions never took a joint action until the great alliance was imposed in late 1968. Consequently, the rise and fall of a faction graphically reflected the rise and fall of its member organizations at the basic levels. Thus, talking about the factions as a whole rather than about their individual member organizations makes more sense in discussing Kwangtung'than it would in discussing Peking. In brief, the conflict structure in Kwangtung was "antagonistic" rather than "non-antagonistic," to use the Chinese jargon.

These characteristics can also be found in other provinces in which the influence of the Party Committee and the PLA was strong and that of the Cultural Revolution Small Group weak. The Small Group could help replace the original conservative Red Guards with more radical Red Guards and could thoroughly repudiate the "theory of natural redness" and the "bourgeois reactionary line" in Peking. But the Small Group could not do this in many cases at the provincial level, since its influence had not reached that level without loss of effectiveness. The only way the Small Group could exercise its influence over the local Cultural Revolutions was through the local Red Guards coming to Peking or the Peking Red Guards going to the provinces for an exchange of experience.

In Kwangtung, the Small Group had attempted to recruit reliable leaders from the provincial cadres after the downfall of T'ao Chu. It initiated secret contacts with the middle-ranking cadres in Kwangtung, and organized them into the Liaison Headquarters of the South Central Bureau. Lacking popular support in Kwangtung, the Liaison Headquarters had to rely on the Small Group's support, and to a certain extent acted as a factional organization of the Small Group. This further alienated the cadres in the Kwangtung Party organization, who rightly regarded the Liaison Headquarters as a factional organization rather than as a mass organization of revolutionaries. When Wang Li and Kuan Feng were purged, East Wind publicly accused the Liaison Headquarters of being their factional organization:

The Liaison Headquarters attempted to set up a telegraphic station to keep in direct contact with the Party Central Committee. They found the telecommunication and post bureaus inconvenient and unreliable for them, and wanted to set up a telegraphic station to privately communicate with the Wang-Kuan-Ch'i counterrevolutionary clique, so that, under the direct command of this counterrevolutionary clique, they could carry out the sinister activities of usurping the Army and seizing power in a big way.[162]

162. "Expose Sinister Conspiracy of Min, Ch'e, Chang Counterrevolutionary Clique to Sabotage Confidential Work," *SCMP,* no. 4274 (9 October 1968), pp. 4-6.

In contrast to the Small Group's precarious position, the PLA was in a good position to shape the course of the Cultural Revolution in Kwangtung. As the PLA emerged as the predominant elite group, the Kwangtung conservatives, who had once been supported by the Provincial Party Committee, rallied around the PLA. Naturally, the PLA supported the conservatives, in part because their interests and ideology coincided, and in part because, as a practical matter, it was the conservatives who supported them. The conflict between the East Wind and the Red Flag factions thus reflected the conflict between the PLA and the Cultural Revolution Small Group, and in turn both elite groups used their client mass factions in their power struggle against each other.

# CHAPTER 8

# The Red Guard Movement After the Wuhan Incident

The tension that had been building between the Cultural Revolution Small Group and the People's Liberation Army since March 1967 finally erupted in the now-famous Wuhan Incident.[1] On July 20, the conservative mass organizations of Wuhan kidnapped Hsieh Fu-chih and Wang Li—two Peking emissaries—at the encouragement (or at least with the acquiescence) of the local military leaders. The Small Group responded to this insubordination by calling on the masses to seize the military power from the "handful of power holders within the army."[2] Thus, the Cultural Revolution entered a new radical phase of armed struggle. But by the beginning of September, the official line had shifted to moderation, and thereafter the de-escalation process steadily continued, interrupted by only a short interval in the spring of 1968, and culminated in a full-scale demobilization in July.

With the announcement of Party reconstruction in October 1967, the main attention of every participant shifted from the Cultural Revolution itself to the question of who would rule China *after* the Cultural Revolution. Inhibited from openly challenging each other by the need to maintain the unity of the Maoist leaders, at least in appearance, the elite groups resorted to manipulating their client mass organizations to consolidate their power bases and form a winning coalition. The power struggle between the Small Group, the PLA, and Chou En-lai's circle was therefore covert—fought behind the

---

1. For the Wuhan Incident, see Thomas W. Robinson, "The Wuhan Incident: Local Strife and Provincial Rebellion During the Cultural Revolution," *CQ*, no. 47 (July-September 1971), pp. 413-418.
2. "The Proletariat Must Take a Firm Hold of the Gun," *Hung ch'i*, no. 12 (August 1967), pp. 43-47.

scenes and hidden from the public eye. But it was clearly manifested in the intensified factional struggle of the mass organizations.

At that time, it appeared that the overall relationship among the three elite groups was still fluid and undetermined. In retrospect, however, it is clear that it was in this period that the coalition between Chou En-lai and Chiang Ch'ing was formed (a coalition that later defeated Lin Piao in 1971). Chou shrewdly allied himself with Chiang Ch'ing's group despite their ideological and policy differences, which stemmed from the question of power distribution in the aftermath of the Cultural Revolution. This chapter therefore focuses on the power struggle between the PLA and the Small Group, particularly as it was manifested in the factional struggle of the mass organizations in the context of the overall process of deradicalization.

## The Wuhan Incident and the Surge of Radicalism

The conflict structure in Wuhan which led to the kidnapping of the Peking emissaries was basically similar to that of other provinces. On January 26, the radical faction made an abortive attempt to seize power. In February, the conservatives denounced the abortive power seizure as a "counterrevolutionary action," and the PLA supported that view. But the radicals insisted that their "main orientation was correct, in light of the general orientation of the movement at that time."[3]

In March, the PLA suppressed the radicals by disbanding the Workers' General Headquarters (the core group of the Wuhan radicals which claimed to have 400,000 members) and arresting five hundred leaders. At the same time, the PLA actively built up the strength of the conservative mass organizations through its militia departments.[4] In April, the radicals retaliated, demanding the rehabilitation of the disbanded organization. They even staged a series of demonstrations and hunger strikes. Instead of yielding, however, the PLA and the conservative mass organizations accused the radicals of sidetracking the great criticism of Liu and Teng.

Meanwhile, the representatives of the leaders of the Wuhan PLA were summoned to Peking in April for negotiations with the Peking leaders. The meeting failed, however, to produce any definite agreement. The PLA continued to defend its March actions, the Small Group accused the PLA of having made mistakes, and Chou En-lai attempted to mitigate the confrontation between the two factions.

The Small Group's relationship with the Wuhan PLA deteriorated to such an extent that the Small Group "sent one of its directors to [the PLA]

3. *News From Chinese Provincial Radio Station,* 24 August 1967, pp. H6-H13.
4. "Inside Facts About Ch'en and Chung's Anti-Party Activities," *SCMPS,* no. 214 (27 December 1967), pp. 19-30.

delegates' living quarters to confiscate their draft of the minutes, and ordered them to make a self-examination."[5] Nevertheless, the PLA representatives informed their colleagues in Wuhan that the Peking meeting had decided that no errors of orientation had been made by the Wuhan PLA, that no reversal of the verdict on the Workers' General Headquarters was necessary, and that the general orientation of the "One Million Heroic Troops" had been correct.[6] The radicals impugned the statement, accusing the PLA delegates of falsifying the decision. The truth, however, was that the conference did not reach any agreement, or, if it did, its decision was in favor of the Wuhan PLA despite the Small Group's opposition.

During June and July, the confrontation between both sides in Wuhan, as in other areas, reached an all-time high. According to Thomas Robinson, more than one thousand persons were killed, and labor strikes reduced the production of over twenty-four thousand factories and mines to less than half of their capacity.[7]

As part of the official policy of sending the central leaders to the provinces on fact-finding missions, Hsieh Fu-chih and Wang Li came to Wuhan to investigate the local conditions. After spending four days talking with various mass organizations, they rendered the following judgment at a meeting attended by the leaders of both factions and the Wuhan military leaders: (1) the San Kang (the three steel-workers' organizations) and the San Hsin (the three student organizations of the Wuhan universities) were "genuine" revolutionary rebels; (2) the military district was mistaken, in both direction and line, in supporting the "One Million Heroic Troops"; (3) the Workers' General Headquarters must be vindicated; and (4) the "One Million Heroic Troops" were a conservative organization, and the San Ssu (the three workers' headquarters) tended to be conservative.

This decision amounted to a total defeat for the conservatives and their patron, the PLA. When Wang and Hsieh returned to their hotel, the "One Million Heroic Troops"—the backbone of the Wuhan conservative forces—stormed the hotel and kidnapped Wang.[8] The Wuhan PLA leaders acquiesced in the kidnapping, excusing themselves on the ground that the spontaneous actions of the workers were beyond their control.

---

5. The PLA defended the dissolution of the Workers General Headquarters, and the Small Group denounced it. Chou En-lai ambiguously said that the Wuhan PLA leaders disbanded the organization before the Center issued the "Ten Articles." "Ch'en Tsai-tao's Examination," *SCMP*, no. 4167 (30 August 1967), pp. 2-3.

6. Ibid.

7. Robinson, "The Wuhan Incident," *CQ*, no. 47, pp. 413-418.

8. It should be noted that only Wang Li was kidnapped. Hsieh Fu-chih was merely detained, and the members of the Red Flag of the Peking Aviation Institute who accompanied them were not subjected to abuse. After his return to Peking, Hsieh was not very critical of the Wuhan PLA leaders. *CNS*, no. 187 (14 September 1967), p. 8.

The Peking authorities reacted swiftly and decisively: they moved in reliable troops, including an airborne division and naval vessels, and at the same time ordered that the Wuhan military leaders ensure the safety of the Peking emissaries. With the help of loyal troops, Wang Li managed to escape from his captors and returned with Hsieh to Peking on July 21. No sooner had the outside troops entered Wuhan than the "One Million Heroic Troops" disintegrated without having put up much resistance.

The basic question regarding the incident is whether it should be viewed as a mutiny of the isolated local military leaders against the central authorities or as the PLA's challenge to the Small Group. The boundary between these two theses is, in fact, very thin, since the Small Group's influence was strong in the Center, whereas the PLA maintained strong influence at the local level. Nonetheless, considering the rising tension between the Small Group and the PLA in general, and the events in Wuhan leading up to the incident in particular, it is more appropriate to view the incident as a clash between the Small Group and the PLA.

This interpretation also takes into account the possible subjective considerations of the Wuhan PLA leaders, who may very well have believed that the Small Group was threatening the basic institutional interests of the PLA and that the entire PLA command structure shared their resentment. If so, they may well have calculated that the PLA's basic interests could not be safeguarded without challenging the Small Group publicly, and that the Peking leaders, although not expected to support their challenge overtly, would be sympathetic. The punishment meted out to Ch'en Tsai-tao, the commander of the Wuhan military regiment, was certainly too light for the crime of mutiny.[9] He was first placed under house arrest, and then allowed to repent. Furthermore, he implied to his interrogator that the Wuhan conservatives did not revolt against the central authorities as such, but revolted specifically against the Small Group.[10]

The Small Group, however, viewed the incident as the PLA's open challenge to the Peking authorities, and so stepped up its attack on the PLA. On July 22, Chiang Ch'ing urged the Red Guards to

defend with weapons and attack with words. We should not be too naive. When the handful of persons who stir up struggle by force takes up arms to attack you, you [revolutionary masses] may take up arms in self-defense. They [the conservatives] do not lay down their arms and are raising rifles, spears, and swords against you, and you lay down your arms. This is wrong. You will get the worst of it. This is what is happening at present in Wuhan.[11]

9. He has now reappeared.
10. "Report on Ch'en Tsai-tao, Chung Han-hua, and Others," *SCMP*, no. 4155 (27 March 1968), pp. 1-4.
11. *CNS*, no. 185 (31 August 1967), pp. 5-6.

*Hung ch'i,* No. 12, published a provocative editorial entitled "The Proletariat Must Take a Firm Hold of the Gun."[12] Allegedly written by Wang Li
and Kuan Feng, it invited the mass organizations to seize military power
from the "handful of power holders in the army," on the grounds that the
"proletarian revolution cannot succeed without controlling guns." Soon the
Peking propaganda machines under the Small Group's control were in full
swing to publicize the editorial.[13]

In contrast to the Small Group's generalized attack on the PLA, the PLA
reacted to the incident with rather mild criticisms specifically directed
against the Wuhan units. Its basic position was that the Wuhan military
leaders, although having made mistakes in orientation and line, could still
atone for their mistakes through self-criticism.[14] Attributing the incident to
the complicated Wuhan situation and to the intrinsic difficulty in the PLA's
job of supporting the left, rather than to the existence of a "handful of power
holders in the army," Lin Piao urged that the incident serve as a lesson,
instead of as an excuse to attack the PLA.[15]

The immediate consequence of the Wuhan Incident was the rise of the
radical forces throughout China. Encouraged by Chiang Ch'ing's July 22 call
to "defend with weapons and attack with words," the radicals were all over
the military units to seize the weapons.[16] Meanwhile, the Small Group was
busy exploiting the Wuhan Incident for its own political gain. Wang Li and
Kuan Feng dispatched "one third of the reporters of the Hsin Hua News
Agency" throughout China to cover the campaign to "drag out the handful
in the army."[17]

As the official line leaned toward the radical direction, even the neutralists
in the factional struggle jumped on the radical bandwagon, thereby swinging

    12. "The Proletariat Must Take a Firm Hold of the Gun," *Hung ch'i,* no. 12 (August 1967),
pp. 43-47.
    13. "Towering Crimes Committed by Counterrevolutionary Clique of Wang Li," *SCMP,* no.
4158 (16 April 1968), pp. 1-8. A crucial question is whether the editorial was approved by the top
leaders. It seems very likely that Chiang Ch'ing and Ch'en Po-ta were consulted, even though the
sources close to the Small Group maintained that the group was not informed. "The 'May 16
Red Guard Corps' of Peking," *CB,* no. 844 (10 January 1968), pp. 1-30. But this seems to be a
device to shield Chiang Ch'ing and Ch'en Po-ta from the final responsibility for the article.
Regarding this problem, Chou En-lai again proved to be more frank than any other leaders.
"We should first of all criticize ourselves. Our propaganda machine was wrong in that we simply
called for dragging out a small handful in the army. It led to antagonism between the masses
and the army, and this was exploited by bad men."
    14. *CFCP,* 29 July 1967.
    15. "Deputy Commander Lin Piao's Important Directives," *SCMP,* no. 4036 (6 October
1967), pp. 1-7.
    16. For instance, within two hours after Chiang Ch'ing's speech, the Red Flag raided the
Kwangtung PLA. Interview with former Red Guard.
    17. These two leaders also organized the Kwangchow Combat Corps and sent it to Canton in
order to "set fire to an attack on the PLA." The Kwangchow Liaison Office to Criticize T'ao Chu
was also established in a hurry, to serve as a commanding headquarters of the Kwangtung
radicals. *San-chün lien-wei chan-pao,* 24 September 1968.

public opinion in favor of the radical forces.[18] In Kwangtung, the radicals set up their commanding headquarters and attempted to seize power in the public security bureaus and the industries under the jurisdiction of the Military Control Commission.[19] With the battle cry of "Drag out Kwangtung Old T'an [Ch'en-lin]!"—referring to Huang Yung-sheng—they attempted to provoke the PLA into a Wuhan type of confrontation.[20]

The PLA patiently refrained from using force against the radicals, in part because it knew very well what the radicals were up to, and in part because the use of force against mass organizations was forbidden. But the PLA leaders developed an equally shrewd method of self-defense. They intentionally neglected the PLA's tasks so that the social order was disrupted, communication and transportation systems came to a standstill, and consumer goods became scarce on the market. They made some concessions to the rebel forces, for instance by allowing the rebel forces to seize outdated weapons, while willingly supplying more sophisticated weapons to the conservatives.[21]

18. Alarmed by the sudden change in the official line, the East Wind also pretended to criticize the Wuhan conservatives whom they had vigorously defended up to that moment. "Tightly Grasp the Opportunity to Launch a General Attack on T'an Chen-lin of Canton," *SCMP*, no. 4020 (13 September 1967), pp. 1-6. The Red Flag rejected the sudden change of attitude. As the PLA appeared to be in trouble, not only did those who had maintained neutrality suddenly come out in support of the Red Flag faction, but also those close to the PLA now endeavored to dissociate themselves from the PLA and to seek the radicals' support. "Important Activities of Political Pickpocket Chang Ken-sheng," *SCMP*, no. 4126 (27 February 1968), pp. 4-12. Those cadres who had sympathized with the Red Flag faction became bold enough to write big-character posters against the PLA. "Drag Out for Public Showing Scoundrels Who Signed the 'August 21' Big Character Poisonous Weed," *SCMP*, no. 4320 (14 September 1968), pp. 7-9. The soldiers who had refused to receive handbills from the Red Flag faction no longer refused; instead, they eagerly read them and even passed them to other soldiers. "Tightly Grasp the Opportunity to Launch a General Attack on T'an Chen-lin of Canton," *SCMP*, no. 4020 (13 September 1967), pp. 1-6.

19. In addition, the Kwangtung radicals established several front organizations such as the Revolutionary Cadre Organization, the rallying center for the cadres supporting the Red Flag faction, and the Red Garrison Headquarters, an armed detachment of the Red Flag faction. Manned by 3,000 armed workers, the Red Garrison Headquarters pledged to seize the public security and the Military Control Commission. "At present, the Red Garrison Headquarters will replace the public security bureau. In the future, it will replace the Military Control Commission and seize the power of the Military Garrison Command." *San-chün lien-wei chan pao*, 3 and 24 September 1968. The Garrison Headquarters actually attempted to seize the power of the Military Control Commission and demanded that the Commission withdraw from the public security bureau. "Public security departments are invaluable, but those under your control are criminals. Do not think too highly of yourselves. While you people have rifles, we have knives. We order you to withdraw all your staff from the public security departments immediately on receipt of this notice." *San-chün lien-wei chan-pao*, 13 September 1968. The Garrison Headquarters actually ordered the power seizure in the public enterprises. "All vital industrial and mining enterprises, such as water works, power plants, railways and warehouses, are to be immediately and completely taken over by the proletarian revolutionaries. Seize power with resolution." *San-chün lien-wei chan-pao*, 13 September 1968.

20. *San-chün lien-wei chan-pao*, 13 September 1968.

21. "Tightly Grasp the Opportunity to Launch a General Attack on T'an Chen-lin of Canton," *SCMP*, no. 4020 (13 September 1967), pp. 1-6.

The PLA's most effective method, however, was to manipulate the conservative mass organizations into attacking the radicals—a tactic designed, according to the charges of the radicals, to divert public attention from the PLA's mistakes and put pressure on the Peking Center.[22] The conservative mass organizations mobilized the peasants into the city to attack the radicals, following the strategy of "surrounding the city from the rural areas." The main slogan of the radicals, on the other hand, was to use "people's war to drag out the handful of power holders in the army and to destroy their social bases."[23] The net result of this maneuver and countermaneuver was large-scale armed struggle and complete chaos.

When the official policy encouraged the mass organizations to defend themselves with weapons without specifying which group was revolutionary and which was not, it accelerated the "armed race" among the mass organizations, which were pursuing a policy of "If you have a sword, [we] must have a gun."[24] The idea of "defend with weapons" changed to "attack with weapons," as each group found it politically advantageous to attack the other first. The conservative and radical mass organizations both organized their own "armed detachments," which crossed the functional and administrative boundaries to other units to help their allies, thus spreading the armed struggle from one unit to another. The power holders and "bad persons with ulterior motives" also attempted to "fish in troubled waters" by inciting the workers and peasants to join the armed struggle.

Worse still, the open attack on the PLA gave rise to "anarchism" and "ultra-leftist tendencies" among the mass organizations. Now each mass organization regarded itself as the only leftist and revolutionary one, while condemning anyone who disagreed with its viewpoint as a "political pickpocket" and "speculator."[25] The radicals declared that "we do not superstitiously believe in any authority" and "all regulations and frameworks should be smashed."[26] Some radicals attacked the entire governing structure by calling for a thorough and violent purge of "all leading cadres" without discriminating whether one was a Maoist cadre or not, and by demanding "an incessant redistribution of social property and political power."[27]

In Peking, the Earth faction responded positively to the call to "drag out the handful of power holders in the army." For instance, the East Is Red group at the Geology Institute openly advocated dragging out the "time

22. During the summer of 1967 Canton observed six large-scale armed struggles with several hundred casualties. Hai Feng, *An Account of the Cultural Revolution in the Kwangtung Area* (Hong Kong: Union Research Institute, 1971), pp. 144-145.

23. *Chu-ying tung-fang-hung,* 8 August 1967.

24. *CNS,* no. 189 (28 September 1967), pp. 6-8.

25. *CNS,* no. 177 (6 July 1967), pp. 1-3; no. 189 (28 September 1967), pp. 1-5.

26. Ibid.

27. *CNS,* no. 188 (21 September 1967), pp. 1-3.

bombs in the military organs [who] utilized the military power which they still held temporarily to slander . . . and to ruthlessly suppress the Cultural Revolution."[28] The Earth faction dispatched well-organized intelligence units to various localities to collect materials incriminating the local PLA leaders, and supported the Assault faction (Ch'ung P'ai) of the central military organs attacking the PLA leaders.[29] The Hsin Peita Commune allied itself with the Revolutionary Rebels of the Three Army Branches (the conservative military organization defending the Peking PLA leaders) and continued to stress the outdated slogan "Love the People and Support the Army."[30]

Both sides engaged in a deadly free-wheeling armed struggle, but the surge of the radical mood gave the advantage to the Earth faction. Encouraged by the Small Group's public criticism that the Hsin Peita Commune was made up of "old conservatives," the anti-Nieh forces, which up to that time had been scattered in the East Is Red group, the Hung Ch'i P'iao P'iao, and the Chingkangshan, unified themselves into the Peking University Chingkangshan and, with the help of the other Earth faction members, challenged the Revolutionary Committee of Peking University.[31] However, PLA unit 4585, which had helped Nieh to organize the Revolutionary Committee, defended the Hsin Peita Commune. The frustrated Earth faction raided unit 4585, holding Cheng Wei-shan, the commander of the Peking Military Region, responsible for the unit's action.[32] The minority radicals at People's University and the Peking Steel Institute also utilized this radical phase to challenge the majority faction supported by the Hsin Peita Commune.

What the Small Group advocated in the summer of 1967 amounted, in effect, to a simultaneous attack on the government leaders and the PLA at the elite level and the conservative mass organizations at the mass level. This strategy proved to be impractical, for it pushed the PLA, the government bureaucrats, and the conservative mass organizations into a united front against the radicals and the Small Group. The strategy was also too radical, for it would certainly have disintegrated the PLA (which Mao later aptly described as the "great wall" because it was the only remaining control mechanism with its organizational capability intact) and the government structures which were essential for discharging day-to-day functions of the state. In fact, the PLA's organizational integrity was in serious danger at that time. The radicals attempted not only to seize the PLA's power from outside,

28. *Tung-fang-hung pao,* 1 August 1967.
29. *Hsin pei-ta,* 25 November 1967. The Assault faction was connected with the May 16 Group. *Hsin pei-ta,* 2 December 1967.
30. *Hsin pei-ta,* 23 September 1967.
31. *Hsin pei-ta* itself admitted that leaders of the CRSG had criticized the Hsin Peita Commune for its moderate orientation. *Hsin pei-ta,* 14 June 1967.
32. *Hsin pei-ta,* 25 November 1967.

but also to instigate internal revolt within the PLA. The radicals agitated the soldiers by saying, "You soldiers get only six yuan a month, while an officer draws a high salary and has a car to ride in."[33]

The government ministries faced complete paralysis. Most seriously disrupted was the Ministry of Foreign Affairs under Vice-Premier Ch'en I.[34] At the instigation of Wang Li,[35] the radicals forcefully took over the Foreign Ministry for five days (some reports say fifteen days) in August 1967. They were led by Yao Teng-shan, the former chargé d'affaires in Indonesia, and the June 16 Group of the Peking Language Institute, both of which were later identified as elements of the May 16 Group. During their control, the rebels "dispatched telegrams to foreign countries, appointed diplomats to foreign countries, searched and closed the Party Committee of the Foreign Ministry, and detained the Vice Foreign Ministers."[36] When the Center condemned the take-over, Wang Li allegedly incited the radicals to raid the British Embassy and set fire to it, so as to justify the take-over.

In the face of this serious situation, Mao had no alternative but to moderate the whole movement, if he wanted to prevent it from degenerating into a civil war. He was also under intensive pressure from the moderate group of the Peking leaders. The radicals close to the Small Group openly declared that "[they] were ready to follow Chairman Mao to the mountains to wage guerrilla warfare, [since] the Chairman did not have the majority support of the Center."[37] Why did Mao not choose this course of action? The answer is probably that his original goal for the Cultural Revolution was to revolutionize the existing ruling structure, instead of completely destroying it.

## The Moderation of the Official Line and the Counterattack by the Heaven Faction

The official line again tilted toward moderation with the exposure of the May 16 Group. On August 11, Chiang Ch'ing and Ch'en Po-ta revealed the existence of the May 16 Group for the first time: "Its spearhead is directed against [Chou En-lai], but is actually directed at the Central Committee, and

33. "Miscellany of Mao Tse-tung's Thought," *JPRS*, no. 61,262 (20 February 1974), Part II, p. 465.
34. For the Cultural Revolution in the Foreign Affairs Ministry, see Melvin Gurtov, "The Foreign Ministry and Foreign Affairs During the Cultural Revolution," *CQ*, no. 40 (October-December 1969), pp. 65-102.
35. "Drag out Yao Teng-shan, Big Political Pickpocket," *SCMPS*, no. 213 (13 December 1967), pp. 4-6.
36. "Towering Crimes Committed by Counterrevolutionary Clique of Wang Li," *SCMP*, no. 4158, p. 6.
37. "Premier Chou En-lai Gives Important Instruction," *SCMP*, no. 4078 (12 December 1967), pp. 1-6.

opposition to [Lin Piao]."[38] By August 20, the official position regarding "dragging out the handful of power holders in the army" was reversed. *Hung ch'i*, No. 13, published a new editorial entitled "The Great Chinese PLA—A Reliable Pillar of Our Proletarian Dictatorship and the Great Proletarian Cultural Revolution."[39] On September 1, Chou En-lai, Chiang Ch'ing, Chang Ch'un-ch'iao, Hsieh Fu-chih, and Yang Ch'eng-wu held an "enlarged meeting of the Peking Revolutionary Committee" in which they delivered "extremely important speeches" described as "clear calls at a crucial and important period in the Great Proletarian Cultural Revolution."[40] It was probably at this meeting that the decisions were made to purge Wang Li and Kuan Feng and to curb radicalism.

Four days later (September 5), Chiang Ch'ing repudiated her own previous slogan "Defend with weapons and attack with words" in her much publicized speech to the Anhwei delegation, which, in fact, fell just short of a humiliating self-criticism.[41] She urged the radicals to lay down their weapons and praised the PLA as a pillar of the proletarian dictatorship, while denouncing the "ultra-leftist tendencies" as if she were not responsible for them. The Center formally ordered all the proletarian revolutionaries to study her speech, and soon all the official propaganda machines were in full gear propagating it.[42]

Following Chiang Ch'ing's speech, the Center took a series of measures, all clearly designed to de-escalate the movement. The rebuilding of the Party and the campaign to rectify the class ranks were announced.[43] Military training was reimposed on the campuses, and Mao's Thought Study Classes were instituted at the various administrative levels. These new organizational formats were followed by an official effort to redirect the mass movement to the criticism of Liu Shao-ch'i and T'ao Chu in general, and to educational reform in particular.[44]

In addition, the attention of the offical propaganda shifted from the student to the workers. The workers were now praised as the main force of the Cultural Revolution and told to "shake off the students' influence."[45] Conversely, the official news media became critical of the students, who now were told that they had made many mistakes, that their main task was to "reform the educational system in each school," and that they should not

38. "The 'May 16 Red Guard Corps' of Peking," *CB*, no. 844 (10 July 1968), pp. 1-30.
39. *JMJP*, 20 August 1967.
40. *Tou-p'i t'ung-hsin*, 22 November 1967.
41. "Comrade Chiang Ch'ing's Comment on a Document," *SCMP*, no. 4026 (22 September 1967), p. 1.
42. "Circular of the General Office of the CCP Central Committee," *SCMP*, no. 4069 (29 November 1967), p. 1.
43. These two themes will be dealt with in Chapter 9.
44. For the official attack on T'ao Chu, see *JMJP*, 11 September 1967.
45. *CNS*, no. 202 (4 January 1968), pp. 1-6.

interfere with the Cultural Revolution in the factories because the "factories have their own masses and the offices also have their own masses, and they can make revolution by themselves."[46] The Red Guards staying in Peking were told to return to their localities; otherwise they would be expelled from the schools and would not be assigned to work after graduation.[47] As noted, the workers as a whole were more moderate than the students, and the Small Group was often criticized for relying on the students—the petty bourgeoisie—rather than the workers. The radical phase of the January Power Seizure began with the merging of the Red Guard movement with the workers' movement. Therefore, the renewed emphasis on the workers and separation of the students from the workers unmistakably portended the forthcoming full-scale demobilization.

Mao personally backed the deradicalization. After travelling to North, Central, and East China to comprehend the local situations, he made a series of comments collectively known as "Chairman Mao's strategic plan." The basic goal of the "strategic plan" was to consolidate whatever the Cultural Revolution had achieved, while simultaneously winding it down by bringing the warring factions into unity. First of all, he suggested narrowing the targets of attack: "We should expand our educational front and reduce our attack front."[48] Second, he indirectly criticized the most important component of the radical ideology—an anti-organizational attitude—by instructing that the repudiation of the "theory of docile tools" should be balanced by a "sense of proletarian discipline, [since] obedience and subordination are conditional."[49] Third, he reaffirmed the moderate policy toward the cadres.[50] Fourth, he removed the distinction between the radicals and the conservatives among the mass organizations:

If there are two factions in a unit, I don't believe that one must be left and the other right. I believe that they can be united. We must carry out ideological work on mass organization, no matter whether it is reactionary or conservative.[51]

Finally, Mao clearly indicated that the PLA's prestige and organizational integrity must be preserved.[52]

The official effort to deradicalize the movement was crystalized in the renewed emphasis on the themes of the Cultural Revolution as the "Great School of Mao Tse-tung's Thought" and the "ideological revolution that touches the people to their souls," the line of interpretation that the PLA had

46. Ibid.
47. *Pei-ching kung-jen*, 23 September 1967; *CNS*, no. 186 (7 September 1967), pp. 4-6.
48. "Chairman Mao's Latest Directives," *SCMP*, no. 4057 (8 November 1967), pp. 1-2.
49. Ibid.
50. *JMJP*, 21 October 1967.
51. "Chairman Mao's Latest Directives," *SCMP*, no. 4057 (8 November 1967), p. 1.
52. "Chairman Mao's Latest Instruction," *SCMP*, no. 4060 (15 November 1967), pp. 1-2.

been advocating for a full year. Compatible with the new interpretation of the Cultural Revolution, the slogan of "Struggle against private interests and criticize revisionism" replaced "Struggle against the power holders taking the capitalist road within the Party." In breaking a long period of silence, Lin Piao delivered on National Day a public speech that related the new definition of the Cultural Revolution to the study of Mao's Thought.[53] Thus, the PLA's view of the Cultural Revolution finally emerged as the official line.

At the same time, an effort was made to dissuade the mass organizations from attacking the Small Group and the PLA for their respective mistakes in the Wuhan Incident and in the subsequent attack on the PLA. The official position on these questions was that, although the PLA and the Small Group had erred, their mistakes should not be used as an excuse for further attack on either of them. For, despite mistakes of some particular PLA units, the PLA as a whole had done a good job, and the nature of the mistakes was different from that of the "bourgeois reactionary line."[54] As for the Small Group's mistakes, it was officially explained that Wang Li and Kuan Feng, rather than the Small Group as a whole, had attacked the PLA.

In addition, the Center pinned the blame for these two incidents on the PLA's complicated task of supporting the left and on the Small Group's overestimate of the PLA's mistakes, rather than on the conflicting political interests of the two groups. As if bad coordination had caused the PLA to challenge the Small Group and the Small Group to attack the PLA, the Center moved to improve communications between the two. The work of the General Political Department, which the Small Group accused of taking "charge of everything," was transferred to three new organs: the political unit, the literary and art unit, and the army newspaper unit, all of which were placed under the direct control of the Military Affairs Commission.[55] It was during this period that Chou En-lai and some members of the Small Group and the PLA appeared as a group, in contrast to the previous practice of appearing in public alone.

Despite this compromise solution, the PLA was gaining power over the Small Group, and the whole movement was being redefined according to the PLA's line. Moreover, it was the PLA, with its newly delegated authority to use force against any attempt to seize its weapons, which was going to unify the warring factions. In the face of a complete breakdown of the government ministries, Chou En-lai reluctantly accepted the establishment of Military Control Commissions in the government ministries.[56] Lin Piao made more

53. *JMJP*, 2 October 1967.
54. *Pei-ching kung-jen*, 28 September 1968.
55. "Talks by Vice-Chairman Lin Piao, Premier Chou, Chiang Ch'ing, and Other Central Leaders," *SCMP*, no. 4148 (28 March 1968), p. 16.
56. *Tung-fang-hung pao*, 22 August 1967. Obviously this news was spread by the PLA leaders to the Heaven faction, which in turn wrote it in the big-character posters. Chiang Ch'ing: "Some

frequent public appearances, which indicated his active involvement in decision-making at the policy level. Yeh Chün, Lin Piao's wife, and Yang Ch'eng-wu, the acting chief of staff, also made more public appearances about that time.[57] *Jen-min jih-pao* began to carry more articles on and by the PLA. Even more visible was the PLA's renewed effort to build up the personality cult of Mao, an effort epitomized in the PLA's phrase "Establish the Absolute Authority of Chairman Mao's Thought in a Big Way and in the Biggest Way." The PLA justified its effort to turn the Cultural Revolution to the study of Mao's Thought by arguing that, "since the PLA had made mistakes due to its insufficient attention to Chairman Mao's Thought, it is necessary to renew the campaign to study Mao's Thought."[58]

In contrast to the rising prestige of the PLA, that of the Small Group declined. The Small Group's key members were purged, its secret May 16 Corps was exposed, and its ideological trend of "ultra-leftism" was criticized. Although the purge was limited to Wang Li and Kuan Feng at the top level, its repercussion on the Small Group's following was devastating. Almost all the members of the Small Group's literary section, under the control of Chiang Ch'ing and Ch'en Po-ta, were purged. Chou Ching-fang, the Secretary General of the Peking Revolutionary Committee, who exercised enormous power, was also purged.[59]

Worse still for the Small Group were the widespread "rumors" that Ch'en Po-ta and Chiang Ch'ing had been criticized by Mao, and had admitted their "errors of left opportunism."[60] Accordingly, the cadres at the various levels, always sensitive to the power relationships at the top, adjusted their survival strategy to the new situation. One power holder reportedly observed:

It looks as if things have begun changing. . . . In the past, the Cultural Revolution Small Group was emphasized and the Party Center was not sufficiently mentioned.

---

people insult the members of Mao's Headquarters under the excuse of suppressing [ultra-leftist trends]. We should prevent them from spreading and suppress the distorted news. Those which were not made public officially should not be copied. Whenever Chairman Mao convened meetings I have almost always been there, but I don't know [about the rumors]." *Hung-chan pao*, 10 October 1967.

57. It was during this time that Lin Piao made his wife the secretary of the Operation Section of the MAC. Later Mao criticized Lin Piao for using his wife as secretary. Chou En-lai commented in early 1968 that "wives of some people" were responsible for creating conflict among the leadership and quoted Chairman Mao's saying that "the wives of leading cadres should not join groups" and he was prepared to issue a circular on this. *Hsiao-ping*, 5 April 1968.

58. *CFCP*, 25 August 1967. As a matter of fact, Mao criticized as early as 18 December 1968. "It is not logical to create 'absolute authority.' There has never been a unique authority. All authority is relative." Edward E. Rice, *Mao's Way* (Berkeley and Los Angeles: University of California Press, 1972), p. 436.

59. The Literary Section of the CRSG was organized on 28 May 1967. For the members, see *CNS*, no. 202 (4 January 1968), pp. 8-22.

60. Rice, *Mao's Way*. p. 430.

... In the past, what Premier Chou said did not draw attention, and only the Cultural Revolution Small Group was listened to. . . . That situation was unreasonable.[61]

The Small Group was increasingly irritated by the PLA's efforts to turn the Cultural Revolution into a study of Mao's Thought. When Lin Piao said that if political work was done properly in the PLA everything would go well, Chiang Ch'ing interrupted: "The former Propaganda Department of the Central Committee and Ministry of Culture also put politics to the fore, but that politics had a bourgeois character. We must put proletarian politics to the fore."[62] Her implication was unmistakable: merely establishing Mao's Thought as supreme was not enough; it must be correctly interpreted and practiced, and it must not degenerate into an empty tribute to Mao.

Chang Ch'un-ch'iao was now recalled to Peking from Shanghai to replenish the undermanned Small Group, and was even franker than Chiang Ch'ing in revealing the tense relationship with the PLA:

They have said that a certain individual of the Cultural Revolution Small Group, they may mean me, is directing the spearhead at the Liberation Army, and has made a mess of things through purging veteran cadres of the Liberation Army. Such [Army] cadres have been deserted by their wives and children, and they have no home to return to. If the Liberation Army is not wanted, they will go to till the land.[63]

The purge of Wang Li and Kuan Feng satisfied neither the PLA nor the Small Group. To the PLA and the conservative mass organizations, limiting the purge of the May 16 Group to Wang Li and Kuan Feng was a compromise that failed to drag out its "backstage boss." The PLA therefore insisted on a thorough exposure of the May 16 Group: "Regarding the organizers and manipulators of the so-called May 16 Group, the counterrevolutionary small clique manipulated by such a handful should be thoroughly exposed and thoroughly destroyed."[64] On the other hand, the radicals regarded the purge of Wang Li and Kuan Feng as the "submission [of the pen] to the pressure of the gun [the PLA]" in the struggle between "the pen [the Small Group] and the gun [the PLA]."[65]

As the conflict intensified between the Small Group and the PLA, Chou En-lai emerged as an arbitrator of the conflict and the holder of the balance of power. In this delicate role, he sided with the PLA for moderating the

61. *Hsin jun-ta* 9 December 1967. They also said that the Cultural Revolution thereafter would be determined by the attitude of the army.

62. "Talks by Vice-Chairman Lin, Premier Chou, Chiang Ch'ing, and Other Central Leaders," *SCMP*, no. 4148 (28 March 1968), p. 16. One of the charges made against Lin Piao was that he used Mao's Thought to advance his own power.

63. "Speeches by Leaders of Central Committee," *SCMM*, no. 611 (22 January 1968), pp. 3-7.

64. *CFCP*, 11 September 1967.

65. "Towering Crimes Committed by Counterrevolutionary Clique of Wang Li," *SCMP*, no. 4158 (16 April 1968), pp. 1-9.

official line, but defended the power of the Small Group. He repudiated the May 16 Group and its ultra-leftist tendency, but personally defended Chiang Ch'ing by stressing that it was she who first saw the danger of extreme radicalism and initiated the criticism against it. He also vigorously defended the Small Group:

In the proletarian headquarters of the Central Committee headed by Chairman Mao, we know that the Cultural Revolution Small Group under the Central Committee is a very important component part. It is equal to the Secretariat of the Party Central Committee, and it is also the General Staff of the proletarian headquarters. In this proletarian headquarters, we individually said something wrong and did something wrong in the process of transmitting the Center's intention. [But] when the mistakes were pointed out, they were immediately corrected and the Party Center resolved the problems by itself.[66]

To prevent the criticism of the May 16 Group from spreading to the Small Group itself, Chou laid down four conditions: (1) the problem of the May 16 Group should not be expanded; (2) only a few bad leaders need to be arrested; (3) the hoodwinked masses should be liberated; and (4) the rightists must be prevented from fishing in troubled waters.[67] This effort certainly helped Chou En-lai in improving his relationship with the Small Group.

What motivated Chou might have been his cold political calculation that his political interest lay not in destroying or decisively weakening the Small Group in favor of the PLA, but in maintaining the balance between the two with himself in between. Or perhaps he was simply trying to make the compromise dictated by Mao workable, whether or not he agreed with Mao's action. But whatever his reasons, he protected the Small Group, which returned his favor by restraining the Peking radicals from attacking him. For instance, when the June 16 Group of the Peking Foreign Language Institute demanded that Chou be dragged out because of his protection of the vice-premiers, Hsieh Fu-chih dissuaded them with the argument that they should forget the Premier's protection of his vice-premiers and concentrate their attacks on Liu Shao-ch'i.[68]

Although the relationship between the Small Group and the PLA was worsening, neither side could directly move against the other in public, since this would undermine the fictitious myth that the Maoist leaders were united, and thereby invite joint criticism from the remaining elite groups anxiously looking for an excuse to retaliate. Nor could the Small Group challenge the official line that was now firmly established for moderation. The stalemate at the elite level was therefore transposed to the mass level.

66. "Premier Chou's Important Speech," *SCMP,* no. 4066 (24 November 1967), p. 2.
67. "Summary of Instruction by Central Leaders," *SCMP,* no. 4088 (28 December 1967), p. 13.
68. "Premier Chou Is Staff Officer," *SCMP,* no. 4060 (15 November 1967), p. 13.

We noted earlier that, in Peking, the Earth faction enthusiastically supported the August radicalism. Immediately after the Wuhan Incident, the more radical Peking Red Guards, led by the Peking Normal University Chingkangshan, advocated the "third round of the great exchange of experience" in order to renew the revolutionary momentum in the provinces, "the seizure of the political power by armed forces" in order to attack the PLA, and the "settlement of the issue by war" in order to assault the rival mass organizations.[69]

As the official line changed to moderation in September, the Earth faction made a sort of self-criticism, largely in order to pre-empt the exploitation of its mistakes by the Heaven faction.[70] Yet, the Heaven faction, led by Nieh Yüan-tzu, K'uai Ta-fu, and Han Ai-ching, stormed Peking Normal University and denounced the Earth faction for being manipulated by Wang Li, Kuan Feng, and Lin Chieh, and for committing the mistake of directing the spearhead against the PLA. The Small Group intervened on the Chingkangshan's behalf and ordered the leadership of the Heaven faction to make self-criticisms. When the latter did so, the Earth faction considered the self-criticisms insincere and false.[71] Resentful of the Heaven faction's exploitation of the purge of Wang Li and Kuan Feng, the Earth faction openly insisted that the purge was due to the PLA's pressure on the Small Group

The Peking leaders generally restrained themselves from making critical remarks against either of the Peking factions, but Chiang Ch'ing was less equivocal. She continued to criticize Nieh Yüan-tzu and the Heaven faction for exploiting the Small Group's misfortunes for their own political gains, and at the same time she defended the Peking Normal Universtiy Chingkangshan by invoking Mao's name.[72] She specifically told the Heaven faction that "it is not worth making a fuss about Wang Li and Kuan Feng, who are but small pawns. If we press the matter further, we shall interfere with Chairman Mao's great strategic plan."[73]

Nonetheless, the Heaven faction continued to exploit the purge for its own political purposes. They concentrated their attack on the Peking Revolutionary Committee, which, as was noted, the Heaven faction opposed from the time of its establishment. *Hung ch'i* constituted another good target, since it

69. "Premier Chou En-lai Gives Important Instruction," *SCMP*, no. 4078 (12 December 1967), pp 1-6,

70. *JMJP*, 19, 23, and 24 August 1967.

71. According to William Hinton, K'uai made self-criticism with tears in his eyes. But a few minutes later, he showed up backstage and commented with a smile that "a proletarian must be a good actor." William Hinton, *Hundred Day War* (New York: Monthly Review Press, 1972), p. 137.

72. "Premier Chou is Chief Staff Officer to Chairman Mao and Vice-Premier,"*SCMP*, no. 4060 (15 November 1967), pp. 4-6.

73. *Chu-ying tung-fang-hung*, April 1968. The CRSG criticized that the Heaven faction "betrayed their trust" in the matter of Wang Li and Kuan Feng.

had initiated the slogan of "Drag out the handful of power holders in the Army," and had been closely associated with the purged men. On September 27, the Heaven faction, aided by the PLA, raided *Hung ch'i*'s offices ostensibly to "drag out the remnants of the Wang Li and Kuan Feng clique."[74] Chiang Ch'ing exploded with rage:

Don't try to pick holes in *Hung ch'i* magazine and the central Cultural Revolution Small Group. Even the problem of Lin Chieh is none of your business. Both Wang Li and Kuan Feng are also none of your business. Don't put up any big-character posters. Those already put up should be covered up with others.[75]

Despite Chiang Ch'ing's defense, the prestige of *Hung ch'i* dwindled rapidly. The reporters of the magazine, who had operated as special Small Group emissaries at the early stages, were now encountering obstacles in their news-gathering activities in the various localities. The magazine was compelled to reprint the *Chieh-fang chün-pao* editorial in its last two issues, for the first time since the beginning of the Cultural Revolution. After its sixteenth issue, published on November 23, 1967, *Hung ch'i* was finally suspended.[76]

The Heaven faction also directly exploited the purge of Wang Li and Kuan Feng by calling for their thorough exposure, a demand which inevitably led to the propaganda machines that these two men had controlled in their capacity as Small Group members, and ultimately led to the Small Group itself. The Heaven action demanded the reorganization of the *Kuang-ming jih-pao*, and *Pei-ching jih-pao*, the Red Guard Congress, the Workers' Congress, and the Peking Revolutionary Committee, on the ground that they were controlled by Wang Li and Kuan Feng through Mu Hsin and Chou Ch'ing-fang.[77]

The Heaven faction did not openly suggest the connection of the purged men to Chiang Ch'ing, Ch'en Po-ta, and Hsieh Fu-chih, but the nature of its criticism of Wang Li and Kuan Feng was such that there was an implied criticism of the remaining Small Group members. For instance, all the criticism against Wang Li and Kuan Feng stated that they had perpetuated bad acts behind the backs of Chiang Ch'ing and Ch'en Po-ta. Moreover, by attacking the less prominent figures of the May 16 Group, such as Chou Ching-fang and Ch'en Ta-lun, the Heaven faction forced them to reveal their Small Group connections.[78] One of the Heaven faction's newspapers reported that P'an Tzu-nien and Wu Ch'uan-ch'i, when captured, were found

74. "News in Brief," *URS* 49, no. 8 (27 October 1967): 110-111.
75. Ibid.
76. *CNS*, no. 208 (22 February 1968), pp. 1-5.
77. *Kuang-ming chan-pao*, 10 November 1967; *Chang-ch'eng*, 3 December 1967.
78. *Tung-fang-hung*, 13 November 1967; *Tung-ch'eng feng-pao*, 23 December 1967.

carrying "many letters with instructions from their bosses,"[79] probably Ch'en Po-ta and Ch'i Pen-yü.

In the face of the Heaven faction's mounting offensive, which was no doubt ultimately directed at weakening the Small Group, the Earth faction stepped up its resistance. As the armed struggle continued, the two warring factions fortified the parts of campus which they occupied by setting up a defense perimeter ("strategic villages"), constructing tunnels connecting their buildings, and accumulating weapons and food.[80] Consequently, many Peking school campuses were transformed into two armed camps.

Despite the stubborn resistance of the Earth faction, the Heaven faction gradually gained the upper hand, thanks to the favorable political atmosphere of the time. At People's University, where the Heaven faction maintained the majority, many members of the Earth faction, represented by the People's University Commune, defected to the Three Banners.[81] The members of the Earth faction at the Central Music Institute, the Nationality Institute, and the Central Finance Institute were subjected to suppression by the Heaven faction.

Even at the schools where the Earth faction was predominant, the Heaven faction challenged the Earth faction and the revolutionary committees it dominated. The Rebel Corps of the Geology Institute and the Second Combat Corps of Peking Normal University demanded the reorganization of the school revolutionary committees on the grounds that these committees were manipulated by Wang Li and Kuan Feng.[82] In the department of Social Science and Philosophy at the Chinese Academy, the conservative General Brigade disintegrated the radical Red Guard Regiment, which was the most active member of the Earth faction and was most closely associated with Wang Li and Kuan Feng.

While the armed struggle continued among the mass organizations, on November 28, 1967, Chiang Ch'ing delivered an important speech to a literary circle in which anti–Small Group sentiment was gaining momentum after the purge of almost the entire Small Group Literary Section. After modestly apologizing for the misunderstanding between the Small Group and the literary circles, she conceded that the "class backgrounds [of the literary workers] are comparatively complicated."[83] Nevertheless, she defended those from bad family backgrounds for the reason that "an individual cannot choose his class background, but can choose his performance."[84] As for the

79. *Hsin pei-ta,* 15 October 1967.
80. *Jen-ta san-hung,* 5 December 1967.
81. Ibid., 15 December 1967.
82. "March Evil Wind of Right Deviation Reversal of Verdicts for Restoration and Overthrow of Vice-Premier Hsieh," *CB,* no. 857 (9 July 1967), pp. 1-30.
83. *Chuan-chu chan-pao,* 16 November 1967.
84. Ibid.

controversy over whether one should be evaluated by his performance during the "fifty days" or the "seventeen years," she suggested consideration of both. Noteworthy in her speech was an ambiguity never found in her previous speeches—the equivocation indicating her conciliatory posture toward the conservatives.[85]

After delivering the speech, Chiang Ch'ing, "mentally exhausted," left Peking for Hangchow, where she stayed until January 22. In Hangchow she was under surveillance by the PLA, which installed a secret monitoring device in the residence of Chairman Mao, where she probably resided. Later she complained: "They shadowed me and they followed me every step I took. They were virtually worse than the Kuomintang reactionaries of the past."[86] She failed to identify who "they" were, but it was obvious that "they" referred to the PLA.

Meanwhile, the deradicalization of the offical line continued in the early part of 1968. *Jen-min jih-pao*'s New Year editorial devoted most of its space to criticizing the "ultra-leftist trends."[87] *Chieh-fang chün-pao* denounced the radicals' refusal to cooperate with the "majority" as a manifestation of "factionalism."[88] Under such continuing and full-scale retreat of the official line, Ch'i Pen-yü quietly disappeared from sight about mid-December, and public criticism of the Sheng Wu Lien, the ultra-leftist secret organization in Hunan, broke out in mid-January.[89] By mid-February, big-character posters criticizing Ch'i Pen-yü as a counterrevolutionary and "secret leader of the May 16 Group" appeared in Peking's central district.

The public campaign against Ch'i Pen-yü and against the ultra-leftist ideology of the Sheng Wu Lien provided the Heaven faction with a good excuse to renew its attack on the Peking Revolutionary Committee. Again it insisted on a thorough public criticism of Ch'i Pen-yü. When Hsieh Fu-chih refused the demand that the Mao's Thought Study Class of the Peking Revolutionary Committee be concentrated on the criticism of Ch'i, the Heaven faction attacked Hsieh for his effort to "keep the lid on."[90] Big-character posters denouncing Hsieh were hung on various campuses about

85. Not surprisingly, Ch'en Po-ta applauded it as her best speech. *Hui-kan*, 21 November 1967.

86. Rice, *Mao's Way*, p. 435.

87. *JMJP*, 1 January 1968.

88. *CFCP*, 28 January 1968.

89. For Sheng Wu Lien, see "Whither China," *SCMP*, no. 4190 (4 June 1968), pp. 1-18. According to Hinton, Ch'i Pen-yü's criticism of Lin Piao's sentence "Today Lao tzu dies in this place" created a great controversy between the Chingkangshan and April 14 groups in Tsinghua. On December 17, he withdrew his criticism of the sentence and admitted that Lin Piao actually wrote the sentence. Then he appeared with Mao and Lin Piao on December 31, 1967, and the appearance was reported in *JMJP*, January 2, 1968. *CNS*, no. 208 (22 February 1968), p. 1. It was his last public appearance. In January there was no public denunciation against him.

90. "Whither China," *SCMP*, no. 4190, pp. 1-18.

March 16, 1968. The two vice-chairmen of the Peking Revolutionary Committee, Nieh Yüan-tzu and Fu Chung-pi (the commander of the Peking Garrison Command), led the anti-Hsieh forces.[91] The Hsin Peita even organized a "special unit for handling the case of Hsieh Fu-chih" that secretly dispatched people to various places to collect adverse materials against him.[92] Later, the Earth faction claimed that Yang Ch'eng-wu, the acting chief of staff, was the mastermind of the conspiracy against Hsieh.[93]

The purge of Ch'i Pen-yü undermined the prestige of the Small Group to the extent that some members of the Heaven faction became bold enough to question the propriety of the March campaign against the "February Adverse Current." These members now publicly argued that Kuan Feng, Wang Li, and Ch'i Pen-yü provoked "you [the Earth faction] to criticize the 'February Adverse Current' and T'an [Chen-lin], Ch'en I, and Yü [Ch'iu-li] as an initial move against the Premier."[94] In a meeting with Chou En-lai and Chiang Ch'ing, a representative of the Ta-ch'ing Commune (Heaven faction) complained that the attack in March 1967 on Yü and other vice-premiers by its adversary, the Peking Petroleum Commune (Earth faction), was a "bombardment of Chairman Mao's Headquarters."[95] Interrupting him with "indignation and agitation," Chiang Ch'ing said:

During the "February Adverse Current" last year, did your school play a role? . . . Only a little? What do you think of the "February Adverse Current"? . . . We are quite clear about that. Which headquarters did you belong to during the "February Adverse Current"?[96]

Chou En-lai asserted that it was correct to criticize the "February Adverse Current," and that the May 16 Group had nothing to do with attacking the "February Adverse Current." Chiang Ch'ing continued:

You always have been conservative. You supported the "February Adverse Current" and opposed us. Ostensibly you supported Chairman Mao and the Vice-Chairman, but actually you bombarded us. Well, you may go on bombarding. Only white-livered devils are afraid of being bombarded. You have been conservative all the way, but you now call yourself correct from the beginning to the end.[97]

Chiang Ch'ing became so hysterical that Ch'en Po-ta cut in: "All right, all right, don't say anything more. You [Ta-ch'ing Commune] have been wrong all along."[98]

91. *Fan-yu ch'ing fu-p'i,* May 1968.
92. Ibid.
93. *Kung-lien,* April 1968.
94. Ibid.
95. "The Premier, Po-ta, on Attitude Toward February Adverse Current Being a Major Issue of Right and Wrong," *SCMP,* no. 4164 (25 April 1968), pp. 1-4.
96. Ibid.
97. Ibid.
98. Ibid.

The government leaders also joined the attack on those who opposed the "February Adverse Current" a year before. Ninety-one senior officials at the Foreign Ministry wrote a big-character poster asserting that Kuan Feng, Wang Li, and Ch'i Pen-yü had manipulated the masses in the attack on Ch'en I. The big-character poster pointed subtly to Ch'en Po-ta as a backstage boss of the anti-Ch'en I force by revealing, for instance, that "within forty-eight hours after Comrade Ch'en Po-ta said, 'See what he had done and help him,' the radicals initiated the attack on Ch'en I."[99] Chou En-lai criticized—or pretended to criticize—the poster on the ground that the attack on Ch'en I was correct, apparently so as not to offend Chiang Ch'ing.[100]

As the Small Group came under public pressure, the PLA became more assertive and intercepted the communications between the Small Group and its mass organizations. Yang Ch'eng-wu and Fu Ch'ung-pi sent PLA personnel to the school campuses in order to determine who was directly communicating what to the Small Group.[101] The rising tension finally erupted in an open confrontation. On March 8, Yang Ch'eng-wu had Fu Ch'ung-pi and armed soldiers arbitrarily enter the Small Group building without permission. When Chiang Ch'ing barred their entrance, Fu challenged her by asking," What is your rank?" This open challenge to the Small Group's authority by the PLA resulted in Yang Ch'eng-wu's purge.[102]

## The Negotiated Settlement in the Provinces

The basic strategy that the Center pursued to facilitate the establishment of the revolutionary committees in the provinces was one of "negotiated settlement." The Center summoned to Peking the representatives of the local groups (including the PLA, the cadres, and the leaders of the radical and conservative mass organizations), and told them to negotiate among themselves under the joint supervision of Chou En-lai, the Small Group, and the PLA. In order to justify the negotiation between the radicals and the conservatives, the Center discarded its previous distinction between revolutionary and conservative mass organizations,[103] and even discouraged the practice of dividing mass organizations into rightists, centralists, and leftists.[104]

99. "Learn from Central Leaders," *SCMP*, no. 4164 (25 April 1968), pp. 4-5; "A Specimen of Rightist Reversal of Verdict," *SCMP*, no. 4191 (5 June 1968), p. 8.
100. *Chung-ta hung-ch'i*, 4 April 1968.
101. *Chu-ying tung-fang-hung*, April 1968.
102. *Studies on Chinese Communism* 6, no. 7 (July 1972): 4-14.
103. Hai Feng, *An Account of the Cultural Revolution in the Canton Area* (Hong Kong: Union Research Institute, 1971), p. 280-281.
104. Chou En-lai told the Kwangtung representatives: "Theoretically, the leftist faction has been right, but not permanently. Correctly speaking not all the leftists of today will be leftist tomorrow, [since] it is not easy to be leftist in practice. Strictly speaking, one can talk about the Right wing, the Left wing, and the middle-roader. But the Right wing is too easily misconstrued

Even after the radicals and conservatives agreed to settle their differences through negotiation, there was no lack of divisive issues. One such issue was how to appraise the past actions of each group. The Center basically maintained that the radical mass organizations had been "correct" in their orientation—such as in attacking the power holders and carrying out the power seizure—but nonetheless had made many tactical mistakes; for instance, seizing power without the proper great alliance.[105] It conceded that the conservatives had displayed a tendency to protect the power holders, but nonetheless defended the claim that they were for revolution. In short, the Center asserted that both sides had committed mistakes and therefore should make self-criticism, instead of talking about the faults of their adversaries. By making a distinction between the mass organizations as such and their bad leaders, and by attributing the mistakes to the bad leaders, the Center attempted to absolve the mass organizations from responsibility for their mistakes.

With the basic issue of how to evaluate the past actions settled, both sides were urged to sign a cease fire agreement. The representatives of the various groups in Kwangtung reached such an agreement on November 2, 1967, and those from Kwangsi did so on March 3, 1968.[106] Then the Center employed two new organizational formats to facilitate the formation of the revolutionary committees: the preparatory revolutionary committee and the Mao's Thought Study Class. The first one—organized in areas in which deep factional cleavage made it difficult to establish a permanent revolutionary committee immediately—served as a forum wherein the representatives of the PLA, the cadres, and the masses worked together for the establishment of the revolutionary committee under leadership appointed by the Center. The preparatory revolutionary committee in turn set up Mao's Thought Study Classes in which the PLA, the cadres, and the representatives of the mass organizations jointly studied Mao's writings and made self-criticisms, in the hope that a consensus would be reached.[107]

Since the cadres' attendance at the study class was the first step toward their eventual reinstatement,[108] each faction tried to enroll as many of their

---

as a rightist faction, because of its conservatism. Then the conservatism is too easily regarded as die-hard conservatism. I would not insist on using the term die-hard conservatives It is not good to regard a mass organization as a rightist faction, since it differs very much from the rightists of bourgeois class." Hai Feng, *An Account of the Cultural Revolution in the Canton Areas,* pp. 280-281.

105. *Chi-yang wen-tzu,* 12 November 1967.

106. For Kwangtung, see *Tzu-liao chuan-chi,* 17 October 1967, and for Kwangsi, see *Wu ch'an-che chih-sheng,* 30 December 1967.

107. *JMJP,* 12 October 1967; *Tou-p'i t'ung-hsin,* 12 November 1967.

108. The *JMJP* made this point clear. "The class to study Mao Tse-tung's Thought is being organized to give a great number of cadres the time and opportunity to receive an education, and on this basis, to make a serious summing up of their experience, draw lessons, strengthen their

own cadres as possible. The preparatory revolutionary committees usually delegated the delicate task of selecting cadres for the study classes to a specially organized "small group" in charge of the cadre question. In Kwangtung, the small group first tried the method of accepting only cadres agreed upon by both factions. However, this method made just seventy cadres eligible for the study class. Therefore, the rule was changed to admit cadres approved by either side, and, as a result, two hundred and thirteen cadres were enrolled in the first Mao's Thought Study Class in Kwangtung.[109]

Who would be represented in the revolutionary committees was the most crucial question to all parties, including the Cultural Revolution Small Group and the PLA, since those who controlled the revolutionary committees would dominate the Chinese political system after the Cultural Revolution. To be sure, both radicals and conservatives endeavored to obtain better representation in the forthcoming revolutionary committees. Particularly divisive was the question of cadre representation. Every participant agreed in principle that those cadres with clean political records before the Cultural Revolution—in addition to proven revolutionary qualities *during* the Cultural Revolution—had to be included in the revolutionary committees.

Such cadres, however, were hard to find. The radicals tended to support cadres who had stood on the rebel side, but many of these persons had other political liabilities—for example, having been disciplined by the Party organization, having been closely associated with the now repudiated Wang Li and Kuan Feng, or having made the mistake of following the ultra-leftist line of attacking the PLA. The cadres supported by the conservative forces had impeccable political records up until the Cultural Revolution, but had made the mistake of carrying out the "bourgeois reactionary line."

A good example of cadres whose political records were dubious, but who nonetheless stood firmly on the rebel side, were the two Szechwan cadres, Liu Chieh-t'ing and his wife, Chang Hsi-t'ung.[110] Liu and Chang had been former Party secretaries of the I-ping special district, but had been dismissed from

---

good points, and correct their shortcomings and mistakes so that they understand and grasp Chairman Mao's line and catch up with the proletarian revolutionary ranks." *JMJP*, 12 October 1967.

109. *Tou-p'i t'ung-hsin*, 12 November 1967. One third of the 213 were supported by both sides and the rest were supported by one side.

110. Another interesting figure was Li Ta-chang, the provincial Party secretary. Although he had a close relationship with Li Ching-ch'üan, the CRSG supported him because he happened to be the one who recommended Chiang Ch'ing to the Party. To the conservatives, the CRSG's support menat the violation of universal rule and they attacked Li as Li Ching-ch'üan's clique. Lo Kuang-en was a literary man who claimed to be the victim of Li Ching-ch'üan and enjoyed the support of the radical groups. Nonetheless, Chou En-lai declared him a bad guy. Liu Ko-p'ing in Shantung and Wang Hsiao-yü in Shansi probably fell into the type of cadres who stood on the revolutionary side but later were found to have dubious political records.

the posts and imprisoned by Li Ching-ch'üan, according to the radicals, for having opposed Li's revisionist line. Not unexpectedly, they joined the rebel group in the Cultural Revolution and were made members of the Szechwan Provincial Preparatory Revolutionary Committee by the Cultural Revolution Small Group. But the conservatives continued to attack them, almost paralyzing the Committee. In a meeting with Szechwan delegates on March 15, Chiang Ch'ing accused Chang Kuo-hua, the new Szechwan Military District commander, and Liang Hsing-ch'u, commander of the Ch'eng-tu Military Region, of not curbing the conservatives and preventing them from attacking Liu Chieh-t'ing and his wife.[111]

Chang Kuo-hua and Liang Hsing-ch'u defended themselves by pointing out that the situation in Szechwan was so complicated that it was not easy to support the rebels and Liu Chieh-t'ing. Furthermore, the PLA leaders maneuvered to repudiate two points of the Ten Articles (of April 6, 1967) which were critical of the PLA. Chiang Ch'ing exploded in anger: "To say that the Ten Articles are out of date means that Li Ching-ch'üan should be reinstated. . . . If you retreat half a step on the Ten Articles, you cannot stand on your feet [on the proletarian side]."[112]

When Chou En-lai agreed with Chiang Ch'ing that Liu Chieh-t'ing was a good cadre, Chang Kuo-hua questioned Chou's sincerity in supporting Liu and the rebel faction in Szechwan. Chou replied: "What is the meaning of asking that? What is the premise? It is the Ten Red Articles. Some people doubt my expression of attitude. What is doubted?"[113] Chiang Ch'ing ended the meeting with a sharp remark to the Szechwan PLA leaders:

I am very tired today and need a rest. Today we bombarded you, but tomorrow you may bombard us. I am not a double dealer. Judging by my whole speech, I am not against the army and I am one supporting Chairman Mao and Vice-Chairman Lin.[114]

Thanks to the direct pressure of the Small Group, the radicals generally did well at the provincial level. Among the thirty-nine positions on the Standing Committee of the Kwangtung Revolutionary Committee (established on February 12), the PLA occupied nine (23%); the cadres, ten

111. The following discussion is based on "Important Speeches Delivered on March 15 by the Leaders of the Center," *SCMPS*, no. 225 (14 May 1968), pp. 1-13. Also a slightly different version is available in "San-yüeh shih-wu jih chung-yang shou-chang chung-yao chiang-hua," 13 April 1968.

112. For the Ten Articles, see *Chung-kung wen-hua ta ko-ming chung-yao wen-chien hui-pien* (Taipei: Chung-kung Yen-chiu, 1973), pp. 157-158. The two articles (nos. 2 and 10) were critical of the PLA.

113. "Important Speeches Delivered on March 15 by the Leaders of the Center," *SCMPS*, no. 225 (14 May 1968), pp. 1-13; "San-yüeh shih-wu jih chung-yang shou-chang chung-yao chiang-hua," 13 April 1968.

114. Ibid.

(26%); and the leaders of the mass organizations, eighteen (46%). An appropriate balance was maintained in the mass organizations between the conservatives and the radicals. Of the eighteen mass organization representatives, eight were members of the Red Flag faction, seven were conservatives, and the other three are thought to have belonged to East Wind.[115] Thus, it was the PLA that constituted the decisive bloc in the Revolutionary Committee.

As a solid bloc in the Revolutionary Committee, the PLA could establish alliances with any other bloc. Not surprisingly, the PLA continued to ally itself with the conservatives rather than the radicals, in part because its interests coincided with those of the conservatives, and in part because the radicals were unwilling to follow the moderate official line in general and the official pressure for a great alliance with the conservatives in particular. At the same time, the moderate official line relieved the PLA from the obligation of supporting the radicals by changing its task from "supporting the left" to "supporting the left, but not any particular faction." This change enabled the PLA to declare that it would support whatever faction was willing to form a great alliance, regardless of its ideological stands. Understandably, it was the conservatives rather than the radicals who were willing to form the great alliance.[116]

As far as the great alliance was concerned, the mass organizations were allowed to negotiate specific procedures under the following guidelines imposed by the Center. First, the mass organizations were encouraged to work for the great alliance and the three-in-one combination at the same time, even though it was more logical to form first the great alliance and then the revolutionary committee.[117] Second, the mass organizations were not disbanded in order to bring about the great alliance, although the great alliance would have been more easily achieved had all the mass organizations been disbanded.

The rationale of this policy was to ensure the independent role of the radical mass organizations, especially the radical mass organizations whose strength, as we shall see, was rather weak at the basic level. The only measure taken by the Center that restrained the role of the existing mass

115. This figure is drawn from the various Red Guard newspapes.
116. A former member of the Red Flag faction observed the strained relationship between the PLA and the Red Flag. "Our failure to be active in pursuing an alliance naturally led to considerable friction between us and the Military Training Platoon. The East Wind, on the other hand, once again cemented its relations with the platoon by expressing enthusiasm for the policy of alliance. Thus, from October to December, the interest of the East Wind and the Military Training Platoon corresponded, and the Red Flag was again suppressed." Gordon Bennet and Ronald Montaperto, *Red Guard: The Political Biography of Dai Hsiao-ai* (New York: Doubleday, 1971), p. 208.
117. *Chih-kung hung-se,* January 1968.

organizations as independent political forces was to separate the students from the workers and to encourage a great alliance in each unit. But even in the policy of forming a great alliance in each unit, a great alliance of the higher level was achieved before that of the lower level.

Under these general guidelines, each faction insisted on methods advantageous to its own political position. In Kwangtung, the conservatives advocated an "unconditional alliance" of the mass organizations, which presupposed the dissolution of the mass organizations; whereas the radicals wanted a "principled alliance"—an alliance with "revolutionary leftists" as the core—and preservation of the independence of each mass organization.[118] The radicals recommended negotiations between the two factions at the provincial level. The conservatives, however, advocated a free election held first at the school level and then at the municipal level, with voting rights restricted to the "Red Guards"—presumably those from the five red categories.[119] Obviously this method would have excluded many radicals with bad family backgrounds from taking part in the voting, while allowing the conservatives to make maximum use of their influence at the basic levels. The radicals denounced the election approach as a "sinister attempt to exclude the rebels from the Revolutionary Committee."[120] Although Chou En-lai agreed with that view, the PLA's preoccupation with the great alliance led it to employ the election method if both factions could not agree on another way to achieve unity, thereby straining its relationship with the radicals.

Apart from the issue of the great alliance, the radicals naturally opposed demobilization. Their distrust of the elite groups compelled them to seize power in their own hands. Many of the discontented groups saw that their opportunity to have their specific grievances redressed would fade away with the demobilization process. Worse still, the Center pressured the radicals to dissociate themselves from specific discontented groups such as the rusticated youth, the contract and temporary workers, and persons with bourgeois backgrounds. Thus, some radicals openly insisted on a continuing and thorough revolution.[121]

118. The Red Flag opposed the "unconditional great alliance." "The rightists, in distortion of the revolutionary great alliance, promote the great alliance for the sake of great alliance, take away the revolutionary spirit [from it], fail to distinguish the rightists, centralists, and leftists, and refuse to recognize that the revolutionary great alliance needs a nucleus." *Kang pa-i,* January 1968.

119. *Hsiao-ping,* 6 November 1967; 17 February 1968.

120. *Tien-shan lei-ming,* July 1968; *Li-hsin-kung* (n.d.).

121. For instance, the militant wing of the Red Flag—known as the August 5 faction—indirectly challenged the moderate wing of the Red Flag by attacking "reformism," "Capitulationism," and Huang Yung-sheng's speech and by publishing a series of articles with provocative titles, such as "More Disorder Is Needed in Canton," and "Calm Before the Decisive

Regarding the radicals' resistance to the moderate official line as a manifestation of the "ultra-leftist" tendency, the conservatives mounted an attack on them. In the spring of 1968, the criticism of the ultra-leftist trends was officially sanctioned, but the conservatives turned the criticism into their primary task by exaggerating the danger of the ultra-leftist trends. The Kwangtung conservatives even defined their conflict with the ultra-leftists as a "class struggle":

The essence of the ultra-leftist trends of thought is whether there will be proletarian dictatorship or a regression to capitalism. Our struggle with the ultra-leftist trends of thought is actually a struggle between two classes, two lines, and two roads.[122]

As a result of these complex interactions, the radicals' influence was diluted in the revolutionary committees on the sub-provincial level, which were organized under the leadership of the provincial revolutionary committees without Peking's interference. The Canton Municipal Revolutionary Committee, for instance, was composed of twelve military leaders, eleven cadres, and ten leaders of mass organizations. Eight of the eleven cadres were identified as pro–East Wind, with only two definitely known to be pro–Red Flag.[123]

The conservatives were even more dominant in the basic units in which the revolutionary committees were organized under the sole supervision of the municipal revolutionary committee.[124] In addition to the conservatives' domination of the standing committees at the lower level, the staffs of the revolutionary committees at the various levels were selected from cadres sympathetic to the conservatives. In the Canton Municipal Revolutionary Committee, "80 percent of the working personnel was pro–East Wind," and, at the lower level, "almost all working personnel of the revolutionary committee were the same groups of the old political department."[125] Worse still for the radicals, East Wind completely dominated the Workers' Disciplinary Inspection Teams—armed detachments organized to ensure the "proletarian dictatorship by the masses" in each factory.[126]

---

Battle." Declaring that the "present contradiction is the contradiction between the laboring people, the educated youth, contract workers and temporary workers [on the one hand] and those who climbed up to the precious position of the workers [on the other]," the radical wings of the Red Flag urged the rusticated youth to "unite with those oppressed and rise to revolt." *Chung-ta hung-ch'i*, 15 March 1967.

122. *Hsiao-ping*, 24 December 1967.

123. This figure is based on the list of Standing Committee members given in Hai Feng's *An Account of the Cultural Revolution in the Canton Areas*, p. 350. During the Spring of 1967 many Red Flag organizations complained that the Canton Municipal Revolutionary Committee rejected the pro–Red Flag cadres nominated to the Revolutionary Committees at the school level. *Hung-se tsao-fan*, January 1968.

124. *Tien-shan lei-ming*, July 1968.

125. *Pa-i chan-tou tui* (n.d.).

126. Originally the teams were to be organized by members nominated by each faction and

Naturally, the radicals were deeply disappointed by the dominant position of the conservatives, while the mass representatives were now relegated to the role of "appendages."[127] What enraged the radicals most, however, was the wholesale reinstatement of the cadres they had attacked from the beginning of the Cultural Revolution. According to the Kwangtung radicals, "the original group of people who carried out the bourgeois reactionary line and defended the Party branches, the work teams, and the puppet preparatory committees have assumed power once again and frantically counterattacked the revolutionary rebels. In one word, a total reversal of the correct decision, a reversal in favor of the bourgeois reactionary line, has been realized."[128] Not only were the old cadres reinstated, but old work methods were revived. For instance, the intelligence unit was re-established to keep watch over the radicals.[129]

The establishment of the revolutionary committees, however, did not end the radical-conservative confrontation. Rather, it brought the confrontation inside the revolutionary committees. Theoretically speaking, the revolutionary committees represented the government authority; but in reality the committee members continued to act as representatives of their factions, thus creating "dual authority structures" composed of radicals supported by the Small Group and conservatives supported by the PLA.[130]

The Heilungchiang Revolutionary Committee, whose experience was widely propagated in February 1967 as a successful way of establishing a revolutionary committee, was almost paralyzed by the factional struggle. The Bombardment faction, consisting mainly of students and strongly supported by the Peking Earth faction, challenged the Committee; whereas the Defense Joint Command, which was mainly composed of workers in the state-owned factories, defended the Committee and its leaders, P'an Fu-sheng and Wang Chia-tao.[131]

In addition, the two factions diverged on how to treat the PLA, the former conservatives, and the erring cadres.[132] Like the radicals in other provinces, the Bombardment faction had suffered a setback in February 1967, and then was subjected to physical assaults in the aftermath of Wang Li's and Kuan

---

approved by the PLA. But since the PLA made their decision in consultation with the security bureau or militia department of each faction, the Inspection Team became a partisan organization of the East Wind. The teams openly suppressed the Red Flag under the pretext of arresting "liu-mang" and speculators.

127. *Kuang-chou kung-jen*, 20 May 1968.
128. *T'ien-shan lei-ming*, July 1968.
129. *Kuang-chou kung-jen*, 22 January 1968; 16 February 1968.
130. *San-erh chih t'ung-hsin*, July 1968. In early 1968, the Center issued a directive that the PLA should respect the Revolutionary Committee. *Li-hsin-kung*, 3 June 1968; *Wen-ko t'ung-hsin*, February 1968.
131. *Harbin feng-lei*, 5 December 1967; *Hung-chün-kung*, 30 June 1967.
132. *Tung-feng chan-pao*, 9 October 1967.

Feng's purge. The Center intervened on behalf of the radicals, and P'an Fu-sheng made a self-criticism of his harsh measures toward the Bombardment faction.[133] Nonetheless, the factional struggle continued, developing into an armed struggle in May 1968.

The Shansi Revolutionary Committee (established in March 1967) did no better than the revolutionary committees of the other provinces. No sooner was the Revolutionary Committee formed than it was split into Liu Ko-p'ing's force and an anti-Liu force led by Chang Jih-ch'ing, the PLA commander who had collaborated with Liu in March. The pro-Chang force set up the Revolutionary Dictatorship Committee above the provincial Revolutionary Committee.[134] The Center summoned the leaders of both factions to Peking, and after one month of negotiation and bargaining, it was acknowledged that Liu Ko-p'ing had been "correct" and Chang Jih-ch'ing had made a "mistake in direction."[135]

Peking's decision, however, did not end the conflict between the two groups. Chang continued to challenge Liu's leadership by collecting materials incriminating Liu. In April 1968, the Peking leaders, including Lin Piao, again urged the Shansi PLA to support Liu K'o-ping.[136] However, the Shansi PLA did not transmit the Peking leaders' instructions to its mass organizations, so armed struggle continued, finally culminating in an attempt on Liu's life.[137]

The Cultural Revolution in Hopei revealed much more complexity than in other provinces, for, because of its strategic importance to Peking, many Peking leaders were involved. The most controversial issue there revolved around Liu Tzu-hou, a provincial Second Secretary. Liu had stood on the Maoist line during the Great Leap Forward, earnestly carrying out the policy of setting high targets for production, as well as for the purchase of agricultural products. But when the Great Leap Forward was cut back in 1961, he was attacked for his leftist line by the provincial First Secretary, Lin Tieh. Probably thanks to his good record in the Great Leap Forward, Liu became the First Secretary in September 1966. Nonetheless, he carried out the "bourgeois reactionary line" of suppressing the rebels at the initial stage of the Cultural Revolution.[138] Over the question of whether he was a good or bad cadre, the Hopei mass organizations were divided.

133. *Chung-kung wen-hua to ko-ming chung-yao wen-chien*, p. 183.
134. *Chingkangshan*, 1 August 1967.
135. *Hung-tieh-chün*, 1 January 1968.
136. *I-yueh feng-pao*, July 1968.
137. *Hou-k'o t'ung-hsin*, July 1968; *Hung-se t'ung-hsin*, 20 July 1967.
138. For the defense of Liu Tzu-hou, see *Pai-wan kung-nung*, 15 December 1967. *Hopei hung-wei-ping*, 15 December 1967; for the attack on him, see *Hung-chan-pao*, 10 November 1967.

The anti-Liu force was strong in the Hopei Red Guard Congress and was supported by the Workers' General Headquarters. The pro-Liu faction, known as Red Tower, was led by the Workers' Congress Preparatory Committee and supported by the Hopei Military District Command.[139] In February 1967, the PLA and the conservatives suppressed the anti-Liu force. However, when the Thirty-eighth Army moved into Hopei, about March 1967, the unit showed sympathy toward the Hopei Red Guard Congress, thus providing each faction with a good excuse for charging the other with being anti-PLA.

To complicate matters further, Yang Ch'eng-wu and the Peking Military Region headed by Cheng Wei-shan sided with the Hopei Military District Command, and reprimanded the Thirty-Eighth Army for supporting the wrong side. When the May 16 Corps was exposed, the Red Tower faction launched a political offensive by linking the anti-Liu force and the Thirty-eighth Army to the May 16 Corps and Lin Chieh. At the same time, Red Tower boasted that it was supported by the formal organizational channels running from Lin Piao to Yang Ch'eng-wu, Cheng Wei-shan, and the Hopei Military District Command.[140]

As the confrontation between the two factions intensified, the Peking leaders ordered them to negotiate in Peking and interviewed them eight times. However, the complexity of the situation in Hopei prevented even the Small Group from clearly supporting one faction. Hsieh Fu-chih showed sympathy toward the radical Hopei Red Guard Congress; nonetheless, he recognized that the rebel force had many members with "impure" class backgrounds and had made the mistake of attacking the PLA and employing violent methods without official sanction.[141] When the Revolutionary Committee was finally established in February 1968, the Red Tower faction dominated it. However, Yang Ch'eng-wu's purge in March 1968 once again pushed Hopei into chaos. The Peking Military Region apologized for its critical statements on the Thirty-eighth Army,[142] and the anti-Liu force mounted an attack on the Red Tower faction, thus creating widespread armed struggle in the summer of 1968.

In Shantung, rebellious cadre Wang Hsiao-yü had collaborated with the PLA leader, Yang Teh-chih, for the successful establishment of the Revolutionary Committee. But the coalition split as the PLA disbanded the mass organizations at the basic level and carried out a Paris Commune style of free election,[143] which no doubt undermined the radicals' power base. The rebels,

139. *Pao-ting hung-wei-ping,* 11 December 1967.
140. Ibid.
141. *Feng-lei-chi,* 26 November 1967.
142. *Tung-fang-hung t'ung-hsin,* July 1968.
143. *Chung-kung wen-hua ta ko-ming chung-yao wen-chien,* p. 181.

supported by Wang Hsiao-yü, challenged the PLA, and the conflict continued into 1969.[144]

In Kwangtung, the PLA and the conservative mass organizations, now entrenched in the Revolutionary Committee, could exercise their power in the Committee's name. However, the Revolutionary Committee discriminated against the Red Flag group by, for example, not supplying the paper necessary for their newspaper, and by dismissing Red Flag members from their jobs and withholding their wages.[145] Yet, the conservatives publicly declared that the proletarian headquarters, the PLA, and the Revolutionary Committee were "three reds," and that anybody challenging these three reds was counterrevolutionary.[146]

When Red Flag challenged the Revolutionary Committee, the East Wind faction denounced Red Flag as a group of "bandits." According to Red Flag:

They [the conservatives] maliciously utilized the opportunity of purging the class ranks, and under the black umbrella of "encircling and suppressing factionalism," they advanced the slogans of "Strike down the landlords, rich peasants, counter-revolutionaries, bad elements, rightists, and the Red Flag bandits," "Catch monsters and freaks," and "Kill all the Red Flag bandits," and they directed the spearhead straight at the revolutionary rebels.[147]

Worse still, the PLA stepped up pressure on Red Flag by suppressing their activities as manifestations of "factionalism" and disbanding their organizations. Later, Red Flag complained that the PLA branded "the struggle between two lines among the masses as factional struggle," thereby "distorting Chairman Mao's strategic plan for struggling against self-interests and criticizing revisionism."[148]

Chiang Ch'ing was increasingly frustrated by the PLA's strategy of verbally supporting the Cultural Revolution while actually suppressing the rebels ruthlessly. She exploded in anger at a conference where Lin Piao was present.[149] She quipped that what was in command was not "proletarian

144. Ibid., p. 220.
145. *Kuang-chou kung-jen,* 22 January 1968; 16 February 1968.
146. *Tien-shan lei-ming,* July 1968.
147. Ibid.
148. The exposure of the Sheng Wu Lien and Ch'i Pen-yü furnished further justification for the attack on the radicals. The Red Flag protested that the East Wind maliciously regarded some Kwangtung rebel organizations as being linked with Wang, Kuan, Ch'i, and the May 16 Group. The Military Training Teams, according to the Red Flag, ordered the disbandment of the Red Flag organizations by "distorting Chairman Mao's strategic plan for struggling against self-interests and criticizing revisionism as the program for the prompt removal of mountain strongholds." Obviously, as was the case with the criticism of the ultra-leftist trends, the PLA and the East Wind could justify their attack on the Red Flag by emphasizing one's attitude toward the revolutionary committee. For their part, the Red Flag regarded the PLA's approach as a "theory taking account of factionalism alone."
149. *San-erh-ch'i t'ung-hsin,* July 1968.

politics but bourgeois politics,"[150] and she was particularly critical of Cheng Wei-shan, the Peking Military Region commander, who had asked for the right to shoot at the masses:

You made a surprise attack on me. You, Cheng Wei-shan, must make a self-criticism. . . . My understanding of the situation is not comprehensive, but, from your asking for the right to fire, we can see your attitude toward the Cultural Revolution Small Group. . . . The Army is the most powerful faction. If you aim at somebody, you can have them.[151]

The Center, however, could not afford to make any major changes in the revolutionary committees, even though it was sympathetic to the rebels' plight. Had the Center changed or dissolved the revolutionary committees, all the precarious effort to build up a new authority structure would have fallen apart. Thus, the official position was that only minor adjustments could be made in the revolutionary committees already established.[152] The Small Group, however, continued its efforts to strengthen the radicals' political position within this broad official line by publicly declaring that only the rebel forces were entitled to leadership positions in the revolutionary committees.[153]

The radicals did not have to wait long to challenge the revolutionary committees and the PLA. The purge of Yang Ch'eng-wu and the campaign against the "four rightist trends" created a new radical upsurge.

150. Ibid.
151. Ibid.
152. "Absorb New Fresh Blood of the Proletarian Class," *Hung ch'i,* no. 4 (14 October 1968), p 11
153. *Hung-ch'i t'ung-hsin,* July 1968. Also see *Kang pa-i,* late June 1968. Chiang Ch'un-ch'iao publicly complained that the PLA did not talk about the right and wrong of both factions in the great alliance.

# CHAPTER 9

# Demobilization

The beginning of the demobilization can be traced as far back as early February 1967, when the effort began to rebuild a new authority structure in the form of the revolutionary committees. After the Wuhan Incident, the Center stepped up the effort. Yet, the formation of the revolutionary committees progressed with disappointingly slow speed. It took almost one full year from September 1967 to set up the committees in all twenty-eight provinces, and the factional struggle continued within the committees. This was mainly because there was no effective political machinery to carry out the Center's will impartially to the various political groups deeply entangled in the factional struggle.

The profound authority crisis, which began with the crippling of the Party's organizational legitimacy, was aggravated when the People's Liberation Army and the Cultural Revolution Small Group became too closely identified with either the conservative or the radical masses to provide effective and impartial leadership. The constant changes in the official line had diluted the effectiveness of the central directives, while leading the Chinese masses to believe that if they exerted enough pressure they would be able to swing the official line to their advantage. Furthermore, the uneven development of the movement in the various provinces made it difficult for the Center to issue any guidelines that were uniformly applicable to all localities. Mao's Thought, although not openly challenged, was selectively interpreted to serve particular interests. And, most important, as the Cultural Revolution came to an end the power struggle among the Chinese elite groups intensified. This helped embolden the masses to disregard any official policy unfavorable to their political interests.

It was therefore obvious that what was needed most for the formation of the revolutionary committees was effective political leadership from the top.

The easiest way to solve this leadership problem would have been to strengthen the legitimacy of any one of the existing elite groups. Yet, Mao could not one-sidedly rely on either the Small Group or the PLA by decisively weakening the other. He could not afford to alienate the PLA, not only because it possessed coercive power but also because it was the only nation-wide organization with the capacity to preserve law and order. Nor did he want to discredit the Small Group, which would have been tantamount to discrediting the Cultural Revolution as a whole.

There was an additional constraint that limited Mao's options. He could not impose his will organizationally from the top to the bottom, since that would mean restoring the methods formerly used by the Party and criticized by him. Moreover, any new political authority had to be acceptable to the elites as well as the masses, and to the radicals as well as the conservatives. It also had to differ in nature from what Mao had destroyed.

Confronted with these dilemmas, Mao improvised a new format, the Workers' Mao's Thought Propaganda Teams, as the interim political authorities which would first bring an end to the factional struggle and then supervise the "campaign to rectify the class ranks" and the rebuilding of the Party. Yet, the power struggle between the radical forces represented by the Small Group and the conservative forces represented by the PLA continued in this last stage of the Cultural Revolution.

## The Last Phase of Radicalism and the
## Workers' Mao's Thought Propaganda Teams

There are good reasons to believe that Mao may well have felt by March 1968 that the official line had gone too far in the moderate direction. Not only had the authority of the Small Group steadily declined, but also the demand to reverse the verdict against the "February Adverse Current" had risen. If allowed to continue, these trends would have undermined whatever the Cultural Revolution had achieved and compelled Mao to purge his own wife.

Apparently, the Peking leaders discussed these problems in a series of high-level meetings in March 1968. After four such meetings at Chairman Mao's residence, the Central Committee finally decided to purge Yang Ch'eng-wu.[1] To minimize the potential adverse reaction by the PLA, Mao and Lin Piao themselves announced the decision at a reception attended by more than ten thousand PLA cadres. The next day, Chou En-lai, Ch'en Po-ta, K'ang Sheng, and Chiang Ch'ing held a "rally of ten thousand people and army cadres." Chou En-lai read the decision, which was signed jointly by the

1. "Important Speech by Vice-Chairman Lin at Reception of Army Cadres on May 25," *SCMP*, no. 4173 (8 May 1968), pp. 1-5.

Central Committee, the State Council, the Military Affairs Commission, and the Cultural Revolution Small Group. The decision was brief: Yang Ch'eng-wu, the acting chief of staff; Yü Li-chin, the political commissar of the Air Force; and Fu Ch'ung-pi, the commander of the Peking Garrison, were all dismissed because they had committed "serious mistakes."[2]

Chiang Ch'ing, who spoke first at the rally, began her speech by disclaiming her connection with Kuan Feng and Wang Li:

They [Wang Li and Kuan Feng] did not ask for instructions, did not report to us, and isolated us, harmed us, and did a lot of bad things. Because we considered them black claws, we dragged them out and hanged them up and did not allow them to intervene with Chairman Mao's strategic plan. However, somebody attempted to utilize this situation in order to deny the victory of the Great Proletarian Cultural Revolution and deny the achievements of the revolutionary masses and revolutionary small soldiers.[3]

Although she did not specify, "somebody" was obviously Yang Ch'eng-wu, who, according to her charges, attempted to seize Hsieh Fu-chih's power over the Peking Revolutionary Committee, and broadcasting stations, *Chieh-fang chün-pao,* and *jen-min jih-pao.* She also accused Yang of having opposed the Cultural Revolution and the mass mobilization, and of having endeavored to establish the personality cult of Mao for his own political gain.

The next speaker, Chou En-lai, focused his criticism on Yang's attempt to exploit Mao's Thought for his own personal political ambitions. Then Chou explained why it was not necessary to artificially establish Mao's personality cult. All these charges might well have been leveled against the PLA as a whole.[4]

In sharp contrast, Lin Piao focused his rather mild criticism on Yang's personal relationship with other PLA leaders, depicting Yang as a factional leader within the PLA.[5] He charged that Yang was Lo Jui-ch'ing's man and had collaborated with Ho Lung, as well as with Wang Li and Kuan Feng. Then he warned that the struggle against Yang should not be extended indiscriminately to his subordinates, supporters, and friends, and that not all persons whom Yang had attacked would be rehabilitated. Lin's speech as a whole creates the impression that he was reluctant to purge Yang and anxious to check the repercussions of the purge on the PLA's organizational integrity.

The Center's official explanation of Yang's purge was that he had opposed the Center in collaboration with Ch'i Pen-yü. This was obviously a device to conceal from the public eye the deepening conflict between the Small Group and the PLA. The truth is that each man was purged for a different ideological reason: Yang, for his conservative orientation, which represented the

2. *Chu-ying tung-fang-hung,* April 1968.
3. Ibid.
4. Ibid.
5. "Important Speech by Vice-Chairman Lin," *SCMP,* 8 May 1968, pp. 1-5.

PLA's stand; and Ch'i, for his extreme radical orientation, which reflected the Small Group's stand. As one of the most active Small Group members, Ch'i was undoubtedly a "backstage boss" of the May 16 Group, and Chiang Ch'ing, regardless of whether or not she was personally involved in the May 16 Group, tried to protect him. After dislodging Ch'i, the PLA, led by Yang Ch'eng-wu, tried to exploit its victory in order to undermine the Small Group. This open challenge to the Small Group compelled Mao to purge Yang.

Yang's purge was therefore a victory for the Small Group, and after the purge the prestige of the Small Group rose again. Chou En-lai and K'ang Sheng lavishly praised Chiang Ch'ing at various public meetings. An instruction given to Hunan delegates on March 30, 1968, specified that one's attitude toward the Small Group was an important criterion for determining whether or not one was a revolutionary.[6] And the Red Guards began to refer to Chiang Ch'ing as the "great leader and standard-bearer of the Cultural Revolution."

Coinciding with Yang's purge, the official line entered the last stage of the Cultural Revolution. This stage was known as the "campaign against the four rightist trends"—that is, rightist reversals of verdicts, rightist split-ism, rightist capitulationism, and rightist opportunism. Chiang Ch'ing again led the offensive. In her March 15 meeting with responsible persons from Szechwan, she declared that, "at present in the entire country, the rightist reversal of verdicts is the principal danger," and she demanded that the PLA support the rebel faction.[7] She reiterated the same theme in a meeting three days later with some delegates from Chekiang: "Rightist split-ism," she said, "has raised its head somewhat from last winter until the present time."[8]

As the new campaign against the "rightist trends" gathered momentum, the official line took a radical direction with regard to two crucial issues. First, the official attitude toward "factionalism" changed. In repudiating their previous practice of condemning "factionalism" as such, *Jen-min jih-pao* and *Chieh-fang chün-pao* defended "proletarian factionalism" in a joint editorial on April 20.[9] According to this new interpretation, if the factionalism were for the proletarian headquarters, it could be good and should not be condemned. This new interpretation was a great relief to the radicals, who were increasingly pressured by the PLA to form a great alliance with the conservatives. Chiang Ch'ing enthusiastically elaborated the implications of this new idea.[10]

6. "Main Points of Instruction Given by Central Leaders on March 30," *SCMP*, no. 4166 (29 April 1968), pp. 9-11.
7. *CNS*, no. 217 (25 April 1968), p. 3.
8. Ibid.
9. *JMJP*, 20 April 1968.
10. *CNS*, no. 215 (11 April 1968), pp. 4-7. Chang Ch'un-ch'iao also said: "It is a mistake to discuss only alliance and not the question of right and wrong. A mistake is a mistake, and a

Paralleling the reinterpretation of "factionalism," the Small Group re-emphasized performance as the major determinant of "class." The first issue of *Hung ch'i,* after it resumed publication in April, declared that anyone who stood on the side of Chairman Mao's line was a "proletarian revolutionary," while anyone who failed to do so was a "bourgeois reactionary," regardless of his actual social origin.[11] Among other provinces, Kweichow further elaborated the new interpretation:

If the people coming from laboring families are not armed with Mao's Thought, they cannot reflect the basic interests of laboring people, and will likely violate Chairman Mao's proletarian revolutionary line.[12]

This new interpretation also represented a reversal of the official line of the preceding stage, to the advantage of the radicals. During December 1967, the Center announced its forthcoming campaign to "rectify class ranks," and even Chiang Ch'ing issued a warning to the radicals that those from an undesirable class should be removed from leadership positions in the mass organizations.[13] The apparent shift to class origin in the official line's emphasis helped the conservatives and the PLA to justify their attack on the radicals with the "theory of natural redness." Some conservative Red Guards publicly argued that "rebellion [against the power holders] depended on proletarian revolutionaries, many of whom were impure class elements," but the class rectification campaign depended on those like themselves who came from good class backgrounds.[14]

This time, it was the radicals who exploited the new official line to their political advantage. In Peking, the Earth faction, which had been on the defense since the exposure of the May 16 Group, launched a strong counter-attack on the Heaven faction. When the PLA appeared to be in trouble, the Tsinghua Chingkangshan and the Red Flag group of the Peking Aviation Institute readily changed their attitude toward the Peking Revolutionary Committee and pledged their support. Again, the major target of the Earth faction was the Hsin Peita Commune and its leader, Nieh Yüan-tzu. The Peking University Chingkangshan raided the dormitory of the cadres supporting the Hsin Peita Commune. Accusing Nieh Yüan-tzu of having supported the "February Adverse Current," the Earth faction invaded the Peking University campus and seized the broadcasting station and other buildings held by the Hsin Peita Commune.[15] When Nieh Yüan-tzu and the

---

conservative organization is a conservative organization." "Excerpts of Speeches by Central Leaders and Leaders of Various Loyalties," *SCMP,* no. 4220 (18 July 1968), p. 4.

11. *CNS,* no. 219 (9 May 1968), p. 8; no. 220 (16 May 1968), pp. 1-5.

12. Ibid.

13. *Yeh-chan tzu-liao,* 2 June 1968.

14. *CNS,* no. 220 (16 May 1968), p. 3.

15. "Niu Hui-lin and His Likes Deserve a Myriad Death," *SCMPS,* no. 224 (6 May 1968), pp. 23-27.

Deputy Commander of the Peking Military Garrison, Li Chung-ch'i, tried to stop the fighting, Nieh was stabbed in the back of her head and Li was beaten.[16]

Hsieh Fu-chih arrived at Peking University and recommended the following four points: (1) the wounded Nieh should be comforted; (2) those who wounded Nieh should be turned in; (3) the Earth faction should withdraw from Peking University; and (4) the PLA should bring an end to the armed struggle and work for the great alliance of both factions.[17]

The recommendations by Hsieh, who was himself a major object of controversy, could not satisfy either side: the Hsin Peita Commune was not satisfied with the Center's moderate attitude toward the stabbing of Nieh; and the Peking University Chingkangshan, which rightly believed Nieh was a follower of Yang Ch'eng-wu, was dissatisfied with the recommendation that appeared to protect Nieh. Also, the use of the PLA to solve the factional conflict would have meant the defeat of the Chingkangshan, which had been at odds with the PLA for a long time.

As in Peking, the radical forces in the provinces found opportunities to attack the conservative mass organizations, the local PLA leaders, and the revolutionary committees. For instance, the Kwangtung Red Flag faction denounced the PLA at public meetings:

In the latter part of last year, the class enemy raised the current of rightist reversal. Exploiting the opportunity to expose the counterrevolutionary clique of Kuan [Feng], Wang [Li], Ch'i [Pen-yü], and Lin [Chieh], they completely repudiated what the Great Proletarian Cultural Revolution had achieved. In opposition to Premier Chou . . . and the Cultural Revolution Small Group, . . . they branded the proletarian headquarters and the revolutionary rebel faction . . . as "ultra-leftists" manipulated by Kuan Feng, Wang Li, and Lin Chieh; and [they branded] the revolutionary cadres who stood firmly at Chairman Mao's revolutionary line as "black hands and capitalist factions."[18]

Some Red Guard newspapers began to raise veiled criticisms of Lin Piao. The East Is Red group of the Geology Institute asked "Thirty-four Why's," which linked Lin Piao with Yang Ch'eng-wu.[19] Another series of questions published by the Kwangtung radicals asked who the backstage boss behind Yang was. They questioned, for instance, "Why is it that, even now, some people still dare to carry on espionage activities against Chairman Mao and other central leaders by installing monitoring devices in their offices and watching their movements? Who is behind them?"[20]

However, the PLA and the conservatives strenuously resisted the new campaign. This time, instead of pretending to conform with the Small

16. Ibid.
17. Ibid.
18. *Chung-ta hung-ch'i,* April 1968.
19. "March Evil Wind," *CB,* no. 857 (9 July 1968), p. 20.
20. "34 Questions," *SCMP,* no. 4210 (3 July 1968), p. 8-12.

Group's wishes, they squarely opposed the campaign. The Kwangtung conservatives continued to attack the radicals, publishing information on how, as part of their "sinister scheme" to seize power from the "proletarian class," the radicals had conspired to attack the PLA and the revolutionary committees.[21]

For their own part, the radicals published copious information on how the PLA and the conservatives had suppressed them under the slogan of "Encirclement and eradication of factionalism."[22] The Kwangtung PLA met the challenge by arresting the leaders of Red Flag, as well as a large number of pro–Red Flag cadres.[23] In brief, the radicalization of the official ideology in the spring of 1968 intensified rather than reduced the conflict between the radicals and the conservatives, as the conservatives, probably encouraged by the PLA, put up a strong resistance to the radicals' challenge.

The armed struggle reached a new peak in June and July of 1968, disrupting social order and paralyzing production and transportation.[24] Weapons seizure again became fashionable. To obtain them, the mass organizations even raided Air Force units in Sinkiang and trains in Kwangsi carrying military aid to North Vietnam.[25] This time, both sides employed every conceivable weapon—in one case, even anti-aircraft guns—apparently determined to physically wipe out their adversaries. Numerous places reported bloody incidents with heavy property damage and casualty figures running into the hundreds.[26]

Among the many devastating repercussions which the renewed armed struggle produced, what most worried the Peking leadership was the deteriorating morale and organizational capability of the PLA. This time, unlike the summer of 1967, the threat to the PLA's organizational integrity came not only from the mass organizations but also from within. Some PLA units—especially those sent to the various localities to support the left— actually supported the radicals. This was highly satisfying to the Small Group, but it created conflict with the regional PLA units.[27]

As noted, the Thirty-eighth Army in Hopei had trouble with the Hopei Military District Command. In Hunan, the Forty-seventh Army came under attack from the conservatives, since it showed sympathy toward the radicals.[28] In Sinkiang, with the acquiescence of the Regional Command, the

21. For instance, see *Kung-chiao nei-han,* June 1968; *Chieh-chu kung-lien,* August 1968.

22. *Kang pa-i,* July 1968.

23. *Chih-tao chung-nan,* 21 July 1968.

24. For instance, see *Kung-lien,* July 1968. As the armed struggle intensified, the conservatives mobilized the peasants to march into urban areas. *Huo-ko t'ung-hsin,* July 1968.

25. *Kang pa-i,* July 1968.

26. *Ta-chun pao,* July 1968.

27. For the conflict between the regional force and the army corps, see Harvey Nelson, "Military Force in the Cultural Revolution," *CQ,* no. 51 (July-September 1972), pp. 444-474.

28. *Hsin kuang-kung,* June 1968.

conservatives attacked PLA unit 7335, which was sympathetic to the radicals.[29] The PLA units under the Kwangsi District Command clashed with unit 6975, which was supporting the rebels.[30] The Nanking Military Commander, Hsü Shih-yu, faced a challenge from his own political commissar, Tu Fang-p'ing, who was supported by the radical faction known as the "Excellent Faction."[31]

In addition to the inter-unit conflicts, insubordination within the units threatened to cripple the PLA's command structure. One of the best known and most complicated cases of insubordination involved Li Ying-han, the deputy commander of the Wuhan Military Region.[32] During the January Power Seizure, Li, with a few other PLA leaders, supported the rebel faction in defiance of his commander, Ch'en Tsai-tao, and even stood behind the rebels when they raided the PLA compound in February. Hsü Hsiang-chien, then the head of the All Army Cultural Revolution Group, supported Ch'en and criticized Li's rebellious activities. However, after Hsü's removal and Ch'en's purge, Li demanded his own rehabilitation and continued to support the radicals, some of whom soon came to clash with the newly appointed commander, Tseng-Ssu-yü.

Alarmed at the widespread armed conflict and the precarious situation within the PLA, some high-ranking PLA leaders, according to an unconfirmed source, petitioned Mao to end the Cultural Revolution and to impose military control all over China.[33] Whether or not this was the reason, the Peking leaders began to move more decisively from June 1967 onward. On June 11, the Peking leaders, including Chou En-lai, the members of the Small Group, Huang Yung-sheng (newly promoted to the post of chief of staff), and Wu Fa-hsien, made a collective decision to stabilize the Army and to purge Li Ying-han.[34] Lin Piao approved the decision on June 13, and Chou En-lai explained its significance:

The central leaders' conference of last night discussed the matter of stabilizing the Army. The Army needs unity at any time, and should have a high degree of concentrated unity, and hence has to maintain a strong stability. The Army certainly should obey orders, follow commands. Disobeying orders is not allowed. . . . Once the Army becomes stabilized, the revolutionary committees can consolidate and develop themselves. You should watch out that, at the moment, some people want to sack the Army; some bad people attack the Army, hoping to destabilize it. That is illegal and cannot be allowed. The Center hopes that Wuhan will produce an example for stabilizing the Army, and that your model will have an influence over other areas.[35]

29. *Tien-shan feng-huo*, 15 January 1968.
30. *CNS*, no. 235 (15 August 1968).
31. Ibid. In Kwangtung the PLA 6968 unit supported the Red Flag. *Chiao-chung hung-ch'i*, 24 December 1967.
32. *Hung-se t'ung-hsin*, 12 July 1968; *Hung-wei-ping t'ung-hsin*, July 1968.
33. *Chung-pao chou-k'an*, 20 July 1968.
34. *Hung-wei-ping t'ung-hsin*, July 1968.
35. Ibid; *Hung-se t'ung-hsin*, 12 July 1968; *Kang pa-i*, July 1968.

At the same time, a decision was made to dispatch specially organized Army units to all the military regions and districts.[36] Known as "Army units to support the left" *(chih-tso pu-tui),* they were placed under the direct command of the MAC. These support-the-left units were vested with enormous power, for they were to supervise the local PLA units and disarm any local units which disobeyed their authority. Their specific tasks were (1) to end the armed struggle; (2) to produce a negotiated settlement; (3) to rehabilitate the rebels; and (4) to carry out a rectification campaign.

What should be noted about this order of June 13 was that the Center still insisted on reaching a negotiated settlement. But by July the Center's patience ran out. In response to the continuing armed struggle, the Center issued two orders (on July 3 to Kwangsi, and on July 24 to Shensi) which flatly stated that anybody engaged in the armed struggle was a "class enemy."[37] This new interpretation finally took ideological justification away from both the radicals and the conservatives by making it illegal to engage in armed struggle for any purpose at all, be it to drag out the "power holders" or to defend the "proletarian headquarters." Soon the official news media were in full swing propagating this significant new point with far-reaching implications.[38]

Considering the difficulties in controlling the factional struggle at the provincial level, one can easily imagine the formidable task involved in ending the factional struggles in the basic units such as schools and factories. By that time, disenchanted with the degeneration of the Red Guard movement into a factional struggle, many students had withdrawn from the Cultural Revolution. But some stubborn and strongly committed students armed themselves with "hot" and "cold" weapons and fortified their buildings and territories within the campuses with electric wire, cement, and underground tunnels. The school campuses were thus transformed into battlegrounds.

Both sides kidnapped members of the opposing faction to extract damaging information and engaged in a free-wheeling armed struggle for the final showdown.[39] Engrossed in their factional struggles, the students completely rejected any kind of outside intervention. For instance, the Shanghai students beat the officials of the municipal revolutionary committee, and the Peking students laughed at the July 3 and July 24 orders on the grounds that the instructions were only applicable in the areas to which they were

36. *Chung-kung wen-hua ta ko-ming chung-yao wen-chien hui-pien* (Taipai: Chung-kung Yen-chiu, 1973), p. 181.
37. Ibid., pp. 186-188. "The July 24 Notice of the CCP Central Committee," *Issues and Studies* 6, no. 1 (October 1969):97-100.
38. For the response of the Kwangtung Revolutionary Committee, see *URS* 53, nos. 1 and 2 (1-4 October 1968), pp. 7-14.
39. For this point, see William Hinton, *Hundred Day War* (New York: Monthly Review Press, 1972), pp. 154-170.

addressed.[40] The radicals even became bold enough to convene a nationwide conference of the rebel leaders of the various provinces, in defiance of the Center's orders to the contrary.[41]

Compared with the students, the workers were less divisive, achieved three-in-one combinations more easily, and set up revolutionary committees more quickly. The reason might be that, as the official Chinese explanation argues, the "petty bourgeois mentality" was stronger among the students than among the workers. Or perhaps the Center simply exerted much stronger pressure on the workers because of the importance of production. Whatever the true reason might be, by February 1968, to give only one example, Wang Hung-wen reported that 99 percent of the Shanghai factories had established a great alliance and 75 percent had effective revolutionary committees.[42] The Peking leaders apparently noticed the differences between the students and the workers as early as October 1967. As we noted, a part of the Center's demobilization strategy was to praise the workers while downgrading the students as the main force of revolution. This trend continued all through the early part of 1968, as some official news media mildly suggested that the students learn from the workers.[43]

It seems natural for the Chinese leaders to have used the workers to control the students; after all, unlike the PLA, the workers were the masses and, more important, the vanguard class, according to orthodox Marxism. Furthermore, the workers were genuinely annoyed with the factional struggles on the campuses and were willing to "help" the students. On July 29, a large crowd of workers gathered in front of the Tsinghua campus, which was now divided and fortified by the two factions fully prepared for the final showdown. As the workers forced their entry onto the campus, the students fired at them, killing five workers and seriously wounding seven hundred.[44] Next day, Mao summoned the leaders of the five major Peking universities and urged them to unify themselves, admitting that he was the "black hand" that had sent out the workers.[45] In addition, he made his support of the workers known to the public by sending mangoes which had been received from a foreign visitor to the Workers' Mao's Thought Propaganda Team stationed at Tsinghua University.[46]

The students understandably protested the workers' intervention on the

40. Hinton, *Hundred Day War*, p. 186; "No Mischievous Acts Will be Allowed," *SCMMS*, no. 235 (23 September 1968), pp. 13-15.

41. Hai Feng, *An Account of the Cultural Revolution in the Canton Area* (Hong Kong: Union Research Institute, 1971), p. 384.

42. *Wen-ko t'ung-hsin*, February 1968.

43. For instance, see "Be Successor to the Revolutionary Cause of the Proletariat," *PR*, no. 22 (31 May 1968), pp. 26-29.

44. Hinton, *Hundred Day War*, pp. 195-202.

45. *Mao Tse-tung ssu-hsiang wan-sui* (n.d., preface dated August 1969), p. 687.

46. "Chairman Mao Sends Treasured Gifts to Peking's Worker-Peasant Mao Tse-tung Thought Propaganda Teams," *PR*, no. 32 (9 August 1968), pp. 5-6.

grounds that the "workers do not understand education [and] do not know the situation in the schools and the history of the struggle between the two lines."[47] The workers, however, easily countered this argument by citing the July 3 and July 24 orders, which made the end of factional struggle the paramount revolutionary task of the moment. The Center, of course, strongly backed the workers. Yao Wen-yüan, the impeccable Maoist leader whose article on Wu Han had opened the Cultural Revolution, laid down the theoretical justification for the workers' involvement on the campus in his article "The Working Class Must Exercise Leadership of Everything."[48] This was an implicit concession on the part of the Small Group to the conservatives who had criticized the Small Group for having relied on "petty bourgeois intellectuals" as the main force of revolution.

All over China, the revolutionary committee leaders were tired of the endless factional struggles, and so responded enthusiastically to the Peking model by sending workers not only to the schools but also to factories with serious factional problems, and in some cases even to Party organs.[49] Gradually the image of the Chinese students in the official news media changed from "heroic small soldiers" to "foul intellectuals" who favored the "theory of many centers."[50]

The Workers' Mao's Thought Propaganda Teams usually consisted of a large number of people drawn from different factories. They dealt with both factions quite fairly, accepting them as de facto revolutionary mass organizations irrespective of their past history in the Cultural Revolution.[51] They first brought an end to the armed struggle by arranging a cease-fire, and then worked to formalize the great alliance by organizing Mao's Thought Study Classes. Interestingly, they organized separate classes for ordinary members and for leaders of the mass organizations, on the assumption that the factional struggle was aggravated, if not caused, by the political interests of the leaders. Then, the teams proceeded to conduct the campaign to purify class ranks and to rebuild the Party structures.

Thus, it is a supreme irony that the Cultural Revolution started with the student revolts—which in turn set off the worker revolts—and ended with workers entering the campuses to control the students. The Maoist leaders, however, explained the irony with class analysis: because they combined both

47. For the workers in the schools, see "Workers in School," *SCMPS*, no. 235 (23 September 1968), pp. 1-26.
48. "The Working Class Must Exercise Leadership in Everything," *PR*, no. 35 (30 August 1968), pp. 3-6.
49. *Kung-jen tsao-fan pao*, 25 August 1968; 19 December 1968.
50. *CNS*, no. 233 (15 August 1968), pp. 11-15; no. 235 (29 August 1968), pp. 1-10.
51. Shanghai reported that 100,000 elite industrial workers were organized into the Workers Mao's Thought Propaganda Team. "Workers in School," *SCMPS*, no. 235, pp. 1-26. The Workers Mao's Thought Propaganda Team sent to the Tsinghua University included steel workers, machine building workers, and textile workers.

"petty bourgeois" and "proletarian" characteristics, the Chinese students were only capable of initiating the revolution; while the historical task of ending the revolution fell on the true proletarians, the industrial working class.

## The Campaign to Purify Class Ranks

The campaign to purify class ranks represented the Chinese leaders' attempt to authoritatively clarify the most divisive and crucial question of who should be the main target. As noted, the Cultural Revolution basically started with a split among the Chinese leaders over the question of how to draw the demarcation line between the targets and the participants. This question was also a root cause of the factional struggles at the mass level. The reason why this seemingly simple question became such a hot issue was that it bore upon the more fundamental ideological questions of how to interpret the Marxist concept of class and where to lead the Chinese revolution in the future. In turn, the ideological questions were directly related to the basic interests of the various political forces in China. Furthermore, the Cultural Revolution underwent several changes, forcing not only cadres but also large numbers of masses to be targets as well as participants. Even Mao expressed his bewilderment over the complicated situation:

In the past, we could easily fight the war of conquering South and North, because our enemy was clear. Compared with that kind of war, the Great Proletarian Cultural Revolution was much more complicated. . . . The main reason was that [the demarcation line between enemy and friend] was unclear, because of the confused mix of ideological mistakes with antagonistic contradictions.[52]

To make matters more complicated, during the two years of prolonged struggle each participant inevitably revealed his weaknesses as well as his strengths at one time or another. In the chaos enveloping the mass movement, it was difficult to separate those who pursued their selfish private interests from those who pursued what they perceived to be the public interest. Some people stood firmly for what they believed to be the right course, but unfortunately they turned out to be on the wrong side—at least from the Maoist viewpoint. Other people, as the conservatives contended, found in Mao's call to criticize the power holders a chance to release their accumulated resentments against the Communist system itself. Still others acted in a purely opportunistic and unprincipled manner, repeatedly chang-ing their allegiance to whichever side seemed to be winning. There was also a group of people known as the faction of wanderers *(hsiao yü p'ai)*, who withdrew from the whole movement, adopted an indifferent attitude, and tried to enjoy themselves. Furthermore, honest people who had reported

52. *Lin Piao chuan-chi* (Hong Kong: Tzu-lien ch'u-pan-she, 1970), p. 37.

their class origin and political history to the Party were victimized by virtue of having bad records; whereas those who had managed to keep their personal records clean by lying could claim to be true revolutionaries.

The open call on the masses to criticize the power holders resulted in an ironical situation in which the veteran revolutionary cadres who had led the Chinese revolution to success were attacked by people who had once stood on the side of the Kuomintang. Some people known as *"san k'ai* party members"—who got along with the Japanese, the Kuomintang, *and* the Chinese Communist Party—could also survive the Cultural Revolution without having passed the "test" of soul-searching.[53] The dedicated Communist cadres who had faithfully carried out the official policies prior to the Cultural Revolution drew heavier criticism from the masses than those cadres known as "old good persons" *(lao hao jen)*. Finally, many foreign agents, especially those from Taiwan, found their best possible opportunities to wreak havoc with the society during the Cultural Revolution, when control mechanisms were completely removed.

If the complexity of each individual's behavior made it difficult to distinguish the good from the bad, the unprecedented large-scale mass mobilization offered an excellent opportunity for a thorough evaluation of each cadre. There was a massive amount of materials collected by the Red Guards which illuminated each cadre's personality, ideological commitment, political records, personal life, and social relations. The Chinese masses came to know their cadres much more intimately and thoroughly during the course of the two-year struggle. By utilizing this massive collective knowledge on the cadres, the Peking regime hoped to separate the "true revolutionaries" from the "sham revolutionaries."

The campaign to purify class ranks thus stressed the involvement of the masses. But at the same time, unlike the chaotic free-wheeling struggle in the preceding stage, the campaign was conducted in a much more controlled manner under the more stable leadership of the Workers' Mao's Thought Propaganda Teams and in accordance with more specific guidelines from the top.

The officially designated categories to be eliminated in the campaign included (1) stubborn bourgeois power holders; (2) renegades and spies; and (3) landlords, rich peasants, reactionaries, bad elements, and rightists who had not been well reformed.[54] Broadly speaking, the selection of these three categories represented a compromise between the conservative forces which had stressed the "five black categories" and the radical forces which held the power holders as the main target. Also the phrases "stubborn" and "not well reformed" represented the Center's attempt to balance class origin with

53. *Kuan-yü ch'ing-li chieh-chi tui-wu tzu-liao hui-pien* (n.d.), p. 31.
54. Ibid., p. 31.

political performance, and thus was another compromise between the radicals and conservatives.

However, this official designation of targets constituted a victory for the conservatives in political terms, for the inclusion of the five black categories indicated an implicit admission by the Center that some people had revolted out of hatred for the existing social and political system—a point which the work teams had accentuated in the Socialist Education Movement as well as in the early stage of the Cultural Revolution, and on which the PLA had justified its suppression of the rebels in March 1967. Initially there was some indication that the campaign was directed only at persons in leadership positions—that is, cadres, PLA officers, members of the revolutionary committees, and leaders of the mass organizations.[55] But as the movement was intensified, the campaign engulfed even the ordinary people, and this also worked to the advantage of the conservatives.

Yet, it is interesting to note that the campaign to purge class ranks originated in Shanghai, a center of radicalism under the jurisdiction of the impeccable Maoist leader, Chang Ch'un-ch'iao. Following the Center's June 6 notice on the problem of "renegades in the Party," the Shanghai Revolutionary Committee organized ten thousand persons into a special investigative team to check more than two thousand cadres.[56]

Furthermore, the campaign was mentioned for the first time in public by Chiang Ch'ing, the vocal defender of the rebels. She touched on the need of such campaigns in a speech on November 11 and then issued an order in December to pluck out the "five black categories" from the leadership positions in the mass organizations.[57] Chiang Ch'ing's belated admission that many dubious characters had infiltrated the rebel organizations may have been a tactical move to defuse the potentially explosive issue by taking it away from the conservative forces. Or the Small Group may have acted out of a genuine concern for the purity of the rebel ranks. Whatever the true motivation might have been, the Small Group's initiation lent legitimacy to the campaign even in the eyes of the rebels.

However, the Small Group took great pains to protect the rebels. First, they tried to combine the campaign with the campaign against the four rightist trends. By a twist of logic, they argued that purifying class ranks was necessary to prevent the trends toward a rightist reversal.[58]

Second, they stressed that the campaign should only investigate cadres, members of the revolutionary committees, and "bad" leaders of the mass organizations, but not the ordinary members of the mass organizations.

55. Ibid., p. 33; *Kang pa-i,* June 1968.
56. *Wen-ko t'ung-hsin,* February 1968.
57. *Yeh-chan tzu-liao,* 1 January 1968.
58. For instance, see *Wen-hui-pao,* 17 June 1968; "Develop the Party's Working Style of Forging Close Links with the Masses," *PR,* no. 27 (5 July 1968), pp. 11-13.

"Bad" leaders were defined narrowly to include only the "renegades, spies, landlords, rich peasants, reactionaries, bad elements, rightists, and capitalists" and cadres purged in the Socialist Education Movement.[59] This was intended to protect the mass organization leaders who had other problems—for example, those who had class background problems or had made various political mistakes during the Cultural Revolution.[60]

Third, while reiterating that purifying class ranks did not mean returning to the "theory of natural redness," the Small Group insisted on balancing class origin and political performance. Chiang Ch'ing argued that "you cannot choose your own position [class]; therefore it is necessary to evaluate one's own performance."[61] Chang Ch'ung-ch'iao stressed the importance of performance during rather than before the Cultural Revolution: "You should not spend much time and energy on a person with an ordinary historical problem, but should see what their present performance is. You should not investigate those who candidly admitted their problems, but should pay attention to present activities."[62]

Fourth, insofar as the "five black categories" were concerned, the Small Group made the concession that they should be dragged out. But by insisting that the "five black categories" consisted only of those who had been so labeled legally prior to the Cultural Revolution, the Small Group tried to prevent the conservatives from labeling anybody with a problematical class background as belonging to the "five black categories."[63]

Despite these precautions, the campaign was bound to hurt the radicals. Once class origin was officially sanctioned as one of the criteria for selecting targets to be purged, the delicate task of maintaining the balance between

59. *Wen-ko t'ung-hsin*, June 1968. Shanghai Workers General Headquarters made distinctions between the bad leaders and those who made this or that kind of mistake in exercising the leadership; between bad leaders and those who assumed the leadership unwillingly, but for some reason; between bad leaders and the organizations they led. *Kuan-yü ch'ing-li chieh-chi tui-wu tzu-liao hui-pien* (n.d.), p. 34.

60. The official documents on the purification campaign made it clear that the campaign should not be directed to the students from an exploiting-class background or to the leaders of mass organizations who made mistakes, even serious mistakes during the Cultural Revolution. In observing that "many students from exploiting classes joined the revolutionary organizations," the Kiangsi decision stipulated that "some with bad family backgrounds, even if they were the leaders of the mass organizations and made some mistakes, should not be investigated." *Kuan-yü ch'ing-li chieh-chi tui-wu tzu-liao hui-pien* (n.d.), p. 32. As for the mistakes made during the Cultural Revolution, only "serious mistakes with serious consequences such as destruction of socialist property and seizure of the confidential files" would be investigated. Ibid.

61. *Wen-ko t'ung-hsin*, June 1968.

62. *Kuan-yü ch'ing-li chieh-chi tui-wu tzu-liao hui-pien* (n.d.), p. 35.

63. Ibid. In short, the CRSG had changed its position from utter disregard of the class origin to recognition of a close relationship between class origin and political performance. The CRSG on some occasions proposed that those with bad class origins should be expelled from the mass organization, but that they still should not be treated as "class enemy."

class origin and political performance fell on the lower-level leadership, who were usually dominated by the conservatives. Even the experience of the Hsin-hua printing shop, which Mao praised as a model, shows that the bourgeois intellectuals and the radical leaders who had bad class backgrounds bore the main brunt of the mass criticism.[64] The campaign brought so much pressure to bear upon the bourgeois intellectuals that nine persons committed suicide at Shanghai Normal University, and Hsieh Fu-chih suggested that the campaign be stopped for a while.[65]

Predictably, the conservatives responded enthusiastically to the campaign, stressing it as if it were the main task of the movement. In contrast, the radicals put up a subtle resistance, privately complaining that the campaign was a "new bourgeois reactionary line directed against the masses."[66] The conservatives denounced the radicals as "conservatives defending the class enemy."[67] The radicals rejoined that the conservatives were diverting the main focus of attention from the power holders, and stressed the point that the main danger of the movement at the moment was the rightest demands for reversals of verdicts. Therefore, they argued, the main task of the moment was the campaign against the four rightist trends.[68]

Mao again set the tone of the campaign by issuing a general guideline:

As for purifying the class ranks, first we must grasp this work firmly; second we must pay attention to policy. We must pay attention to policy in dealing with counter-revolutionaries and those who have made mistakes. The target of attack must be narrowed, and more people must be helped through education. The stress must be put on the weight of evidence and on investigation and study. It is strictly forbidden to extort confessions and accept such confessions. As for good people who have made mistakes, we must give them more help through education.[69]

The revolutionary committees, the Workers' Mao's Thought Propaganda Teams, and the PLA set up special investigative teams organized along the principle of the three-in-one combination to collect and analyze materials on each case. The special investigative teams operated under the dual supervision of the masses and the higher-level leadership. Mass participation in the campaign was encouraged, but following the masses blindly was discouraged. Although it is difficult to determine how much weight the opinions of the masses carried, mass participation in deciding who was a "class enemy"

64. Ibid., pp. 5-8.
65. Ibid., p. 40; *Ho-chu t'ung-hsin*, July 1968; *Hung-se t'ung hsin*, 12 July 1968; "Hsieh Fu-chih's Talks Concerning the Work of Purifying Class Ranks in Peiping," *Issues and Studies*, July 1971, pp. 104-109.
66. *Kang pa-i*, July 1968; *Tien-shan lei-ming*, July 1968.
67. [A Red Guard Leaflet] published by Chang-sha chan-pao (n.d.); *Wen-ko t'ung-hsin*, July 1968.
68. *Hung-ch'i t'ung-hsin*, July 1968.
69. *DR*, 10 January 1969, p. DDD5.

certainly constituted a definite departure from the Party practice prior to the Cultural Revolution.[70] The upper-level leadership kept a close eye on the campaign; any decision made had to be approved by them or the decision was declared void.[71]

In addition to satisfying both the masses and the upper-level leadership, the special investigative teams had to balance various sets of contradictory considerations.[72] The most obvious contradiction was between class origin and political performance. One's class status had to be based on the class he had been assigned to prior to the Cultural Revolution, not on the labels applied by the masses during the Cultural Revolution. Those with bourgeois class backgrounds were divided into "ordinary bourgeois elements" and "bourgeois rightists," and the children of the bourgeoisie were divided into those of "ordinary landlords and rich peasants" and those of "exploitative landlords and rich peasants."[73] Persons with historical problems were subdivided into those whose cases were known to the organization prior to the Cultural Revolution and those whose cases were not known.

Political performance was evaluated not only in terms of the desirability of the behavior but also in terms of the intention that produced the particular actions. Those who had written or uttered something critical of the regime were distinguished from those who had actively engaged in subversion. Persons who had used the Cultural Revolution to advance their own personal interests were divided into those who had done so "sporadically" and those who had done so "systematically."[74] Even for persons who had surrendered to the Kuomintang, a distinction was made between those who had surrendered to or had been captured by the Kuomintang and those who had cooperated with the Kuomintang by selling out their comrades. It was urged that people belonging to the first group should be treated leniently and those in the second group severely.

In addition to the above factors, the special investigative teams had to take into account one's present attitude in passing out sentence. As shown in the slogan "Dead evidence and living attitude" a willingness to rectify one's mistakes was considered palliative.[75] Voluntary disclosure of one's own problem was taken as a sign of reform, and such a person was recommended for lenient treatment:

Disclosure [of one's problem] is better than no disclosure; early disclosure is better than later disclosure; thorough disclosure is better than reserved disclosure. If one

70. According to Shanghai *Kung-jen tsao-fan pao* (21 February 1968), the masses said to each other: "In the past the public security organs made decisions, the people's court sentenced, and we masses only saw the final decision. But Chairman Mao now gives that power to us."

71. *Kuan-yü ch'ing-li chieh-chi tui-wu tzu-liao hui-pien* (n.d.), pp. 28, 34-35.

72. Ibid., p. 28; *Kung-jen tsao-fan pao*, 19 December 1968.

73. Ibid.

74. *Kung-jen tsao-fan pao*, 17 August 1968.

75. Ibid., 19 February 1968.

sincerely discloses his whole criminal story and admits his crimes to the people humbly, he will be treated leniently and given a way for safe conduct, and his case will not affect his family.[76]

In one of the last stages of the campaign to purify class ranks, a final decision was made on the disposition of each cadre's case. Before that moment, the cadres had been in an awkward position: almost all of them had been criticized and attacked by the masses, but "they were neither removed from their positions nor reinstated to their former positions, and their cases were neither settled nor managed."[77] By the time their cases *were* settled, the official policy on cadres had relaxed remarkably. This was due in part to the stubborn resistance of the cadres, who made it crystal clear that without an accommodation to their political interests the restoration of order would be impossible. But another factor was that Mao's intention in the Cultural Revolution had always been "educating" people rather than striking them down. In any case, Mao issued another set of strategic instructions which stated that (1) the masses should welcome the cadres; (2) the cadres should be allowed to study; (3) the cadres should be allowed to make revolution again; and (4) the cadres should learn from their mistakes.[78] Thus, even those cadres who had made mistakes in the Cultural Revolution were to be given a new opportunity to atone for their sins.

In response to Mao's call, the Hsin-hua printing shop in Peking adopted the following pairs of distinctions, which would have saved almost all of the power holders if observed fairly: (1) persons who merely had contact with the counterrevolutionary revisionists in the organizational setting were to be distinguished from those who had conspired with the counterrevolutionary revisionists; (2) persons who had simply carried out a counterrevolutionary revisionist line imposed by higher levels were to be distinguished from those who had earnestly supported the wrong line; (3) persons who had used bad elements through a lack of vigilance in the class struggle were to be distinguished from those who had conspired with the bad elements; (4) persons who had made erroneous remarks by mistake were to be distinguished from those who had intentionally opposed the socialist system; (5) persons who had taken part in collective decisions that turned out to be wrong were to be distinguished from those who had actively initiated wrong decisions; (6) persons who had neglected to supervise a bad inferior were to be distinguished from those who had conspired with a bad inferior; and (7) persons who had carried out the bourgeois reactionary line in ignorance were to be distinguished from those who had carried out the wrong line consciously.[79] These elaborate distinctions were intended to absolve from liability the cadres who

76. *Kung-jen tsao-fan pao,* 17 August 1968; 19 December 1968.
77. Ibid., 10 April 1969.
78. *Tung-fang-hung t'ung-hsin,* July 1968.
79. *Kung-jen tsao-fan pao,* 10 April 1969.

had merely carried out organizational decisions while purging factional cliques. Undoubtedly, they would have drastically reduced the number of cadres to be purged.

The actual process of reaching a final decision on individual cases involved several layers of study classes. A special investigative team first convened its own study session to unify its members' understanding of the official guidelines. Then, a study group of the masses was organized to criticize Liu Shao-ch'i's cadre line and to study the correct official line, which was characterized as "neither extreme rightist nor extreme leftist," and which called for "neither extreme leniency nor extreme strictness."[80]

At the same time, the cadres under investigation were also put into study classes to reform themselves. On the basis of their performance, they were divided into three groups: those who would be graduated from the class; those who would remain in the class to undergo further study; and those who would be expelled. Those who were graduated were liberated; those remaining in the study class would have another chance; while those who were expelled were, in fact, purged.[81] To balance the authority of the leaders and the spontaneity of the masses, "closed-door investigations" and the wholesale "discarding of leadership" were widely denounced as erroneous.[82] When the masses were divided on cadres, they were allowed to discuss and debate until they reached an agreement on the interpretation of the official guidelines, the available evidence, and the final conclusion.[83]

What we have discussed so far is an ideal model. There are not enough materials to ascertain how all the numerous and somewhat contradictory guidelines were actually used for each case and how fairly they were applied. But it must be noted that the proliferation of categories reflected the regime's effort to limit the purge to as small a number of persons as possible and to those who were genuinely opposed to Mao.

Broadly speaking, the rules were more likely to be applied to the lower-ranking cadres, whereas political considerations played a more important role in the fate of the higher-ranking cadres. The rule stressing evidence and consensus would, however, have helped even the high-ranking cadres if they wanted to request a new investigation on the ground that the rules were not fairly applied to them. It is also likely that those who had been "hoodwinked" by Liu's "Self-cultivation" had a better chance of surviving than

80. Ibid. The guideline for the Mao's Thought Study Class included the following points: (1) study on policy line; (2) discussion of the goal and implication of settling the case of cadres; (3) grasping the target of settling the case; (4) criticism of Liu Shao-ch'i's cadre line; (5) considering the repentence of the targets. On the other hand, allowing masses to purge whomever they wanted was warned against. *DR*, 26 December 1968, pp. H7-9.

81. *Kung-jen tsao-fan pao*, 19 December 1968.

82. Ibid., 10 April 1969.

83. Ibid., 19 December 1968.

those who had formed factions and engaged in factional struggles. Cadres with clean personal records also would have done better than those with suspicious records. However, contrary to the Center's intention, the participation of the masses offered a better chance of survival to those cadres with weak personalities ("old good persons") than to the organizational men with rigid and forceful personalities who had ruthlessly carried out unpopular policies.

As an effort to authoritatively and definitively distinguish right from wrong, the purification campaign revealed several underlying assumptions of the Chinese notion of justice. First, the Chinese approached justice with the moral concept of good and bad rather than the legal concept of innocent and guilty. However, the boundary line between good and bad was not absolute and rigid; it was rather relativistic and flexible, as shown in the phrase about "good persons making mistakes." Nonetheless, the moralistic approach to justice attached a much greater importance to intention than a legalistic approach would have. The investigators drew on the principles of Marxist class analysis to determine elusive intentions by inferring intention from class origin. Yet, as was noted, they knew very well that class origin was not an absolute criterion for good or bad. Thus, performance was equally stressed.

Performance was, however, as elusive a notion as intention in the context of the Cultural Revolution, since the definition of what constituted good and bad behavior had changed. Moreover, it was obvious to the Maoist leaders, who were endeavoring to generate a genuine commitment on the part of the cadres and the masses, that too much stress on performance would only produce formalistic and contrived compliance. As was noted, a possible justification for the bureaucrats' having carried out the bourgeois reactionary line was that it was the official policy coming down through the formal organizational channels, although the true reason was that it served their interests. Many of the radicals attacked the power holders in the name of revolution, but actually in order to obtain redress for their specific grievances. Because of this complicated situation, the Chinese leaders endeavored to balance intention with performance in evaluating each cadre, and they judged performance on the basis of the records of one's entire career—including the records for the "seventeen years" and the "fifty days."

Furthermore, the Chinese seem to have firmly believed that punishment is neither punitive nor retributive, but a means to "educate." This bold assumption was derived in part from the traditional Chinese view which underplayed the free will of the individual but underscored man's susceptibility to wrong ideas and influences, as well as man's malleability. The Marxist view that man's actions are the reflections of the social structure further reinforced the traditional Chinese view of man. The optimistic confidence in education is also grounded in the Chinese Communists' unwavering faith in the validity of their ideology and their cause. Without this overriding moral conviction, it is unthinkable that even Mao would have attempted to rehabilitate cadres who had been attacked so severely in the Cultural Revolution.

Also, the Chinese seem to see justice not solely as a matter for the individual involved but additionally as the concern of the whole community. In other words, each action was évaluated not only in terms of its intrinsic merits and demerits but also in terms of the community's perception of that action. For instance, the Chinese leaders stipulated that "the degree of resentment of the masses" should be taken into account in evaluating the cadres.[84] This collectivistic approach to justice contrasts sharply with the Western notion of individually oriented justice based on inalienable human rights in a democratic society. The Chinese form of justice may accurately reflect the collective sentiment, thereby helping to build up a community consensus, but there is a great danger that it might be subjected to the capriciousness of the masses. The fairness of this political approach to individual culpability ultimately depends on the fairness of the leaders and the members of the collective to which one belongs.

## The Reconstruction of the Party

To the surprise of many Western observers, Mao, who had initiated the attack on the Chinese Communist Party, also ordered its reconstruction. With hindsight, it seems clear that even the most ardent Maoist leaders never intended to abolish the Communist Party. From the beginning, they made a subtle distinction between persons occupying official positions in the Party and the Party as such. As early as April 1967, Mao predicted the revival of the Party structure within six months or a year. Around National Day, 1967, when the initial steps of the moderate official policy had already been taken, Mao instructed Chang Ch'un-ch'iao and Yao Wen-yüan to study when and how to convene the Ninth Party Congress.

Yao spent twenty days gathering the opinions of the masses in the Shanghai area and submitted a report to the Center on October 10, 1967.[85] The Center first distributed Yao's report to the various levels for discussion and then issued an official document entitled "Notice on the Opinions about Convening the Ninth Party Congress."[86] This Notice was based on Yao's report and was accompanied by the instruction that the local revolutionary committees should organize selected units to discuss the revised Party constitution.

84. Ibid.
85. Untitled Monograph [Materials on Party Reconstruction], n.d., in *Hung-wei-ping tzu-liao hui-pien* (released by the Center for Chinese Research Materials), pp. 5029-5042.
86. Ibid.

It must be noted that Mao entrusted the task of Party reconstruction to the Shanghai radicals. The reason might have been simply that Shanghai was the most advanced area in terms of the progress of the Cultural Revolution. But other political motives may also have been involved. Since the Party reconstruction portended the end of the Cultural Revolution, Mao may have wanted to provide the Small Group with the opportunity to undertake this task in such a way that the process would not undermine its political interests.

Whatever the reasons, Yao's report recommended a method of Party reconstruction that would not decisively weaken the radicals' position.[87] First, he recommended the earliest possible date for the Ninth Party Congress, preferably in the first half of 1968. In view of the rising conservative trend, convening the Ninth Party Congress at the earliest possible date would be advantageous to the radicals. Second, as to the question of whether the national Party or the local Party congress would convene first, Yao suggested that the national congress should be held first, to be followed by the lower-level congress. Observing that only the Eighth Party Congress had been organized in the "bottom-to-top" fashion, Hsieh Fu-chih endorsed Yao's idea as a way "to ensure the majority of the rebel Party members and the quality of the Party."[88] Third, Yao advocated "negotiation by the various parties," instead of democratic elections, to select the national delegates. This method, combined with the second point, would have effectively barred the conservatives, who still commanded majority support at the basic levels, from making their influence felt directly at the upper levels.

The official document also prescribed that the national Party congress should embody three three-in-one combinations: one composed of the PLA, the cadres, and the masses; another, of the workers, the peasants, and the soldiers; and the third, of the old, the middle-aged, and the young. In addition, the document stated that "many comrades suggested that the Ninth Party Congress should announce in a big way that Vice-Chairman Lin is the close comrade-in-arms of Chairman Mao and Chairman Mao's successor, and this should be written down in the reports and resolutions to further enhance the prestige of Vice-Chairman Lin."[89] Although it is impossible to tie this sentence to any particular political group, in view of the fact that Yao's report did not contain the sentence it seems certain that it was inserted at the top level.

Simultaneously with the preparation for the Ninth Party Congress, the decision was made to reactivate the Party structures. On December 2, the Center dispatched a document entitled "On the Opinions Regarding the

87. Ibid.
88. *Wen-ko t'ung-hsin,* 11 December 1967.
89. Untitled Monograph (Materials on Party Reconstruction) in *Hung-wei-ping tzu-liao hui-pien,* pp. 5029-5040.

Rectification, Restoration, and Reconstruction of the Party Structure."[90] Accompanied by a note soliciting the opinions of the lower levels, the document laid down the basic guidelines for the resumption of Party life, the expulsion of Party members, and the absorption of new members.

However, these general guidelines drew different responses from the various revolutionary committees, depending on whether the radicals or the conservatives dominated them. For instance, the response of the Shanghai Revolutionary Committee revealed that it was very much concerned with the possible comeback of the power holders, whereas the Kwangtung Revolutionary Committee was less concerned with this problem.[91] Emphatically stressing that the reconstruction of the Party should not be interpreted as a return to the structures which existed prior to the Cultural Revolution, the Shanghai Revolutionary Committee objected to the use of the term "restoration."[92] In contrast, the Kwangtung Revolutionary Committee simply stressed the importance of the Party reconstruction and the need to strengthen the Party leadership. Moreover, the Kwangtung Revolutionary Committee warned that the Party reconstruction should not direct the spearhead against the ordinary Party members, and that vigilance should be maintained against the enemies disturbing the great orientation and against leftist slogans such as "Destroy the old Party constitution."[93]

Besides these general differences, the two revolutionary committees also diverged substantially on several other crucial questions. The first difference centered on whether or not the non-Party rebels should be allowed to take part in the process of Party reconstruction and who should be admitted into the Party. The Shanghai Revolutionary Committee insisted that, since some rebels had actually been performing the functions of the Party members, the rebels should be allowed to take part in the "nuclear meeting of the Party."[94] At the same time, it emphatically criticized the conservatives' argument that the "non-Party-member rebel faction cannot control the Party."[95] After discussing these problems in general terms, the Kwangtung Revolutionary Committee decided to allow the leaders of the mass organizations to attend the "nuclear Party meeting," but without any voting rights.

The Kwangtung Revolutionary Committee also stressed good class background as an important qualification for the new Party members, while the Shanghai Revolutionary Committee did not mention the point, and instead emphatically stressed political performance in the Cultural Revolution.

90. Ibid.
91. For Shanghai, see Untitled Monograph (Materials on Party Reconstruction), and for Kwangtung, *Chuan-ta sheng ko-ming wei-yuan hui cheng-chih kung-tso* (n.d.).
92. Ibid.
93. Ibid.
94. Ibid.
95. Ibid.

As for the method of selecting the Party core groups, Shanghai recommended the "combination of top to bottom with bottom to top, the alliance of inside and outside, sufficient fermentation, and repeated negotiation," a method that ensured the broad participation of the rebels.[96] Kwangtung, in contrast, decided to give the final authority in selecting the Party core groups to the Party core groups at higher levels. In short, the Shanghai Revolutionary Committee stressed the aspect of rectification, whereas the Kwangtung Revolutionary Committee underscored the normalization of the Party structure.

Subtle as the differences between the two approaches were, they had a decisive bearing on who would control the reconstructed Party; the Kwangtung approach restricted the voice of the rebels in Party affairs, whereas the Shanghai line intended to ensure the voice of the rebels.

In Peking, the Geology Institute followed the Shanghai approach, while Peking University followed the Kwangtung line. Under Nieh Yuan-tzu's leadership, Peking University only allowed Party members to select the Party core group.[97] At the Geology Institute, where the head of the Revolutionary Committee was not even a Party member, the Revolutionary Committee disbanded the temporary school Party Committee and appointed a Party core group that included Wang Ta-pin and Nieh Shu. Wang and Nieh had not been Party members, but were given Party membership without waiting for the normal probationary period.[98] Moreover, the lower-level Party core group of the Geology Institute was composed of non-Party members who were "revolutionary soldiers trusted by the comrades."[99]

Peking University defined the functions of the Party core group as "management of the organizational life, organization of the study group of Mao Tse-tung's Thought, and promotion of the political and ideological works of the Party members."[100] In sharp contrast to the limited powers given to the Party core group at Peking University, the Party core group at the Geology Institute possessed enormous powers—in particular, the power to rectify the Party, develop Party organs, and handle Party membership.[101]

The Party members of the Geology Institute challenged the Party core group led by non-Party members as a "seizure of the Party power by non-Party members."[102] The Hsin Peita Commune supported the opponents of Wang Ta-pin, denouncing the practice of including non-Party members in the Party core group.[103] The East Is Red faction of the Geology Institute justified its action by publishing old instructions issued by the Party during the land reform movement that stipulated that non-Party members might

96. Ibid.
97. *Hsin pei-ta,* 2 December 1967.
98. *Tung-fang-hung pao,* 5 December 1967.
99. Ibid.
100. *Hsin pei-ta,* 2 December 1967.
101. *Tung-fang-hung pao,* 16 December 1967.
102. Ibid., 5 December 1967.
103. *Hsin pei-ta,* 2 December 1967.

participate in the Party rectification campaign.[104] After making a dubious distinction between joining the Party organizationally and ideologically, East Is Red argued that the rebels could be considered to have joined the Party ideologically, though not organizationally, and that they were better qualified to carry out the Party rectification campaign than those who had joined the Party organizationally but not ideologically.[105] Then East Is Red declared that the "proletariat [rebels] cannot make an inch of concession insofar as the rectification question is concerned."[106]

The conflict over how to organize the Party core groups at the school level was merely the tip of the iceberg. Beneath lay the gigantic power struggle over the issue of who would control the reconstructed Party machine. It seems very likely that the major contestants were the PLA with Lin Piao at its head and the emerging coalition of Chou En-lai and the Cultural Revolution Small Group. The PLA probably wanted to put Lin Piao's name in the Party Constitution as Mao's successor, and the Chou-Small Group coalition probably opposed it. Although there is no direct evidence on this point, there is some indirect evidence.

By December 1967, the effort to name Lin Piao as Mao's successor in the Party constitution was known to the public, and the Hsin Peita Commune supported the idea.[107] The Earth faction in Peking opposed the idea by launching an extensive public campaign against the Khrushchev type of ambitionists conspiring to usurp the political and military power. An article entitled "How Khrushchev Came to Power," published by the Earth faction, explained that Khrushchev had exploited Stalin's trust to become his successor, putting his followers in the important posts while attacking other comrades.[108] The implication of the article was obvious: Khrushchev did not mean Liu Shao-ch'i but the PLA leaders who gained most from the Cultural Revolution, particularly Lin Piao. The implicit meaning was made explicit by the pro-PLA students:

According to their [Earth faction] view, the large number of people who mounted the historical stage to assume the leadership positions were not loyal to Chairman Mao, but ambitionists of the Khrushchev type. In their view, those people are Khrushchevs, and the first task is to drag out the Khrushchevs in the proletarian headquarters, as they dragged out the handful in the army in the past.[109]

But despite the radical-conservative dispute over how to reorganize the Party, the Party reconstruction continued through 1968. It was carried out

104. *Tung-fang-hung pao,* 5 December 1967.
105. Ibid., 9 December 1967.
106. Ibid.
107. *Hsin pei-ta,* 31 December 1967.
108. *Tzu-liao chuan-chi,* June 1968; *Tung-fang-hung pao,* 16 December 1967.
109. *Hsin pei-ta,* 31 December 1967.

first in the areas where the provincial revolutionary committees were established and the campaign to purify class ranks was finished. When the last province (Sinkiang) set up its Revolutionary Committee on September 5, 1967, the Party reconstruction gained full momentum. For the first time since the beginning of the Cultural Revolution, *Hung ch'i* (No. 4) exalted the Chinese Communist Party, although the thin distinction between the Party as such and the power holders in the Party was maintained:

Our Party is a great, glorious, and correct,Party. But because of the influence of the bourgeois revisionist line, it was infiltrated by a small number of power holders.[110]

Meanwhile, the Twelfth Plenum of the Eighth Party Congress was held in October 1968. Lin Piao delivered the political speech to the Congress attended by the rebels, the revised draft of the Party Constitution was adopted, and the decision was made to expel Liu Shao-ch'i from the Party. The meeting was followed by the Ninth Party Congress, held in April 1969. With the convening of the Ninth Party Congress, the Great Proletarian Cultural Revolution that had officially started with the Eleventh Plenum of the Eighth Party Congress came to an end, thus enabling the Maoist leaders to maintain the fictitious posture that the Cultural Revolution had been carried out under the leadership of Chairman Mao and the Chinese Communist Party.

110 "Absorb Fresh Blood from the Proletariat," *PR*, no. 43 (25 October 1968), pp. 4-7.

# CHAPTER 10

# A Test of the Radical-Conservative Hypothesis: A Case Study of the Kwangtung Cultural Revolution

So far, we have used the terms "radicals" and "conservatives" without fully defining and substantiating them. This chapter will test the validity of the radical-conservative thesis by systematically analyzing the differences between the two Kwangtung factions as reflected in their newspapers.

## Distribution of the Red Guard Newspapers

Let us first examine the total number of each faction's publications. As shown in Table 9, the Red Flag faction published almost four times as many titles as the East Wind faction.

Assuming that the number of titles reflects the degree of heterogeneity of each faction, this distribution indicates that Red Flag was more heterogeneous than East Wind. This is consistent with the assumption that Red Flag was a coalition of discontented groups with diverse group interests. In fact, it was the Red Flag member organizations that published newspapers specifically to air the grievances of the rusticated youth, the pedicab drivers, and persons who were stigmatized by the Party in the early stages of the Cultural Revolution. East Wind did not have many grievances to air, since it was organized for the better-off social groups in the top-to-bottom fashion by the existing leadership structures, such as the labor unions, the political and militia departments, the Party Committees, and the PLA, in order to stave off the rebels' challenge to the political status quo.

Figure 2 illustrates that Red Flag's publication usually increased during the radical phases, while East Wind's publication usually increased during

Table 9. *Distribution of the Kwangtung*
*Red Guard Newspapers by Faction*

|        | East Wind | Red Flag |
|--------|-----------|----------|
| Titles | 30        | 118      |
| Issues | 75        | 232      |

*Source:* The Stanford Collection of the Red
Guard Newspapers is used for this table.

the moderate phases. In March 1967—when, according to Red Flag, the "West Wind Prevailed over the East Wind"—the number of Red Flag publications dropped to zero. With Chou En-lai's visit to Kwangtung in April, the number of Red Flag publications rose, reflecting its renewed public campaign and rising strength. The post-Wuhan radical phase is reflected in the continuing rise in the number of Red Flag's publications and the decline in East Wind's.

The steady rise in the number of Red Flag publications in October was due in part to the time lag between the Center's adoption of a moderate policy in September and its actual impact on the activities of the Red Guard movement at the local level. This rise was also due to the specific support that the Center had shown to Red Flag. During October, both factions tried to strengthen their bargaining positions by launching extensive public propaganda campaigns. Thus, the falling trend in the number of Red Flag publications after October 1967 reflects Red Flag's declining fortunes caused by the full implementation of the moderate official line, the strengthening of the PLA's power, and the diminishing influence of the Cultural Revolution Small Group after the purge of Wang Li and Kuan Feng. During the same period, most of the East Wind publications were extensively covering the criticisms of the May 16 Group and the "ultra-leftist trends."

The new increase in the number of Red Flag publications in January 1968 was due to the split of the Red Flag faction into militant and moderate groups in the face of the impending establishment of the revolutionary committees. With the establishment of the Provincial Revolutionary Committee in Kwangtung, the coalition of East Wind and the PLA suppressed Red Flag for its opposition to the newly established revolutionary committees. This suppression caused a sharp drop in the number of Red Flag publications. At the same time, the number of East Wind publications increased sharply.

This situation again changed in April, when the campaign against the "four rightist trends" was launched. The upsurge of radicalism was reflected in the sharp and continuing rise in the number of Red Flag publications until July. But when the Center again strengthened the PLA's authority in July

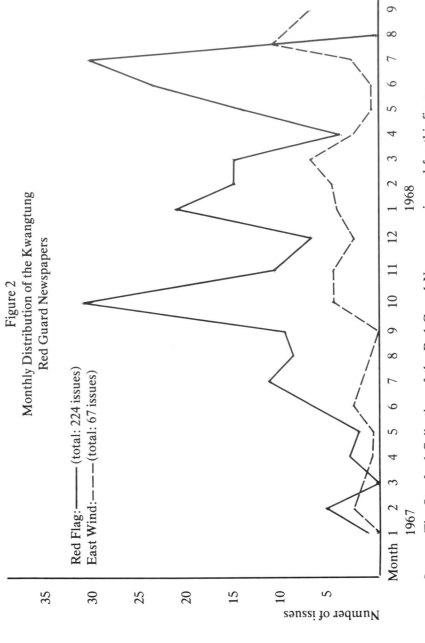

Figure 2
Monthly Distribution of the Kwangtung
Red Guard Newspapers

Red Flag: ——— (total: 224 issues)
East Wind: — — — (total: 67 issues)

Number of issues

35    30    25    20    15    10    5

Month 1 2 3 4 5 6 7 8 9 10 11 12 1 2 3 4 5 6 7 8 9
      1967                          1968

Source: The Stanford Collection of the Red Guard Newspapers is used for this figure.

1968, this action was immediately reflected by a sudden and dramatic drop in the number of Red Flag publications. In comparison, East Wind continued to publish its newspapers—denouncing Red Flag's anti-PLA activities—until September 1968.

Supposing that the number of newspapers published by each faction indicates its political strength, the discussion above clearly shows that the rise and fall of each faction depended to a large extent on the tone of the official line. To determine the degree of this dependency, we examined how frequently each faction carried speeches by the Peking leaders and reported on the Cultural Revolution in other provinces. Table 10 is constructed from a sample of forty-seven issues selected from each side (see Appendix 1).

Table 10 clearly indicates that East Wind had less communication with— and therefore was less influenced by—the Center, while Red Flag maintained a close relationship with the Center. This is not surprising, in view of the fact that the Cultural Revolution's radical impetus (which, as we shall see, was defined by the attack on the power holders entrenched in the governing bodies at the various levels) came from the Center. East Wind, which was strong at the lower levels, neither needed nor wanted the Center's interference.

East Wind was also not active in horizontal communication with other provinces.[1] This again shows that East Wind had maintained such strength in each administrative or geographical unit that it did not need support from other units. In contrast, the radicals, who challenged the existing leadership in each unit, needed this outside support, as is shown in their frequent

Table 10. *Distribution of Articles
Reporting on the Central Leaders and the
Cultural Revolution in Other Provinces*

|  | East Wind | Red Flag |
|---|---|---|
| Speeches of the leaders | 5 | 28 |
| Reports on the Cultural Revolution in other provinces | 0 | 10 |

*Source:* Forty-seven Red Guard newspapers from each faction (see Appendix 1 for the titles).

1. Although it did not rely on outside forces, the East Wind supported the conservative forces of other provinces such as the One Million Heroic Troops in Wuhan and the Kwangsi Great Rebel Army. The September 15 faction of the Seventh Machine Ministry had supported the Cheng-tu Industrial Army. *Tsao-fan yü-li pao,* 14 May 1967.

horizontal communication. In brief, Red Flag was more dependent on the Center than was East Wind, and had more frequent contacts with the rebels of other provinces.

## The Responses to the Official Lines

Let us now consider how official policies were treated in our sample. The articles dealing with the official policies are shown in Table 11.

As we observed, East Wind was very critical toward the Provincial Kwangtung Provincial Joint Revolutionary Rebel Committee, which Red Flag organized after the January 22 power seizure; whereas Red Flag did not mention its abortive and hence perplexing attempt to seize power in January.

East Wind responded positively to the "great alliance" and the "three-in-one combination," while Red Flag reacted passively or negatively. The reason is very obvious: the great alliance and the three-in-one combination enabled East Wind and the PLA to claim their full share in the power seizure; without these, Red Flag could have laid an exclusive claim to power. For this reason, Red Flag first resisted the great alliance and the three-in-one combination, and then, once these policies became firmly established officially, it attempted to interpret them in its own way to correspond to its group interests. The same is true of the revolutionary committees at the various levels. But when the Small Group called for the campaign against the "four rightist trends," East Wind completely ignored the call and continued to attack Red Flag, which published twelve articles on the subject. As was discussed elsewhere, Red Flag defended "factionalism," whereas East Wind denounced it. The issues of educational reform and rehabilitation, since they have not been discussed previously, need fuller descriptions.

The re-emphasis on the issue of educational reform was a part of the retrenchment policy initiated in September 1967, and paralleled the shift in focus from power seizure to "ideological transformation," the latter being the trademark of the PLA.[2] When the issue of educational reform became of primary importance, the radicals found themselves in an awkward position and the conservatives again gained the upper hand. As they had done in the first stage of the Cultural Revolution, East Wind responded enthusiastically to the issue of educational reform by widely publicizing the fact that students from the five red categories had been discriminated against by the old system.[3] On the one hand, again attributing the responsibility for discrimination to the teachers, they insisted that even middle-school teachers belonged

2. For the official order of educational reform and "reopening of class," see *Chung-kung wen-hua ta ko-ming chung-yao wen-chien hui-pien* (Taipei: Chung-kung Yen-chiu, 1973), p. 125.
3. *Chiao-yü hao-chiao*, December 1967. For the conservatives' response to the educational reform, see *Hsiao-ping*, 9 November 1967; 24 December 1967.

Table 11. *Distribution of Articles*
*Dealing with the Official Policies*

|  | East Wind | Red Flag |
|---|---|---|
| The Joint Revolutionary Rebel Committee (January 22 power seizure) | 7* | 0 |
| The Great Alliance and the Three-in-One Combination | 12 | 5* |
| The formula of the Revolutionary Committee | 8 | 8* |
| Factionalism | 4* | 2 |
| The campaign against the "Four Rightist Trends" | 0 | 12 |
| Educational reform | 8 | 2 |
| Rehabilitation | 2 | 17 |

*Source:* Forty-seven papers from each faction (see Appendix 1 for the titles).

*Indicates articles criticizing the official lines.

to the category of bourgeois authorities. On the other hand, they minimized the responsibility of the power holders for the mistaken educational line:

The major mistake in our leadership was the policy of surrendering and conceding to the bourgeois intellectuals, allowing them to control the authority in functional affairs [in general] and the big power in schools [in particular].[4]

Red Flag initially resisted the renewed movement for educational reform on the ground that "reopening class suppresses revolution."[5] When educational reform became the firmly established official policy, Red Flag interpreted this in its own way to correspond with its interests. First, the Red Flag radicals insisted on combining the educational reform with "struggle, criticism, and reform of each unit," so that they could continue the attack on the power holders.[6] Second, they considered criticism of the elite schools to be the major task of educational reform.[7] Third, they demanded as a precondition of successful educational reform a "thorough liberation" of the teachers, who had been stigmatized as "rightists" by the Party organization during the first stage of the Cultural Revolution.[8] Fourth, and most important, they

4. *Hung-ch'i p'ing-lun: Kang pa-i chan pao* (combined issue), February 1968.
5. *Hsiao-ping,* 9 December 1967; 24 December 1967.
6. *Kang pa-i chan-pao,* January 1968.
7. *Pa-i feng-pao,* January 1968; March 1968; *Kuang-ya 8.31,* March 1968; *T'iao-chan,* March 1968.
8. *Hung-ch'i p'ing-lun: Kang pa-i chan-pao* (combined issue), February 1968.

regarded the power holders as responsible for the wrong educational policy and minimized the responsibility of the bourgeois authorities on the ground that the power holders, by imposing on the intellectuals the principle of "Follow me and live, oppose me and die," actually left them no alternative but to obey.[9] Some Red Flag members were more straightforward in defending intellectuals: "Even some teachers from the old society also belong to the masses," and "the teachers who have not reformed the old bourgeois world view are still revolutionary teachers."[10] East Wind interpreted Red Flag's conditional acceptance as opposition to educational reform.[11]

In the school Party Committees, Red Flag directed its attack against high-ranking officials. In one report on "power holders," Red Flag opposed five out of seven Party Secretaries or Principals, one Deputy Party Secretary, and one Vice-Principal. On the other hand, those who were approved by Red Flag included only one Party Secretary, one Deputy Secretary, and three low-ranking cadres.[12] Meanwhile, at Chungshan University, East Wind attacked a Deputy Secretary and eight professors as the "backstage bosses" of Red Flag.[13] What is more striking is that all of East Wind's victims were denounced as bourgeois authorities from bad class backgrounds.

In the schools, the conflict between the power holders ("reds") and the bourgeois authorities ("experts"), wherein each one passed the buck to the other, was aggravated by several factors. First, prior to the Cultural Revolution the reds and experts had been in the process of assimilation. Second, as I have noted above, in order to protect themselves the power holders pre-empted Mao's Cultural Revolution by purging the bourgeois authorities, an action that was later officially denounced as a "bourgeois reactionary line." Third, the educational reform which the Party had originally emphasized and which the radicals had downgraded, re-emerged after one turbulent year with official sanction as a crucial feature of the Cultural Revolution, thus providing each side with a partial justification of its position. East Wind took this re-emergence as a vindication of its earlier activities. On the other hand, Red Flag insisted that most of the victims of the early stage were innocent persons framed by the power holders, and it demanded their thorough rehabilitation.[14] Related to the conflict between power holders and bourgeois authorities was the controversy over the "seventeen years" versus the "fifty days of the work teams and the white terror," which we have examined in our study of the movement in Peking. Needless to say, Red Flag emphasized the

9. Ibid.; *Hung-ch'i pao,* 20 February 1968.
10. *Hung-ch'i p'ing-lun,* 1 January 1968.
11. *Hsiao-ping,* 9 December 1967.
12. *Hung-se tsao-fan-che,* June 1968.
13. "Another Batch of High-ranking Black Advisors Including Wu Ch'uan-ping and Ch'en Chia-pao Is Thoroughly Finished," *SCMP,* no. 4340 (17 January 1969), pp. 13-16.
14. *Pa-i chan-pao,* January 1968; *Ts'ui-hui tzu-fan hsien,* February 1968.

importance of the "fifty days," and East Wind that of the "seventeen years."[15]

The differences over these two issues—power holders versus bourgeois authorities, and seventeen years versus fifty days—were again reflected in the controversy over the rehabilitation of those persons attacked by the power holders at the initial stage of the movement. To be sure, the official policy was that all the "innocent victims" should be rehabilitated. It was, however, not easy to determine whether one had been attacked "rightly or wrongly."

East Wind tried to restrict (if it did not totally oppose) the rehabilitation of as small a number of victims as possible, denouncing wholesale rehabilitation as "class revenge against the proletarian dictatorship," "restoration of the old," and "reversal and negation by the rightists of what the Cultural Revolution has achieved."[16] East Wind based its arguments on the irrefutable fact that the victims of the initial stage had usually made many mistakes in the Cultural Revolution. Red Flag insisted that the mistakes were excusable in such a complicated movement, while East Wind maintained that the mistakes were not accidental, but rather the expression of hatred of the proletarian dictatorship. Although there was a grain of truth in East Wind's position, an extreme form of its position amounted in effect to a repudiation of the official position that the power holders had intentionally framed innocent persons in order to defend themselves at the initial stage.

Red Flag, on the other hand, tended to expand the rehabilitation category to include even those persons who had been disciplined before the Cultural Revolution and those who had been "correctly" branded as rightists.[17] Red Flag did so by stressing the mistakes of the "bourgeois reactionary line." In order to defend persons from bad family backgrounds and those who had once served in the Kuomintang, the radicals developed an interesting but theoretically crucial argument that one's personal status *(shen-feng)* should be distinguished from his functional role or job classification *(chih-wu)*.[18] The essential point of this argument was that not all those who had served in the past in the Kuomintang regime automatically came to have a counterrevolutionary status. However, this extreme position was tantamount to a total reversal of the verdicts on the "monsters and freaks."

The controversy posed a quandary for the Center, since it was obvious that

---

15. For the Red Flag's view on this issue, see *Kang pa-i chan-pao*, February 1968; *Ko-ming wen-i chan-pao*, 15 May 1967. For the East Wind's view, see *Wen-i hung-ch'i*, 15 April 1967.

16. *T'i-yü chan-pao*, 18 March 1968.

17. For instance, the radicals wanted to rehabilitate those who were disciplined in the 1957 anti-rightist campaign and in the Socialist Education Movement, those who were disciplined by the Party organization for various reasons, such as being "provincialists," and those who were correctly branded as "monsters and freaks" by the Party Committees at the early stage of the Cultural Revolution. *Pa-i chan-pao*, January 1968; *Hung-ch'i p'ing-lun* (combined issue), February 1968.

18. *Chieh-fang pao*, March 1968.

both sides had tried to manipulate the issue for their own political advantages, and neither the judgment on the mistakes of the "bourgeois reactionary line" nor the verdicts on the "monsters and freaks" could be completely repudiated. Chou En-lai defended the preceding year's campaign against the "monsters and freaks":

> Recently, in his comment on a document, Chairman Mao defined the monsters and freaks as landlords, rich peasants, reactionary bad elements, and rightists who are not rectified. The scope of last year's campaign to drag out [the monsters and freaks] was too broad. Some part of the State Council made mistakes. At present, Chairman Mao adds a new definition—that is, landlords, rich peasants, and reactionary bad elements who are not reformed well. Those who are reformed well cannot be called "monsters and freaks."[19]

Ch'en Po-ta took a more provocative position. Declaring that the power holders who had victimized the masses (especially those "who know the inside story of the Party Committees"), were monsters and freaks, Ch'en regarded the rehabilitation as an essential part of criticizing the bourgeois reactionary line.[20] Moreover, he openly conceded that "without rehabilitation, the masses still would not dare to rise in revolt against the power holders taking the capitalist road, and the Cultural Revolution could not proceed thoroughly."[21] Conversely, without a thorough struggle against the power holders, the rehabilitation would be ineffective:

> There can be a real rehabilitation only when the bourgeois reactionary line is thoroughly struck down, and the power holders taking the capitalist road are thoroughly struck down. Otherwise—that is, if there is only a formalistic rehabilitation— . . . the masses cannot be thoroughly liberated.[22]

Naturally, Ch'en's view was welcomed by Red Flag, but not by the PLA, which had the authority to make the final decision on rehabilitation. Faced with the subtle opposition of the Kwangtung Military Commission, Red Flag sent its representatives to Peking to complain. The Center summoned the representatives of the Kwangtung Military Commission to Peking, and ordered them to negotiate with Red Flag.[23] As a result, the Kwangtung Military Control Commission ordered the rehabilitation of the following persons:

(1) People who have been branded as "counterrevolutionary," "anti-Party elements," or "rightists," and were forced to quit or were discharged unreasonably under false

19. *P'ing-fan tzu-liao hui-pien,* January 1968.
20. *Chieh-fang pao,* March 1968.
21. Ibid.
22. Ibid.
23. *Ts'ui-hui tzu-fan hsien,* February 1968. Also for the visit of the Red Flag to Peking, see "Visit to the CR Joint Reception Room of the CCP Central Committee Office and the State Council," *SCMP,* no. 4119 (15 February 1968), pp. 1-15.

charges, or because of mistakes made before the Cultural Revolution, or because they criticized the leaders of the work teams. [This clause included those who had been designated as targets of the Cultural Revolution by the Party Committees because of their past mistakes or because they challenged the Party organization.]

(2) Children of landlords and rich peasants who have been wrongly purged during the campaign to clean up the elements of the four [bad] categories; those who have been wrongly classified as landlords and rich peasant elements; those who have historical blemishes about which a settlement was made before the movement, who were not labeled as four elements before the movement, and are not active saboteurs, but have been labeled as four-category elements during the movement. [This clause included those who were suppressed during the Cultural Revolution because of their class backgrounds.]

(3) Apart from those to whom the above conditions apply, those people whose verdicts should be reversed in the spirit of the Party Central Committee's policy and regulations on the Great Proletarian Cultural Revolution, but which have not been reversed.[24]

It was one thing for the PLA to agree to a broader rehabilitation under the Center's pressure, but it was another thing to carry out the agreement. The Kwangtung PLA issued a supplementary regulation which specified that those who had "violated the state law" during the Cultural Revolution should not be rehabilitated.[25] Using "violation of the state law" as a criterion for non-rehabilitation was, in the eyes of Red Flag, an excuse to oppose the rehabilitation, since almost everyone had violated the state law in seizing power and attacking the power holders or the PLA. These rebellious activities, plus the bad class backgrounds and bad political records of the past, made Red Flag vulnerable to the charges that it had violated the state law. Red Flag therefore regarded the supplementary regulation as an abrogation of the previous rehabilitation order of September 2, and tried, by taking a strict legalistic approach, to limit the PLA's authority to classify anyone among the "four elements." Red Flag insisted that a person could be branded as one of the "four bad elements" only (1) if the public security office, the prosecutor, and the court declared so; (2) in accordance with the guidelines laid down by the ten-member small group of the Center; (3) when the person himself, the members of his work unit, and the police station of his residential area were notified.[26]

To summarize the responses to the official policy lines, each faction reacted to the official positions selectively on the basis of their self-interests. As shown in Table 12 and in more detail in Appendix 2, East Wind tended to favor moderate policies and Red Flag tended to support the radical policies initiated by the Cultural Revolution Small Group. These tendencies can be

24. "Kwangtung Provincial Military Control Commission's Instruction on Reversal of Verdict," *SCMP*, no. 4151 (2 April 1968), pp. 6-7.
25. *Ts'ui-hui tzu-fan hsien*, February 1968; *P'ing-fan tzu-liao hui-pien*, January 1968.
26. *Ts'ui-hui tzu-fan hsien*, February 1968.

Table 12. *Distribution of the Contents of*
*Quotations from Mao by East Wind*
*and Red Flag*

|  | East Wind | Red Flag |
|---|---|---|
| Radical content | 8 | 18 |
| Moderate content | 22 | 11 |

*Source:* Forty-seven papers from each faction (see Appendix 1 for the titles).

easily noted by the content of Mao's quotations published in each faction's publications. The most popular quote of Mao in Red Flag's publications was "The Cultural Revolution is a class struggle under socialism"; in East Wind's publications, it was Mao's "strategic instruction" issued in October.

## The Power Holders Defined

The most divisive issue in the Cultural Revolution centered on who would be the main target of the mass movement. At the initial stage, as was noted, the conservatives emphasized the "monsters and freaks" (generally the intellectuals and remnants of the bourgeois class) as the major targets; whereas the radicals directed their attention mainly to the "power holders taking the capitalist road within the Party." Even in 1967, when power seizure became an irrefutable reality, East Wind maintained that the main targets of the movement were the "monsters and freaks."[27]

When the power holders became the officially sanctioned targets, the trend was for Red Flag to concentrate its attacks on the institutionalized power base, the Party Committees, and for East Wind to personalize the targets by concentrating on individuals. As shown in Table 13, East Wind attacked more persons in its publications than did Red Flag. At first glance, this might seem ironical, but a careful examination reveals that attacking so many persons in a newspaper article was a way for East Wind to limit the impact of the Cultural Revolution. Attacks on persons rather than on institutions (such as the Party Committees) personalized the targets, thus tending to limit the spillover from the Party leaders to the Party organization itself.

East Wind also concentrated its attacks on the central and provincial leaders who had already been officially purged or publicly attacked by Red Flag. Also severely attacked were the low-ranking cadres and the leaders of

27. *Jen-wu yü ssu-hsiang,* 15 October 1968, pp. 30-32.

Table 13. *Distribution of Articles Criticizing Persons**

|  | East Wind | Red Flag |
|---|---|---|
| Central leaders<br>officially purged | 46 | 23 |
| Provincial leaders<br>officially purged | 15 | 8 |
| Lower-ranking cadres<br>and leaders of mass<br>organizations | 35 | 2 |
| Party Committees or<br>other "power holders" | 2 | 7 |
| Total | 98 | 40 |

*Source:* Forty-seven papers from each faction (see Appendix 1 for the titles).

*The articles are classified on the basis of their titles rather than their contents, because the contents of the articles are so complicated, dealing with many persons and issues, that it is extremely difficult to classify them by content. Also, in order to give "weight," I have counted the pages of the articles, so the coordinates in the table indicate the *number of articles by pages.*

the mass organizations, but these attacks were soon prohibited by the Center as "turning the spear downward." Red Flag, on the other hand, concentrated on the organizations themselves, frequently referring to its targets in imprecise terms like "power holders," a term which was defined by one's position in the organization.

At the last stage of the Cultural Revolution, the question of which cadres would survive the movement became the main focus of the cadre problem. All cadres made a desperate attempt to be "liberated." Even the revolutionary masses were preoccupied with the question, since they knew very well that what they had fought for in the past two years would depend on which cadres would remain in their original posts.[28] Red Flag and East Wind agreed to retain 18 percent of the cadres and to overthrow an additional 38 percent. On the remaining 44 percent they were unable to reach any agreement.[29]

In order to see what each faction meant by "power holders," I have collected data on 169 cadres whose official Party positions were known and who were criticized by either faction or by both. This data is presented and analyzed in Tables 14 to 20, below.

First, I calculated how many Party Secretaries and members of standing committees were criticized by each faction (Table 15).

28. *Hung-ch'i lien-wei,* 12 February 1968; *Chi-kuan hung-ssu t'ung-hsin,* 9 January 1968.
29. *Chi-yang wen-tzu,* 22 January 1968.

Table 14. *Numbers of Cadres with Known Positions*
*Who Were Criticized (a) by Either Faction or*
*(b) by Both Factions**

| Criticized by East Wind | Criticized by Red Flag | Criticized by both | Total |
|---|---|---|---|
| 72 | 64 | 33 | 169 |

*I collected data on cadres from three levels—the Central-South Regional Bureau, the Kwangtung Provincial Party Committee, and the Canton Municipal Party Committee. My source was the Kwangtung Red Guard newspapers collected by the Program on Contemporary China at the University of Chicago. The fact that a particular cadre in the sample is criticized by one faction does not necessarily mean that he was supported by the other faction. But given the increasing conflict between the two factions over the cadre issues, it would not be methodologically unreasonable to compare the characteristics of the groups criticized by each faction. To avoid the fallacy of interpreting the unavailability of information on an individual as a denunciation by one faction, I have tried to define the category "criticized by one faction" very strictly. However, when I knew that a person was an active member of a faction but was nevertheless denounced by his own groups because of pressure from the Center, I classified him as being criticized by one side only, disregarding the denunciation by his own faction. For example, K'o Feng was the most active member of the radical faction, but, because of pressure from Chou En-lai, the radicals dropped their support of him. The time period covered ends in March 1968.

East Wind denounced only three Party Secretaries who cannot be identified as having been also criticized by Red Flag (4.2 percent of those criticized by East Wind); whereas Red Flag criticized eighteen Party Secretaries (28 percent of all those criticized by Red Flag). Needless to say, Table 15 indicates that Red Flag tended to attack the real locus of power in the CCP, while East Wind attacked the cadres other than the Secretaries and members of standing committees. In fact, two of the three Secretaries criticized by the conservatives appear not to have been real power holders.[30]

The contention that East Wind concentrated its attacks on low-ranking cadres while Red Flag tended to attack high-ranking cadres is also substantiated by Table 16, which compares the number of criticized persons whose official positions were known to the number of criticized persons whose positions were unidentified.

Table 16 shows that East Wind denounced ninety-two cadres whose positions were not identified, whereas there were only three such persons criticized by Red Flag. If one assumes that the cadres whose positions were not

30. Two of the three high-ranking cadres criticized by the East Wind were Li Erh-chung, a member of the Standing Committee of the Central-South Regional Bureau, and Po Hui-chi, a secretary of the Canton Municipal Party Committee. Both men appeared to be intellectuals rather than Party bureaucrats: Li was the director of Central-South Branch of the Chinese Academy of Sciences, and Po worked as a director of the Department of Higher Education in 1958 and was identified as a deputy director of the Propaganda Department of Central-South Bureau.

Table 15. *Criticisms of Party Secretaries and Members of Standing Committees*

|  | Criticized by East Wind | Criticized by Red Flag | Criticized by both |
|---|---|---|---|
| Party Secretaries and Standing Committee members | 3 | 18 | 15 |
| Other | 69 | 46 | 18 |

identified were low-ranking, the data in Table 16 clearly reveals that the conservatives attacked more low-ranking cadres than the radicals. In fact, East Wind charged that the radicals regarded the "cadres at and below the departmental level as basic masses," and that "all 12th-, 13th-, and 14th-grade cadres belong to the rebels."[31]

In Table 17, we see how many chiefs and deputy chiefs of departments and bureaus were attacked by each faction. Standing committee members and Party Secretaries are classified as chiefs.

Table 17 clearly indicates that Red Flag tended to attack the chiefs, whereas East Wind tended to attack deputy chiefs. Unlike the schools and factories, where sometimes the chief is an expert and the deputy chief is a political leader, in the Party Committees the chief represents the formal organizational structure and the legitimacy of the Party organization.

In Table 18, we see how the division between the radicals and the conservatives was related to the attacks on cadres in political and functional fields. The "political" category includes Party Secretaries at all levels (including

Table 16. *Identified and Unidentified Positions of Criticized Cadres*

|  | Criticized by East Wind | Criticized by Red Flag | Criticized by both |
|---|---|---|---|
| Position known | 72 | 64 | 33 |
| Position unkwown | 92 | 3 | 0 |
| Total | 164 | 67 | 33 |

31. *Chung-ta chan-pao*, 11 January 1968.

Table 17. *Criticism of Chiefs and Deputy Chiefs*

|  | Criticized by East Wind | Criticized by Red Flag | Criticized by both | Total |
|---|---|---|---|---|
| Chiefs | 23 (31.9%) | 46 (71.9%) | 24 (72.7%) | 93 |
| Deputy Chiefs | 49 (68.1%) | 18 (28.1%) | 9 (27.3%) | 76 |
| Total | 72 | 64 | 33 | 169 |

$$X^2 = 27.0$$
$$df = 2$$
$$p < .001$$

Secretaries of the Party factions in a given department), staff personnel (e.g., the chief of the secretariat), and cadres in political departments (e.g., the Political Department for Finance and Trade of the Canton Party Committee). Others are classified as "functional."

Table 18 indicates that Red Flag tended to attack cadres in the political field, whereas East Wind tended to attack cadres in the functional fields. In a sense, this tendency is a continuation of the initial controversy among the students over the issue of "bourgeois academicians" versus "power holders." The conservatives had maintained that those from bourgeois families were the main target of the Cultural Revolution, thus leaving the cadres with their real political power intact.

Besides the question of who was criticized by which side, I also attempted to examine why they were criticized. It is extremely difficult to compile quantitative evidence on the types of criticism made by each side, although it is easy for a careful reader to grasp the qualitative differences between the criticisms of each faction. Among the cadres who were criticized by East Wind, there were easily discernible sub-groups (Table 19).

Table 18. *The Fields of the Criticized Cadres*

|  | Criticized by East Wind | Criticized by Red Flag | Criticized by both | Total |
|---|---|---|---|---|
| Political | 27 (37.5%) | 38 (59.4%) | 21 (63.6%) | 86 |
| Functional | 45 (62.5%) | 26 (40.6%) | 12 (36.4%) | 83 |
| Total | 72 | 64 | 33 | 169 |

$$X^2 = 9.2$$
$$df = 2$$
$$p < .01$$

Table 19. *Cadres Criticized by East Wind*

| *Members of the Central-South Liaison Headquarters* | *Signatories of the August 21 Big-character Poster* | *Others* |
|---|---|---|
| 71 (43%) | 61 (37%) | 32 (20%) |

Of the cadres criticized by East Wind, 43 percent were identified as members of the Central-South Liaison Headquarters, the Cadres' Revolutionary Committee, or the Red Garrison Command, three well-known radical cadre organizations in Kwangtung. Thirty-seven percent of the cadres were identified as having signed the big-character poster criticizing the PLA's handling of the armed conflict on August 21, 1967, and as having supported the radical faction.[32] For only 20 percent of those criticized by the conservatives was no organizational affiliation cited. In light of the fact that the criticism of the Central-South Liaison Headquarters centered on its anti-PLA activities,[33] it can be concluded that the conservatives criticized cadres who failed to support the PLA. This is confirmed by the data in Table 20.

In drawing up Table 20, I selected five factors that constituted major elements of the criticism by both factions: (1) Personal background, including class background, past affiliation with the Kuomintang, and "historical problems." (2) A close relationship with leaders denounced by both sides or by one side. T'ao Chu and Wang Jen-chung were denounced by both, Lin Li-ming and Chao Lin-i were denounced by the radicals, and Min I-fan was denounced by the conservatives. (3) "Provincialism"—the only major potential source of conflict among the Kwangtung Party leadership prior to the Cultural Revolution. Not surprisingly, those who were charged with being "provincialists" had revolted against the Party Committees at an early stage of the Cultural Revolution and supported the radicals. However, when the Center officially denounced the "provincialists," the radicals dropped their support of them. (4) Anti-PLA activities. (5) A close connection with the May 16 Group, the radical organization in Peking.

The figures in Table 20 represent the numbers of persons attacked by each faction according to the types of criticism. If a person was criticized several times for the same reason, he is counted only once; if a person was criticized several times for different reasons, each type of criticism is counted.

Table 20 illustrates the differences in the sort of charges that were made by the conservatives and the radicals. The East Wind conservatives based nearly

32. "Drag Out for Public Showing the Scoundrels Who Signed August 21 Big Poisonous Weed," *SCMP*, no. 4320 (17 December 1968), p. 7.
33. *Kuang-chou hung-wei-ping*, 28 August 1968.

Table 20. *Types of Criticism*

|  | Criticized by *East Wind* | Criticized by *Red Flag* |
|---|---|---|
| Personal background | 22 | 8 |
| Personal relationships | 22 | 62 |
| Provincialism | 23 | 11 |
| Anti-PLA | 81 | 0 |
| May 16 Group | 23 | 0 |
| Total | 171 | 81 |

half of their charges on "anti-PLA activities"; the rest were distributed equally among the four other types of criticism. On the other hand, the Red Flag radicals concentrated on "personal relationships." It is also interesting to note that the radicals never denounced any cadre on the ground that he had engaged in anti-PLA activities or was connected with the May 16 Group. In contrast to the radicals' charges, which were generally based on the single factor of personal relationships, the conservatives criticized many of the individual cadres for several different reasons, which were sometimes inconsistent. For instance, one cadre was charged with being both T'ao Chu's man and a "provincialist."

While the radicals did not criticize any cadres for their actual behavior in the Cultural Revolution, the conservatives made more than half of their charges on this basis. The conservatives seem to have denounced cadres only when the latter revolted against the Party organization and broke organizational norms and inhibitions. It would seem that such denunciations constituted defensive measures taken by the conservatives in response to the political challenge put forward by the cadres they criticized. As for the radicals, they would obviously have denounced those cadres who supported the conservatives. Nevertheless, since it was the radicals who made the initial attacks, their selection of targets among the cadres were less influenced by the latter's subsequent behavior in the Cultural Revolution than were the choices made by the conservatives, who emerged as a group at a later stage. Interestingly, however, the positions of the radicals and the conservatives were reversed on the issue of how to identify the "masses," for the definition of whom the conservatives relied on social factors such as class background, whereas the radicals emphasized behavioral factors such as performance in the Cultural Revolution and attitude towards the power holders.

Table 21. *Position and Function of*
*43 Radical Cadres*

|  | Chief | Deputy Chief |
|---|---|---|
| Political | 4 | 14 |
| Functional | 5 | 20 |

Finally, on the question of what factors contributed to the revolt of the radical cadres, I examined the position and function of forty-three cadres identified as members of the Central-South Liaison Headquarters, referred to above as the backbone cadre organization of the radical faction.

Without comparing either the characteristics of the conservative cadre organizations or the distribution of all the cadres in the Kwangtung Party organs according to these four variables, Table 21 does not completely define the characteristics of the radical cadres. However, in light of the fact that the characteristics of the members of the Central-South Liaison Headquarters coincided with the characteristics of the cadres criticized by the conservatives (see Tables 17 and 18), it is possible to argue that "deputy chief" and "functional" were factors closely related to the cadres' radicalism. Furthermore, it was the deputy chiefs who were in a position to carry out the Maoists' call to attack the Party organization, for, although the deputy chiefs were part of the Party organization, they were less likely to be power holders and were therefore less tied to maintaining the structural legitimacy of that organization. Whatever their particular motivations, however, they revolted against the Party organization and thus became targets for attack by the conservative mass organizations.

The preceding discussion demonstrates that Red Flag tended to attack the real locus of power in Chinese society, whereas East Wind attacked persons without real power. The following section will examine the charges which Red Flag and East Wind made against each other.

## Charges and Countercharges

Although there is probably much distortion and falsification in the charges made by each faction, a careful examination of the charges reveals a certain pattern and consistency. First of all, East Wind devoted twice as much space to criticizing Red Flag as Red Flag devoted to criticizing East Wind (see Table 22). This suggests that the attacks by East Wind on Red Flag were part of a defensive move to prevent Red Flag from challenging the political status quo.

In terms of the content of the charges, both factions agreed on certain points, differing only on the importance given to these points. East Wind

Table 22. *Distribution of
Articles Criticizing the
Opposition Faction*

| East Wind | Red Flag |
|-----------|----------|
| 86 | 42 |

*Source:* Forty-seven papers from
each faction (see Appendix 1 for
the titles).

attacked Red Flag for its bad class background and for its "ultra-leftist" tendency, while Red Flag attacked East Wind for its conservatism and its proximity to the establishment. East Wind boasted of its "pure class background," and persistently charged that the members of Red Flag came from "impure and complicated" class backgrounds and collaborated with the "social dregs, landlords, rich peasants, reactionaries, and rightists, as well as their children who persisted in the reactionary standpoint."[34] One typical charge read:

The handful of Red Flag leaders . . . relied on and trusted some of those [persons] released from labor camps and those with serious political problems, because the latter dared to shoot and dared to assault [which was, in fact, class revenge]. On the other hand, they regarded as die-hard conservatives the revolutionary workers and revolutionary students who came from the poor classes but defended the Party and the state confidential materials with their lives.[35]

As for the controversy over the issue of class origin versus political performance, East Wind invariably stressed class origin, accusing Red Flag of one-sidedly emphasizing political performance:

They faithfully carried out the rightist opportunist line of P'eng Chen's "emphasis on appearance" and opposed the class analysis. . . . They regarded all those agreeing with their view as "revolutionary" and those disagreeing as "conservatives and Trotskyites." In their view, only those daring to shoot and assault were really revolutionary, and the others were opposing the revolution.[36]

The radicals claimed that they were the true revolutionary rebels who faithfully followed Chairman Mao's call even at great risk to their personal safety. They characterized themselves as "those who (1) struggled against the power holders of their units at the risk of being labeled counterrevolutionaries, right after Chairman Mao's August 1 big-character poster; (2) dared to challenge the white terror of the bourgeois reactionary line after the publication of *Hung ch'i*, No. 13 [of 1966]; (3) rose to seize power from the power

34. *Hsiao-ping,* 9 December 1967.
35. *Chung-ta chan pao,* 6 March 1967.
36. Bid.

holders of each unit after the Shanghai January Power Seizure; and (4) dared to expose the mistakes and helped to criticize and supervise the mistakes after the PLA made mistakes in the process of supporting the left."[37]

East Wind agreed that Red Flag had displayed a "daring" spirit in its revolt, but insisted that Red Flag's motivation was bad:

When they [Red Flag] were suppressed, they possessed a certain amount of rebel spirit *(fan-k'ang hsing)* in order to liberate themselves; objectively there was a certain amount of revolutionary spirit. Nevertheless, they revolted from private interests (even from the interest of their own class). They started from the interest of the individual or his faction (even from the standpoint of the reactionary class), observed the situations, estimated the gains and losses, and decided shrewdly.[38]

From the bad class backgrounds of Red Flag's members, East Wind inferred that "if the Red Flag faction controls power, all the Party members, Chinese Youth League members, revolutionary cadres, and revolutionary workers will be the targets of its dictatorship."[39] Once the motivation of the Red Flag members had been inferred from their bad class backgrounds, then Red Flag's activism became a source of vulnerability rather than an asset.

In attacking Red Flag, East Wind first presented all the behavioral characteristics of the radicals, particularly their opposition to the moderate official policies and to Mao's strategic instructions, their close ties with the purged members of the Cultural Revolution Small Group, and their attacks on the PLA. Then, East Wind simply interpreted these observable characteristics, which even Red Flag could not deny, as concrete examples of the "sinister attempts" of the class enemies to overthrow the "proletarian dictatorship." By the same reasoning, East Wind's defense of the PLA against Red Flag's attacks had a "true proletarian revolutionary spirit." East Wind could therefore assert that its conflict with Red Flag was "between revolution and counterrevolution," a struggle between two lines and between restoration and anti-restoration in the revolution."

East Wind's attack on Red Flag inevitably raised the complicated question of how to appraise Red Flag's revolt against the power holders. With regard to this question, East Wind attacked both the power holders *and* Red Flag:

At the beginning of the movement, some people carried out the bourgeois reactionary line and oppressed certain persons. Later, when the bourgeois reactionary line was criticized, those oppressed rose up in revolt and oppressed those who had carried out the bourgeois reactionary line, thus making the mistake of criticizing the bourgeois reactionary line with a *new* bourgeois reactionary line.[40]

Although, because of the Center's restraints, East Wind did not publicly and

37. *Kuan-yü ch'ing-li chieh-chi tui-wu tzu-liao hui-pien* (n.d.), p. 49.
38. *Hsiao-ping,* 9 December 1967.
39. *Hung-ch'i p'ing-lun,* January 1968.
40. "Whither the General Faction?" *JPRS,* no. 43,357 (16 November 1967), p. 5.

specifically demand a reversal of the verdicts against the power holders, its attack on the power holders' attacker, Red Flag, was undoubtedly intended to protect the power holders, or at least had that effect.

While the conservatives attacked the radicals for their "complicated and impure" class backgrounds, the radicals zoomed in on East Wind's close connection with the power holders:

[East Wind] is a power-holder-sponsored organization formed . . . by the conservative and right-wing forces which collapsed in the January storm. It is the social foundation of the handful of capitalists in the Party and the Army, and the bourgeois reactionary line is its political line. It serves as the able henchman of the handful of capitalists in the Party and the Army against the revolutionaries and the Great Proletarian Cultural Revolution.[41]

Red Flag also charged that East Wind had "four mores and one fewer"— that is: (1) more persons of the original Revolutionary Committee organized by the Party Committees; (2) more persons of the original Red Guards organized by the Party Committees; (3) more persons who carried out the bourgeois reactionary line; (4) more activists selected by the power holders taking the capitalist road; and (5) fewer victims of the bourgeois reactionary line.[42]

Instead of denying the bad class background of its own members, Red Flag argued that East Wind's very emphasis on class background was a sinister attempt to revive the "theory of natural redness," and hence constituted opposition to the official line in order to "suppress the real rebels, to reverse the verdicts on the power holders, and to protect the interests of the 'privileged students and worker aristocracy.' "[43] With regard to the accusation that it had opposed the moderate official policies, Red Flag counter-charged that the conservative forces had distorted the true spirit of the policies in the process of implementing them.

In brief, the basic controversy between the conservatives and the radicals centered on how to define "class" in China, where the private ownership of the means of production had been abolished since the Communist Party had taken power seventeen years earlier. The conservatives defined "class" along narrow Marxian economic lines, and thus made the "bourgeois class" the target of the Cultural Revolution. The radicals, on the other hand, defined "class" more broadly and politically, and thereby justified their attack on the power holders as a sort of "class struggle." Obviously, both sides pushed their views to opposite extremes in order to maximize their political interests.

41. Ibid.
42. *Chien-hsin,* December 1967.
43. *Hung-ch'i p'ing-lun,* January 1968.

# CHAPTER 11

# Conclusion

## The Genesis of the Great
## Proletarian Cultural Revolution

In the literature on the Cultural Revolution, two theoretical approaches stand out. One approach, influenced explicitly or implicitly by the model of "totalitarianism," views the Cultural Revolution as a power struggle within the elite which had no real effect on the interests of the various social groups at the mass level. By restricting the focus of research to elite behavior, this approach fails to relate the actual process of the Cultural Revolution (presumably the method employed to resolve the elite conflicts) to its possible causes (the elite conflict that precipitated the Cultural Revolution).

The other approach, theoretically more complicated than the first, states that the basic issue in the Cultural Revolution was the clear-cut division between the elite and the masses in the Chinese political system. This approach takes into account the great complexity of the Cultural Revolution —for example, the complex issues it raised, the length of time it took, the high costs it exacted, and the repercussions it generated for the Chinese political system. A rigorous application of logical inference from this approach leads us to examine the bureaucratization of the Chinese Communist Party and its social implications in the broader context of the continuing Chinese revolution.

After it came to power in 1949, the CCP underwent profound changes, all of which could be loosely called bureaucratization. The reasons for the changes are not difficult to see. First of all, it seems inevitable that any revolutionary movement undergoes institutionalization, if for no other reason than the revolutionaries' desire to consolidate their power. As the Party's main task changed from the relatively simple one of defeating the Nationalist Party to the much more complex one of ruling hundreds of millions of people, a certain amount of routinization and functional specialization within the CCP was unavoidable. The ambitious aim of totally restructuring the society and rapidly developing a complex modern economy further necessitated this bureaucratization.[1] Although these changes might have enhanced the CCP's capabilities, they also vitiated its revolutionary élan.

Consider the membership of the CCP as an illustration. The CCP's membership jumped from 1.2 million in 1949 to 17 million in 1961 to 23 million in 1973. As of 1971, 80 percent of the Party members had joined the Party since 1949, 70 percent since 1953, and 40 percent since 1965.[2] The increase in Party membership entailed both an increase in the number of Party functionaries managing Party affairs and a concomitant increase in power disparities within the Party. Moreover, as the Party expanded, various social conflicts crept in, transforming the Party into a sort of gigantic interest-articulation machine.[3]

The enormous capability of the Party for reward and punishment might well have drawn a large number of applicants whose major concern was their private career rather than dedication to the revolutionary cause.[4] Older members who joined the Party in its early years of struggle had proven themselves, but it was difficult to test the loyalty and commitment of the newer ones to the goals of the revolution. Moreover, when the Party became the establishment in China, it tended to recruit only those who were willing to conform to its organizational interests, principles, norms, and patterns of behavior.[5] In other words, the routinized promotion process within the CCP favored the conformist type of personality rather than the rebellious revolutionary type, thus encouraging Party members to develop an organizational mentality—a "slave mentality" in Red Guard jargon—while penalizing those who challenged the organizational norms in the name of political principles.

The changes within the Party organization generated changes in the Party's relationship with the social forces at large. Once in power, for example, the CCP found it necessary to impose its will even on the proletariat, who often did not perceive their interests as the CCP defined them.

1. For bureaucracy in general, see Anthony Downs, *Inside Bureaucracy* (Boston: Little, Brown and Co., 1967); Nicas P. Mouzelis, *Organization and Bureaucracy* (Chicago: Aldine Publishing Co., 1967); Charles Perrow, *Complex Organization* (Chicago: Scott, Foresman and Co., 1972).

2. Yuan-li Wu, ed., *China, a Handbook* (New York: Praeger, 1973), p. 209.

3. James R. Townsend, "Intraparty Conflict in China: Disintegration in an Established One-Party System," in Samuel P. Huntington and Clement H. Moore, eds., *Authoritarian Politics in Modern Society: The Dynamics of Established One-Party Systems* (New York: Basic Books, 1970), pp. 284-310.

4. Michel Oksenberg, "Local Leaders in Rural China, 1962-1965," in *Chinese Communist Party in Action*, ed. A. D. Barnett (Seattle: University of Washington Press, 1967), pp. 155-215.

5. Philip Selznick, "Co-optation: A Mechanism for Organizational Stability," in *Reader in Bureaucracy*, ed. Robert Merton, pp. 135-140.

For instance, when the landless peasants became property owners they tended to defend their private plots, and even within communes families with more labor power emerged as rich peasants. Moreover, as a ruling Party responsible for modernizing and industrializing society, the CCP sometimes found it useful to have the support of the bourgeois class. Consequently, despite its claim to be the vanguard party of the proletariat, the CCP's ties with any particular social group weakened, making the Party itself—rather than its ties to particular social forces—the source of political authority in China. Indeed, as bureaucratization and routinization proceeded, the opportunities for the masses to participate in decision-making drastically declined, further divorcing the Party from its original social base.

Thus, the organization which was initially created purely as an instrument for realizing ideological goals developed organizational interests divergent from those goals—in particular, divergent from the goal of equality. Regardless of their original class backgrounds, all those who rose to prominence in the new social hierarchy found themselves with common interests distinguishable from the interests of other groups located at the bottom of the hierarchy. Originally, the CCP was quite effective in leveling inequality, especially of the economic sort, but now with its own organizational interests at stake and under pressure from client social groups, the CCP found itself in support of the political status quo and could not effectively fight for political equalization. In sum, the Party itself had become a source of new social stratification.[6]

The notion of inequality is, of course, intrinsic to that of hierarchical order.[7] The need to rule, however, was not the only source of inequality. The need for expertise was another.[8] Modernization and industrialization require experts. After the disastrous failure of the Great Leap Forward, the CCP attempted to combine the ideas of "red" and "expert" in order to use the experts' knowledge for revolution. But, in reality, as reds became experts they tended to think and act only in terms of practical concerns, losing their revolutionary commitment. Party structure was affected as experts were co-opted into the important Party committees at all levels.[9]

The educational system, the most important avenue for upward mobility in China, was also affected. Specifically, the effort to combine redness and expertness worked primarily to the benefit of the children of the bourgeoisie and the children of the cadres. The first group owed their access to the

6. T. B. Bottomore, *Class in Modern Society* (London: George Allen and Unwin, Ltd., 1965).

7. Ralf Dahrendorf, *Class and Class Conflict in Industrial Society* (Stanford: Stanford University Press, 1957).

8. Kingsley Davis and Wilbert E. Moore, "Some Principles of Stratification," in *Class, Status and Power*, ed. R. Bendix and M. Lipset (New York: Free Press, 1966), pp. 47-52.

9. *Hsin pei-ta*, 25 November 1967.

educational facilities to their excellence in academic achievement, and the latter group to their indisputable redness.[10]

It was over this question of how to deal with the bureaucratization of the Party and the restratification of Chinese society that Mao differed from his handpicked successor, Liu Shao-ch'i. Mao regarded even a formal organization as a collectivity of people rather than an impersonal structure of differentiated roles. To him the role structure of an organization, important though it may be, was secondary to the actual individual people who personally perform the roles. Hence, Mao was very critical of the prevailing bureaucratism. To him bureaucratism meant, not efficiency, but evasion of responsibility, formalistic execution of work, subjectivism, commandism, empty words unsupported by action, unnecessary procedural rules, overstaffing, selfishness, disregard of the basic needs of the masses, and, most of all, isolation from the masses.[11]

In contrast to Mao, Liu understood organization as a structure of functionally differentiated roles that are designed to utilize the differences among men in intelligence and skill.[12] Liu took a legalistic stand by emphasizing procedural rules such as majority rule and hierarchical rules. His emphasis on procedural rules led him to the ironical conclusion that when the ends are themselves in dispute it is the means that can define the ends, and wrong methods can make correct ends incorrect.[13] As for the possibility of bureaucratism in a socialist country, Liu's view was similar to that of Stalin— namely, that once socialism is achieved, there is no danger of bureaucratism.[14]

Though the differences between Mao and Liu at first glance appear to be an empty ideological dispute, they had far-reaching ramifications for Chinese politics. First, according to Liu's view, the organization defines the ideology. In other words, the correct ideology is whatever the Party decides upon in accordance with its normal procedures. For Mao, on the other hand, the ultimate goal of communism takes precedence over the Party as an organization, and the CCP is a means to realize the communist ideology.

Second, for Mao, a good cadre is someone who sticks to the correct ideology. Mao insisted that if one is correct in his ideology he may use irregular methods to achieve his goals. But, to Liu, observance of organizational discipline required that every Party member be dedicated to the collective interests, and defiance of organizational discipline was indicative

10. *T'iao-chan*, March 1968.

11. "Chairman Mao Discusses Twenty Manifestations of Bureaucracy," *JPRS*, no. 40,826 (February 1970), pp. 40-43.

12. Liu Shao-ch'i, *Collected Works* (Hong Kong: Union Research Institute, 1969) vol. 1, pp. 370, 372.

13. Ibid., vol. 1, pp. 361, 365; vol. 2, p. 9.

14. Ibid., vol. 2, p. 9.

of self-interest. For Mao, it was the other way around. If a person knowingly obeys an organizational command that he knows to be wrong, Mao would call him selfish, because in an organizational setting, private interest, especially that of personal advancement, requires one to please his superiors. In brief, Mao's view justified challenges to superiors by subordinates, to majorities by minorities, and to the Party by the people, while Liu's view prohibited such challenges.

Mao and Liu also differed on two crucial points regarding the concept of class. The first point was whether class is to be defined by economic factors. The second point was whether members of a class must have a subjective awareness of their identity. As shown in his strong emphasis on correct ideology, Mao tended to interpret class politically, and stressed the subjective awareness of class over the objective conditions. Liu, on the other hand, tended to define class strictly by economic factors, and stressed the objective conditions—that is, class origin—over the subjective awareness.

Again, the ideological differences between Mao and Liu over the definition of class had immediate ramifications for Chinese politics. If class is defined solely in economic terms, the logical target of the class struggle would be the remnants of the bourgeois class, which did not have any political power. When class origin is stressed, only those persons from proletarian family backgrounds can take part in the class struggle. In contrast, when political consciousness is emphasized, children from bourgeois families can lay claim to "proletarian class consciousness" obtained through the study of Mao's Thought, and thus they can take part in the class struggle. If the concept of class is defined by political consciousness, the target of the class struggle might well include the Party organization itself, the locus of political power. In other words, the definition of class in terms of political consciousness would allow those who were located outside the locus of political power in China to attack the Party bureaucrats, while invoking the concept of class struggle to justify their attack.

Despite the obvious differences between the two outlooks, Mao's political ideology and Liu's organizational philosophy appeared to work together, complementing each other until the Great Leap Forward. But the disastrous failure of the Great Leap Forward shattered the confidence of the Chinese people in Mao's Thought and his personal power. In 1959, Mao retired from the chairmanship of the People's Republic of China. In contrast, Liu rose rapidly and gained ready acceptance after he became the Chairman of the state. The Party organization found Liu's ideology congruent with its own interests, his leadership style orderly and disciplined, and his policy orientation pragmatic, and so it readily shifted its loyalty to the new leader. The Chinese masses also became familiar with Liu, as he made more frequent public appearances, speeches, and trips abroad, and became the principal feature in the news media. His essay on "How to Be a Good Communist" was republished with great fanfare, serialized in *Jen-min jih-pao,* and made required reading for Party cadre training.[15]

Thus, ideology and organization, the unity of which Franz Schurmann once considered the most important factor in the success of the Chinese revolution,[16] became separated from each other, the first symbolized by Mao and the second by Liu.

The elements of power struggle also entered the conflict between Mao and Liu. From 1956 onward, Mao made several attempts to reverse the trends of bureaucratization in the Party and stratification in the society at large. The belief that bureaucratism stems from the cadres' isolation from the masses and ignorance of their conditions led Mao to initiate the policy of *hsia-fang* (sending the high-level cadres down to work at lower levels). In addition, regular manual labor for the cadres and the "four togethers" with the masses were adopted. Mao increasingly emphasized the importance of correct ideology for the cadres, particularly of the leaders among them, calling for democracy within the "democratic centralism."[17]

On two occasions prior to the Cultural Revolution, Mao attempted to reduce the gap between the elite and the masses: first, in the Hundred Flowers Movement of 1956;[18] and then again in the Socialist Education campaign of 1963-1965.[19] But on each occasion his efforts met with strong resistance from the Party organization, and Mao became completely disenchanted with Liu Shao-ch'i by the end of the Socialist Education Movement.[20] Thus, Mao made the same effort again in the Cultural Revolution, defining its objective as revolutionizing the superstructure by purging the "power holders taking the capitalist road within the Party."[21]

## The Actors in the
## Great Proletarian Cultural Revolution

### Mao Tse-tung

While numerous political forces and factors combined to produce the complexity of the Cultural Revolution, Mao's role stands out as the most

15. Lowell Dittmer, *Liu Shao-ch'i and the Chinese Cultural Revolution* (Berkeley and Los Angeles, University of California Press, 1974), pp. 52-53.

16. Franz Schurmann, *Ideology and Organization* (Berkeley and Los Angeles: University of California Press, 1966).

17. "Comment on Peking Normal College Investigation Material Report," *CB,* no. 891 (8 October 1969), p. 50.

18. Roderick MacFarquhar, *Contradictions among the People, 1956-1957* (New York: Columbia University Press, 1974).

19. Richard Baum, *Prelude to Revolution* (New York: Columbia University Press, 1975).

20. *Wen-ko t'ung-hsin,* 9 October 1967; "Premier Chou's Criticism of Liu Shao-ch'i," *SCMP,* no. 4060 (15 November 1967), pp. 7-10.

21. "A Talk by Chairman Mao to Foreign Visitors," *SCMP,* no. 4200 (18 June 1968), pp. 1-7.

prominent and the most decisive. It was Mao who was most responsible for setting the entire process in motion, first by removing or weakening the controls exercised by the Party organization, and second by granting the masses almost unlimited political freedom under the slogans of the "four big freedoms," and "to rebel is justified." Furthermore, Mao continued to make key decisions at each stage of the movement, radicalizing or deradicalizing it as the situation demanded. And, at the end, Mao terminated the mass movement by ordering the reconstruction of the Party apparatus.

To emphasize Mao's role, however, is not to say that he was absolutely powerful and free of any constraints. Certainly, he attempted to impose his will on events, but he was also constrained by the events themselves. His letter to Chiang Ch'ing shows how the power struggle among his colleagues at the top levels restricted his options.[22] Similarly, the polarization of the masses into radicals and conservatives also constrained his freedom of action. In short, Mao was constrained by the expectations and pressures of various political groups, by his own ideological pronouncements, by his commitments to ideological goals, and by the resources available to him at any given moment.[23]

If Mao's basic objectives were to revolutionize the superstructure and to purge some capitalist roaders within the Party, the first problem he confronted was where and how to obtain support for his objectives. The problem was not an easy one to resolve. After all, he wanted to reform the entire ruling structure and the whole population, while finding the necessary impetus for the reform from *within* the ruling structure and the population. Moreover, while revolutionizing the ruling structure, he had to maintain the continuity of the regime, of production, and of a certain degree of civil order.

Mao saw mass mobilization as the solution to his problem. First, mass mobilization would reduce the gap between the elite and the masses by drawing the masses into the political process. Second, it would help the bureaucrats to understand the real conditions at the basic levels, and would facilitate the information flow between the elite and the masses. Third, mass mobilization would be consistent with the view that "a world outlook cannot be imposed on anyone, and [that] ideological remolding represents external factors acting on internal factors, with the latter playing the primary role."[24] Fourth, mass mobilization would combine the enthusiasm of the cadres and the masses, permitting each to check the possible deviation of the other. Fifth, the method would be particularly well suited to a situation in which the masses rather than the Party leaders were to determine who should be

22. *Hsing-tao jih-pao*, 4 November 1972.
23. Michel Oksenberg, "Policy Making Under Mao Tse-tung, 1949-1968," *Comparative Politics* 3, no. 3 (April 1971): 322-350.
24. "A Talk by Chairman Mao to Foreign Visitors," *SCMP*, no. 4200 (18 June 1968), p. 1-7.

purged. Finally, mass mobilization would enhance Mao's own power by linking him directly to the masses.

The basic component of Mao's strategy of mass mobilization was to exploit the existing social contradictions by shifting his support from one group to another, according to the groups' positions on a particular issue and according to the practical needs of the moment. This strategy enabled him to supplement his diffuse power with genuine support from particular political groups, and at the same time allowed him maneuverability in his actions. He relied on the masses to criticize the elite and to break the coalition of reds and experts within the elite. But, at the same time, he continued to recognize the need for leadership from the top and actually used the organizational capability of the PLA to maintain control from the top. He mobilized the radicals to attack the power holders and to compel the privileged social groups to renounce their privileges. On the other hand, he depended on the conservative mass organizations to put pressure on the bourgeois experts and to check those with bad family backgrounds from directly challenging the Marxist class line.

As was noted, Mao's objectives in the Cultural Revolution stemmed from his commitment to a Marxian egalitarian view, but his strategy was based on the realistic calculation of the relative power positions of the various political forces. The contradictions he exploited did not exactly correspond with a Marxian class analysis based on economic factors. He politicized the notion of class to explain the existing social cleavages in China; yet he did not go to extremes to explain all contradictions in class terms—the class label was applied only to the power holders taking the capitalist road. In this respect, Mao's basic strategy resembled a united-front policy.

Lyman Van Slyke stresses three preconditions for such a policy: (1) the proletarian class is not strong enough to achieve the given task; (2) other classes also have some common interests with the proletariat; and (3) a temporary alliance would not change the nature of the proletariat.[25] These three conditions seem to describe the situation that faced Mao in the Cultural Revolution. Some members of the proletarian class in old China rose to the top of the new social hierarchy and hence defended their advantageous social positions, while other members, although located at the bottom of the society, were "hoodwinked" by the Leninist principle that the Party is always right.

On the other hand, the remnants of the bourgeois class and other aggrieved social groups were willing to challenge the advantaged social groups. In a striking parallel with the united-front policy, the labels used for the various political forces were based not on class terminology but on the

25. Lyman P. Van Slyke, *Enemies and Friends* (Stanford: Stanford University Press, 1967), p. 121.

political terminology of "leftist," "middle-roader," and "rightist." As in the united-front policy, Mao, at least verbally, endeavored to keep the target as small as possible. The slogans of "Unite with 95 percent of the masses" and "Ninety-five percent of the cadres were good" unequivocally lack any class analysis or Marxist justification.

At a much more concrete level of observation, one can find in Mao's leadership the following discernible patterns.

First, although the bureaucratization of the Party motivated Mao to launch the Cultural Revolution, this does not mean that he began with a master plan, as the "plot" thesis implies. As he once frankly admitted, only in the process of the Cultural Revolution did he find the solution to the problem of unequal distribution of power, which had concerned him for such a long time. During the Cultural Revolution, he usually made decisions in an ad hoc manner, reacting to the various specific problems as they arose, rather than in accordance with a prearranged blueprint. Mao attempted to impose his will on events, but he was also constrained by the events themselves. In this dilemma, he followed a "dialectical" approach by continuously adjusting subjective wishes to objective conditions. Basically, he tried to manipulate the intrinsic dynamics of the mass movement in order to lead the movement in the direction he wanted it to go, all the time endeavoring not to be completely carried away by the events. When the objective conditions pushed him toward taking a measure which was at odds with his declared ideological commitments, he improvised new methods. For instance, he criticized the Party for its organizational control over the student movement and for sending out the work teams, but when the need arose to reimpose control over the students, he devised the Workers' Mao's Thought Propaganda Teams, which were abundantly similar in form and function to the work teams.

Second, instead of issuing specific orders on his own initiative, he usually issued broad ideological instructions in response to the initiatives of the masses or other leaders. Another method he used frequently was to allow or even to promote conflict among groups, and then intervene personally at a decisive and critical moment. He also intentionally moved slowly, in some cases allowing the chaos to last for quite a while. These methods provided the masses and the other leaders with an opportunity to pursue the conflict by themselves, and also enabled Mao to use his personal power most effectively by giving him a wide range of options and freedom in selecting the proper time for his intervention.

Third, in leading the whole movement in the direction that he wanted it to go, Mao followed a zigzag pattern rather than a continuous and steadily incremental approach. The Cultural Revolution thus underwent a series of radicalization and deradicalization phases, displaying the cyclical pattern suggested by Skinner.[26] Despite its obvious merits, this strategy had its share of disadvantages: for example, it enhanced the expectations of both the radical and the conservative mass organizations, thus making it even more difficult to resolve their conflicts. The zigzag pattern may also be explained by the contradictory considerations that Mao had to take into account for any decision. Unlike a counter-elite challenging a ruling elite to a life-and-death struggle, Mao always remained responsible for maintaining minimal order, production, and continuity, even while trying to revolutionize the ruling structures.

Fourth, Mao's dual role also explains the peculiar mix of conflict and compromise among the Chinese elite during the Cultural Revolution. Despite the sharp internal conflicts among the elite, compromise was possible because the elite groups all had a large stake in keeping contention among themselves within certain manageable boundaries, preventing it from developing into an open civil war threatening the basic foundation of their entire system. But a more important factor was that Mao acted as a centripetal force: he had to be fair to all the contentious factions, for otherwise he could not lay claim to the position of supreme leader, demanding the allegiance of all formal and informal structures. In this respect, the conflicts in the Cultural Revolution differed from those in the international system of balance of power. There it is power alone rather than fairness that matters.

Fifth, Mao's unique role makes it difficult to distinguish the formal from the informal groups in the Cultural Revolution setting.[27] First of all, Mao derived his authority, power, and influence from both formal and informal structures. He was the supreme leader in terms of the formal Party structure, and the recognized guardian of official ideology. But he was still a factional leader who worked through informal structures to eliminate his political opponents and realize his goals. Mao probably justified his use of informal groups on the grounds that those whom he wanted to purge were themselves acting as informal factional leaders rather than as Party leaders. In other words, Mao understood, as do many social scientists, that bureaucrats may utilize formal organizational structures to advance their private interests.

### The Cultural Revolution Small Group

Organized by the May 16 Notice, the Small Group was initially composed of three power groups: the young intellectuals led by Chiang Ch'ing; Party leaders such as T'ao Chu, Wang Jen-chung, Chang P'ing-hua, and other

26. G. William Skinner and Edwin A. Winckler, "Compliance Succession in Rural Communist China: A Cyclical Theory," in *A Sociological Reader on Complex Organization,* ed. Amitai Etzioni (New York: Holt, Rinehart & Winston, 1969), pp. 410-438.

27. Tang Tsou, "Prolegomenon to Study of Informal Groups in CCP Politics," *CQ,* no. 65 (January 1967), pp. 998-1103.

provincial First Secretaries; and PLA representatives such as Liu Chih-chien and Hsieh T'ang-chung. But as the Cultural Revolution progressed, those members who were closely affiliated with the Party and the army were purged, and only the Chiang Ch'ing faction survived.

The core members of the Small Group were the ones who had actively taken part in the polemics on literature and the arts since 1962, thus developing close personal ties with Chiang Ch'ing. Except for K'ang Sheng and Ch'en Po-ta (both of whom were alternative members of the Politburo of the Central Committee), most of them were minor officials from the middle or lower ranks in the Chinese leadership hierarchy, with career backgrounds in cultural and propaganda fields and without any work experience in functional fields. Because of these characteristics in its membership, the Small Group exhibited none of the restraint and prudence that high-ranking officials should possess, nor any of the practical sense that experienced cadres in the functional fields would have had.

Within the Small Group, K'ang Sheng and Hsieh Fu-chih could be termed power holders: they were older, higher in rank, had more political experience, and were more moderate than the rest of the members. Chang Ch'un-ch'iao and Yao Wen-yuan were more moderate than members such as Kuan Feng, Wang Li, and Ch'i Pen-yü, whose rashness caused them to be purged in the later part of the movement. But despite the variety of its members, the Small Group acted as a whole, since all of its members shared a common interest in changing the status quo of the pre-Cultural Revolution political system.

Located initially outside the formal power structure of the Chinese political system, the Small Group as a whole had no special interests to protect and no stake in preserving the status quo. Consequently, its ideology, policies, and power interests made it more radical than any other elite group. Since the Small Group owed its political power and legitimacy to Mao, the direct translation of Mao's Thought into policy served its own power interests. The Small Group strove to establish the cult of Mao's Thought, and took it as the final standard for judging right and wrong. To the Small Group, the key concept of Mao's Thought was the class struggle, and therefore the main task was to carry out—not to study—that struggle. Thus, they underscored the Cultural Revolution as a "struggle between two lines," while choosing to ignore the PLA's interpretation of it as an "ideological revolution touching the masses to their souls."

The Small Group consistently pursued a radical policy: it argued for an uncontrolled rather than a controlled mass mobilization; for a struggle against the power holders rather than against the experts; for the predominance of class consciousness rather than class origin; and for an unlimited rather than a limited power seizure. It considered political action more important than intention, and behavior during the Cultural Revolution more important than behavior during the previous seventeen years. Despite their numerous problems, the Small Group backed the radical mass organizations throughout the entire Cultural Revolution.

The Small Group expanded its power gradually, and only in the radical phases of the mass movement. Under the pretext of carrying out Mao's line, it expanded its function of leading the Cultural Revolution in the educational institutions to include all the segments of Chinese society and all the aspects of political power. Because it was small and closely knit, it could freely expand the target to include the entire formal struture of the Party organization, while recruiting supporters from within the formal organization by using personal ties, in complete disregard to normal organizational principles. The policy of "freely mobilizing the masses," which for the party organization meant the loss of its control over the movement, provided the Small Group with an opportunity to cultivate its own power base among the masses.

By pursuing a thoroughly radical policy line in the name of Mao's Thought, the Small Group completely ignored the objective constraints that any responsible decision-maker would have to take into account. Not surprisingly, its opponents distrusted the Small Group as a political faction interested only in the aggrandizement of its own political power. This distrust helped the Cultural Revolution to degenerate into a simple form of power politics. But for all its shortcomings and mistakes, the Small Group managed to survive the Cultural Revolution and emerged as one of the most important groups in the political system which followed.

*The Party Organization*

During the Cultural Revolution, the Party organization displayed typical organizational behavior in a strained situation. When Mao pressured the Party to reduce the gap between the elite and the masses, it was unable to faithfully carry out his wishes without compromising its own organizational integrity and its vested interests in the status quo. However, instead of openly and squarely challenging Mao's demands, the Party organization persisted in its tactic of stalling and subverting them. For example, it sent out the work teams ostensibly to lead the movement in the direction that Mao wanted, but in reality to impose its own control over the mass movement and restrict its development.

Mao's order to withdraw the work teams marked the end of the "structural legitimacy" of the Party; thereafter the Party leaders took part in the movement as individuals representing Mao's Thought rather than as representatives of the organization. When the movement entered the power-seizure phase, these individuals lost their claim to represent Mao's ideology, and they were thereafter involved in the movement solely as the objects of criticism and attack.

A few summary observations regarding the behavior of the Party organization can be made.

First of all, there was a wide discrepancy between what both the public and the Party professed to be right and proper and what the Party organization actually did. But concealment was no longer possible once the masses were mobilized to examine the Party's internal affairs. The more actively the Chinese masses became involved in the political process, the clearer it became to everyone that the Party bureaucrats had been distorting Mao's Thought.

Second, the Party's defense centered on extolling the principle of organizational integrity. By stressing its "structural legitimacy," the Party attempted to bar the Chinese people from interfering with its internal affairs. By stressing the need of leadership in the mass movement, it attempted to maintain its prerogative to determine the scope and the method of mobilization and to determine who were to be the targets.

Third, the Party organization tried to turn the movement against relatively innocuous targets—in particular, the remants of the "bourgeois class" as defined in traditional Marxist economic terms. Consequently, the Party organization was always one step behind the Maoists in attacking top officials. The Party moved to attack Wu Han's academic position only after the Maoists had begun to attack his political position; it moved to attack the "bourgeois authorities" only after the Maoists had begun to attack the "black gang"; and it moved to attack the "black gang" only after the Maoists had begun to talk menacingly about the "power holders taking the capitalist road within the Party."

Fourth, the Party organization tried to limit the participation of the masses to the social groups that were favorably inclined toward the Party. Through the various existing mass organizations, it mobilized the Party and CYL members, "the five red categories," and the relatively privileged workers—in other words, those social groups that would not have threatened the basic interests of the Party even if they had been freely mobilized.

Fifth, the Party organization heavily utilized its organizational resources to lead the mass movement in the direction it wanted. For instance, the security personnel of the Party organization collected information on those persons who were considered threats to its "structural legitimacy," presumably in order to retaliate against them in the future. When Mao ordered the Party to release these "black materials" to the public, it resisted the order, first by mixing them with its confidential documents, and then claiming that the Party leaders were the only qualified judges of which papers were "black materials" and which were confidential materials vital to national security.

Sixth, responsibility within the organization was passed back and forth from one person to another, and nobody assumed any definitive responsibility. Responsibility was also passed downward through the chain of command so as to protect the higher-ups under the pretext of protecting the organization. This tactic is known in Chinese jargon as "sacrificing pawns to protect the king." When pressure from Mao and the mass organizations built up, some "pawns" revolted against the "king," exposing the Party's deviousness.

Seventh, as pressure on the Party organization increased, communication inside the organization became increasingly secret and unintelligible to outsiders; the struggle for political survival became increasingly desperate and confused; and personal ties of friendship and trust replaced formal organizational ties and organizational lines of communication. Once the "structural legitimacy" of the organization was finally discredited, the organizational ties became a source of vulnerability rather than of strength for Party leaders. The Party leaders then tried to utilize their personal ties to manipulate the mass organizations that shared common interests with them, employing various tactics, such as "economism," "sham power seizure," and support of the conservative mass organizations.

## The People's Liberation Army

The role of the PLA in shaping the Cultural Revolution was second only to that of Mao and the Small Group, and it emerged as the most powerful political force at the conclusion of the movement. The PLA had direct influence at both the policy-making and the implementation levels: it exercised its influence in the policy-making process through Lin Piao and the Military Affairs Commission; and as the Party disintegrated, it was entrusted with the task of carrying out the policy.

The PLA's vast apparatus, although enabling it to expand its political power, also hindered it from operating as a unified political group. With its complex system, numerous organizations, and various factions, the PLA had many internal cleavages, conflicts, and interests which weakened its cohesion and limited its freedom of action. The discernible cleavages included the Field Army factions, and the divisions between the political commissars and the military commanders, the local garrison forces and the centrally controlled strategic armies, and the central and the local military organs. The relative importance of each type of cleavage in influencing the overall behavior of the PLA changed with the various stages of the Cultural Revolution.

But despite these divisions, the PLA by and large participated in the Cultural Revolution as a unified actor, mainly because two basic desires united its leaders: the first was to preserve its organizational integrity; and the second, to maintain a minimum degree of law and order in Chinese society. As a military organization, it was essential for the PLA to preserve its well-established hierarchical command structures. As a part of the establishment in China, it was also not in its best interests to see a complete change in the basic political status quo.

The PLA went along with the Small Group to the extent that this would not undermine its two basic interests, and it also engaged in the inner-elite struggle against the Party organization within these limitations. But when the masses and the Small Group finally threatened these two basic interests, the PLA no longer followed Mao. Not even Lin Piao was willing to disregard the interests of the PLA in pursuing his own personal ambitions.

The other PLA leaders also engaged in some "factional conflicts," but, again, only within the above limitations. As was noted, factionalism in a formal organization appears only when its structural legitimacy is weakened or removed. At no time in the Cultural Revolution was the organizational legitimacy of the PLA decisively weakened, although it did come under attack for a brief period in the summer of 1967. Thus, it can safely be said that the PLA's common organizational interests were more decisive in influencing its behavior than were its internal cleavages or its desire to integrate itself with the radical leadership.

The PLA expanded its influence mainly during the moderate phases, which usually came after the extreme radical phases. It played a pioneering role only at the initial stage of the Cultural Revolution, when the movement was directed against a limited number of Party leaders—for example, Wu Han, Chou Yang, and P'eng Chen—and when the ideological issues in dispute had no direct political ramifications. Even at that early stage, only certain top PLA leaders and the PLA propaganda machines were involved. In the summer of 1966, during the initial stage of the mass mobilization, the PLA played a somewhat less active role, only providing logistical support to the emerging Red Guards and applauding their activities in general terms. But the PLA soon lost its "pace setting" role. When the Red Guards divided into radicals and conservatives, the PLA failed to come out in support of the radicals. Lin Piao appeared to be notably more conciliatory toward the Party organization after becoming Mao's designated successor at the Tenth Plenum. The central leadership of the PLA was restricting the mass movement within the army at the very time when the civilian Cultural Revolution was expanding from the Party organizations to other institutions.

When the Cultural Revolution finally entered the stage of power seizure, the discrepancy between the radical rhetoric of the PLA and its actual behavior became very wide. The January Power Seizure confronted the PLA with two dilemmas: (1) should there be a power seizure within the PLA?; and (2) what role should the PLA play in the power seizure from the Party organization? The PLA understandably opposed any notion of power seizure within the army, which would obviously have meant demolishing its own command structure. A compromise was reached: power seizure was forbidden within the PLA, but the army was given the task of supporting the power seizures outside—a task known a "two military and three supports"—thus drawing the local PLA leaders involuntarily into the Cultural Revolution. However, it was impossible for the local PLA leaders to support the leftists as the Small Group demanded, unless they were willing to sacrifice their basic institutional interests. Following the example of the Party organization, the local PLA leaders attempted to resolve the dilemma by implementing the official policies only in such a way that they would not undermine the army's own interests.

When this was recognized by the radical masses as a distortion of the official orders, the radicals challenged the PLA leaders, and this led to their suppression by the PLA. In the summer of 1967, the radicals advanced the slogan of "dragging out the handful of power holders in the army." The rising conflict between the local PLA leaders and the radical mass organizations which the Small Group now fully supported put the central PLA leaders, especially Lin Piao, in an impossible position: they were under conflicting pressures from the Small Group and the local PLA leaders, but could not afford to alienate either of them. Thus, the central PLA leaders vacillated, exacerbating the conflict between the Small Group and the local PLA leaders.

In retrospect, Lin Piao's later downfall can probably be traced back to the conflict that arose between the PLA and the Small Group during this period. Lin Piao became Mao's designated successor by accepting the radicalization of Mao's Thought and forming a coalition with the Small Group. But once he did so, he realized that his political interests now conflicted with his earlier ideological pronouncements. He could not translate his radical ideas into policy, and this resulted in a widening gap between his rhetoric and his policy positions.

Even his ideological pronouncements were not as radical as many observers thought at the time. His two most radical speeches were given during the early stages of the movement, one at the Politburo meeting on May 16, 1966, and the other at a mass rally on October 1, 1966. The rest of his speeches were delivered after the Wuhan Incident and were clearly geared to bringing an end to the Small Group. In terms of content, they appear to be incongruent with the way the movement was unfolding. Even at the most radical phase of the Cultural Revolution, Lin continued to push for the "study of Mao's Thought" and "politics in command," his two basic themes, which were at first considered radical by the Party, but which were later widely used by the PLA to moderate the movement during the period of power seizure. In brief, the political ambition of a few of its central leaders, coupled with its own organizational interests, inevitably created a wide gap for the PLA between its professed ideology, on the one hand, and the actual implementation of that policy, on the other.

## The Government

Although the central ministries of the government were forced into the movement either as participants or as objects of attack, they were the least active of the four elite groups. They neither gained as much from the movement as the PLA did, nor did they lose as much as the Party organization. This was in part due to the peculiar position of the government within the total Chinese political system. The government was not the locus of political decision-making and policy-formulation, nor was it invested with the mystique of legitimacy, as were Mao, the Party, and the PLA; rather, it was merely an administrative organ carrying out decisions made by the Party. Its function, however, was more important than that of the Party for the day-to-day administration of policy, and particularly for the management of the Chinese economy. The Party structure operated within the government units, and this dual structure helped the government to maintain its institutional integrity even when its Party structure came under attack. Moreover, since the government agencies were concentrated in Peking, the government leaders were spared from involvement in the more complicated, spontaneous, and capricious local politics.

The involvement of the government leaders in the movement did not start until September 1966, when students chased some work teams back to the government ministries that had sent them out. The next stage of their involvement came when the Cultural Revolution spread to the factories, and the discontented workers were mobilized. In January 1967, many government ministers came under public attack, and government ministries were subjected to a power seizure. In February 1967, taking advantage of the newly adopted formula of the three-in-one combination, the government leaders manipulated the power seizure by handing over power to a "reliable" mass organization of their own creation. The radicals and the Cultural Revolution Small Group challenged this as a "sham power seizure," and branded the action as part of the "February Adverse Current." But despite persistent challenges from the radicals and the Small Group, and despite the subsequent chaos, particularly in the Foreign Ministry in August 1967, the government leaders managed to defend the February power seizure, sometimes resisting the radicals' attack and sometimes compromising with them.

Chou En-lai's skillful leadership also contributed to the successful survival of the government. By consistently pursuing a moderate middle-of-the-road approach throughout the movement, and by emphasizing the need to balance revolution and production, Chou was able to minimize the disruptive effects of the Cultural Revolution on the government. Unlike other top political leaders, who swung from one extreme to the other, Chou shifted his position gradually toward the radical direction, in keeping with the changing demands of the movement, but always in a moderate and flexible fashion (particularly when compared with that of the Small Group). He also tried to protect the minimum interests of the government, as well as other institutional groups, an attitude which undoubtedly earned their support.

After the Wuhan Incident, when the conflict deepened between the Small Group and the PLA over who would control the newly reconstructed Party organization at the sub-provincial level, Chou again wisely decided to support Chiang Ch'ing against the PLA generals, notwithstanding the attacks that her radicals had made on him and his subordinates, and notwithstanding his sympathy for the PLA's policy orientation.

*The Radical Mass Organizations*

The members of the radical mass organizations were recruited mainly from the social groups that had held grievances against the establishment. Among the students, they were those with "bad" family backgrounds, those who had been sent to the rural areas, and those who had revolted against the work teams. Among the workers, they were those from the smaller, poorer factories, the contract and temporary workers, the apprentice and unskilled workers in the larger factories, and the individual laborers. Among the cadres, they were the low- or middle-ranking cadres, those with "bad" family backgrounds, and those who had been disciplined or "rectified" by the Party organization prior to the Cultural Revolution. The grievances of these discontented groups were aggravated by the initial tendency of the Party organization to turn the major thrust of the movement against them, labeling them "reactionaries," "rightists," or "anti-Party elements."

The initial demands of these groups were limited; they simply wanted exoneration and the removal of the labels or "hats" that the Party had put on them. But as the movement turned against the Party, they saw that their interests lay in bringing about a basic change in the distribution of power in the society. In this respect, their interests coincided with those of the Small Group, and the two thus collaborated closely.

Several observations can be made regarding the radicals in the Cultural Revolution. First, their ideology was directed against the entire establishment, particularly against those who held a monopoly on political power. They defined "class" politically, thus drawing their justification for attacking the Party from the thesis of "class struggle." Some of the extreme radicals even used the term "red capitalists" to refer to the Party and to government bureaucrats.

Second, the radicals tended to concentrate their attacks on Party cadres, particularly the chiefs of the various departments, as well as those in the political fields in the Party organization; they displayed more leniency toward intellectuals and specialists. On the whole, they stressed organizational ties as a basic criterion in selecting targets, a tendency that expanded the targets along the formal lines of the Party organization. Consequently, it was the radicals rather than the conservatives who displayed the conspiratorial and anti-organizational activities that were frequently found in the factional struggle.

Third, as challengers to a highly organized CCP, they criticized "organizational principles" as such, denouncing them as the product of a "slave mentality." At the same time, they emphasized general political principles by which each individual could exercise his personal judgment. They also questioned in a subtle way the specific legitimacy of various past policies and campaigns, such as the "anti-rightist" campaign and the Socialist Education movement. It is not surprising that, in the eyes of the conservatives, the radicals were attempting to "reverse the achievements of the CCP in the past seventeen years."

Fourth, the radicals' actions resembled those of an "interest group." Although the conservative mass organizations also articulated their interests, their approach was more passive, as they attempted to defend their interests only as these interests were threatened. The radicals, in contrast, engaged in active propaganda campaigns to dramatize their grievances and justify their radicalism, taking examples from daily life, particularly from the darker side of Chinese society.

Fifth, with the exception of the intellectuals at the highest level who had been co-opted by the Party, those persons who were more educated tended to be more radical. In general, students rather than workers, college students rather than middle-school students, and intellectuals rather than Party cadres joined the radical organizations. This can be explained by the fact that the intellectuals tended to come from "bad" families, and that only those with some education could accurately perceive the power struggle going on at the top level and be in a position to exploit these conflicts for their own purposes.

Finally, the radicals maintained good relationships only with the Small Group. Their relationships with the government bureaucrats and the PLA were tense. During the January power seizures, they attacked both government functionaries and the PLA, and were in turn suppressed during the "February Adverse Current." Right after the Wuhan Incident, they armed themselves and launched a campaign of "dragging out the handful of power holders in the army." But when the PLA consolidated its power at the last stage of the movement, they were again subjected to repression.

## The Conservative Mass Organizations

Social groups which were well off in the period prior to the Cultural Revolution tended to become conservatives. These included Party and Chinese

Youth League members, the children of cadres and the PLA, regular workers, skilled workers, and workers in big factories. They were initially mobilized by the existing leadership structures operating through the work teams, the Party Committees, the government organizations, the trade unions, and the CYL. Their involvement in the movement was defensive rather than offensive.

The original Red Guard groups, organized under the influence of the regular Party organizations, drew their membership from persons in the "five red categories." On the strength of their "good" social backgrounds, these Red Guards were qualified to launch and to take an active part in educational reform and the campaign against the "four olds," advocating the "theory of natural redness." But when the movement was turned against the Party, their social backgrounds hindered them from continuing their active participation. By the end of 1966, the original Red Guards in Peking had been replaced in their leadership roles by the radicals from "bad" family backgrounds. In the provinces, however, this kind of displacement did not generally occur, and the original conservative Red Guard units survived to compete with the radical Red Guards right up to the final stages of the Cultural Revolution.

Several characteristics of the conservative mass organizations should be noted. First, the conservatives tended to concentrate their attacks on the "bourgeois class" ("bourgeois academicians," "bourgeois specialists," and "monsters and freaks"), de-emphasizing the "power holders" and seldom using the term "revisionism." They tended to attack lower-ranking rather than higher-ranking cadres (deputy chiefs, for example, rather than chiefs), and cadres in functional rather than in political fields. At the initial stage of the movement, they also attacked their fellow students who had "bad" family backgrounds, clearly displaying a tendency to deflect the movement against the mass organizations rather than the elite.

Second, the conservatives tended to restrict the scope of their attacks, usually resisting the radicals' attempts to widen the targets. This meant that they usually spent more time and energy in denouncing persons who had already been officially denounced, following one step behind the radicals, rather than initiating their own public criticism campaigns. For instance, they attacked Liu and Teng only after their downfalls had become obvious, and they attacked T'ao Chu only after his purge had been officially announced.

Third, they supported the concept of the "five red categories," based on the "theory of natural redness," which emphasized class origin over current political consciousness and performance. They seldom raised any questions over the special privileges enjoyed by the stratum to which they belonged, but they frequently denounced the radicals for their "bad" class backgrounds.

Fourth, these groups tended to support the more moderate policies, such as the great alliance and the three-in-one combination, and stressed unity, discipline, order, and obedience to the authority of the higher levels. Often in the majority, they, rather than the radicals, demanded free elections. They tended to emphasize the study of Mao's Thought, the revolutionizing of one's ideology, educational reform, and the campaign to rectify class ranks—issues which did not have an immediate effect on the distribution of power.

Fifth, they tended to be loyal to the PLA. In fact, one's attitude toward the PLA was their major criterion for being considered revolutionary. At the same time, they subtly attacked the Small Group and probably supported the PLA's effort to have Lin Piao named as Mao's successor in the new Party Constitution.

## The Limited Conflict at the Elite Level and the Development of Vertical Cleavages

The four elite groups—the Cultural Revolution Small Group, the Party, the PLA, and the government leaders—were actively involved in the Cultural Revolution, forming coalitions with one another for defensive as well as offensive purposes. However, unlike the conflict in an international balance of power system in which order is maintained by the configuration of each actor's power rather than by a higher authority, the conflict among these four elite groups was regulated by two external constraints: first, a set of rules; and second, the supreme leader.

The rules of the game were ambiguous, and the degree to which they were observed varied according to the type of rule in question, the actor, and the period. Nevertheless, they were generally adhered to by all the actors.

The first rule was to acknowledge the supremacy of Mao's Thought, regardless of how ambivalent such adherence might be, and to respect Mao's supremacy, regardless of how arbitrary it might be. Mao's Thought and his supreme position became the ultimate justification for any action. During the two turbulent and chaotic years of the Cultural Revolution, no major actors—not even purged leaders—openly challenged this rule. Rather, the actors resorted to the tactic of flexibly interpreting Mao's Thought and of enlisting his support in order to protect their own interests. Thus, all the conflicts and even the armed struggles ironically had to take place in the name of supporting Mao Tse-tung's Thought.

The second rule of the game was the prohibition of any major actor from openly challenging the raison d'être of the Cultural Revolution. No one publicly questioned the need to purge the "black gang," the "bourgeois authorities," or the "power holders." They differed, however, on the relative importance of these abstract categories and on the question of how they should be applied to particular persons.

The third rule concerned the predominant role of the masses in the Cultural Revolution. The principle of "freely mobilizing the masses" was accepted by all the actors, although they differed on its actual meaning and on the degree of control the masses should exercise over the movement. Even the Party organization adopted the tactic of hindering the mass mobilization within the very framework of mass mobilization. Manipulation of the masses by the elite, particularly through factional ties and for factional interests, was in conflict with official policy, but it occurred frequently.

The third rule often came into conflict with the fourth: that the leaders not only were free to have direct contacts with the masses, but indeed were compelled to. In practice, this provided the elite with many opportunities to manipulate the masses.

The fifth rule was to follow the official line. Despite the divisions and struggles among the elite groups, Mao established the official line all through the movement. Although the official line was often equivocal and inconsistent, anyone who openly defied it risked retaliation, particularly from his opponents.

The sixth rule prohibited anyone from pursuing narrowly defined interests, be they private, factional, or institutional. Theoretically, everyone was engaged in conflict only in pursuit of the public or proletarian interest, although in reality the boundaries between the conflicting groups were often very thin. This rule allowed for the punishment of anyone who openly advocated interests which were too narrowly defined, engaged in secret conspiratorial activities, publicly attacked particular institutions, or revealed the existence of conflict among the allegedly united Maoist groups. Conflict among the Maoist elite was supposed to be kept secret from the masses. When Wang Li and Kuan Feng violated this rule by publicly attacking the PLA and the government, Mao was compelled to purge them.

These rules of the game derived partly from the fact that, despite their sharp internal conflicts, the elite groups all had a huge stake in keeping the contention among themselves within certain manageable bounds, preventing it from developing into an open civil war which would threaten the basic foundation of their entire system. Mao was particularly adamant in this regard, for it was he who was responsible not only for triggering the Cultural Revolution but also for resolving it. Mao could not lay claim to the position of supreme leader, commanding the allegiance of all the formal and informal structures, without applying these minimal rules fairly to each elite group. Even had he wanted to overlook violations of the rules by any one group, he could not have done so, because of the pressure from the others. In particular, any extremely partisan act by Mao would have greatly under-mined his legitimacy in the eyes of the masses. Thus, some of the rules were so firmly established that they bound even Mao himself.

Besides these rules of the game, Mao's unique position as the final arbiter of any dispute contributed to the mitigation of the conflicts among the elite. The four elite groups had to interact indirectly, mainly through Mao himself; there was no institutionalized channel through which any group could confront another to bargain for a compromise. What horizontal coordination did exist occurred on the basis of informal and personal relations. This system of parallel bureaucracies which lacked a horizontal mechanism of coordination and depended on a single higher authority accorded Mao enormous power and freedom of action, which he used to regulate the conflicts among the elite groups and maintain some semblance of unity among them.

During the Cultural Revolution, the masses were less culpable for their mistakes and were thus freer in their actions than the elite groups were. The movement was basically directed against the members of the elite. Moreover, it was a rule of the game that, if they were penitent, the masses should be forgiven for their mistakes, on the ground that they were inexperienced in politics. This resulted in an interesting phenomenon: conflict initiated at the elite level usually erupted into open confrontation at the mass level. The elite groups undoubtedly exploited the freedom of the masses by manipulating them to oppose a particular policy, to attack a particular group, or to mount pressure on Mao.

For instance, to counter the expansion of the movement into the factories, the Party organization and some government leaders resorted to passive resistance by abandoning their responsibility to control the economic de-mands of the masses, rather than challenging Mao at the policy-making level. Moreover, when the PLA was pressured to support the radicals instead of directly challenging the order at the top level, it encouraged the conserva-tives to attack the radicals, so as to create civil chaos and indirectly put pressure on Mao. In the later stages, the Small Group encouraged the radicals to attack the PLA, which in turn encouraged the conservatives to attack the Small Group.

In exerting their control over the mass organizations, the elite groups relied mainly on the manipulation of political symbols, communication patterns, organizational connections, and personal ties. Originally, the Maoist leaders expected that symbol manipulation alone would be sufficient to control the masses and create consensus among them. But the schisms within the original Maoist coalition (e.g., the cleavage between the PLA and the Small Group), the radicalization of symbols, the high-level generality of the official ideology, and the masses' tendency to interpret ambiguous symbols according to their own interests all undermined the effectiveness of symbol manipulation as a means of controlling the masses.

Each elite faction attempted to change the dominant political symbols to conform to its own interests, since it was political symbols that legitimized the particular policies desired by each elite group. The Party organization supported the slogan of natural redness, whereas the Small Group opposed it; the PLA tended to characterize the Cultural Revolution as "the great school of Mao Tse-tung's Thought," whereas to the Small Group it was "a struggle between two lines." If some symbol was so firmly established that no elite group could challenge it, the various factions exploited its generality to protect their own interests. For instance, the Small Group interpreted power seizure as the capture of public offices by the masses, whereas the government leaders and the PLA interpreted it as seizure from above in order to check economism.

One of the tactics adopted by the Maoist leaders to destroy the organizational integrity of the Party was to uproot the prevailing communication pattern; instead of the intra-organizational communication through well-established hierarchical channels, they switched to direct contact between the top leaders and the masses. This new communication pattern was characterized by a multiplicity of channels and a lack of "gate-keepers" to regulate the flow. Usually the communications from the top leaders to the masses were transmitted by editorials in major periodicals such as *Hung ch'i, Jen-min jih-pao,* and *Chieh-fang chün-pao.* The unprecedented number of speeches made by the Maoist leaders at both big rallies and small group interviews filled in the ambiguities of the editorials and provided authoritative and detailed interpretations of current policies.

To obtain an upward flow of information, the Maoist leaders encouraged the Red Guards to bring their complaints to Peking, and even to send letters to the Center without using postage stamps. In effect, the multiplicity of communication channels (including Red Guard rallies, revolutionary exchanges of experience, speeches delivered by the leaders, big-character posters, and the Red Guard newspapers) was effective in destroying or decisively weakening the power monopoly of the Party organizations. At the same time, these communication channels provided the elite groups with ample opportunities to manipulate the masses for their own interests.

The direct and uncontrolled information flow between the masses and the elite groups, however, created new problems for the Maoist leaders. First of all, it readily exposed the policy differences existing among the Maoist leaders, thus intensifying the conflicts among the mass organizations. Second, the removal of the "gate-keepers" in the communication channels exposed the top leaders to direct pressure from the mass organizations. Third, when there was a policy difference among the Maoist leaders, the mass organizations tended to communicate only with the leaders who were sympathetic to their specific interests, thereby intensifying the line of cleavage from the bottom to the very top.

As formal communication channels and organizational norms broke down, factional structures based on personal and informal relations began to rise. It was especially the radical cadres, those with fragile positions in the formal organizations, who relied heavily on informal relationships such as personal friendships to challenge the power holders and to seize their power. Factional ties thus became operative vertically as well as horizontally. Each elite group took advantage of its formal relationships with the mass organizations to cultivate informal and secret relationships which were better suited to carrying out officially prohibited activities.

Nonetheless, the vertical alliances did not only permit the elite to manipulate the masses; for their part, the mass organizations utilized the support of their elite patrons for their own interests. Hans Toch has suggested three criteria for testing the degree of manipulation of the masses by the leaders:

1. If a group of persons behaves in a way that has a favorable consequence for the individual in authority, it can be assumed that this result has been intentionally achieved.
2. If a group of people behaves in a way that is not in its own best interests, it can be inferred that they have been manipulated.
3. If people are drawn into irrational or illogical solutions to their problems, they are probably being manipulated.[28]

As a whole, the first condition applies to the mass organizations. The other two, however, do not apply to the Cultural Revolution. The radical and the conservative mass organizations all behaved in ways which appear to have been consistent with their best interests. They all had real stakes in the outcome of the Cultural Revolution, as well as in the rise of their representatives. The vertical link-ups, by and large, were founded on a base of common interests between the patron elite and their client mass organizations.

Thus, the mass organizations had some leverage over their patrons. If the patrons betrayed their interests, the organizations had the option of deserting to the opposition. This threatened the patron groups, not only with the loss of their power base, but also with the exposure of their illicit activities. It is precisely for this reason that collecting materials on the elite groups and organizing other intelligence-gathering activities constituted a most important part of the work of the mass organizations. In their efforts to collect

28. Hans Toch, *The Social Psychology of Social Movement* (New York: The Bobbs-Merrill Company, 1965).

incriminating materials against the opposing faction, the mass organizations used both coercion and bribery. By exaggerating and making distorted inferences from materials, each group tried to discredit its adversaries and impugn their motives. In sum, the emergence of vertical factional alliances based on mutual interests made it extremely difficult to resolve conflicts through compromise at either the elite or the mass level.

# List of the Sample

EAST WIND

*Chung-ta chan-pao:* 6 March 1967; 11 January 1968; 1 March 1968; 3 March 1968; 4 March 1968; 14 April 1968; 21 May 1968; 3 August 1968; 4 August 1968; 17 August 1968; 22 September 1968

*Hsiao-ping:* 9 October 1967; 9 November 1967; 9 December 1967; 24 December 1967; 5 April 1968

*Kuang-chou hung-wei-ping:* 10 February 1967; 28 August 1968

*T'i-yü chan-pao:* 30 October 1967; 11 October 1967; 18 February 1968; 18 March 1968

*Chan chung-nan:* 21 July 1968; 3 August 1968; 23 August 1968

*125 chan-pao:* 3 April 1967; 9 June 1967

*Kung-an chan-pao:* 1 August 1967

*Kung-jen p'ing-lun:* Mid-March 1968; late June 1968; late August 1968

*Chien-chu kung-jen:* 1 January 1968

*Hung chan-pao:* 10 October 1967; 29 November 1967

*Hsin chu-ying:* 1 August 1968

*Hsin hsing kung-jen:* 16 February 1968

*Hsin hsing kung-she:* 30 December 1967

*Kung-jen chan-pao:* 9 July 1967

*Ta fang-hsiang:* 8 July 1967

*San-chün lien-wei chan pao:* 25 July 1968; 14 August 1968; 10 August 1968; 17 August 1968; 1 September 1968; 7 September 1968; 8 September 1968

RED FLAG

*Chu-ying tung-fang-hung:* 1 October 1967; 31 October 1967; 1 April 1968

*Chung-ta hung-ch'i:* 30 July 1967; 13 January 1968, 15 March 1968; 1 April 1968; 27 May 1968; 12 June 1968

*Kang pa-i:* 4 October 1967; mid-December 1967; 1 January 1968; January 1968; February 1968; mid-July 1968

*Kung-an hung-ch'i:* 31 October 1967

*Kuang-chou chan-pao:* January 1968; May 1968; June 1968; 10 July 1968; 16 July 1968

349

*Chung-hsüeh hung-wei-ping:* 31 December 1967; late May 1968; early July 1968; late July 1968
*Chih-tien chiang shan:* 1 October 1967; 27 October 1967
*Tung-fang-hung:* 11 July 1967; 2 August 1967; 21 November 1967; 15 March 1968; 8 April 1968; late June 1968
*Hung-ch'i kung-jen:* 28 August 1967
*San-ssu chan-pao:* 14 June 1967; 5 June 1967; 3 November 1967
*Hsin i ssu:* 17 May 1967
*Chan kuang-tung:* 10 July 1968
*I-yüeh pao-feng:* January 1968; May 1968; July 1968
*Sheng-chih hung-ch'i:* January 1968
*Pu-tui hung-ch'i:* October 1967
*Hung chan-t'uan:* December 1967

# Major Issues and the Responses of the Conservatives and the Radicals

| Issues | Conservatives | Radicals | Initiators of the Issues |
|---|---|---|---|
| Educational Reform (May–July 1966) | + | – | Mao and Party |
| Campaign against the "Four Olds" (August–September 1966) | + | – | Party |
| Work Teams (August–December 1966) | – | + | CRSG |
| Class Origin (August–December 1966) | + | – | Party |
| Power Seizure (January 1967) | – | + | Mao and CRSG |
| Involvement of the PLA | + | – | Mao |
| Power Holders | – | + | CRSG |
| Educational Reform (September–December 1967) | + | – | Mao |
| Rehabilitation | – | + | CRSG |
| Formation of the Revolutionary Committee | + | – | Chou and Mao |
| Campaign against the "Four Rightist Trends" | – | + | CRSG |

# Index